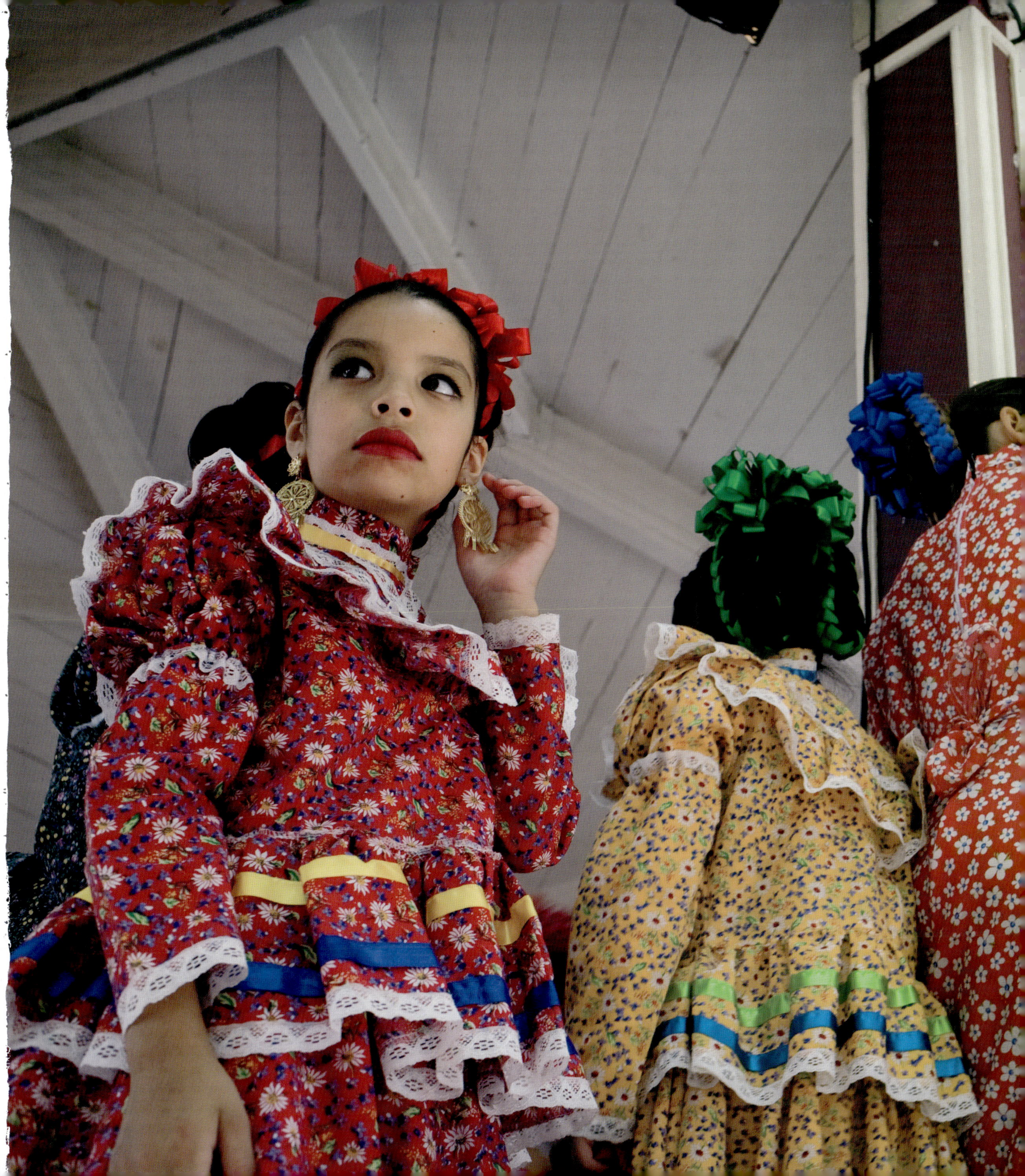

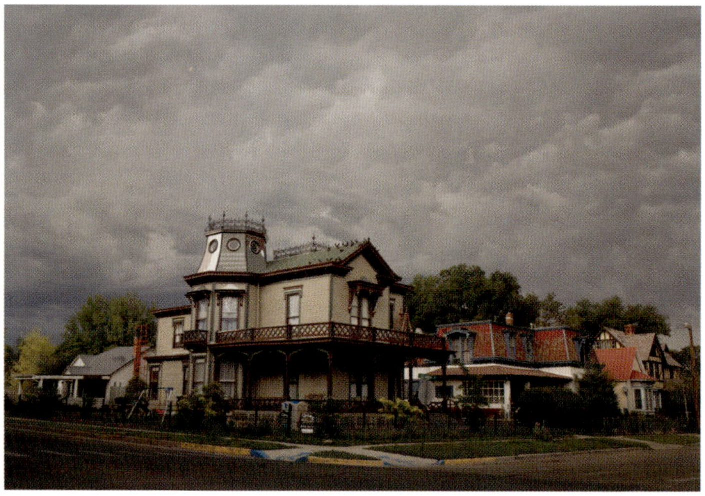
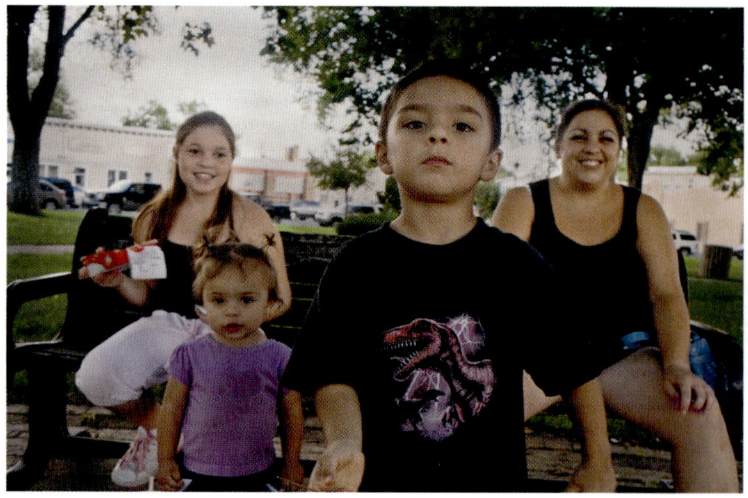

Learning Las Vegas

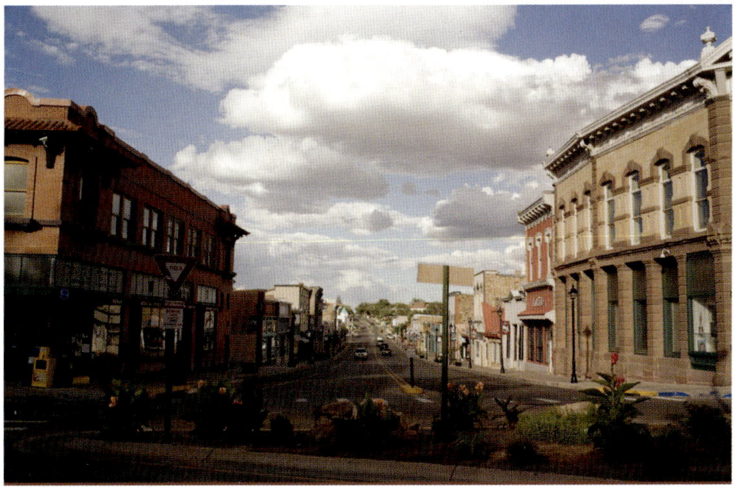

PORTRAIT

OF A

NORTHERN

NEW MEXICAN

PLACE

Text and Photography

Elizabeth Barlow Rogers

Museum of New Mexico Press
Santa Fe

in association with

Foundation for Landscape Studies
New York City

 Museum of New Mexico Press is a division of New Mexico Department of Cultural Affairs.
Project editor: Mary Wachs
Art direction and production: David Skolkin
Design associate: Jason Valdez
Composition: Set in Perpetua with Mona Lisa display
Maps: Deborah Reade
Manufactured in China
10 9 8 7 6 5 4 3 2 1

Library of Congress Cataloging-in-Publication Data
Rogers, Elizabeth Barlow, 1936-
Learning Las Vegas : portrait of a northern New Mexican place / text and photography, Elizabeth Barlow Rogers.
pages cm
Includes bibliographical references and index.
ISBN 978-0-89013-578-5 (clothbound : alkaline paper)
1. Las Vegas (N.M.)--History. 2. Las Vegas (N.M.)--Social life and customs. 3. Oral history--New Mexico--Las Vegas. 4. Las Vegas (N.M.)--Biography. 5. Las Vegas (N.M.)--Pictorial works. I. Foundation for Landscape Studies. II. Title.
F804.L3R64 2013
978.9'55--dc23

2012040175

Photography Credits
Courtesy Las Vegas City Museum: 76 (2008.19.1-14); 77 (76.4.46); 83 (62.42.1); 84 (68.17.17).
Courtesy Palace of the Governors Photo Archives (NMHM/DCA): 74 top (neg. 061255); 74 bottom (neg. 014386); 77 (neg. 014695); 79 top (neg. 170730), bottom (neg. 127374); 80 (neg. 122065).

Museum of New Mexico Press
PO Box 2087
Santa Fe, New Mexico 87504
www.mnmpress.org

FOR SUSAN HERTER

Contents

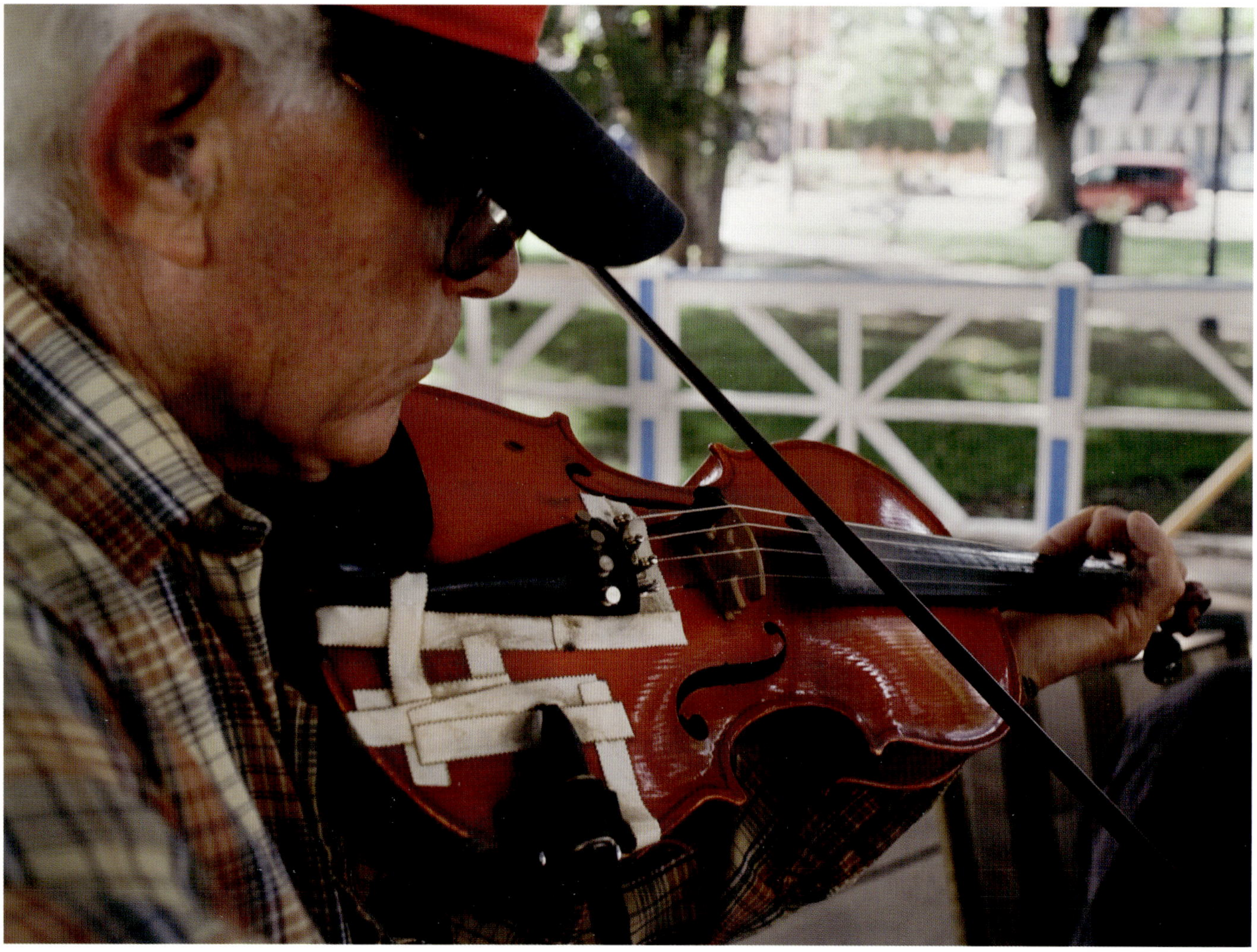

Introduction

When we speak of "a sense of place," what do we mean? What is it exactly that we sense? How do we perceive a place—its nature, its character, its "genius"? Can we articulate certain inherent attributes that denote place and mark each individual place as distinct and different from all others?

Learning Las Vegas: Portrait of a Northern New Mexican Place[1] is an attempt to examine a place and its people as a configuration of natural forces, human actions, and social and economic circumstances. It avoids being overly analytical, however, for place reveals itself ambiguously and never completely, even to the most diligent geographer, historian, political scientist, or anthropologist. To know a place in all its complexity is impossible. But it is possible to learn a place well enough to delineate its physiognomy and personality and thus create a portrait in time.

"The other Las Vegas," as it is sometimes called, exists within a setting that is one of the most storied and scenic parts of America, and much of its population has roots in Northern New Mexico that go back four centuries. Its status as a relic of a bygone period of the nation's settlement history makes it the kind of place that inspires nostalgia for a past that is imagined as more innocent, even idyllic. As an added attraction, here you can buy a large period home for a fraction of the cost you would pay for a much smaller one in Santa Fe or Taos. Moreover, in contrast to the world-famous Nevada city of the same name or the many anonymous, forgettable urban conglomerations spread across the American landscape, New Mexico's Las Vegas continues to live securely within its own well-defined image of itself. Unlike the citizens in other historic places who invite restoration redevelopment in order to become tourist meccas, Las Vegans have allowed their town to be used as a setting for movie shoots but have so far resisted strategies for improving the perennially ailing economy by theming its colorful past. The shorthand expression for this attitude is, "We don't want to be like Santa Fe."

Toby Sena

All settlements are dependent on the availability of water, and those in the arid West are especially challenged in this regard. To exist they must effectively secure reliable sources and manage their distribution with ingenuity. To grasp the development of Las Vegas in both physical and political terms, it is necessary therefore to appreciate the role of the small Gallinas River in the town's formation and continuing existence. Tracing the river upstream into the Gallinas Canyon and visiting the communities along other nearby tributaries of the Pecos River makes clear the fact that all the Spanish colonial settlements in the Sangre de Cristos—or "Blood of Christ," as this southernmost range of the Rockies was named by the conquistadores—were restricted to the narrow valleys along such stream courses. Likewise, it is important to understand the *acequia* system of irrigation as a way of distributing water for crops through a series of river-fed ditches. Its reasonable allocation made a communal form of local governance mandatory, and the cooperative digging of the *acequia madre*, or mother ditch, was a prior condition of permanent settlement in Las Vegas as in other Northern New Mexican villages.

The complexion of Las Vegas is colored by its relationship to the rest of its home county, San Miguel, as well as Mora County to the north. The rich grasslands encompassing Las Vegas historically served as the economic base for the town's prosperity. Viewing this immense, uninterrupted range, so productive in the raising of sheep and cattle—and so coveted by Anglo-American and Spanish-American societies with their vastly different systems of property law and grazing rights—brings into focus the fraught history of New Mexico's land-grant system. In addition, a visit to Fort Union, built in 1851 by the United States Army a few miles north of Las Vegas near the juncture of the mountains and the plains for the purpose of protecting Santa Fe Trail caravans from Indian raiders, makes tangible an important chapter in the history of the American West.

To comprehend the layout of Las Vegas and study its architecture it is necessary to walk its streets; to see its outlying villages and ranches, as well as the traces of the Santa Fe Trail at Fort Union and elsewhere, requires traveling away from town by automobile. To read its history entails poring over books and dissertations in the library. To visualize its past it is necessary to look in local photographic archives. To follow what goes on day-to-day one must subscribe to the town newspaper. To feel the pulse of the present it is important to immerse oneself in the life of the town, which creates the pleasant necessity of attending events—fiestas, processions, pageants, football games, graduations, and other celebrations and social gatherings. To fit together the many pieces of the mosaic of impressions that constitute a varied and nuanced portrait of place one is compelled to sit down and talk with numerous individuals.

This book records both in words and photographs my walks in Las Vegas, field trips throughout San Miguel and Mora counties, research in local archives, and conversations with the many Las Vegans who have graciously invited me into their homes and places of business. Like the travelers along the Santa Fe Trail, for this literary, visual, and oral-history journey, I have had only a rudimentary road map, and that has enhanced the sense of surprise and wonder that accompanied my discovery of this extraordinary place.

As with all journeys, this one had a starting point. Mine began one day in 2007 when I walked through the old plaza with my camera in hand to the small gazebo that functions as a bandstand, stage for events, and place for teenagers and other townspeople to hang out. I began photographing a man of slight build who was playing a battered violin held together with adhesive tape. Beside him a burly companion was striking the notes of a keyboard with an uncertain index finger. After hesitating a moment, I took the plunge. "Hi," I said, "my name is Betsy Rogers, and I'm taking pictures and writing a book about Las Vegas." "My name is Toby Sena," he replied, "and I'm teaching my friend to play music."

Learning Las Vegas

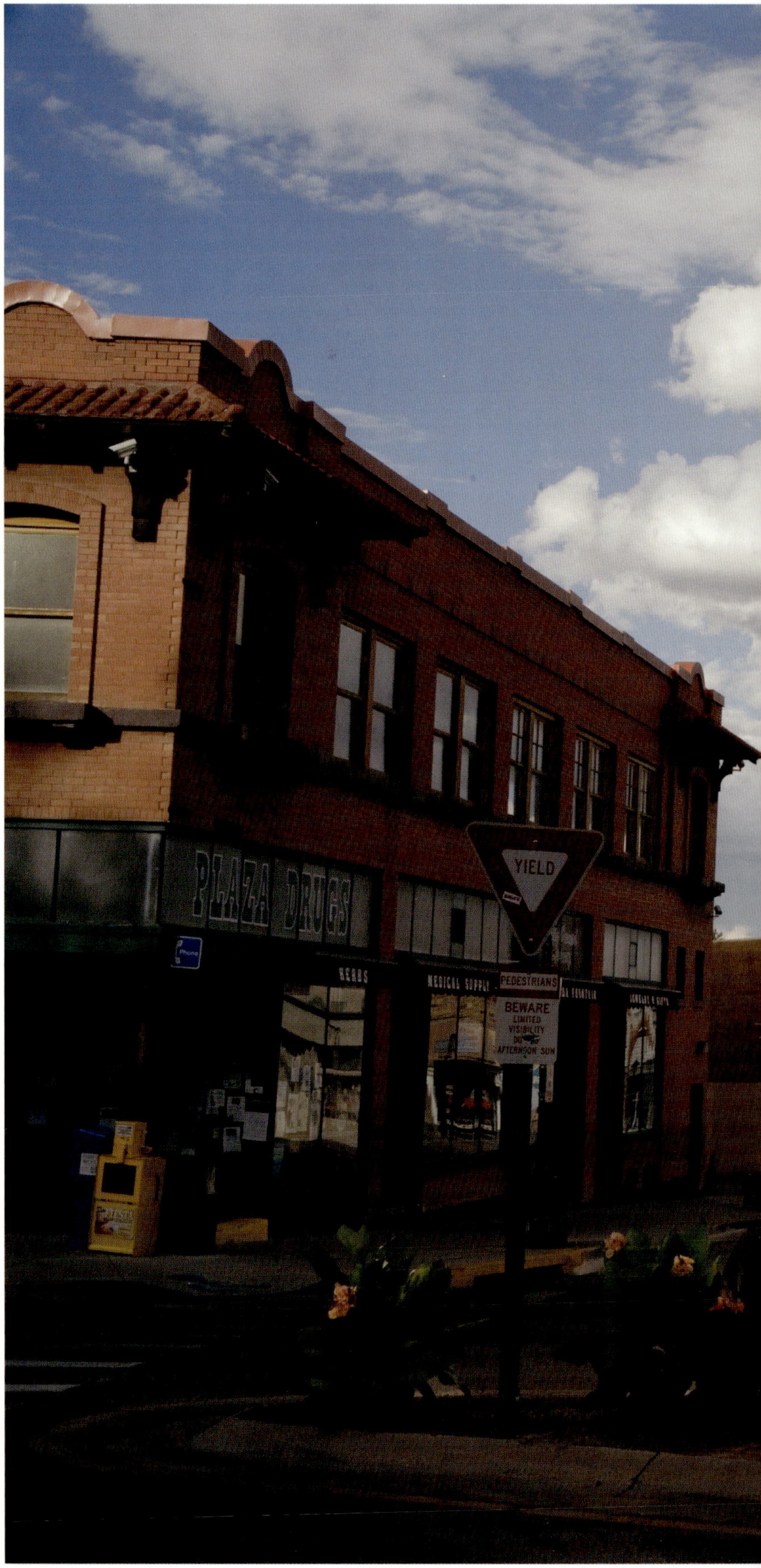
PLAZA DRUGS
YIELD
MEDICAL SUPPLY
PEDESTRIANS
BEWARE
LIMITED
VISIBILITY
AFTERNOON SUN

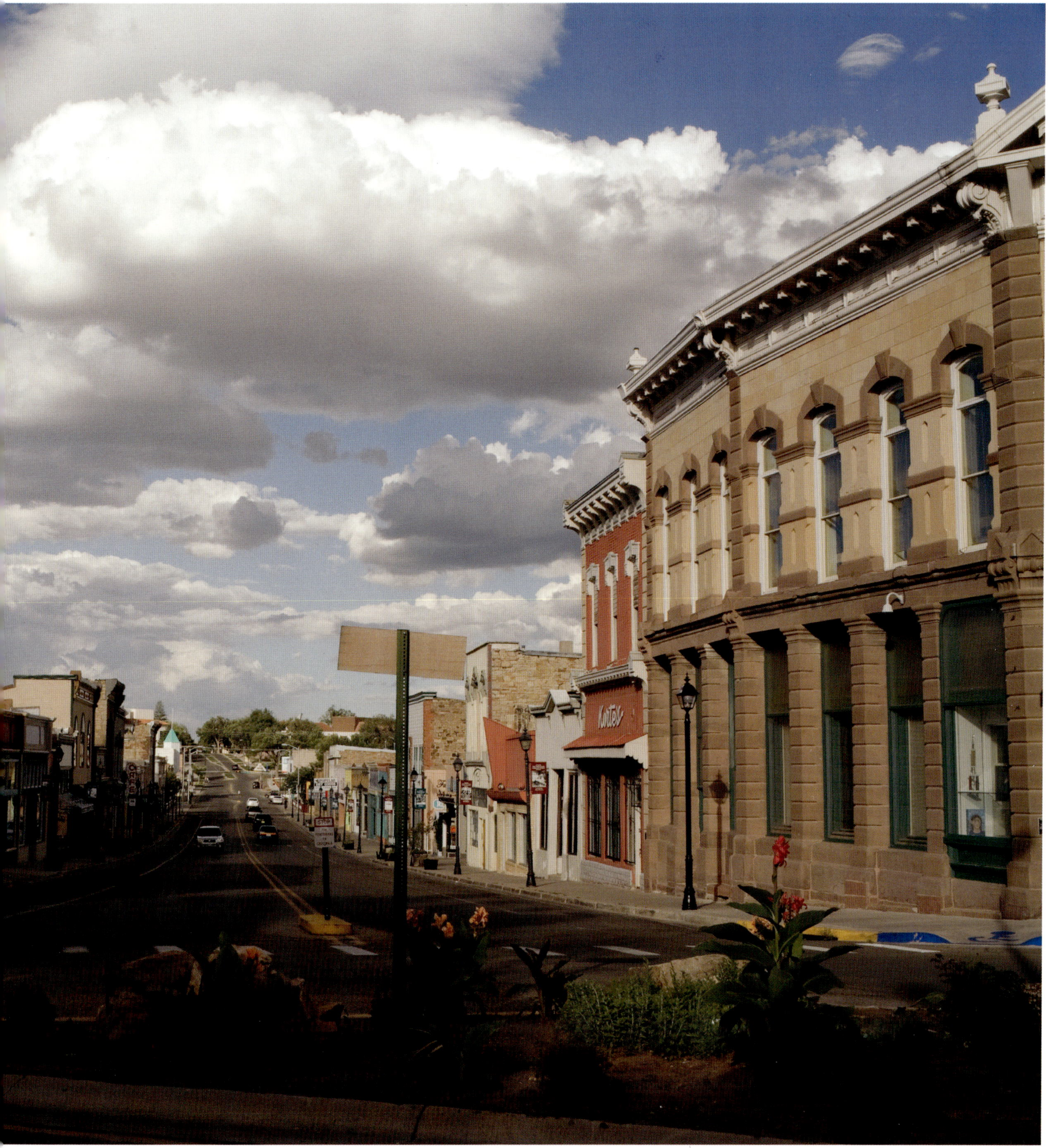

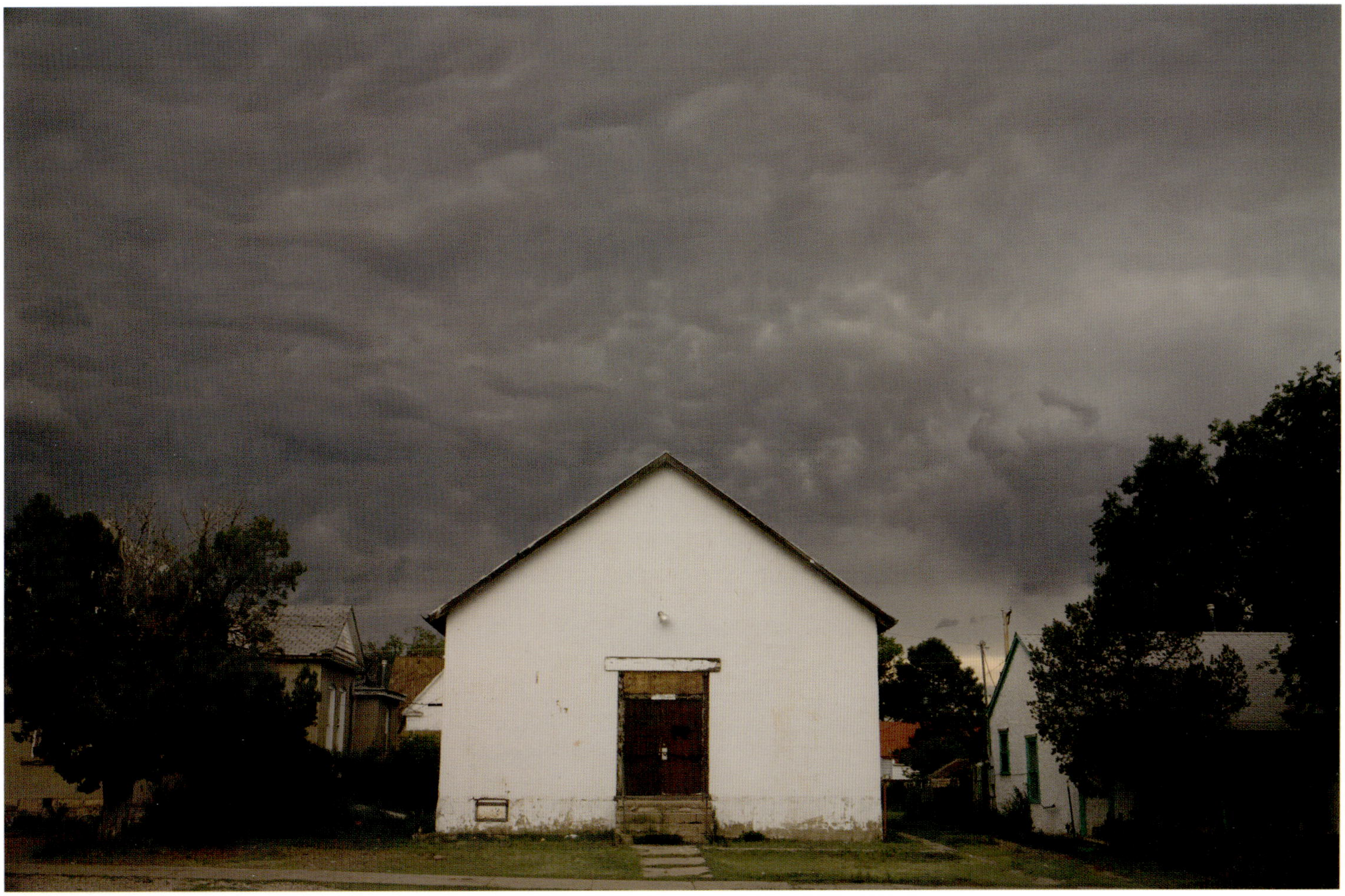

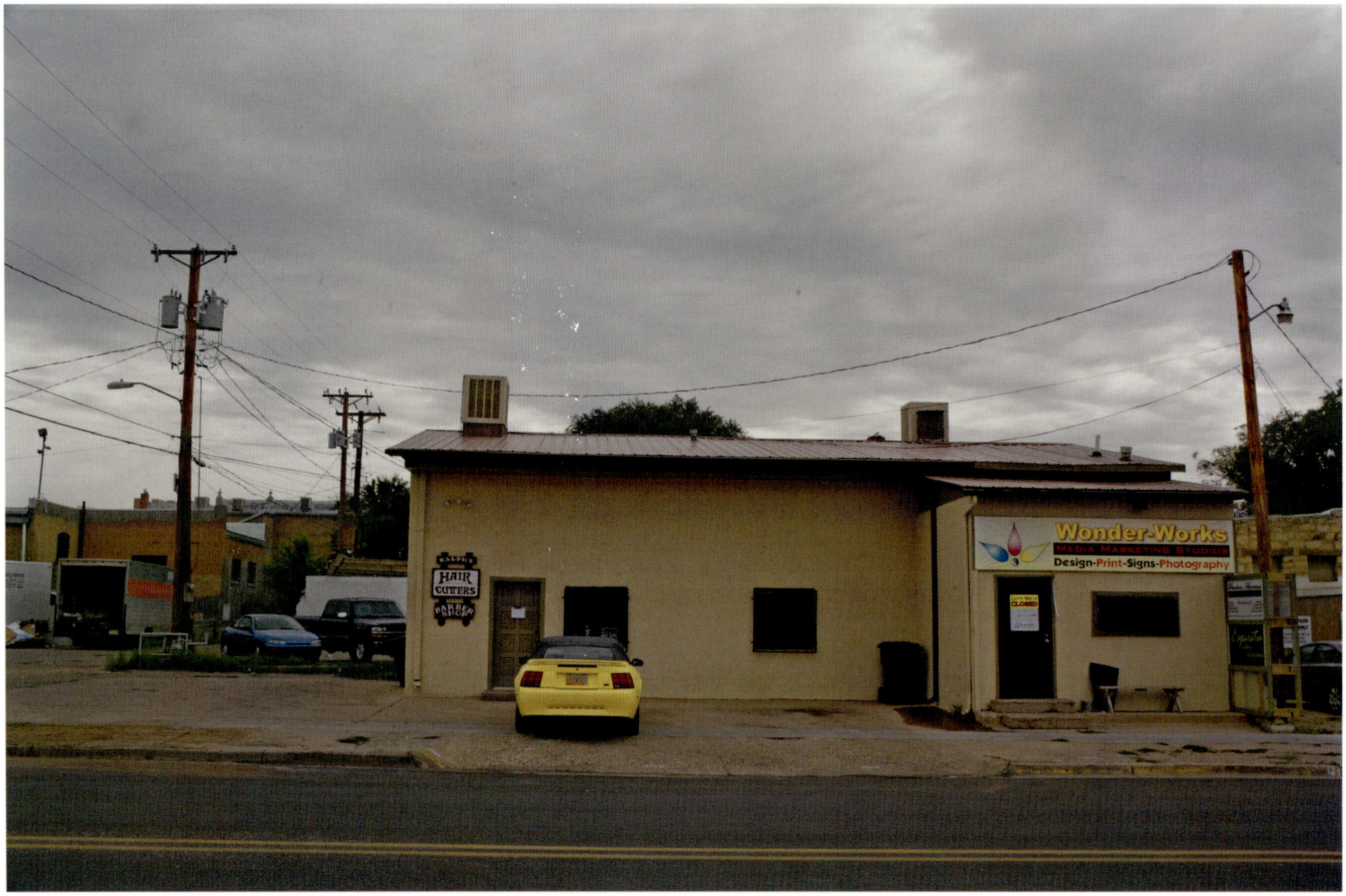
RALPH'S
HAIR CUTTERS
BARBER SHOP
Wonder-Works
MEDIA MARKETING STUDIOS
Design-Print-Signs-Photography
CLOSED

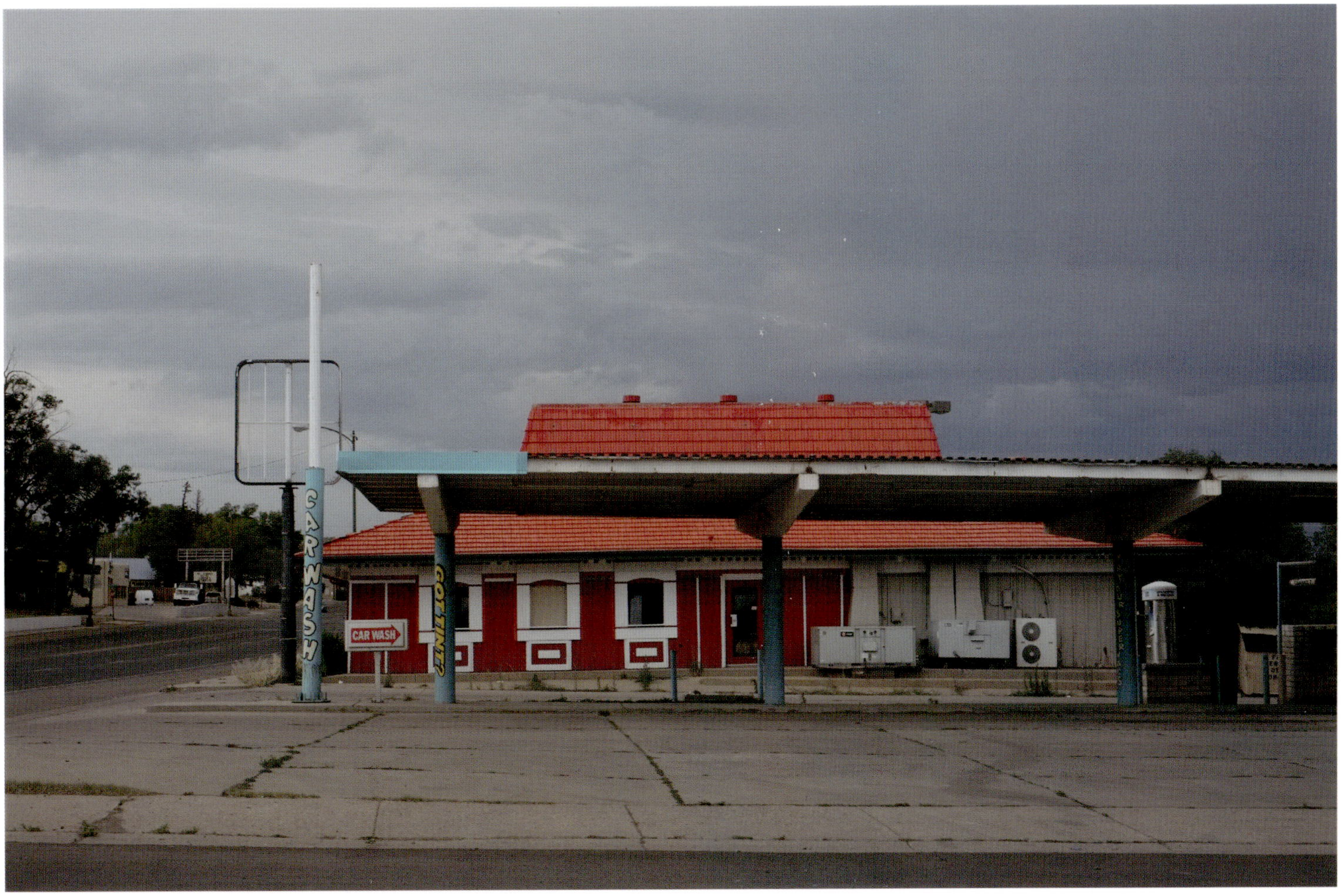
CAR WASH
CAR WASH
GOT TINT?

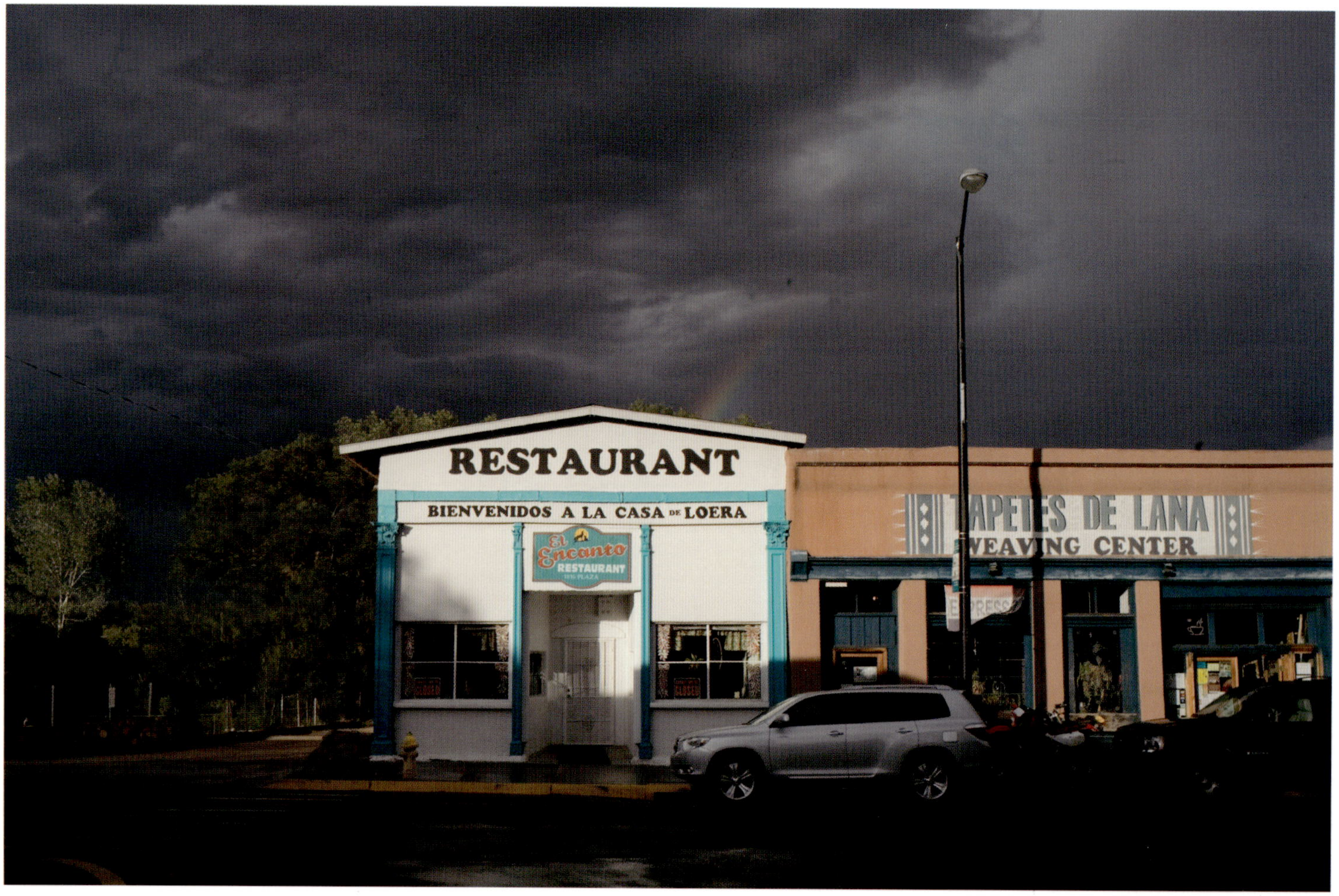
RESTAURANT
BIENVENIDOS A LA CASA de LOERA
El Encanto
RESTAURANT
TAPETES DE LANA
WEAVING CENTER
CLOSED
CLOSED

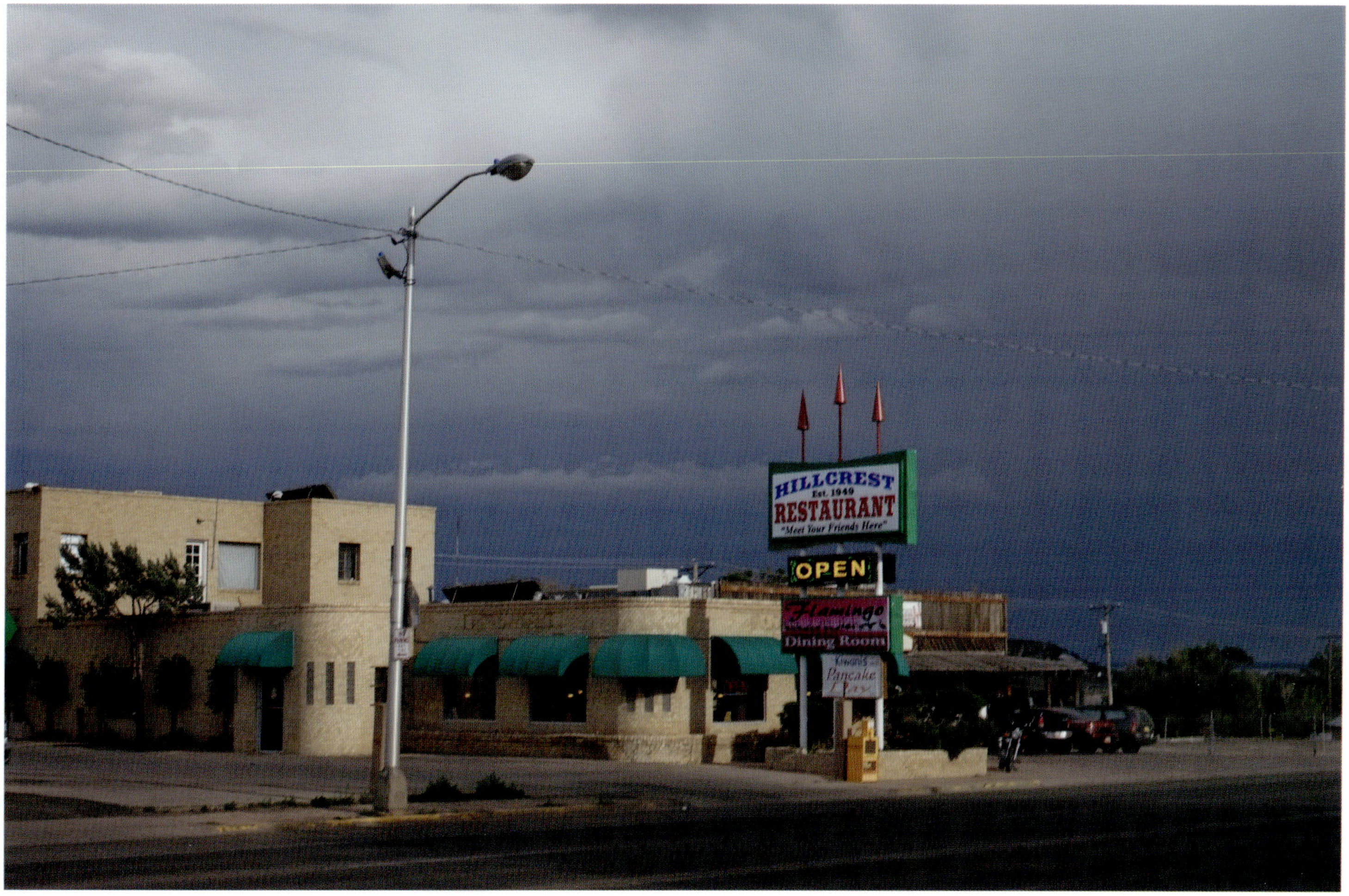
HILLCREST
Est. 1949
RESTAURANT
"Meet Your Friends Here"
OPEN
Flamingo
Dining Room
Pancake

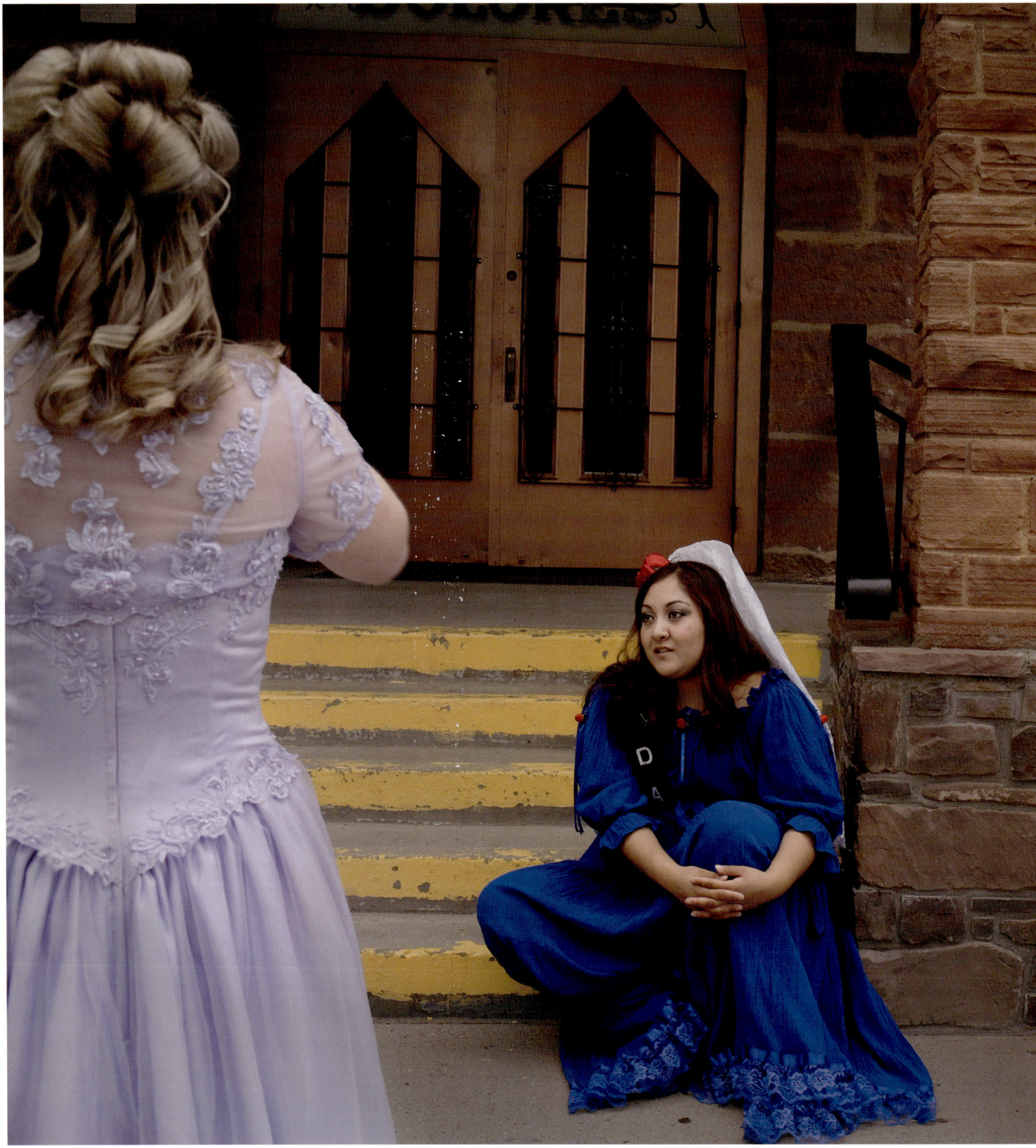

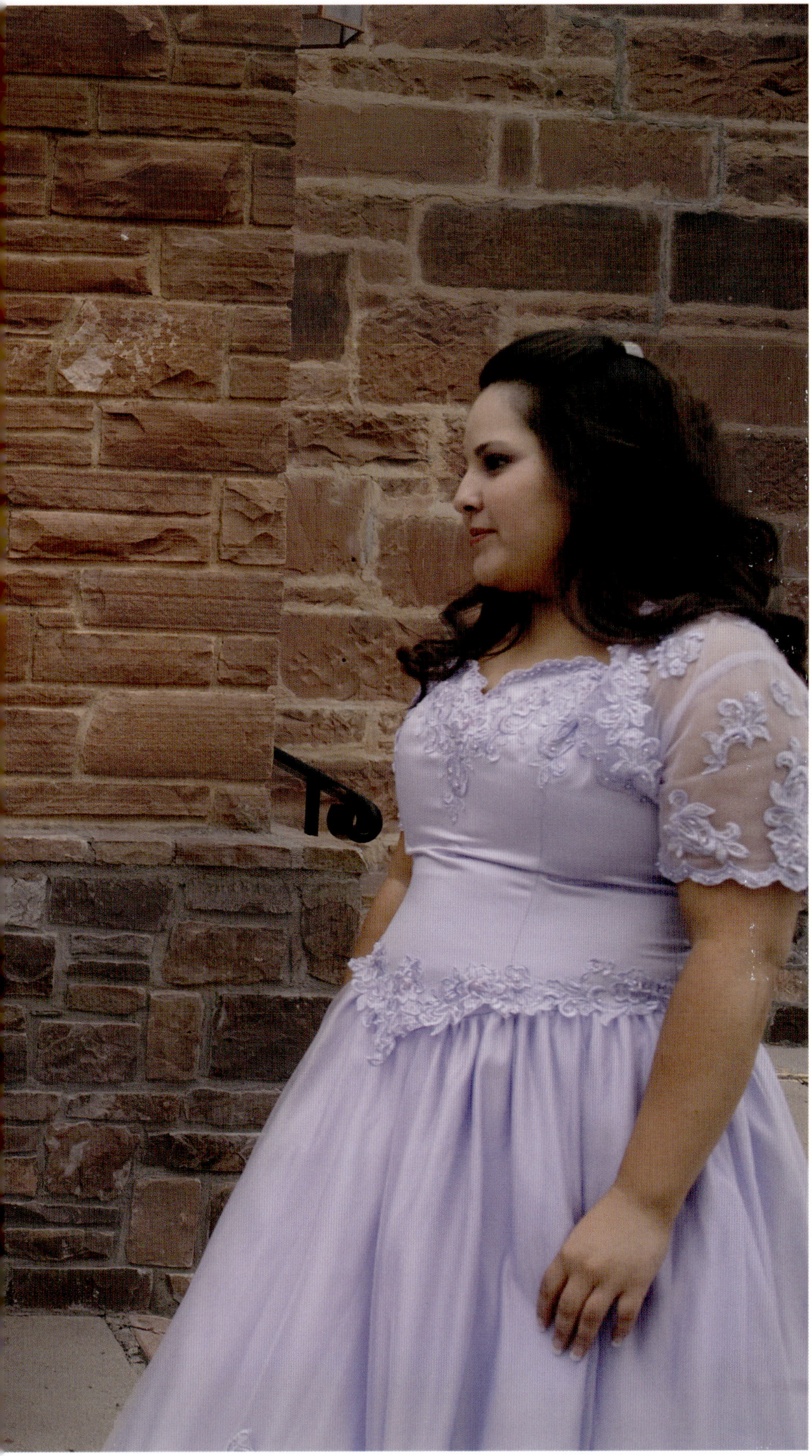

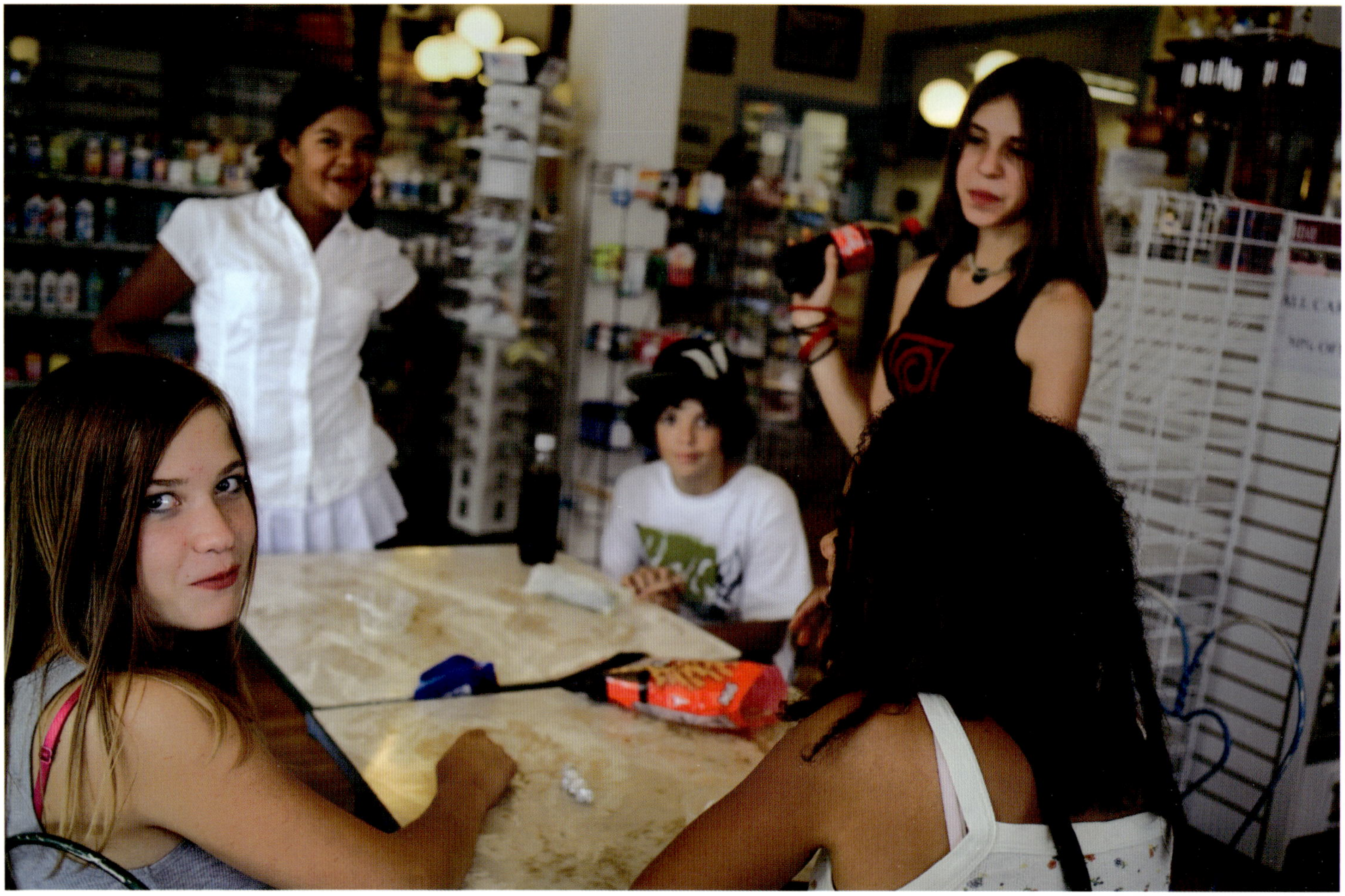

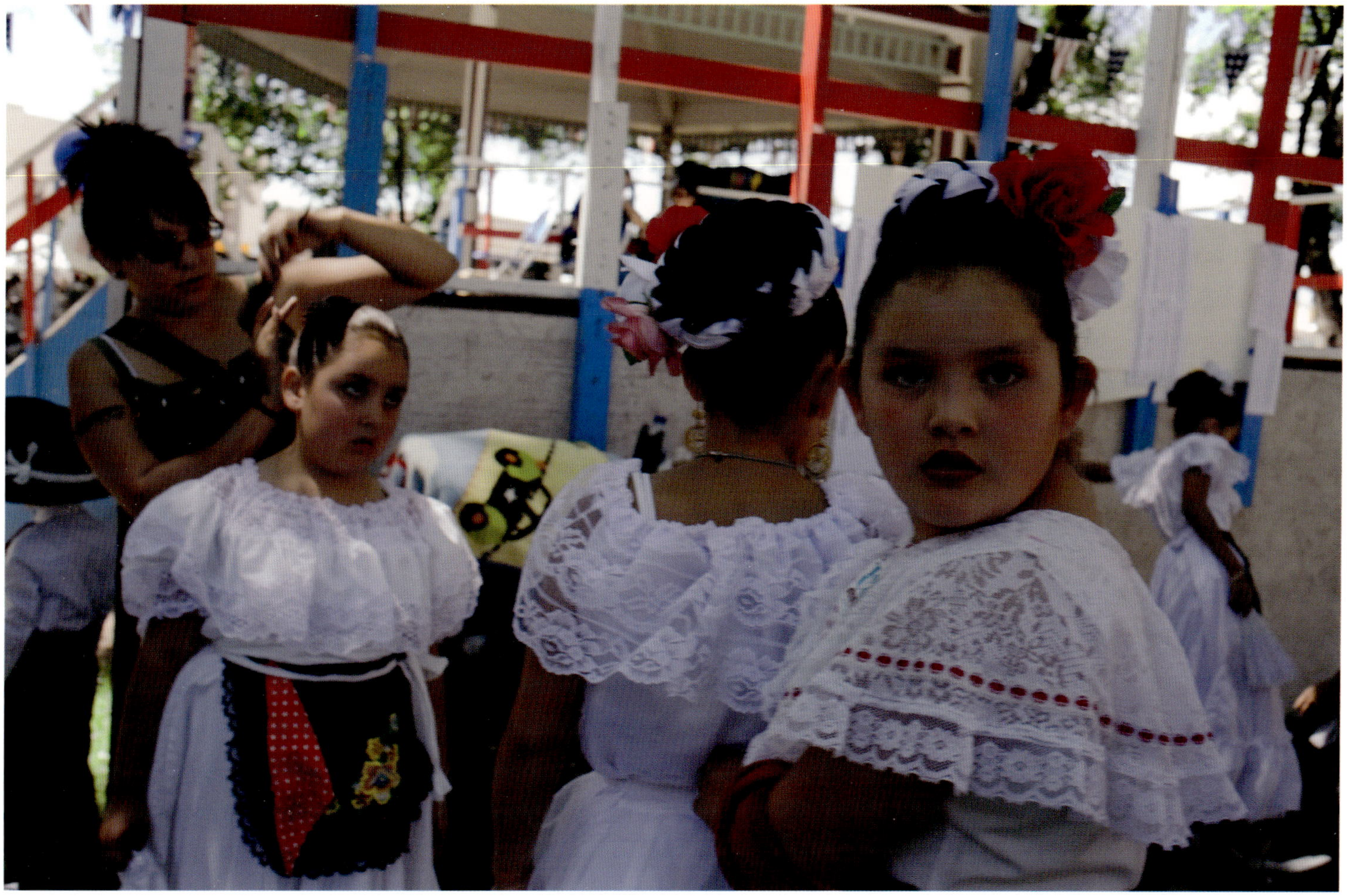

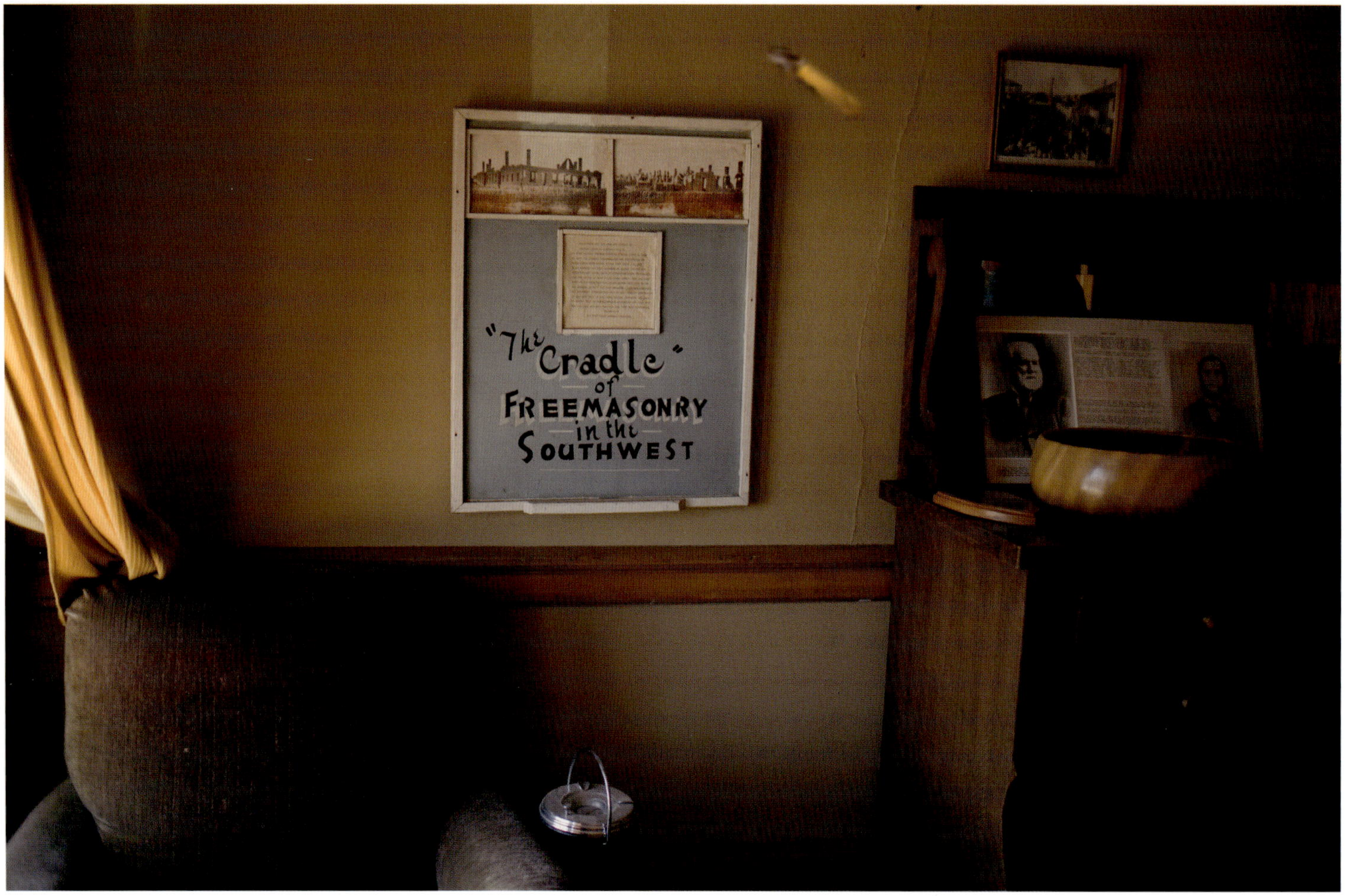
"The Cradle" of FREEMASONRY in the SOUTHWEST

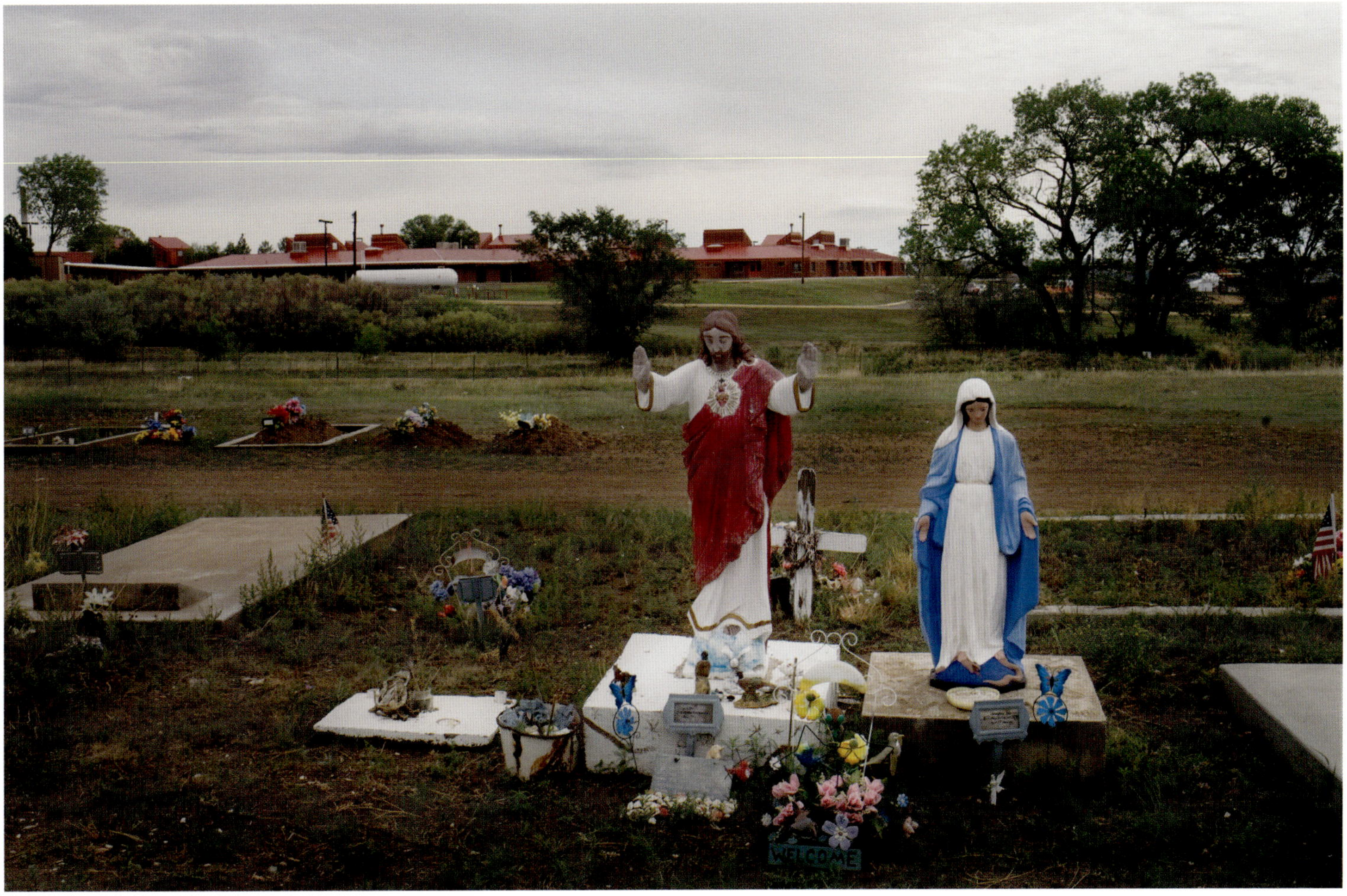
WELCOME

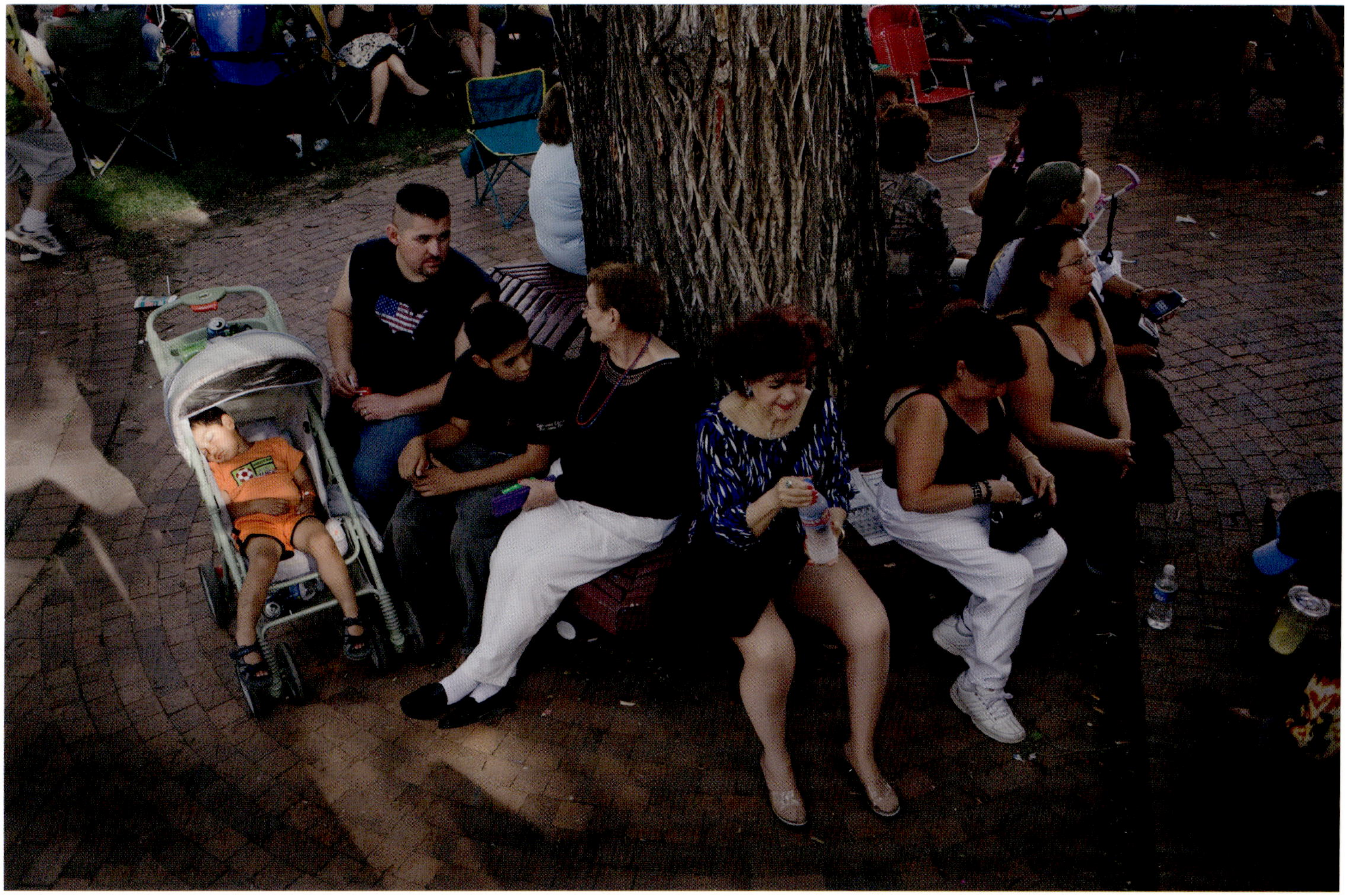

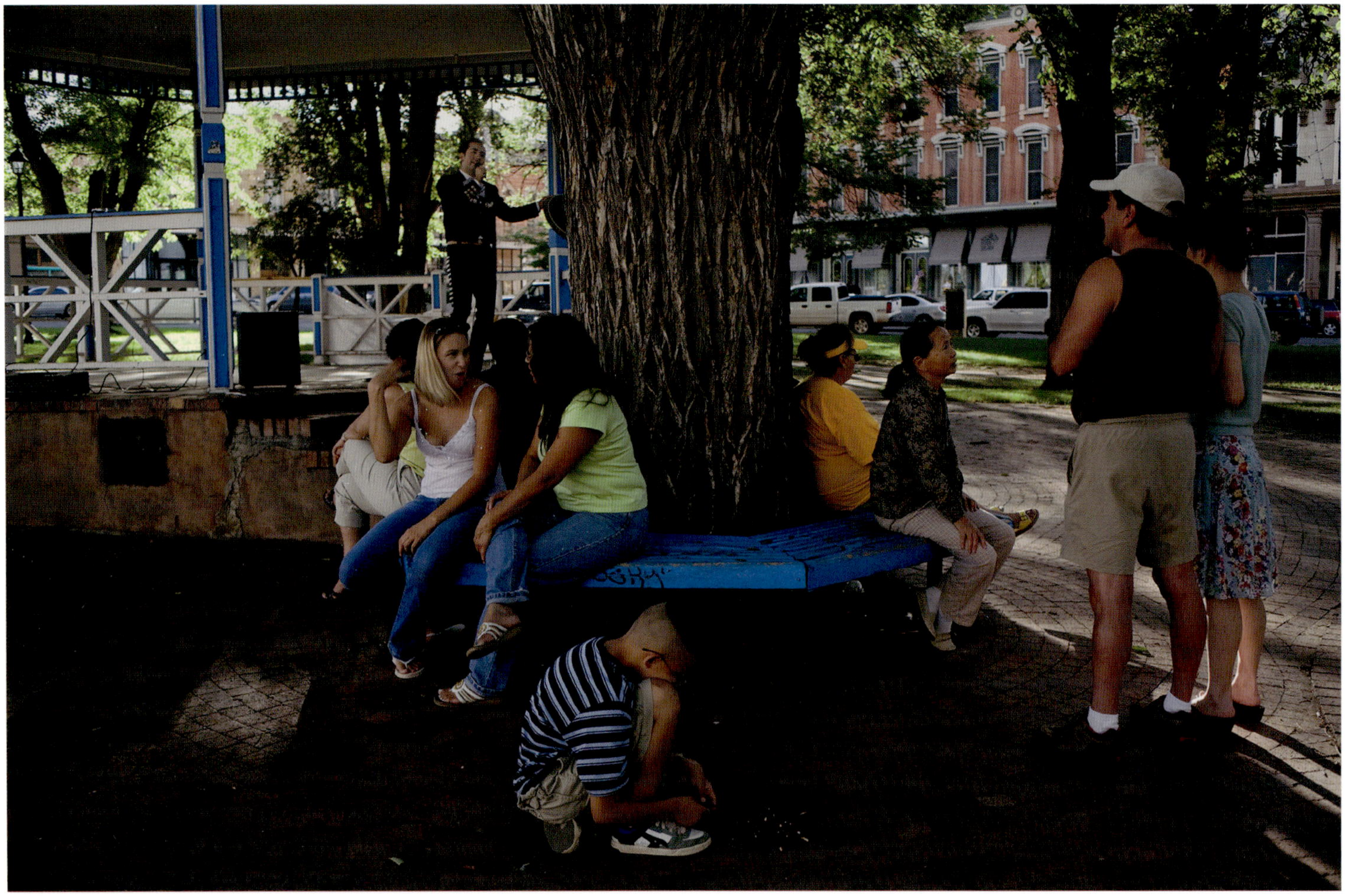

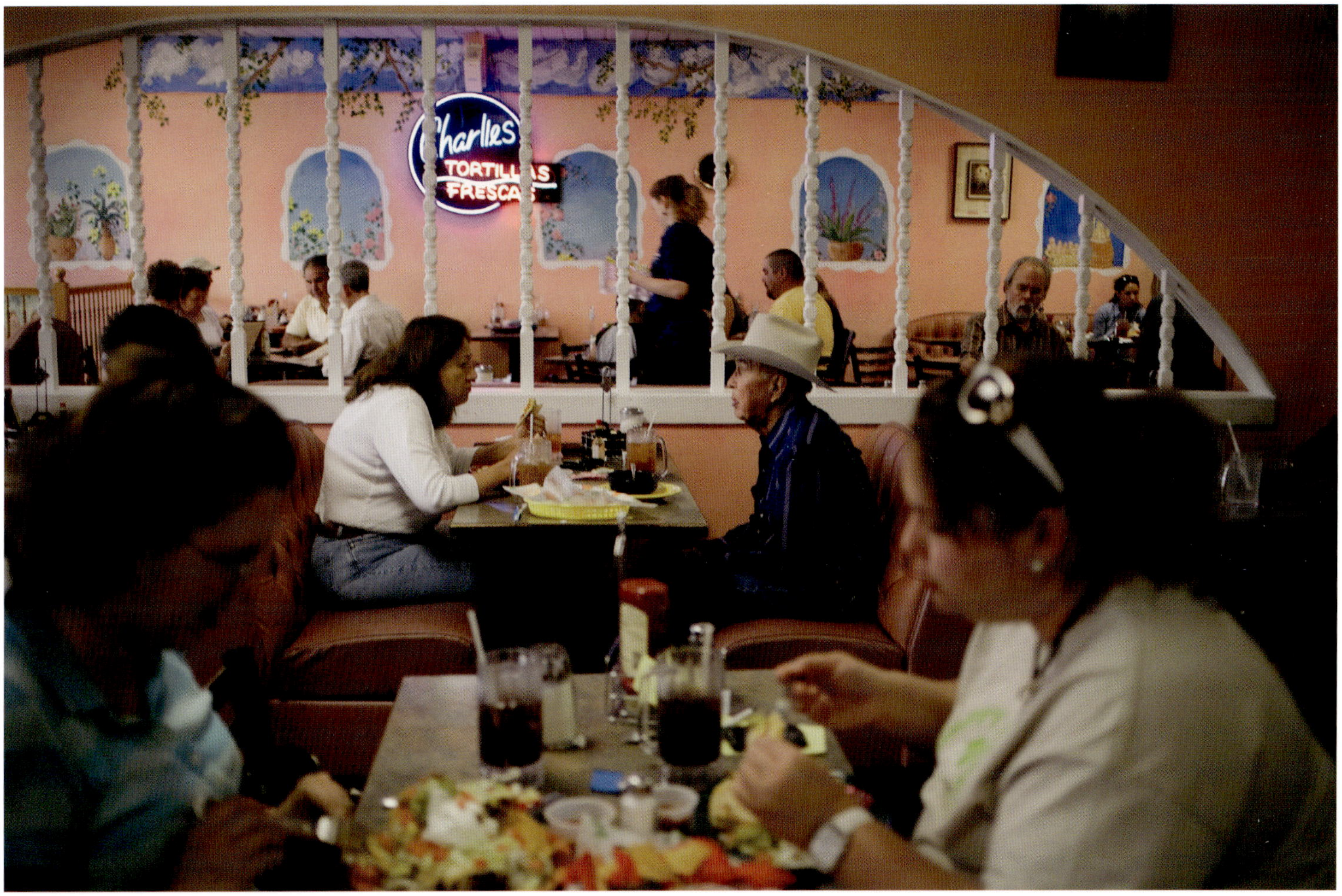
Charlies
TORTILLAS
FRESCAS

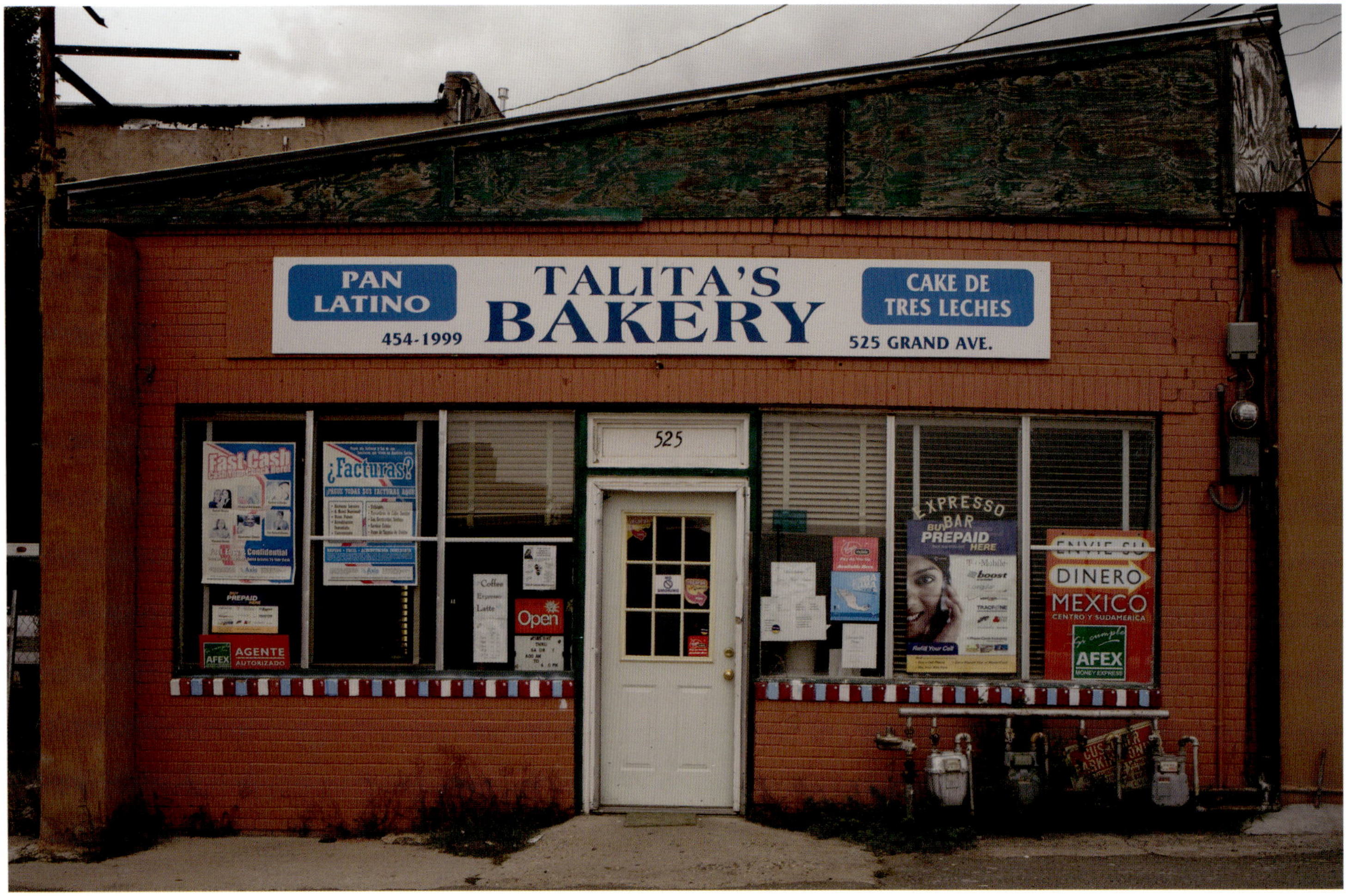
PAN LATINO
TALITA'S BAKERY
CAKE DE TRES LECHES
454-1999
525 GRAND AVE.
525
Fast Cash
¿Facturas?
AGENTE AUTORIZADO
Open
EXPRESSO BAR
PREPAID
ENVIE SU DINERO MEXICO
CENTRO Y SUDAMERICA
AFEX

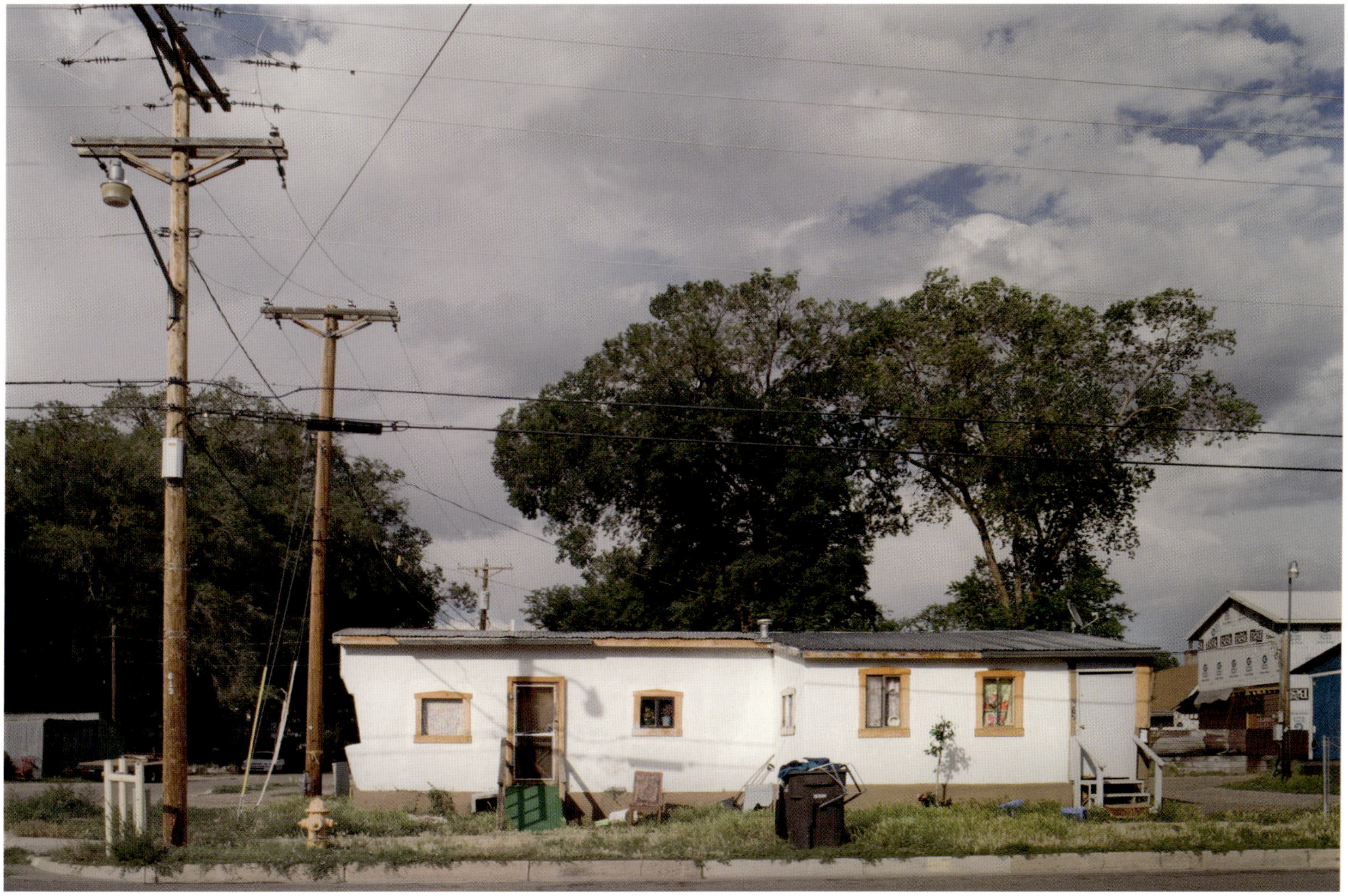

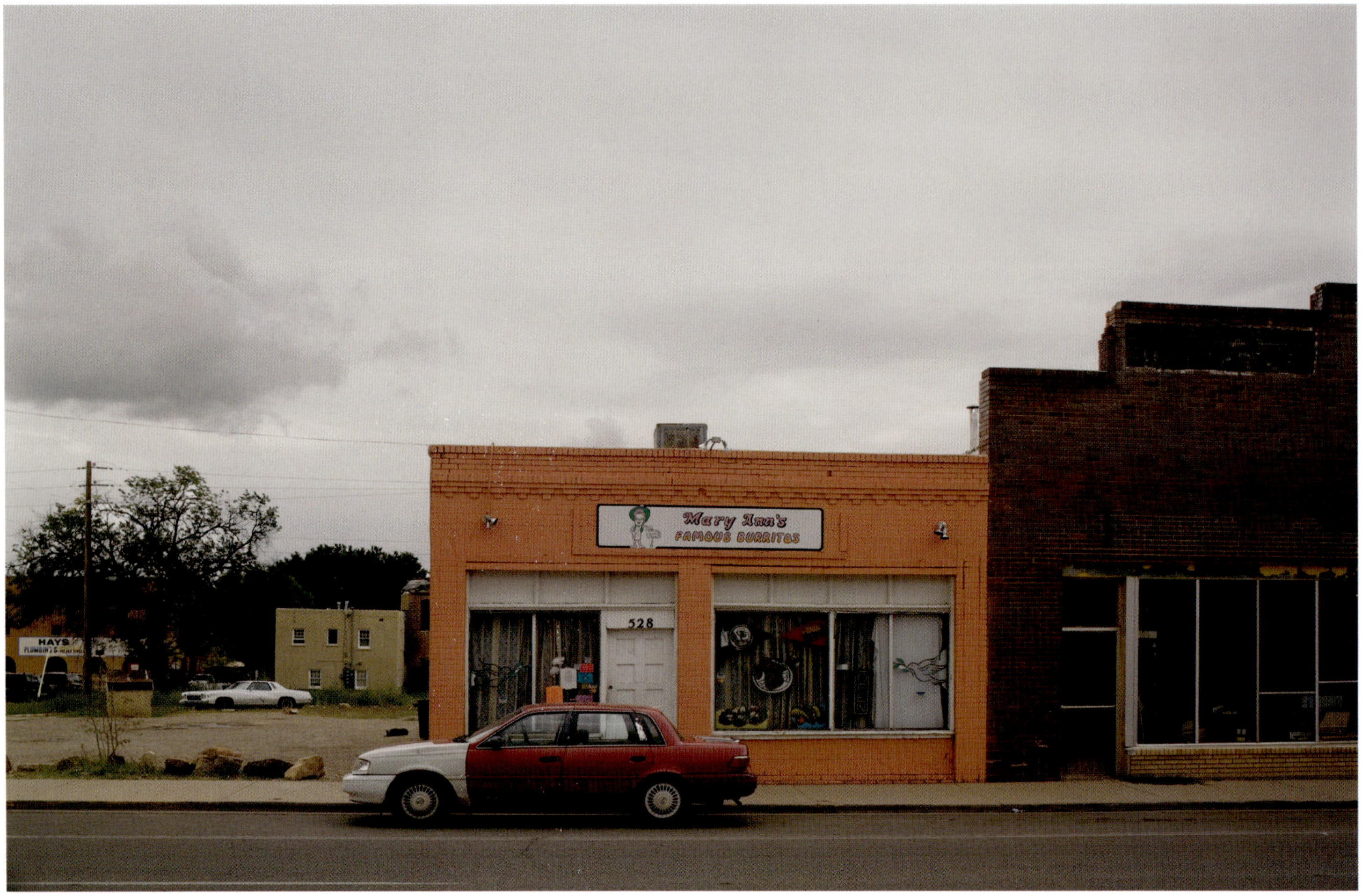
Mary Ann's
FAMOUS BURRITOS
528
HAYS

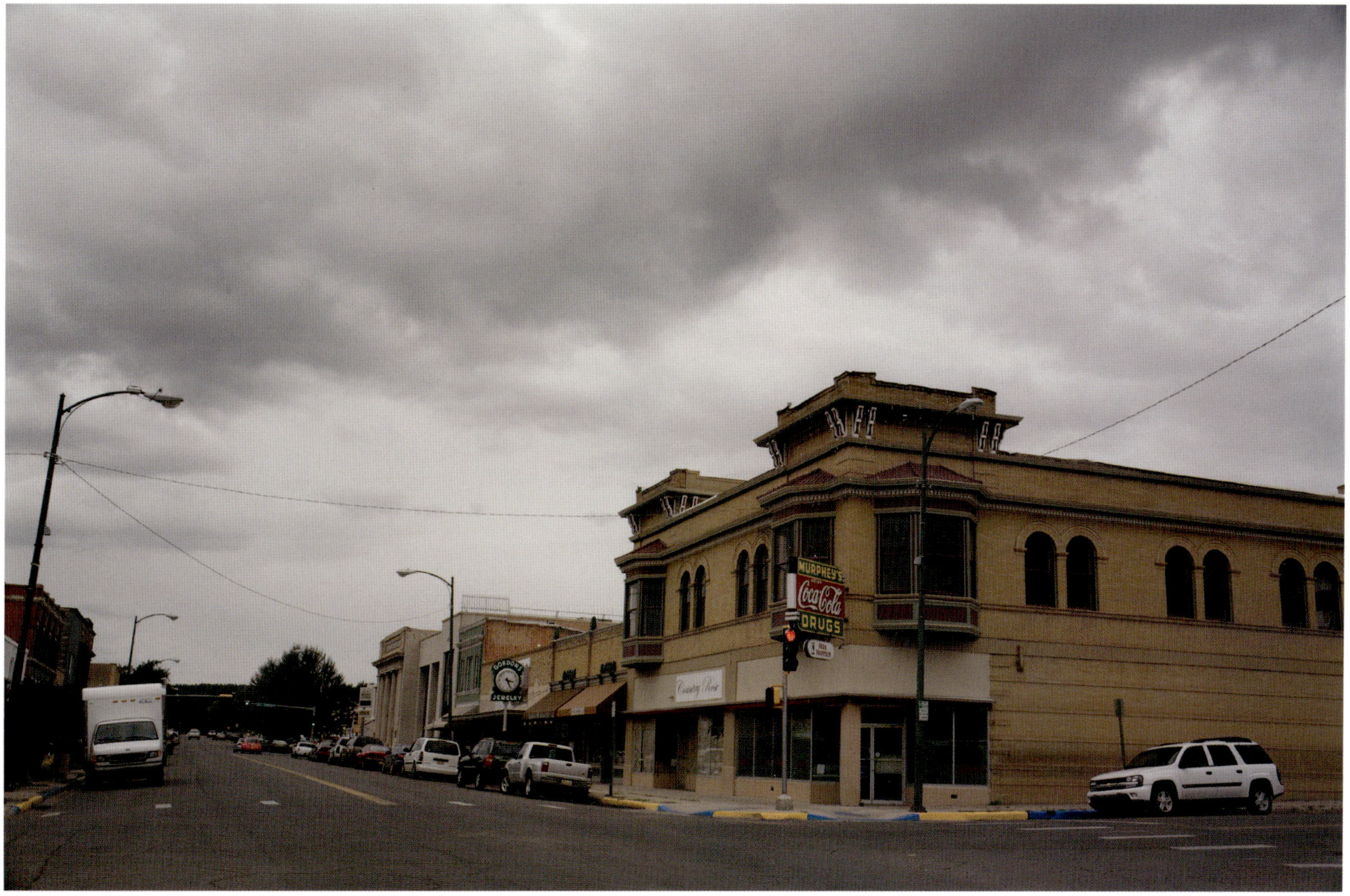
GORDONS
JEWELRY
MURPHEY'S
Coca-Cola
DRUGS
Country Rose

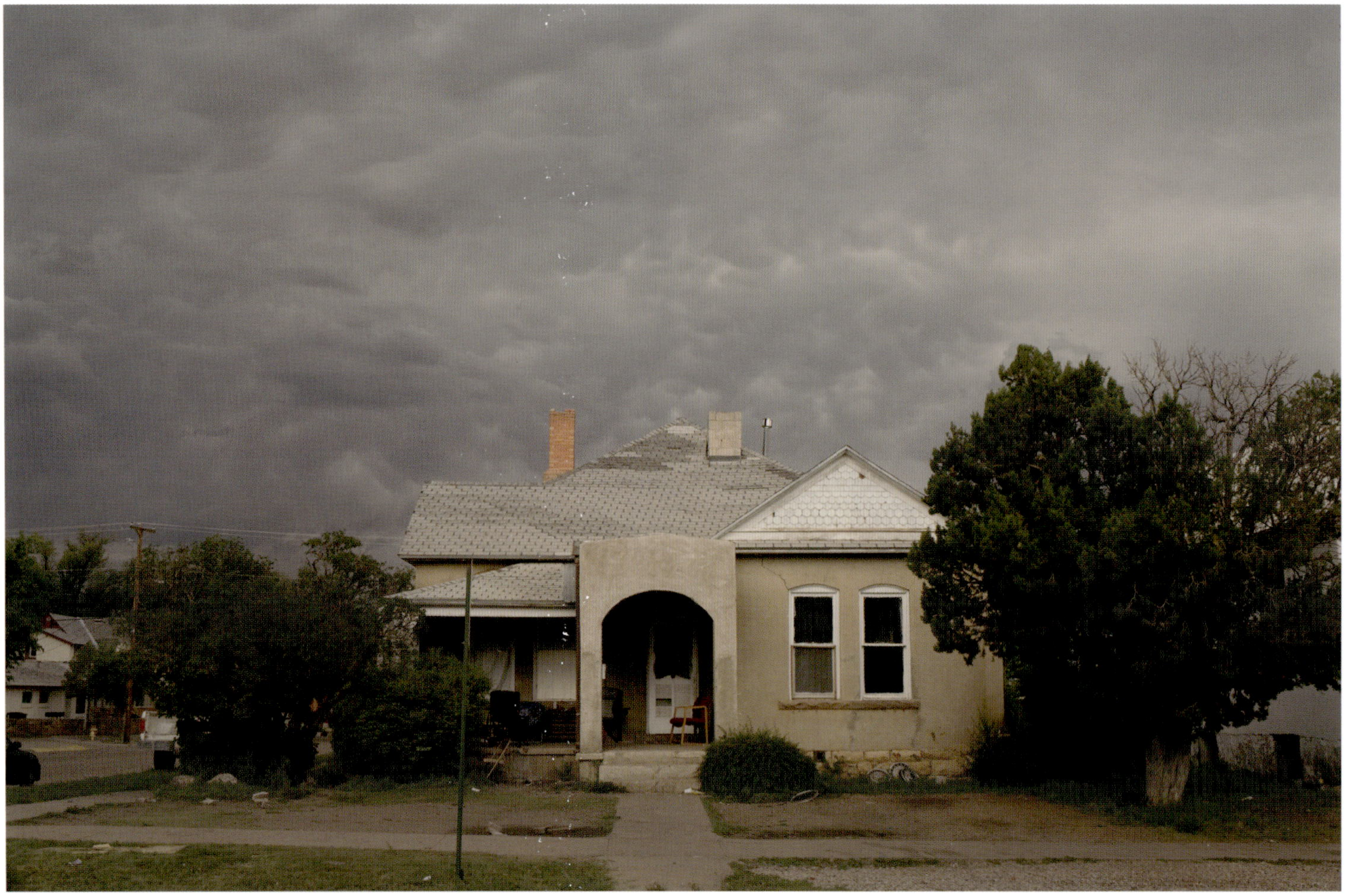

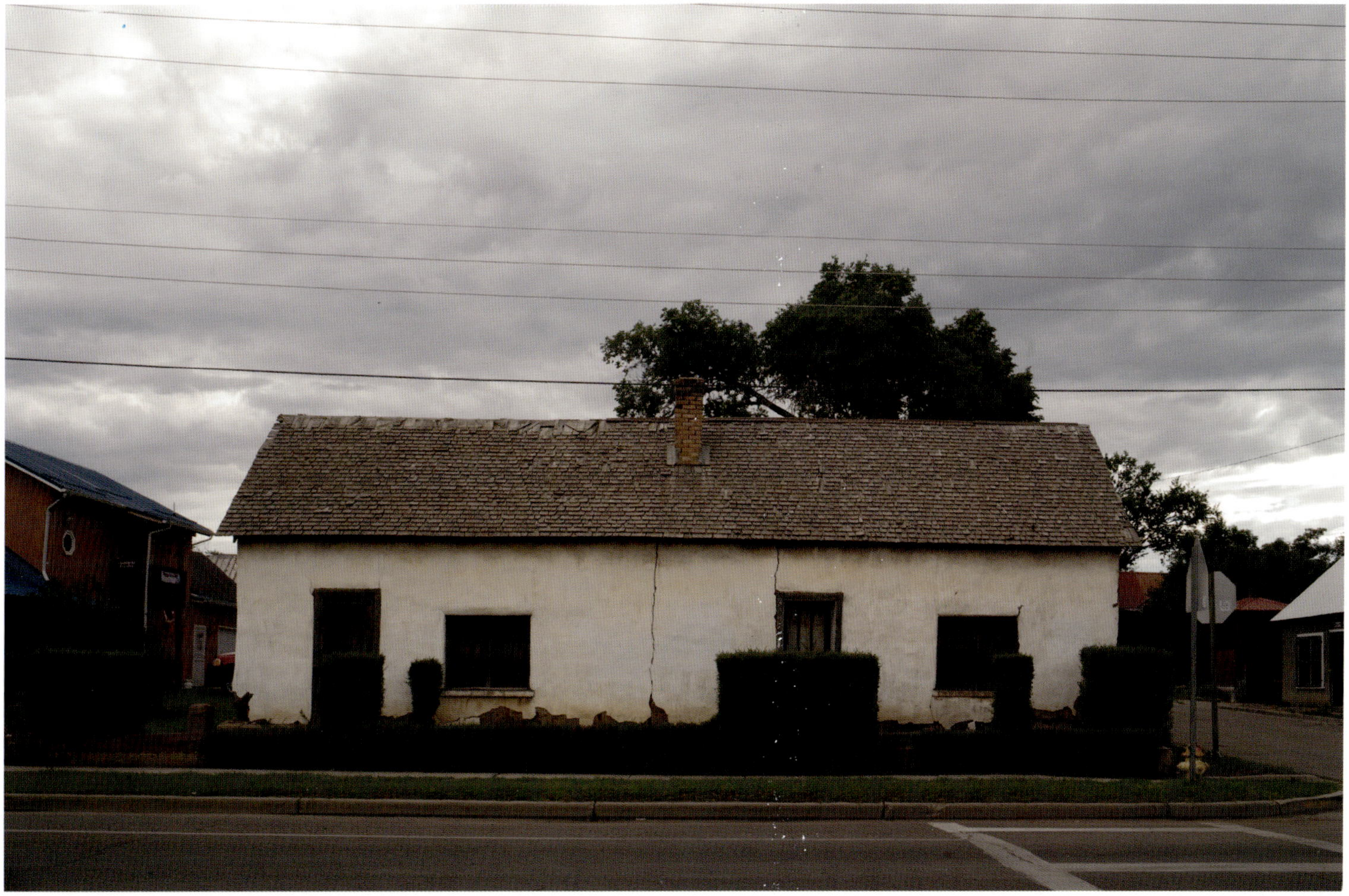

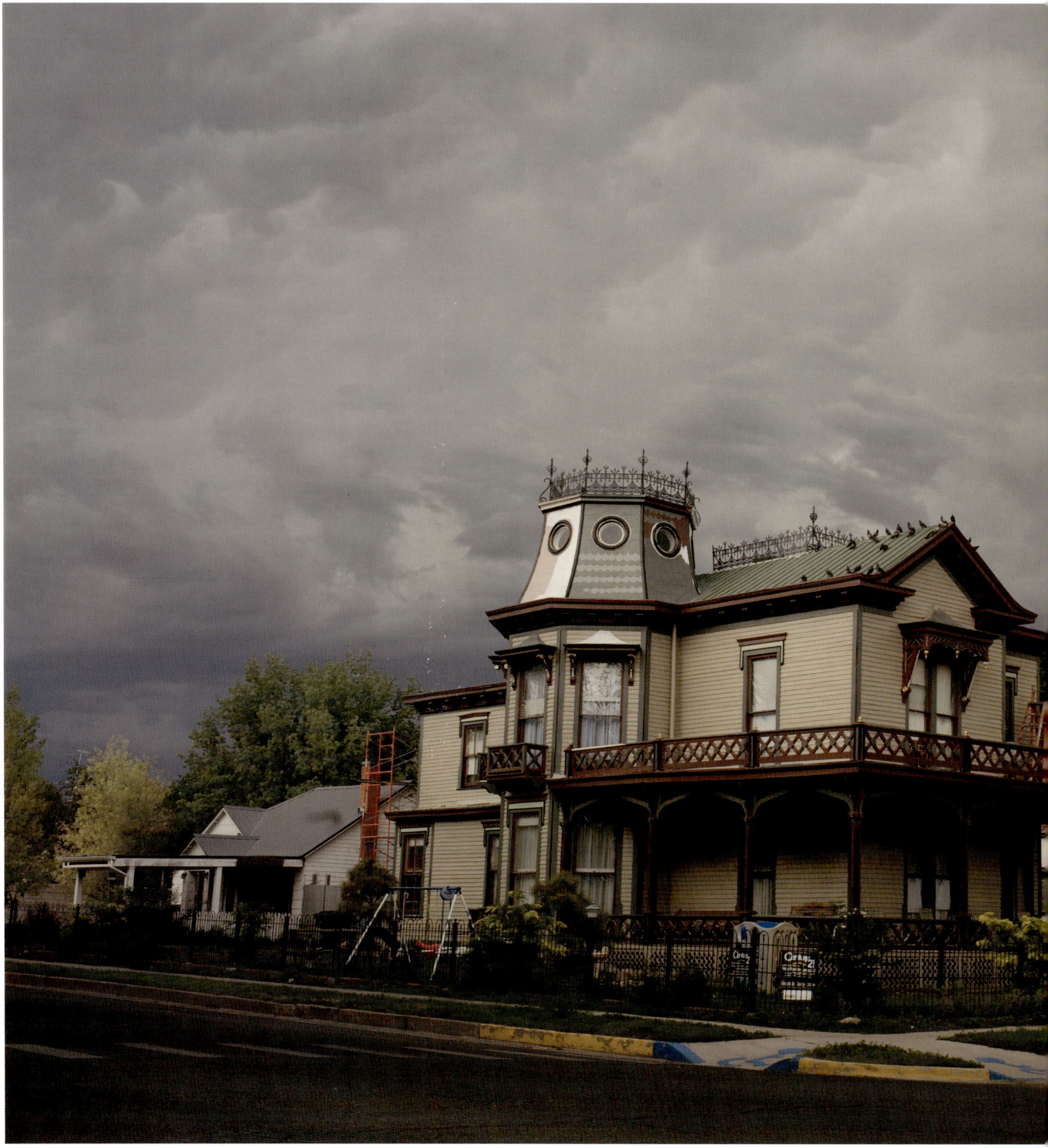

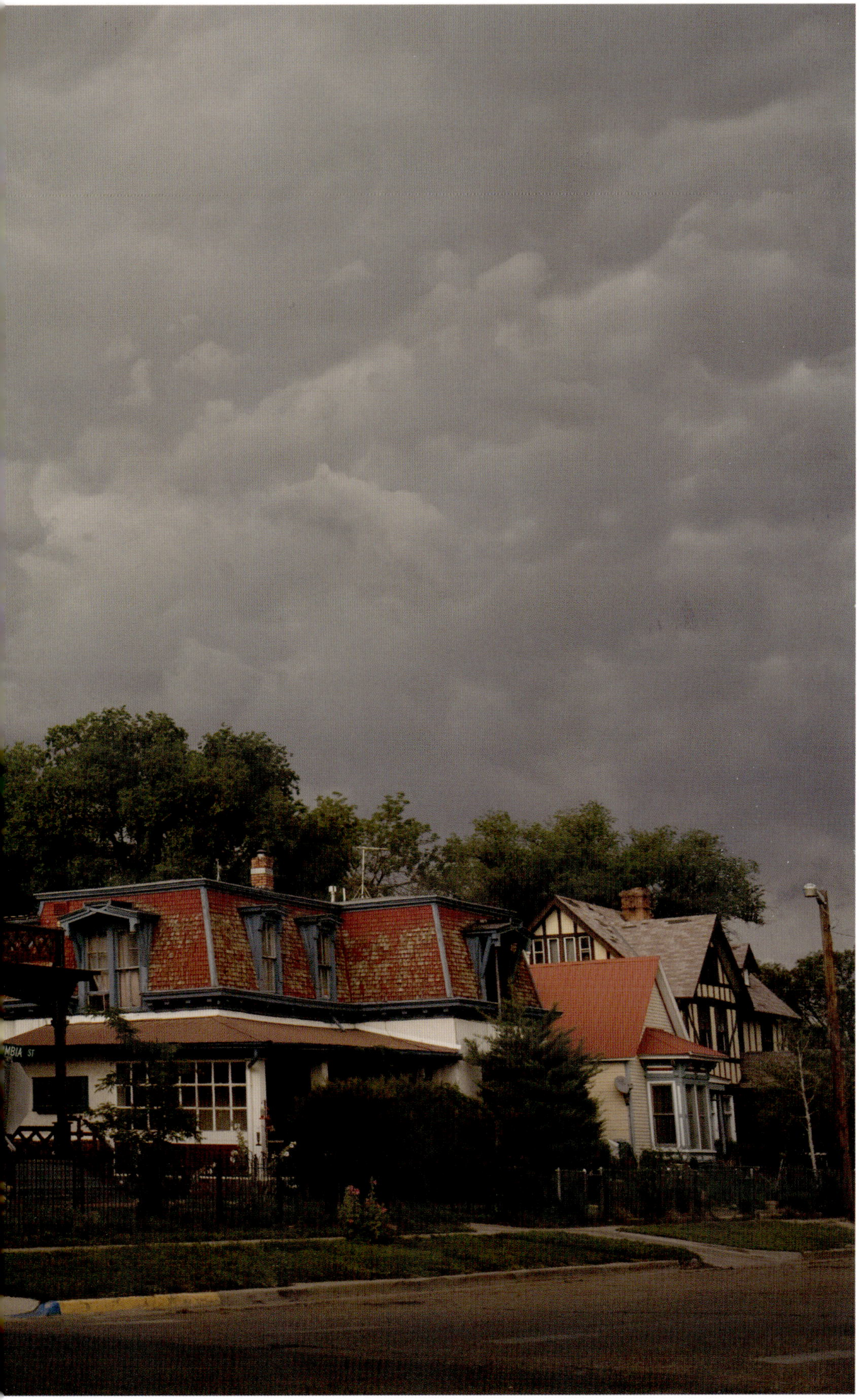

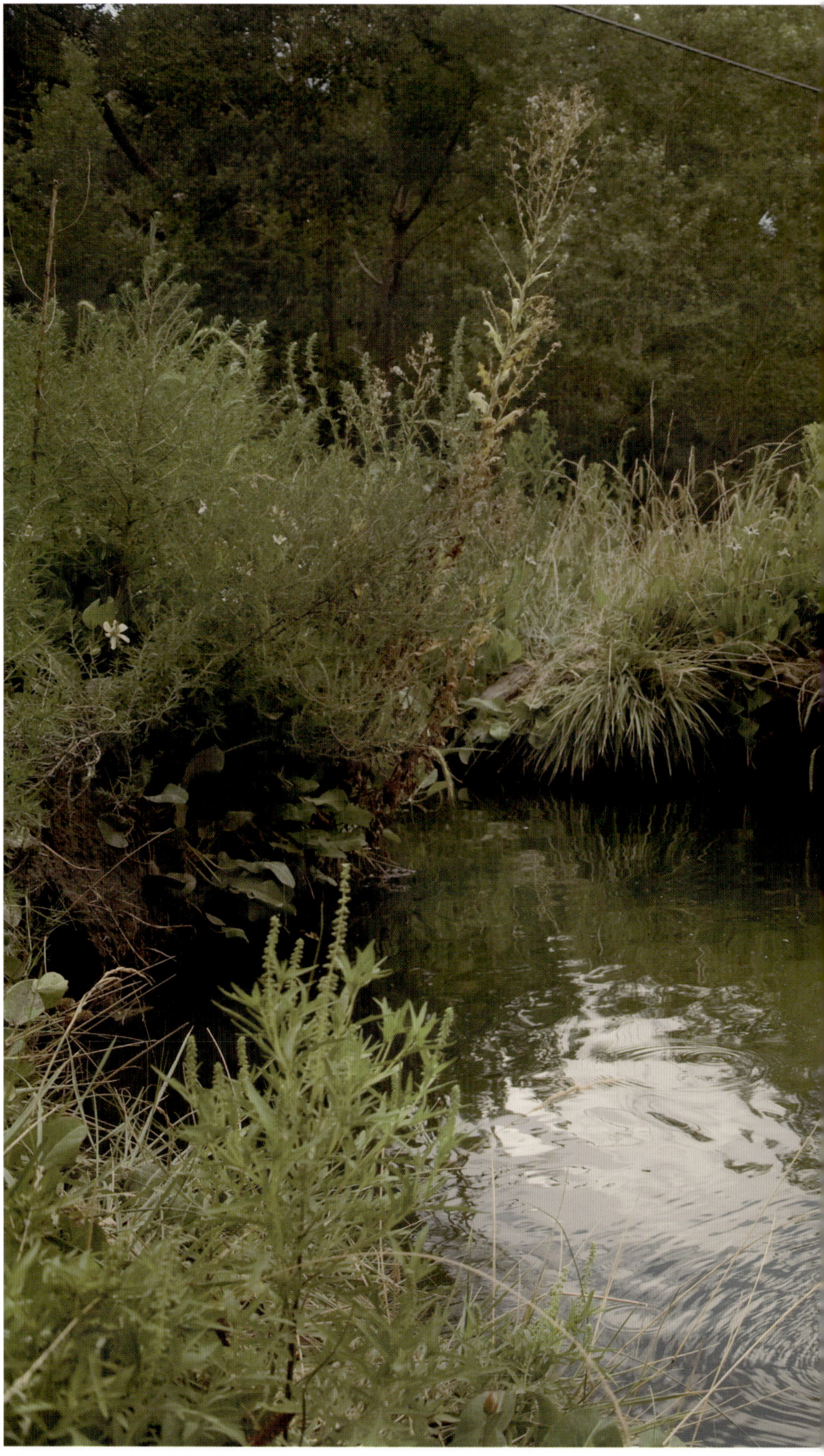

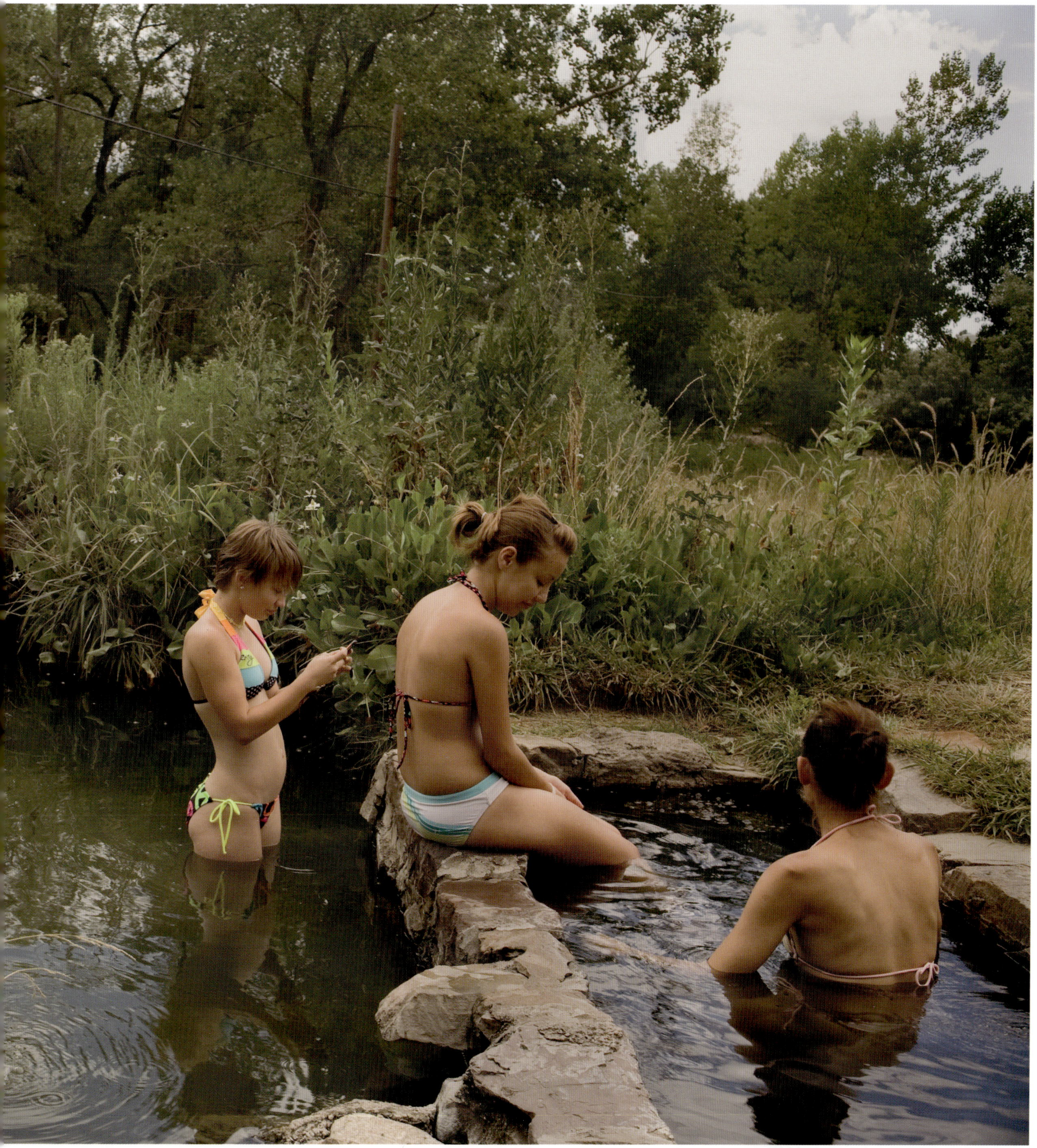

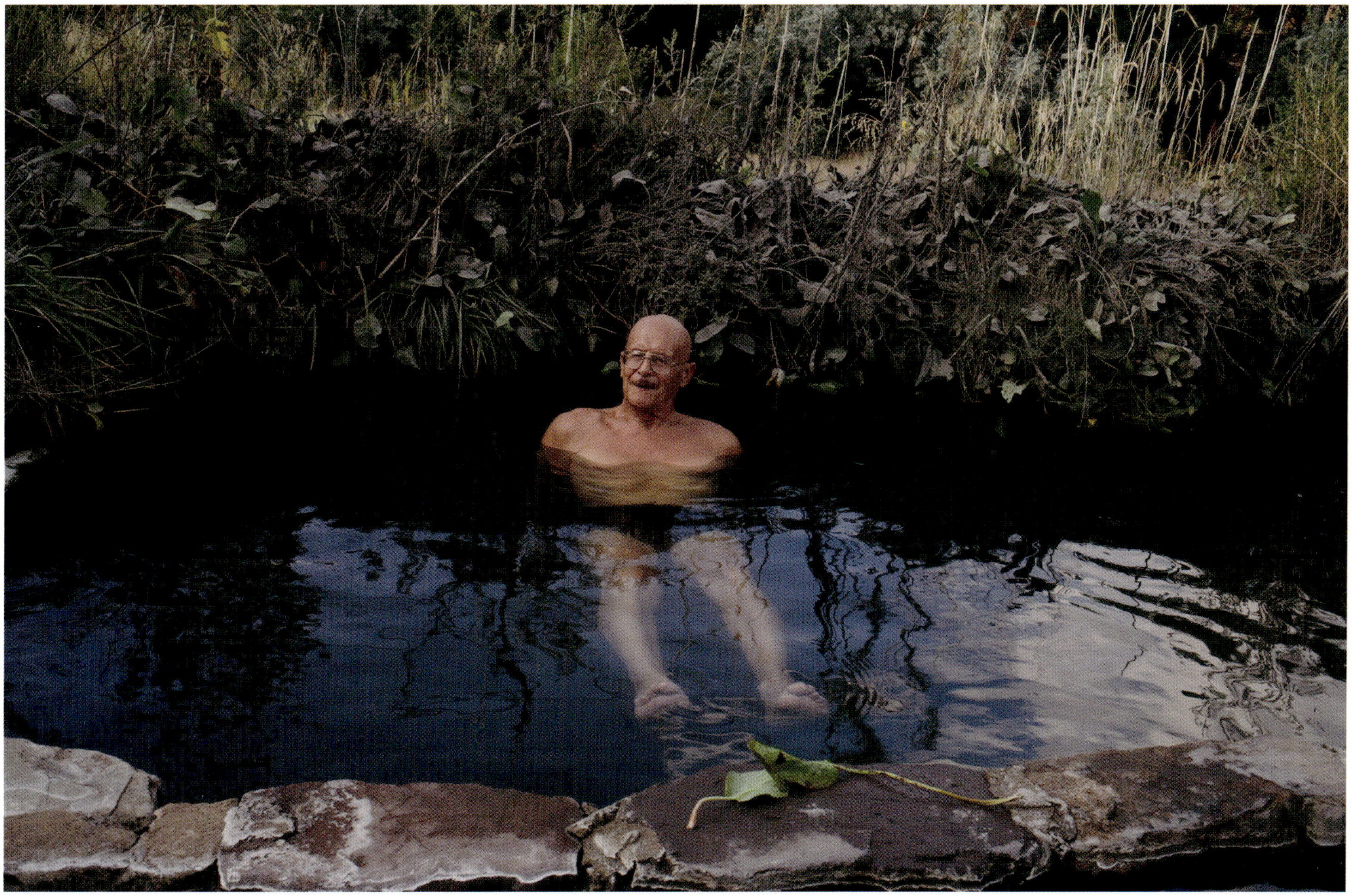

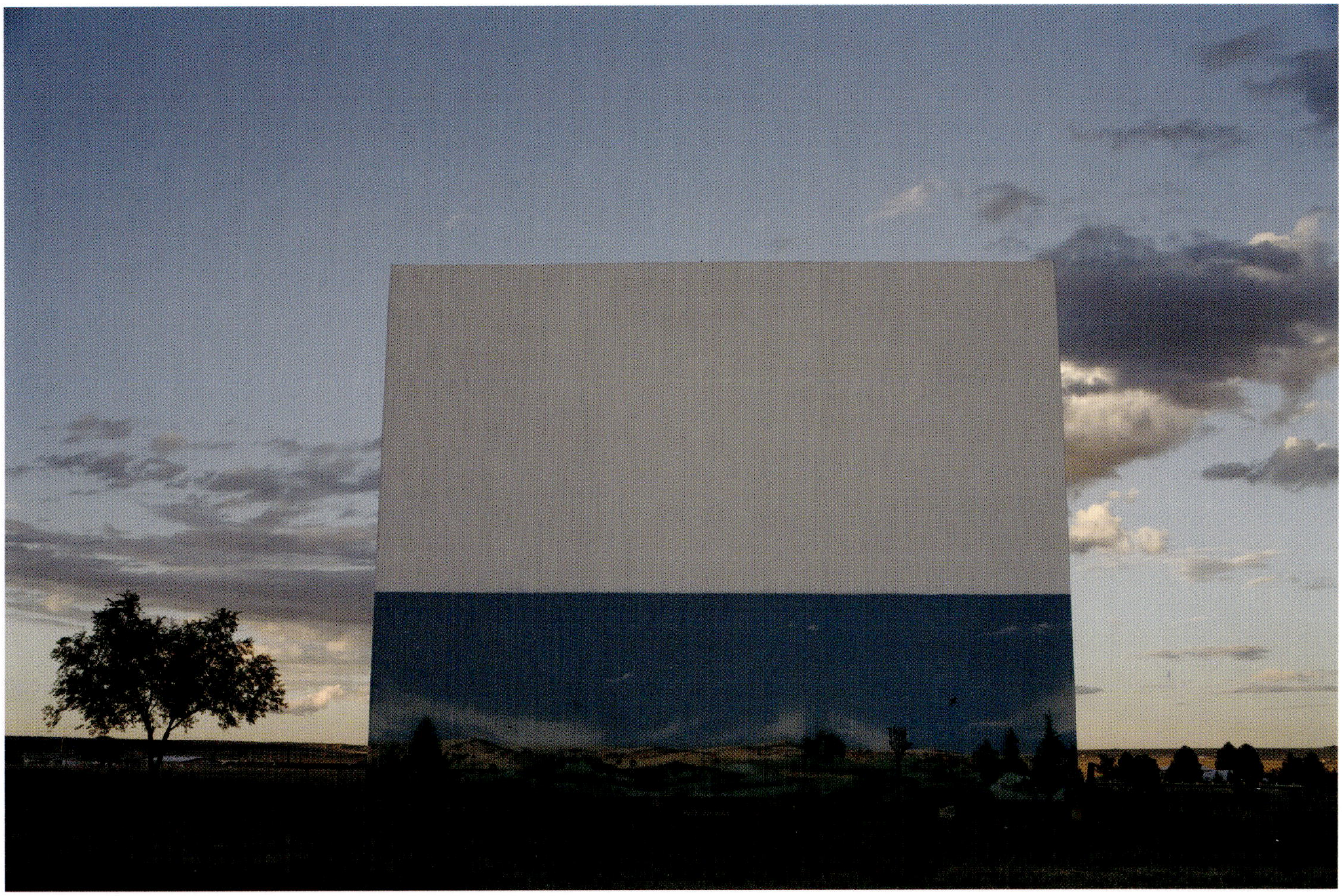

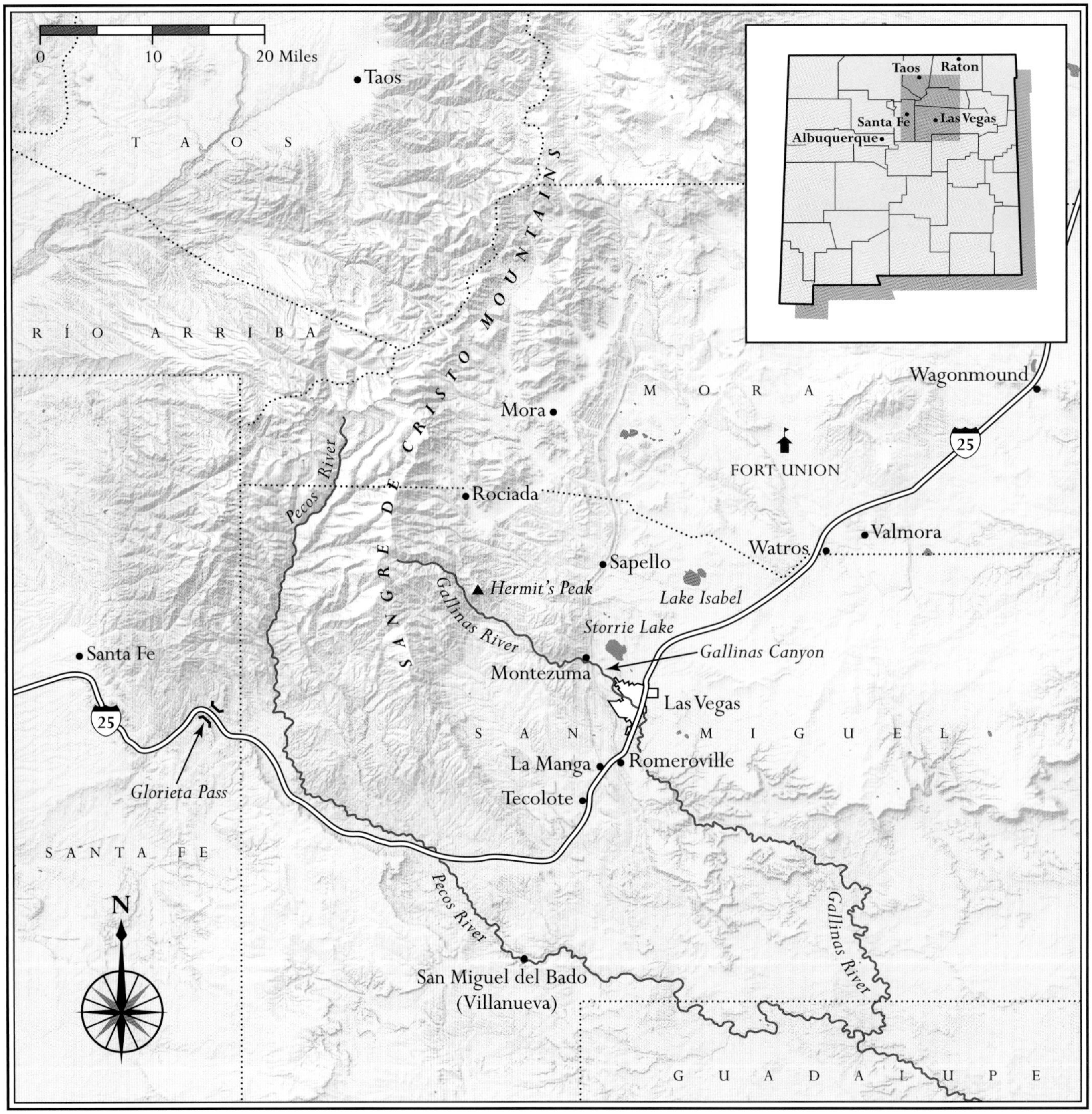

Deborah Reade

Chapter One: Discovering Las Vegas

To start with topography, *Las Vegas* translates as "The Meadows." The name refers to the series of spacious grasslands fanning out from the slopes of the Sangre de Cristo Range where the mountains form the western terminus of the Great Plains. If you climb to the top of Hermit's Peak and gaze eastward into the infinitude of flat prairie, you feel with a vertiginous thrill this meeting of mountain and plain. It is similarly awe-inspiring to stand in the tall grass beside the military ruins at Fort Union, now a National Park Service Historic Monument, and gaze westward to Hermit's Peak, then beyond it to other ridges along this most southerly range of the Rocky Mountains.

Las Vegas lies sixty miles east of Santa Fe, the much older settlement that was established in 1609 close to the northern edge of Spain's New World empire. After the opening of the Santa Fe Trail to prairie commerce in 1822, Las Vegas was the first settlement travelers saw after leaving Fort Leavenworth, Missouri. Wagon trains stopped there before lumbering onward to Glorieta Pass, the gap in the mountains that allowed access to Santa Fe, New Mexico's territorial capital. If the Anglo merchants who plied the trail in increasing numbers sought direct opportunities for trade with Mexico, they could continue south from Santa Fe along El Camino Real de Tierra Adentro (The Royal Road of the Interior Land), the well-trafficked 1,600-mile route to Mexico City forged by Spanish conquistadores at the end of the sixteenth century.

Although the trail's connection to the Camino Real remained important to the commerce between Mexico and the United States, Las Vegas soon became a nexus of considerable significance for additional reasons. Wool from the large herds of sheep and hides from the cattle that grazed the rich grasslands of the *vegas,* along with the pelts of beaver trapped in canyon streams, were important commodities, and manufactured goods from the East found a ready market on this new Western frontier.

Taking advantage of the town's location as the last stop on the trail and its position as a growing hub of trade with outlying towns and forts, a number of enterprising merchants set up mercantile establishments in Las Vegas in the middle of the nineteenth century. The coming of the railroad in 1879 magnified the town's importance, and it rapidly grew to become an important commercial city. By the first half of the twentieth century, however, Las Vegas lost this preeminence as economic circumstances changed and prosperity dwindled. What had been much more than a mere boomtown became a by-way. With its failure to rebound, Las Vegas settled into what it is today: an exceedingly pretty small town with a declining population. Because stasis has thwarted its overall physical transformation, you can read much of its history in its layout and architecture. With a discerning eye you can also see how history is inscribed in the outlying landscape of ranches and Hispanic villages along the Gallinas and other small rivers that thread their way through the canyons of the Sangre de Cristos.

Walking Around Town

Discovering physical Las Vegas does not take long, for you can easily walk from one end of town to the other. On New Mexico Avenue and South Pacific Avenue and their cross streets—Moreno, Valencia, Bernal, Sapello, Perez, Santa Ana, Tecolote—you are in the older part of town. Here is where you will find, set close to the street, some of the long, single-story adobe houses built as family compounds around a *placita*, or small communal courtyard. These relics are now few in number, for Las Vegas, unlike Santa Fe, has not mandated adobe construction as its distinctive architectural brand. Indeed, most of the houses you see in this section are interesting because of their stylistic diversity, colorful exteriors, and their evidence of having been built, repaired, cared for, or neglected by their owners. Architecturally hard to classify, some buildings show Greek Revival and Queen Anne influence, and others have elements of a style that architectural historians

Aerial view of West Las Vegas

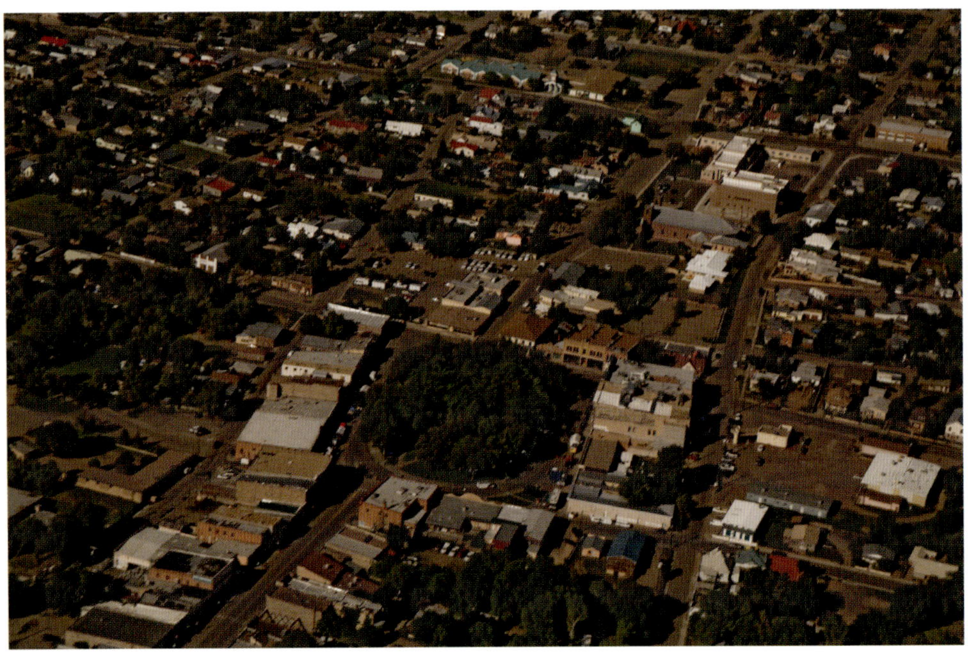

have christened World's Fair Classic—a combination of neoclassical and Colonial Revival features popularized in 1893 at Chicago's Columbian Exposition. As you move away from the center of town, you begin to see "double-wides," mobile houses assembled on site from two separate industrially fabricated units. In all, West Las Vegas presents a fascinating array of architectural idioms representing successive building technologies, local availability of materials, stylistic fashion, and individual needs, tastes, and means.

The heart of West Las Vegas—and one might say the spiritual heart of the entire city—is the plaza, the rectangular open-space center found in most Spanish Colonial towns, which was originally enclosed by contiguous adobe houses embracing an east-facing church. Landscaped in the 1880s after the arrival of the railroad made the Santa Fe Trail obsolete and the plaza was no longer a place where ox-drawn wagons and mule carts collected, it remains a pleasant, tree-shaded park framed by handsome commercial buildings, witnesses to the degree of prosperity that Las Vegas achieved during the last part of the nineteenth century. As varied as the residences in West Las Vegas, these range in style from adobe to New Mexican Territorial to the Italianate Victorian exemplified by the Plaza Hotel.

On the slope one block to the northwest of the plaza is Our Lady of Sorrows Church—Nuestra Señora de los Dolores—which can be classified as a provincial version of Gothic Revival. Begun in 1862 to replace the original adobe church built on the plaza by the town's founders, the construction of a building of this size and material—finished red sandstone quarried twenty-five miles away—represents a testament to the power and influence of New Mexico's famous Archbishop Jean-Baptiste Lamy (1814–88), especially since the building with its 150-foot-long, 60-foot-wide nave and pair of high, square towers was completed a decade before the coming of the railroad and at a time when little mechanical building equipment was available.

Aerial view of East Las Vegas

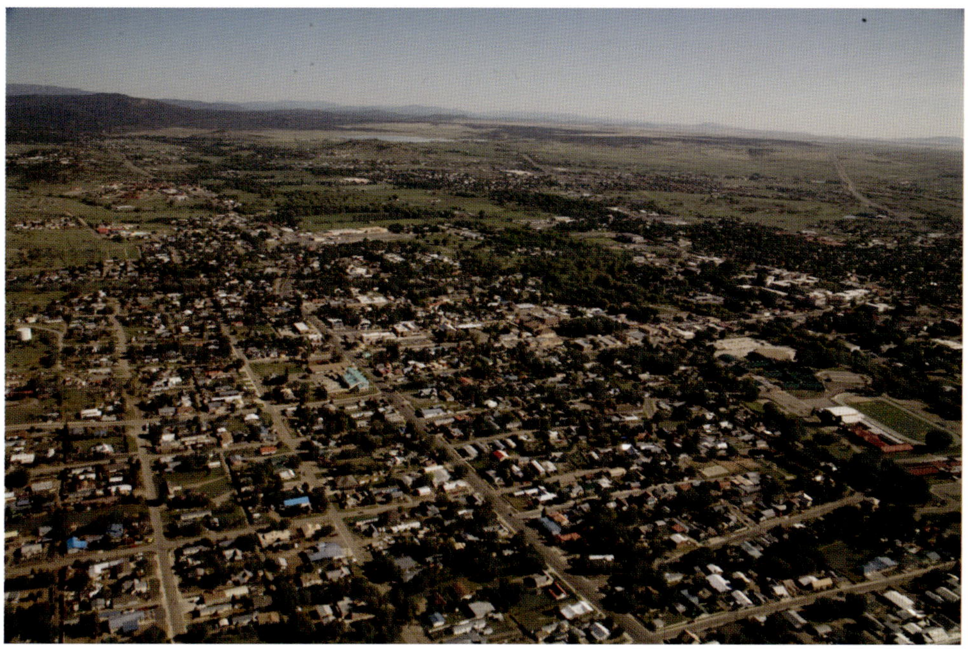

The architecture along Bridge Street, which runs a couple of blocks from the plaza to the Gallinas River, is similar to that around the plaza—handsome, mostly pre-1900 commercial structures,

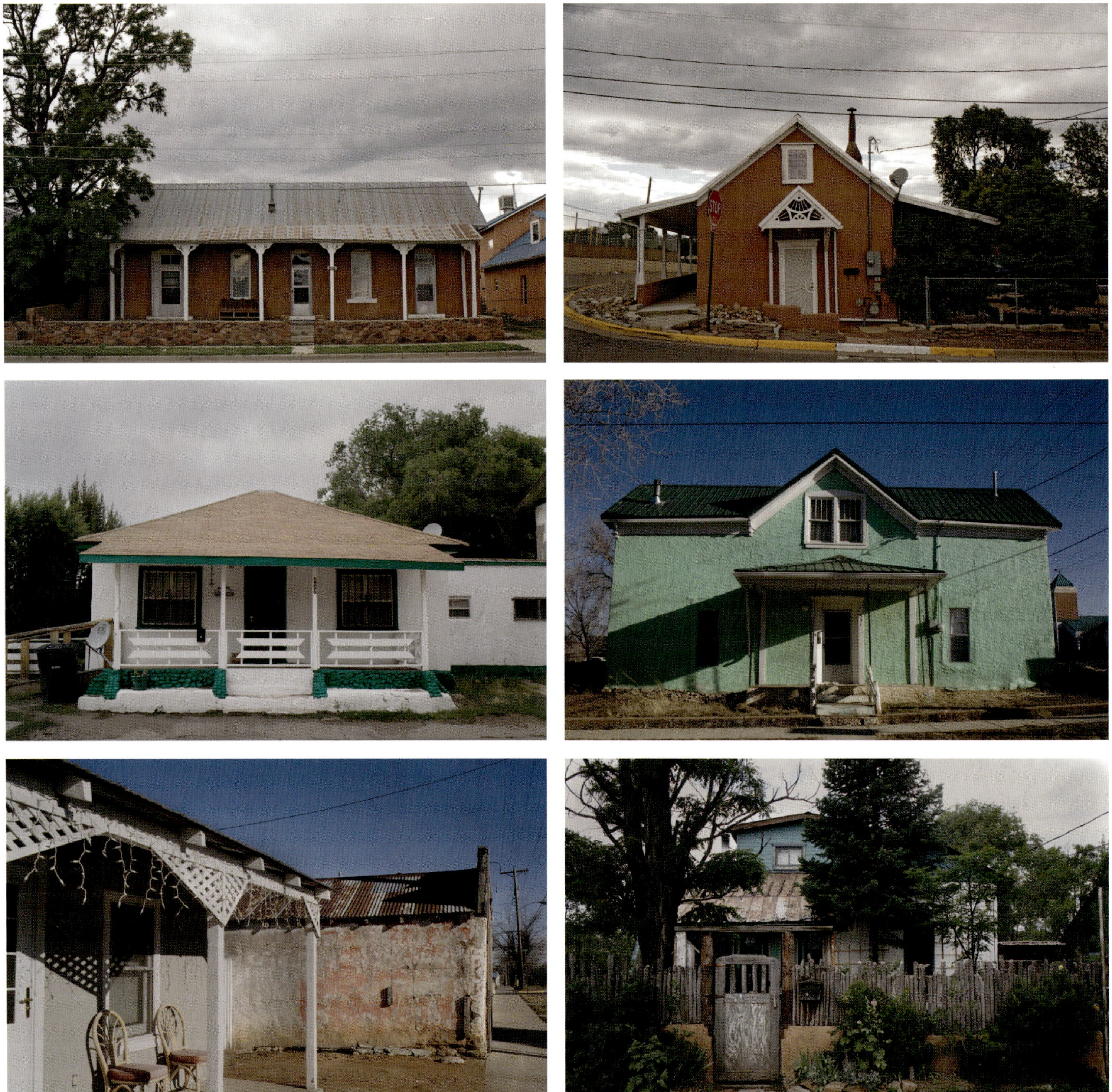

West Las Vegas houses

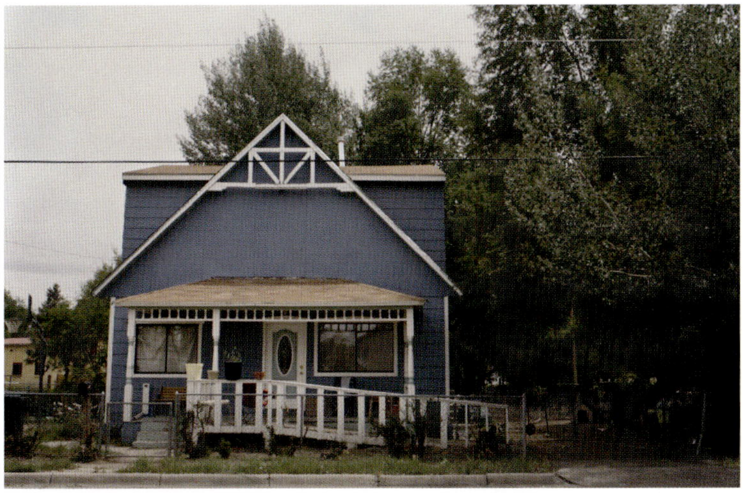
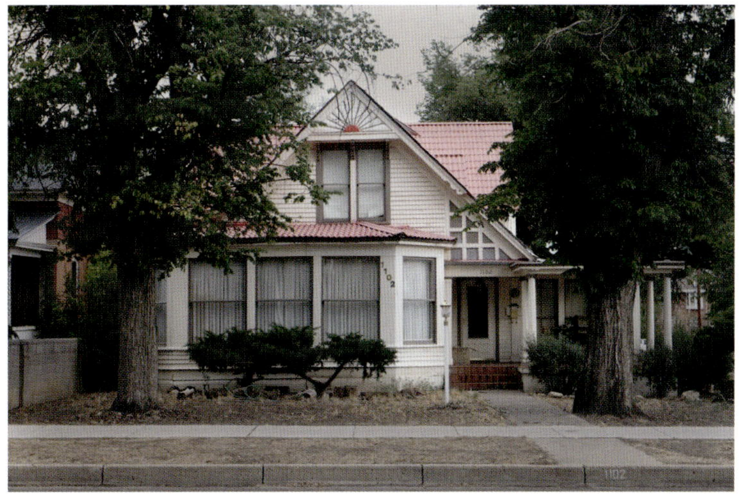
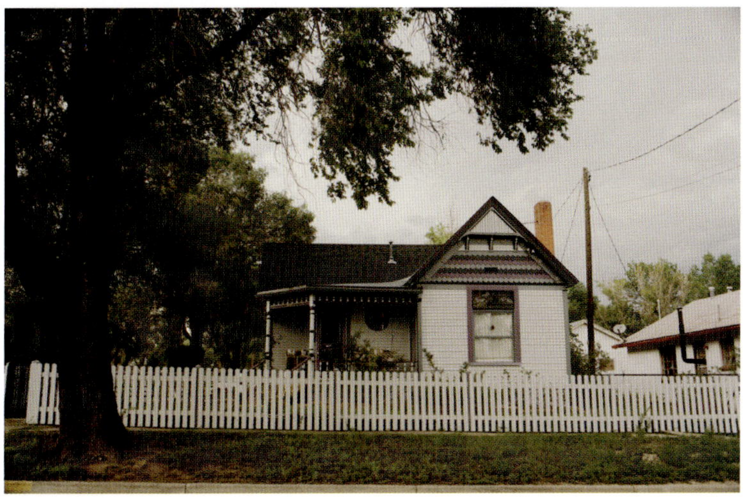
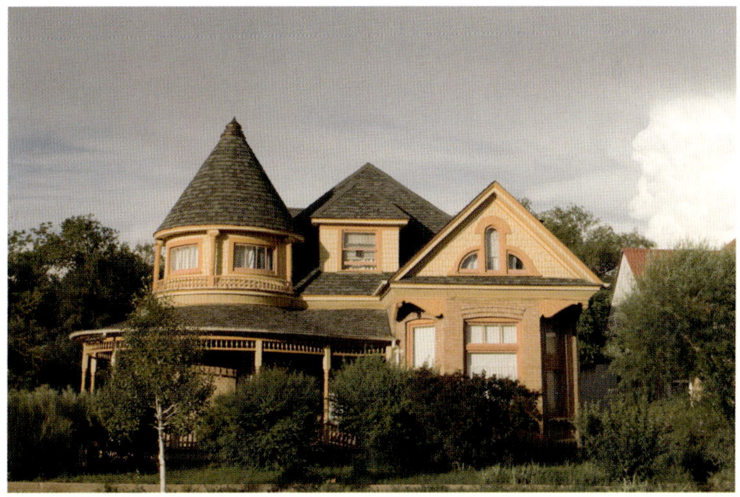
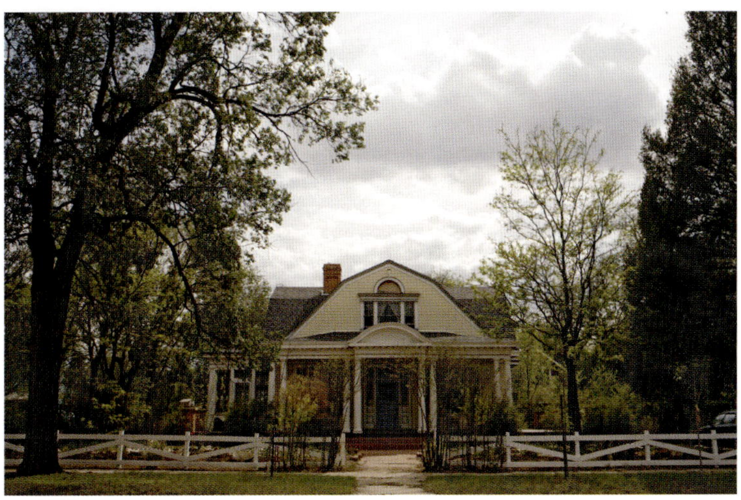
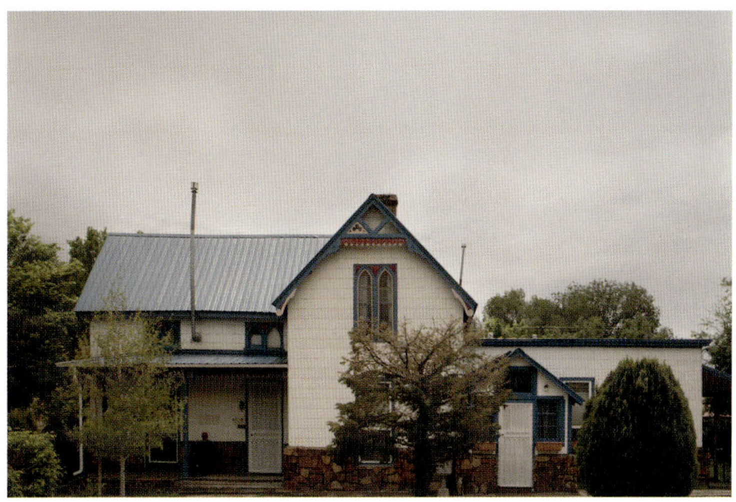

East Las Vegas houses

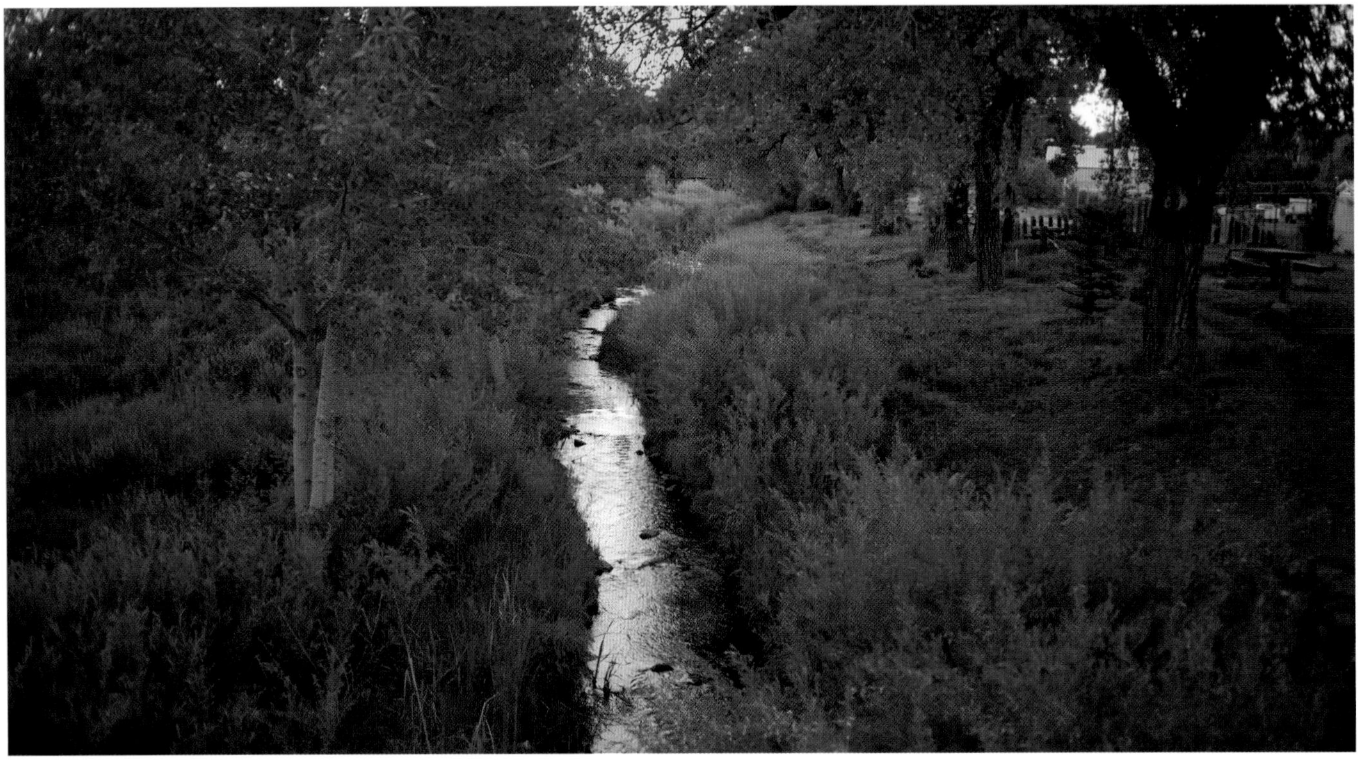

Gallinas River

some in serious disrepair, some in a state of partial renovation, and some refurbished to serve a variety of uses. Among the buildings on the south side are E. Romero Hose and Fire Company, the Rialto restaurant, Popular Dry Goods selling western apparel, and the Kiva, an Art Deco–style movie theater. On the north side you will find a tattoo parlor, Estella's Café, the bookstore Tome on the Range, the New Mexico Mental Health Center, and a storefront housing a not-for-profit organization called the Citizens Committee on Historic Preservation. Among other activities, this volunteer group organizes tours of the city's commercial, institutional, and residential landmarks.

The Gallinas River forms a distinct boundary between West Las Vegas (called Old Town), where the plaza and the layout of the surrounding streets evince the town's Hispanic origins, and East Las Vegas (New Town), built according to the street grid laid out by surveyors to accommodate the Anglo settlement that sprang up with the coming of the Atchison, Topeka and Santa Fe Railroad. The river, which dwindles to creek-size in town, is the principal source of drinking water for Las Vegans. It is also part of New Mexico's time-honored system of irrigation whereby *presas*, or diversion dams, tap important streams at various points in order to channel water into the hand-dug ditches, the *acequias*, that distribute water to cultivated fields.

Once you have crossed the bridge that gives Bridge Street its name, you are in New Town. At this point Bridge Street becomes National Avenue, a tree-lined thoroughfare that runs to Grand Avenue. Located on either side of National Avenue on the hill rising above the Gallinas River, the campus of New Mexico Highlands University, with a student body of 3,700, boasts a number of fine buildings, including the Adele Ilfeld Auditorium, a handsome sandstone 726-seat theater designed by the early-twentieth-century architect E. W. Hart and built between 1914 and 1921. Along with other thoroughfares evidencing the Union patriotism prevalent in Territorial New Mexico in the wake of the Civil War—Washington, Douglas, Lincoln, Columbia, Grant—National is intersected by perpendicular streets, also tree-lined, named according to the numerical sequencing of the nineteenth-century surveyor's plat. Fifth, Sixth, Seventh, and Eighth are especially attractive, with many fine brick mansions interspersed with frame houses and comfortable Arts and Crafts–era bungalows. The white dome and columns of the neoclassical Carnegie Library, which looks like a small-scale version of Monticello, give a pleasant gravitas to the leafy square surrounding it, as does the large, contemporary Gothic Immaculate Conception Church facing it at the corner of Sixth Street and National. St. Paul's Chapel on Eighth Street and Columbia was originally the Montefiore Congregation's synagogue, built in 1884. At the intersection of Eighth and National, on what was once called Zion Hill, stand St. Paul's Episcopal Church (1890) and the Methodist Church (1923), a pale yellow brick structure with a 390-pipe organ, oak pews, and stained-glass windows shipped in from St. Louis.

Where National meets Grand Avenue is the historic Municipal Building, a 1940 Works Progress Administration project. Since 1961 it has been the City of Las Vegas Museum and Rough Rider Memorial Collection. Railroad Avenue, running parallel to Grand, marks the eastern edge of town. Here you will find the California Mission Revival–style train station[1] and the adjacent boarded-up Castañeda Hotel. Originally operated by the Fred Harvey Company, whose chain of hostelries kept pace with the building of the country's transcontinental rail lines, the Castañeda was in Las Vegas's heyday a lively spot staffed by young women known as Harvey Girls. A short distance south is the railroad's large

Highlands University campus

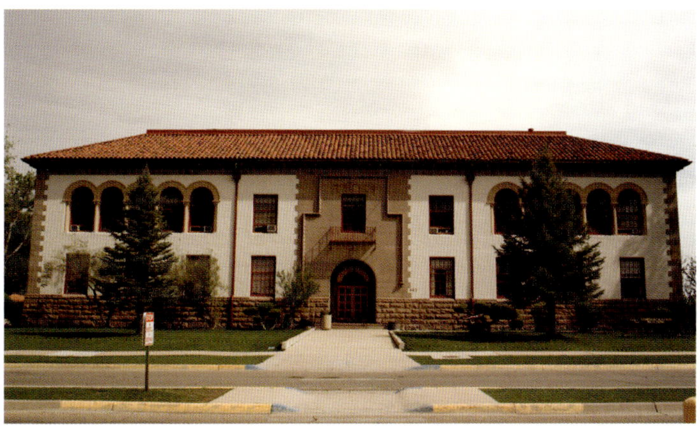

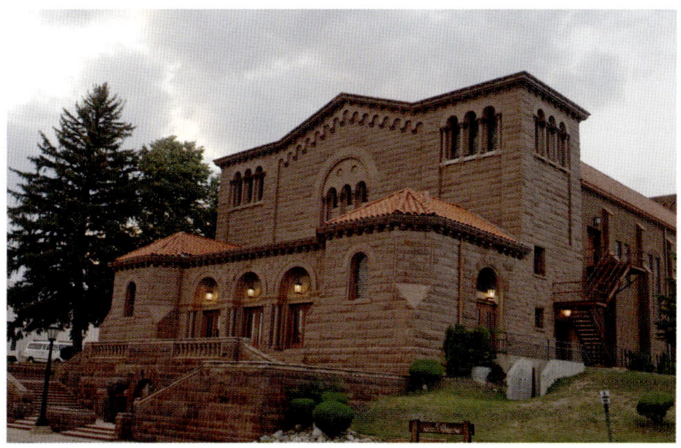

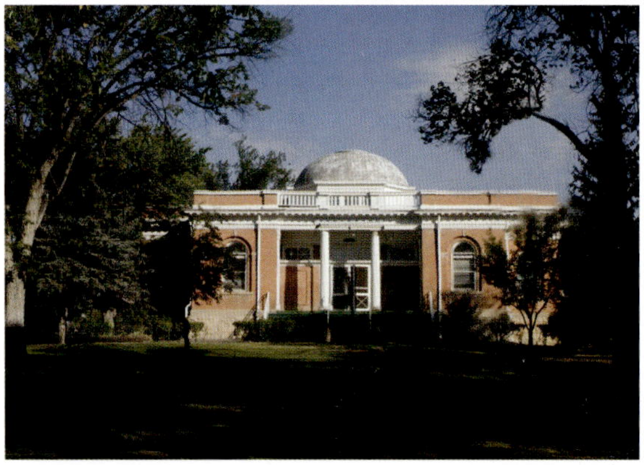

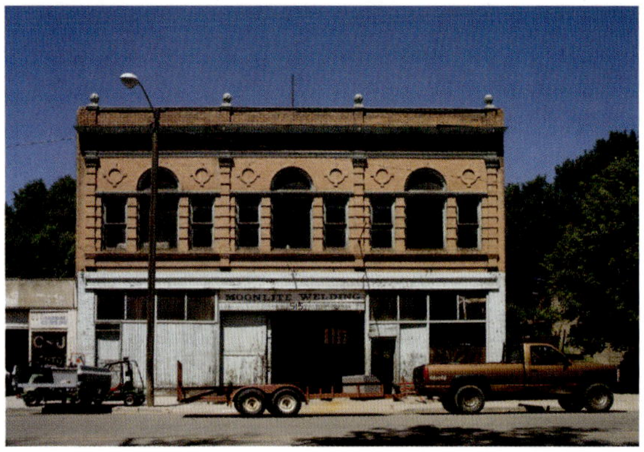

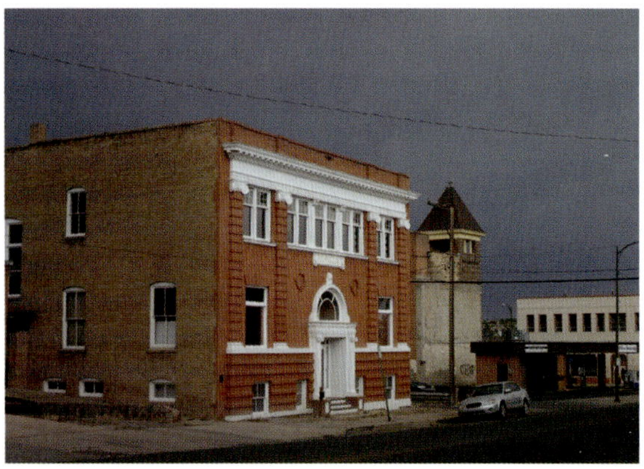

Carnegie Library

515 Railroad Avenue

YMCA

nine-bay roundhouse, which was used for warehousing after the railroad company decommissioned its division headquarters in Las Vegas in 1959. On the west side of Railroad Avenue are some mostly abandoned or deteriorating warehouses and former retail establishments, historic structures of considerable architectural distinction.

Because of its proximity to the train tracks, many of the dwellings in the area around nearby Lincoln Park—the New Town counterpart to the Old Town plaza—were once inhabited by railroad company officials and trainmen. This section of town is an architectural history textbook of locally inflected building idioms dating from the early 1880s, when the railroad company laid out East Las Vegas. Because of the ease with which stone could be brought in from nearby quarries after the arrival of the railroad, there are several large masonry houses in an eclectic medley of Italian Villa, Second Empire, Classical Revival, and Queen Anne styles. Derived from Picturesque cottage pattern books, an array of modest-sized wooden houses with gable roofs and bracketed columns supporting front porch eaves preserve the pleasant aspect of late Victorian America. Two apartment houses, a building type well in advance of its time in New Mexico, were also erected in this area around the turn of the twentieth century.

The old mercantile center encircling the plaza and running down Bridge Street was not entirely eclipsed as the town's commercial core by the coming of New Town. However, the business district that grew up around Sixth and Douglas—praised as "the best example of a turn-of-the-century commercial and institutional center remaining in New Mexico"[2]—testifies to New Town's former preeminence. Today you walk these blocks with a sense of regret for the loss of their once-vibrant economic life.

On the corner of Douglas and Grand sits a large hotel. Built as The Meadows in the early 1920s when automobile transportation increased western tourism, it was later given a Spanish Colonial Revival façade and renamed El Fidel. Next door on Douglas is the town's most architecturally significant building, the 1895 Chapman Masonic Lodge # 2 designed by I. H. Rapp and Associates. This rusticated, locally quarried, dark reddish-purple sandstone structure with its impressive carvings flanking the main entrance "is probably the finest Richardsonian Romanesque building erected in New Mexico," according to architectural historian Chris Wilson.[3] At the corner of Douglas and Sixth stood the Duncan Opera House. Though less distinguished than its neighbor, until its demolition in 1965 its combination of Italianate and Romanesque Revival styles offered additional testimony to Las

Vegas's architectural aspirations. A block further west on Douglas is the Southwest Capital Bank (originally the First National Bank and later the Bank of Las Vegas), built in 1921. Instead of the ruggedness of Richardsonian Romanesque, here the architects Rapp and Rapp employed the Neoclassical Revival, the architectural style associated with financial solidity. For building material they chose Missouri sandstone, which was cut, carved, and polished in St. Louis.

The corner of Sixth and Douglas is anchored by the 1898 Crockett Building, also designed by Rapp and Rapp, a landmark structure now nostalgically identified with its longtime first-floor corner tenant, Murphy's Drug Store. It was recently remodeled and reopened as the First Community Bank, with the result that the prominent Murphy's Drug Store corner sign, considered by some to be a landmark in its own right, was demoted to souvenir status and placed less conspicuously on a side wall. On the opposite side of the street the site of the demolished Duncan Opera House is the drive-up auxiliary of the bank. In spite of the lack of vitality that has characterized the area following the migration of shopping to the commercial strip along Mills Avenue north of town, Charlie's Spic & Span bakery and café between Seventh and Eighth Streets on Douglas draws a large breakfast and lunchtime crowd.

Erected around the corner on Sixth Street between 1892 and 1896, the Old City Hall, currently the Las Vegas Police Station, was the first municipal building in New Mexico. The handsome red-brick YMCA adjacent to it was constructed in 1905 according to a design by Rapp and Rapp. In its original state it boasted a reading room, gymnasium, swimming pool, activity lobby, and sixteen bedrooms.[4]

Outside the Town

Once you have explored the town on foot, the environs of Las Vegas are likely to inspire your curiosity. Heading north on Eighth Street as it follows the course of the Gallinas you will come to Upper Town, called Plaza de Arriba, which was founded in 1841, six years after the original Las Vegans had received their community land grant. In typical fashion, the settlers of Upper Town, also called San Antonio in honor of the community's patron saint, built their church facing east on a wide plaza. Although it once thrived as a farming and sheep-raising community, San Antonio is now a semirural suburb of Las Vegas. Its old plaza is an overgrown vacant space used for parking during church services.

You can get an added sense of the deep roots of Spanish colonial history by exploring other river-valley settlements nearby. By following the frontage road along Interstate 25 running south from Exit 343 to the

Train station

Castañeda Hotel

Chapman Masonic Lodge #2

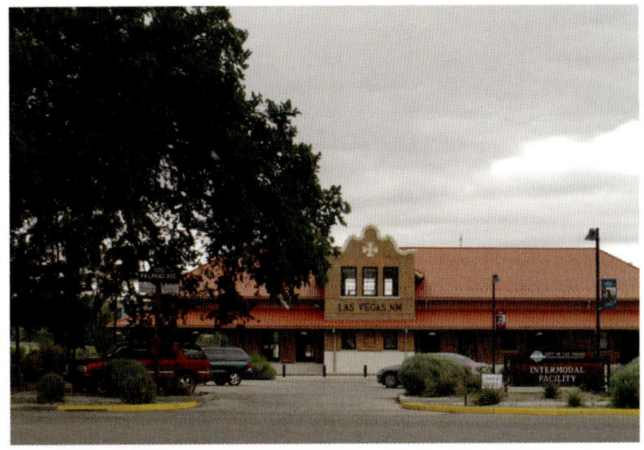

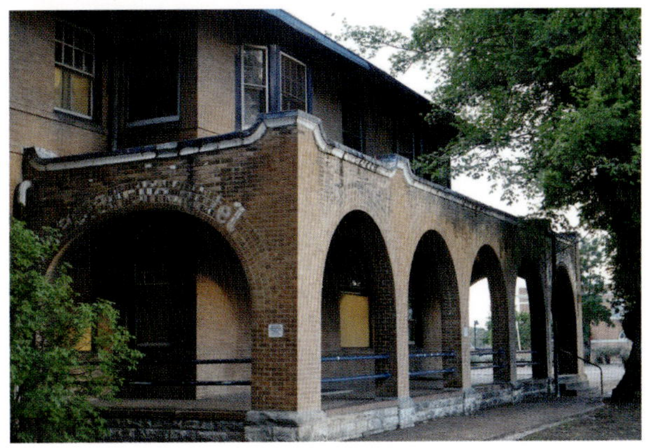

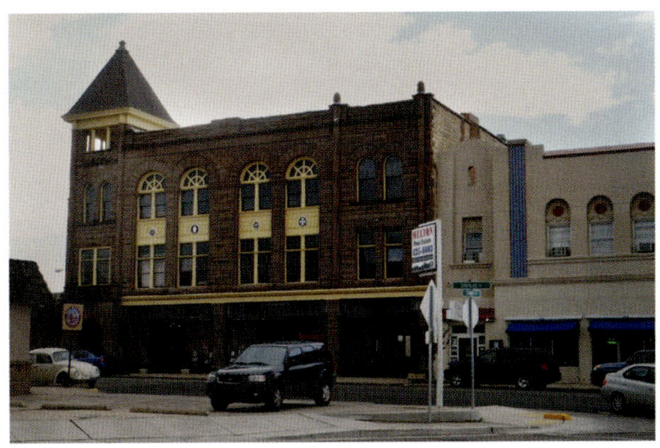

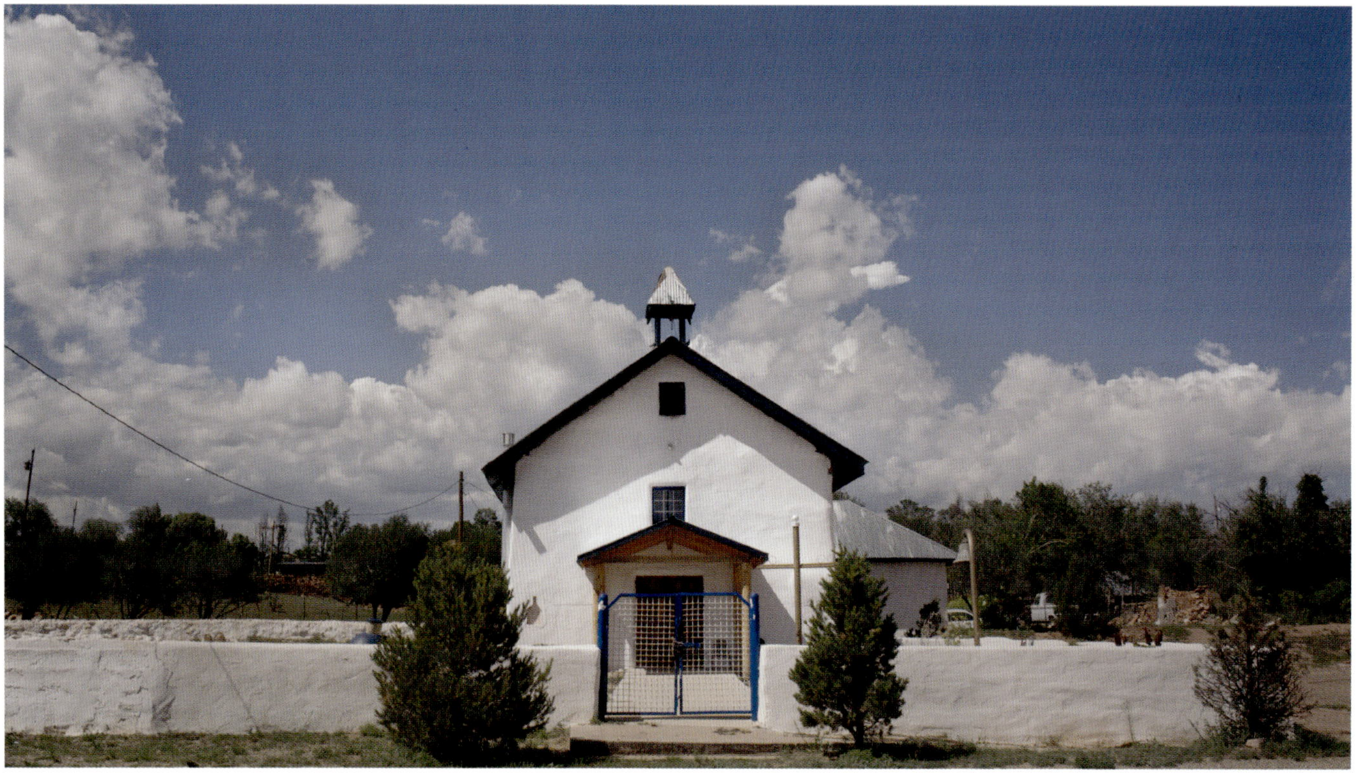

Tecolote Church

dirt road that leads you into the San Augustín canyon, you will come upon a chain of mostly abandoned villages along the Gallinas River as it wends its way toward the Pecos River—San Augustín, Lourdes, Concepción, La Liendre, Los Torros, Chaperito. Or, if you take the Tecolote exit eight miles south of Las Vegas on Interstate 25, you will cross Tecolote Creek, the site of Tecolote—meaning "owl"—a village occupying a Mexican land grant, originally over 48,000 acres.[5] Like all the small Hispanic settlements in Northern New Mexico, it has as its center a modest adobe church, which in this case has been whitewashed. In addition to being historic structures, such village churches are living works of folk art, part of a distinctive tradition richly represented in this part of the Southwest. Most have adjacent *camposantos*, burial grounds with lavishly decorated graves. Inside, some have devotional statues of painted plaster such as those in contemporary Catholic churches, but many retain their original wooden *retablos* (painted panels), reredos (altar screens) and *bultos* (sculptures) by local *santeros* (carvers of figures of saints).

Also built of whitewashed adobe, the present-day church in San Miguel del Bado, thirty miles south of Las Vegas, is considerably larger than the other village churches nearby. Its beautiful interior is adorned with statues of saints in the more familiar contemporary Catholic style rather than the indigenous northern New

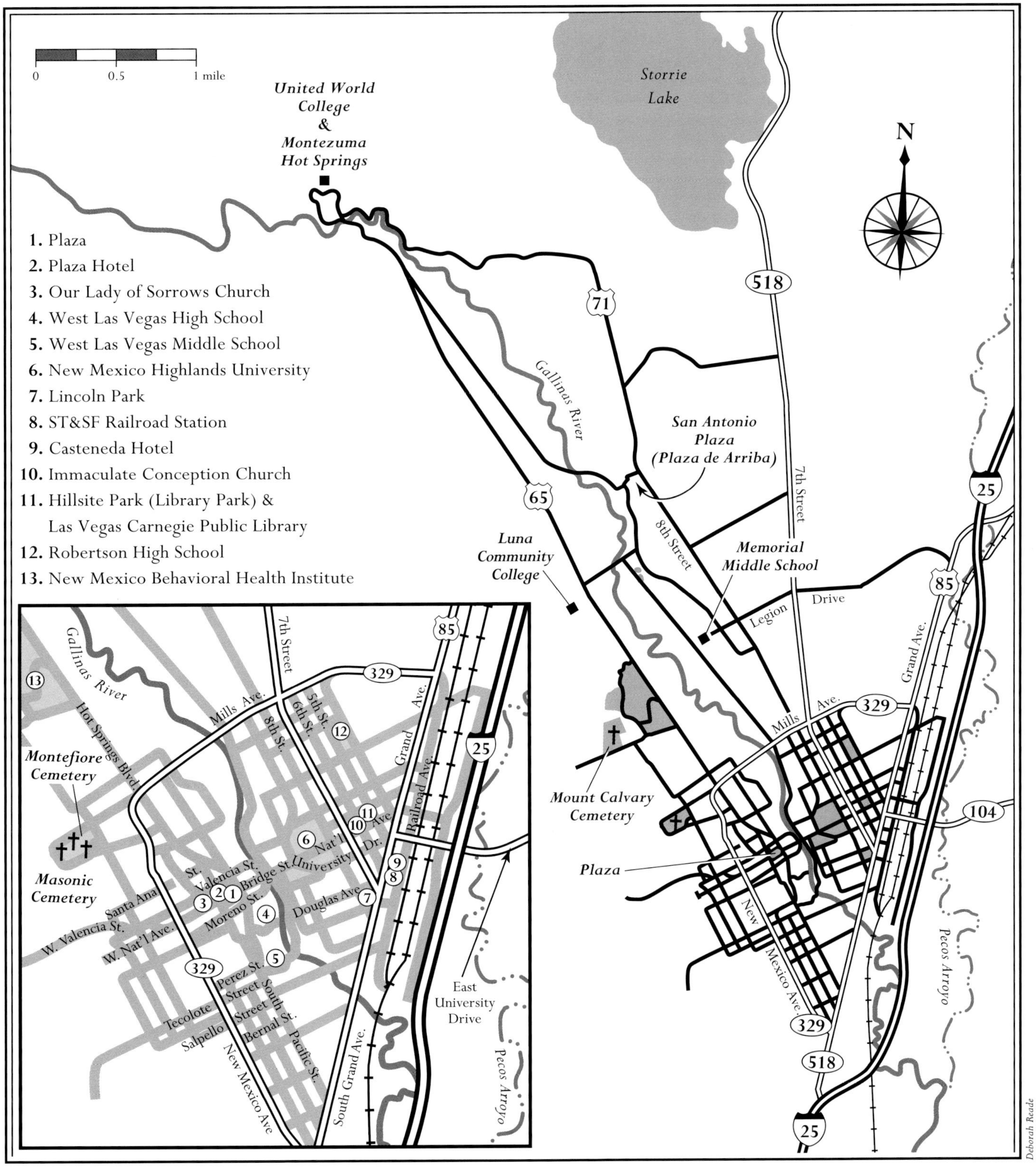
0
0.5
1 mile
United World College & Montezuma Hot Springs
Storrie Lake
N
1. Plaza
2. Plaza Hotel
3. Our Lady of Sorrows Church
4. West Las Vegas High School
5. West Las Vegas Middle School
6. New Mexico Highlands University
7. Lincoln Park
8. ST&SF Railroad Station
9. Casteneda Hotel
10. Immaculate Conception Church
11. Hillsite Park (Library Park) & Las Vegas Carnegie Public Library
12. Robertson High School
13. New Mexico Behavioral Health Institute
518
71
Gallinas River
San Antonio Plaza (Plaza de Arriba)
7th Street
65
25
8th Street
Luna Community College
Memorial Middle School
Legion Drive
85
Grand Ave.
Mills Ave.
329
104
Mount Calvary Cemetery
Plaza
New Mexico Ave.
Pecos Arroyo
518
25
Gallinas River
13
Hot Springs Blvd.
Montefiore Cemetery
Masonic Cemetery
Mills Ave.
7th Street
329
85
8th St.
5th St.
6th St.
12
Grand Ave.
Railroad Ave.
25
11
10
Ave.
Nat'l
University Dr.
6
9
8
Valencia St.
St.
2
1
Bridge St.
3
Santa Ana
W. Valencia St.
W. Nat'l Ave.
Moreno St.
4
Douglas Ave.
7
329
Perez St.
5
Street
South
Tecolote
Street
Salpello
Bernal St.
Pacific St.
New Mexico Ave
South Grand Ave.
East University Drive
Pecos Arroyo
Deborah Reade

Mexican. The community whence the original settlers of the Las Vegas land grant migrated, San Miguel is the first of a string of villages running along the Pecos River through what Las Vegans call The Valley. If you drive to the last of these, Villanueva, you will arrive at a state park.

To the north of town, at the end of Hot Springs Boulevard, lies the beautiful Gallinas Canyon. The canyon begins as a low ridge, or *crestón,* on the eastern slope of which are three cemeteries. The substantial granite markers of Montefiore cemetery are a reminder of the role Jewish merchants played in transforming Las Vegas into an important mercantile center. The contiguous Masonic cemetery is also the burial place of many important former town leaders, both Jewish and Gentile. Mount Calvary lies a short distance to the north.

Occupying 300 acres next to Mount Calvary Cemetery between Hot Springs Boulevard and the ridge of the crestón is the New Mexico Behavioral Health Institute, previously known as the State Hospital and before that as the Insane Asylum. Among the forty-seven buildings spread across its campus are a number of low, red-brick buildings, some of which look like college dormitories. These have evocative New Mexican names such as Tesuque, Zia, and Zuni; Ponderosa, Yucca, and Sandia. Behind these facilities are two cemeteries where patients were buried in earlier times and an area that was once a farm garden where they cultivated their food.

Beyond the New Mexico Behavioral Institute on Hot Springs Boulevard crowning the crestón is Luna Community College. Built as Camp Luna, the site served as a training ground for one of the three regiments of Theodore Roosevelt's Rough Riders, the volunteer cavalry recruited in 1898 to fight in Cuba during the Spanish American War. The college's sports mascot, a cavalryman on a fleet horse, is a reminder of this important chapter in American history.

If you continue north along the Gallinas River you will come to the village of Montezuma. The name reflects the nineteenth-century misconception that prehistoric southwestern ruins were built by Aztecs who had traveled north from Mexico. By now you have entered the canyon where steep cliffs plunge to the roadbed that parallels the river. Geologists explain the sharp declivity as a fault zone where the bedrock once fractured and slipped, making the strata discontinuous on either side of the surface where the break occurred. In this part of the Sangre de Cristo chain, the igneous Hermit's Peak Precambrian granite forms a basement layer that acts like a hot plate to produce the geothermal currents heating the water that flows deep belowground. Blocked at the fault line, the water pushes back to the surface, forming hot springs that can be trapped in pools of varying degrees of temperature. Like other such hydro-geological phenomena elsewhere, this natural feature was a therapeutic attraction to native populations and has remained one ever since.

High on the slope above the hot springs stands the main administration building of United World College. Built by the railroad as an elite resort hotel in 1886, it attracted vacationers who came by train from the East and Midwest. In contrast to its

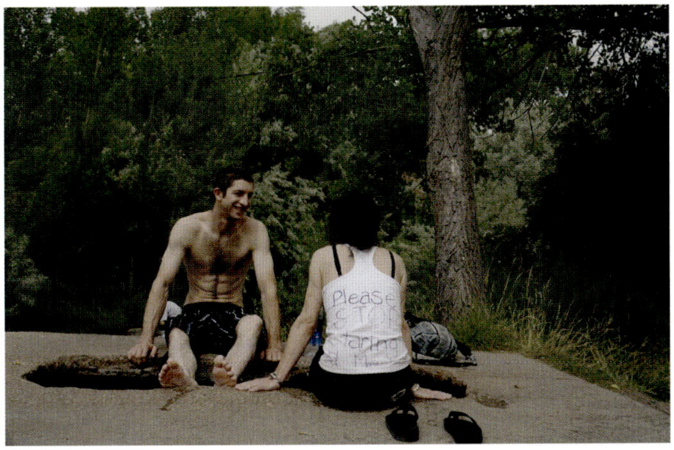

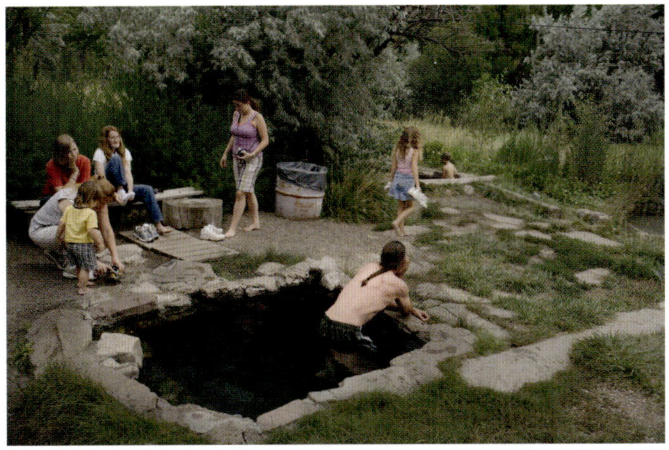

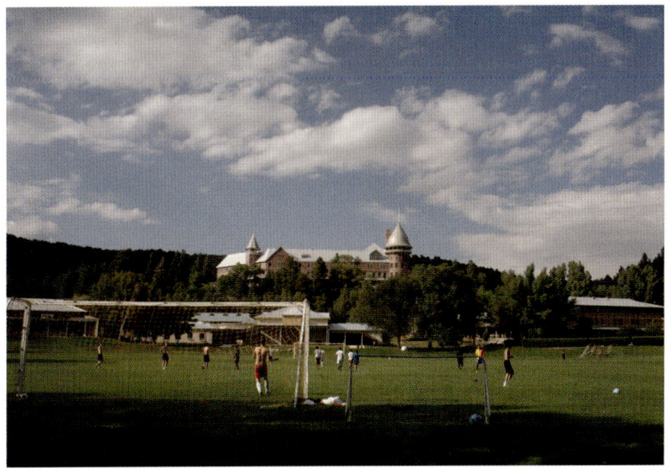

once-fashionable clientele strolling amid Victorian flower beds, students now play soccer on the grounds below the "castle," as the handsome turreted Queen Anne–style building is popularly known. If you are of a mind to soak in the warm lithium-rich water of the old concrete-lined pools or take a swim in the fast-flowing clear Gallinas, you can park alongside the road and follow one of the well-used trails that lead downhill through the spongy meadow grass.

Continuing northward, the road begins to wind through the mountains as you approach the Santa Fe National Forest, part of the 223,333-acre Pecos Wilderness, with trails along slopes covered with stands of pine, fir, and aspen. Before it became federal property, the head of the Gallinas canyon was the site of a dude ranch built beside the river by Margarito Romero in 1890. Situated at the foot of El Cerro del Tecolote, or Owl Mountain—better known as Hermit's Peak—the ranch, which Romero named El Porvenir ("The Future"), is now a Christian summer camp for church groups and a recreational campground managed by the U.S. Forest Service.

Montezuma Hot Springs

Student soccer game, United World College

Hermit's Peak and the rest of the eastern Gallinas Canyon wall forms the regional topographical divide marking the end of the Great Plains and the beginning of the Rocky Mountains. To explore the flat landscape of cattle and grass on the other side, with its vast sky filled with impressive cloud formations no matter what the time of day or weather, you will want to drive north on Interstate 25 toward Raton. Now you are able to experience the exhilaration of great scenic breadth, with rangeland sweeping out to the horizon on one side and the view of the mountains you are skirting on the other. At an elevation of 10,263 feet, east-facing Hermit's Peak is no Mount Rainier towering above the crests around it, but its tall, granitic face stands out prominently as a landscape marker. For travelers on the Santa Fe Trail, sighting Hermit's Peak meant that their journey across the endless sea of grass was nearing an end.

On the plains east of Hermit's Peak lies Fort Union, where the Cimarron cutoff converged with the northern branch of the Santa Fe Trail. If the light is at the proper angle, you can see that the two trails were actually concentrations of many sets of ruts left by the iron wheels of mule- or ox-drawn wagons. They lead to a cluster of military ruins. Today Fort Union is a National Monument, a 721-acre federal property where National Park Service rangers offer guided tours of what were once officers' quarters, married soldiers' housing, bachelors' barracks, and a sutler's

Aerial view of Gallinas Canyon

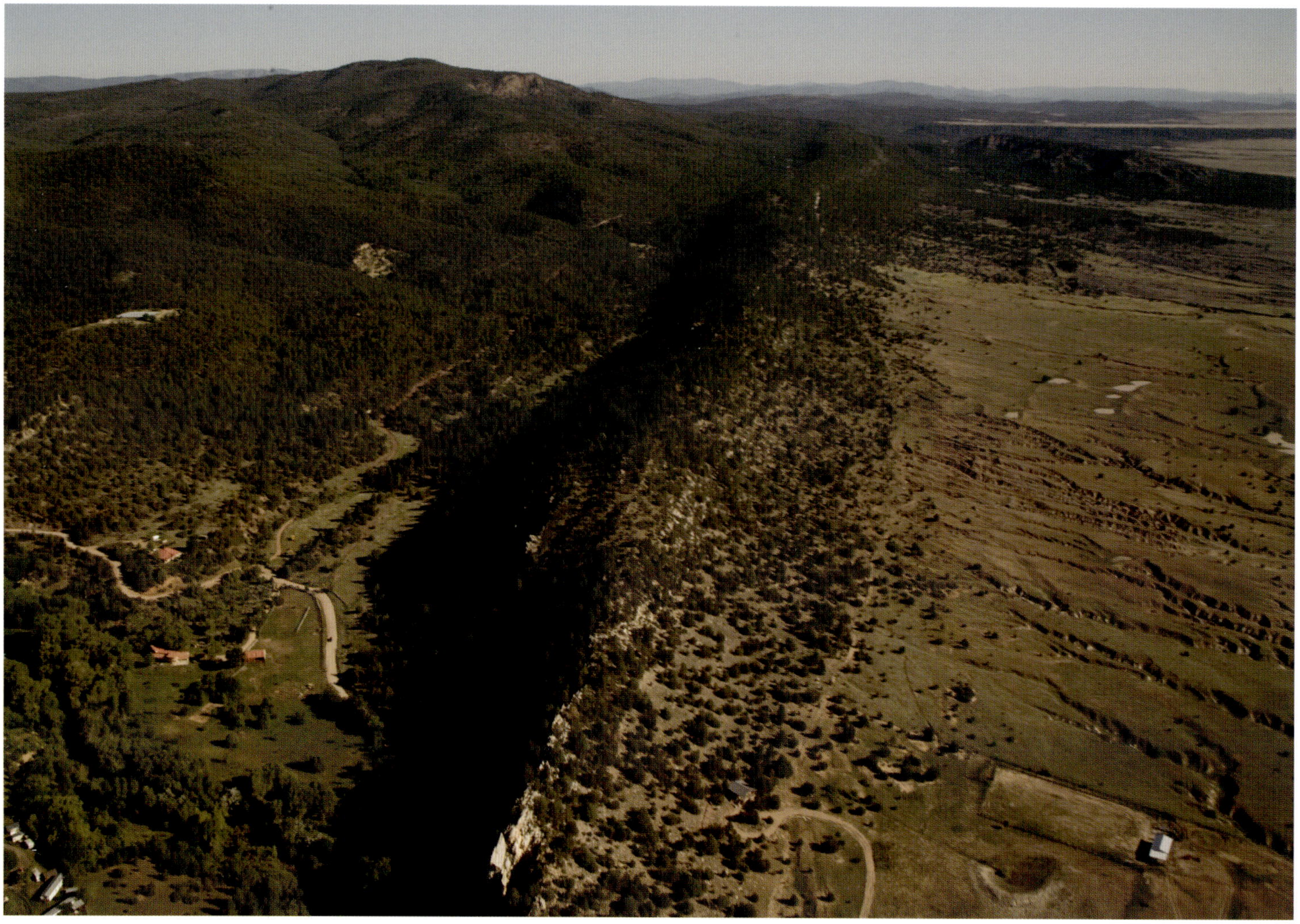

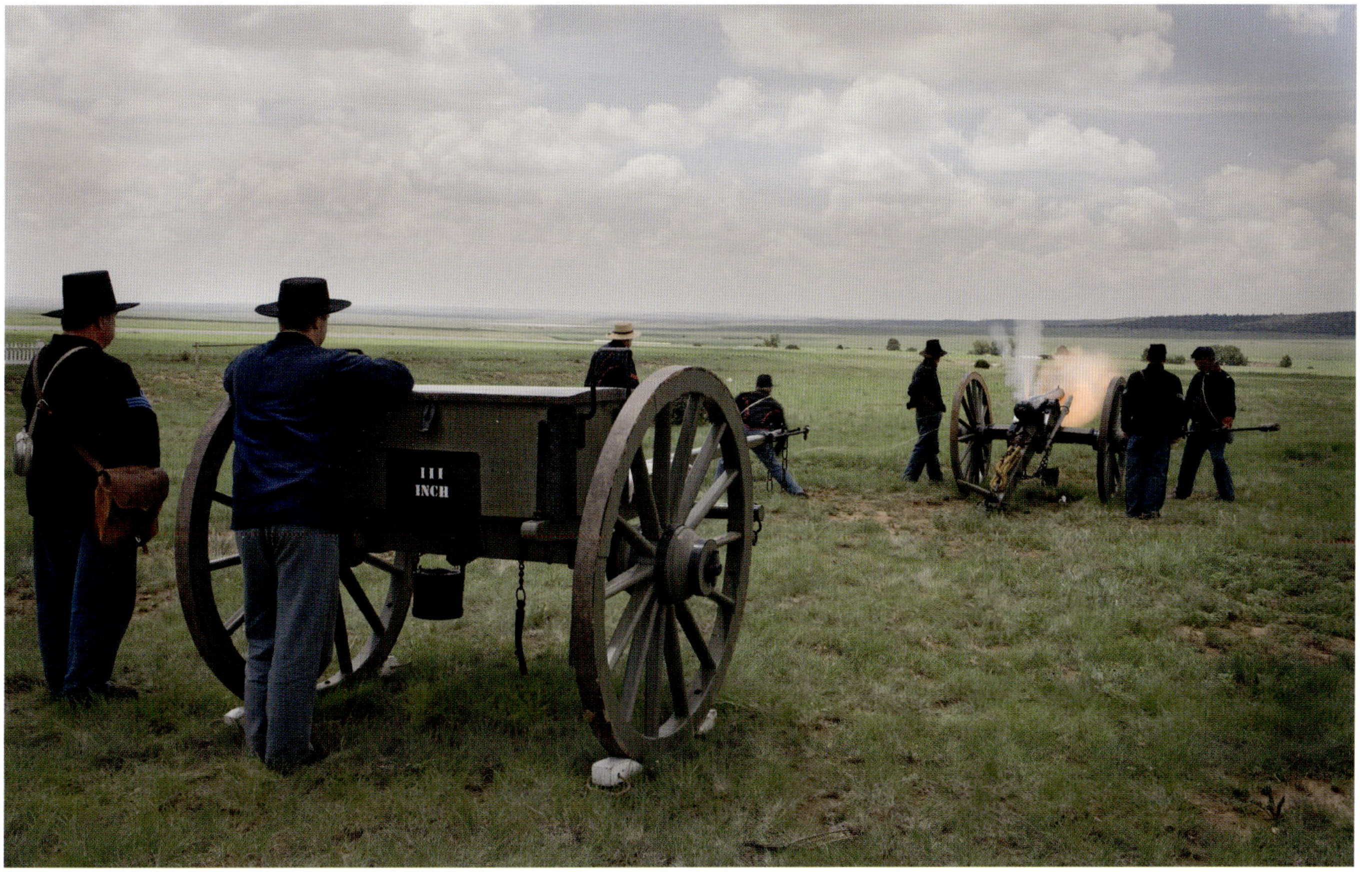

Civil War reenactors, Fort Union

store. Members of the various chapters of the Santa Fe Trail Association, who like to match the historical record with physical evidence or simply enjoy a site imbued with the romantic aura of its colorful past, often supplement their regular meetings with field excursions to this spot. In addition, since Union soldiers were attached to the fort during the Civil War, military history buffs who belong to clubs dedicated to the simulation of the army life of the period hold re-enactment events on the grounds in which appropriately costumed members of the National Park Service educational staff participate.

One day, to take in the entire breadth of this awe-inspiring landscape, I decided to challenge myself with a hike up Hermit's Peak. Starting at El Porvenir, the trail winds its rock-strewn course in a series of endless-seeming switchbacks. Looking at the massive stony cliff face rising 2,700 feet above me, I had qualms. However, it was so pleasant walking through tall ponderosa pines and Douglas fir that I kept climbing, enjoying the quiet solitude, filtered light, and forest smells. Occasionally I stopped to rest, once watching a hammering woodpecker making a nest hole in the top of a dead tree trunk. Then on and on, switchback upon switchback, I continued climbing.

Eventually I came to a place where the trail crosses a spring. Finally, with more persistent climbing, I saw the forest thin out into a grassy clearing marked here and there with campers' fire rings beneath a scattering of tall pines and nothing beyond but light and sky. Walking forward a few paces, I stood on a rocky ledge jutting over the sheer rock face and could see so far that it was hard to discern the horizon line. Transfixed upon my vertiginous balcony, I stared out across the unfathomable flat distance once traversed by Comanche horsemen, vaqueros, sheepherders, ranchers, adventurers, merchants, and homesteaders and tried to imagine how all this diverse humanity contributed in one way or another to making Las Vegas the important place it once was. I conjured up the sight of prairie schooners—so called because their white canvas covers looked like sails crossing the grassy sea. I thought of the large herds of sheep that provided the abundance of wool that merchants shipped to brokers in the East, trading this commodity for agricultural implements, dry goods, firearms, mining equipment, and other products needed in the developing West. I considered how wagon and then rail freighting of raw materials and goods had turned Las Vegas into a major center of trade, how its advantage as a transportation hub had been eclipsed, and how—after several mostly futile attempts to restart its economic engine—it had settled into a long period of quiescence. I unwrapped my sandwich and, still somewhat dazed from the long climb and breathtaking view in front of me, settled down on a sunny rock to eat my lunch.

Afterward I lay back, staring up at the intensely blue New Mexico sky pondering how to make sense of the historically permeated panorama. I realized that walking the streets of a city, driving around the countryside, and finding a high perch from which to gain a broad view are good means of reading a landscape. However, since I was interested in a more complete narrative of the past, I understood that this kind of impressionistic discovery needed to be augmented by historical research. Sitting on top of Hermit's Peak, I knew it was time for me to begin reading books about Las Vegas.

In 1610, three years after the English founded Jamestown, the recently settled community of Santa Fe became the headquarters of the newly declared "Kingdom of New Mexico" at the northern perimeter of Spain's vast transcontinental empire. Accompanying the conquistadores who came to claim the territory were Franciscan missionaries charged with converting and subduing the indigenous population they found settled in pueblos, compact agricultural villages of adobe structures organized around a central plaza. With promises of protection from raiding nomadic tribes, together with assurances of the efficacy of the Catholic God in promoting the fertility of crops, the Spaniards were able to subdue these Native Americans into a state of vassalage under their *encomienda* system.[1]

This military, spiritual, and economic bargain proved tenuous, however. After suffering at the hands of the Spanish, their purported protectors, as well as from a long period of drought that made them question the efficacy of the new religion, the subjugated Native Americans revolted. In 1680, after murdering a number of mission priests, the united Pueblo tribes were successful in expelling their rulers. The Spanish, however, were determined to regain their northern borderland, and by 1692 they had accomplished their second conquest, known as the Reconquista—a historic event still celebrated by New Mexican Hispanics today—thereby establishing Santa Fe once again as the capital of New Mexico.

The continuing threat of attacks by Comanche, Apache, Navajo, and other mounted raiders delayed Spanish colonial expansion into the fertile valleys of the eastern slopes of the Sangre de Cristos. To advance colonization, the Spanish land-grant system evolved from its original encomienda version to one whereby the governor, with the recommendation of his subordinate official, the *alcalde*, could confer community as well as individual grants. Community grants were assigned to groups of prospective settlers who petitioned the territorial government. The grant was awarded based on careful evaluation of the petitioners' qualifications and the suitability of the land for occupation. Settlement proceeded according to a prescribed formula. Each settler was given a house lot and a plot, typically a long, narrow strip of land running from wooded foothills across an open field to the river. Nearby was the main irrigation ditch, known as the *acequia madre.* The rest of the grant, called the *ejido*, was common land where all the settlers had grazing, hunting, and fishing rights as well as rights to gather herbs, firewood, and rock for building material.[2]

Early Settlers

The mother colony for the Las Vegas land grant was San Miguel del Bado, "bado"[3] being a derivation of *vado,* meaning ford or river-crossing. Its grant dates from 1794, and it can therefore be considered a pioneer settlement within the community land-grant system that populated the valleys along the Pecos River and its tributaries during the first third of the nineteenth century. Its fifty-two *pobladores*, or colonists, were from Santa Fe and Peña Blanca and included several families who were mestizo (mixed-blood) and *genízaros* (Christianized Indians descended from slaves).

Safety was a primary concern. In the beginning there were only twenty-five firearms among the fifty-two settlers. Looking on the settlement as a frontier line of defense for the territorial capital in Santa Fe, Governor Lorenzo Márquez enjoined them "to exert [them]selves to supply all the firearms and ammunition that it may be possible to procure."[4] The high percentage of genízaros—thirty-nine among the original population—provided an advantage in protecting the frontier, since these detribalized Indians were familiar with the tactics of the nomadic raiders. As community grants became the norm after Mexican independence from Spain, the elite members of the highly stratified Hispanic society were not necessarily the preferred recipients of large tracts of land, which were now more readily bestowed as community grants to men of mixed blood who were better able to protect their property. Large tracts of communal land were awarded to the founders of nearby San José (1803), Tecolote (1824), and Anton Chico (1822).

Successful defense was still not a given, for raiding Plains Indians forced the settlers of these grant lands to abandon their initial villages. Less vulnerable grantees further away from the plains were able, however, to establish small farming villages within the relative safety of the Sangre de Cristos in locations where water was available. The most obviously desirable location for grazing cattle and sheep, the big meadows at the eastern edge of mountains, or *las vegas grandes* as they are called in Spanish, were the most exposed and therefore remained the hardest to wrest from their nomadic warrior occupants. But eventually the settlers prevailed and the San Miguel del Bado, San José, Tecolote, and Anton Chico grants achieved permanence.

The year 1821 marked a watershed in the history of New Mexico when Spanish authority over Mexico and its territories was replaced by autonomous Mexican rule. The new government ended the Spanish embargo on trade with the United States. This change was not lost on William Becknell, the trader who pioneered the Santa Fe Trail in order to connect Missouri merchants with New Mexico's capital and the trade in silver coins, furs, wool, and mules via the Camino Real from Chihuahua to Santa Fe.

Located directly on the route of the Santa Fe Trail at the spot where the wagons forded the Pecos, San Miguel del Bado became a portal of entry on the final leg of the journey to Santa Fe, and the tolls that were charged at the crossing were a source of prosperity for the little community. Real wealth, however, was counted in cattle and sheep, and the accession of native Mexicans to the seat of government offered a fresh chance for acquiring grant lands in places where there were abundant grazing opportunities. Thus, in the same year that Mexico achieved its independence and Becknell took advantage of the lifted embargo on trade with the United States, Luis María Cabeza de Baca (the surname is commonly abbreviated as "C. de Baca"), one of eight men who had previously attempted to occupy the big meadows, petitioned the newly created Provincial Deputation of Durango, Mexico, for a grant for himself and his seventeen children. Two years later the alcalde of San Miguel was instructed by the political chief of New Mexico to grant C. de Baca a *sitio* of approximately 500,000 acres. After the petition was confirmed in 1825, he and his sons occupied a portion of their vast holding, at least seasonally, grazing 3,000 sheep along with some cattle, milk cows, and a large herd of horses. They were, however, unable to actually settle and begin cultivation except in a very rudimentary way because of continual raiding by Apache, Comanche, Navajo, Pawnee, and Ute Indians. Pawnee raiders finally succeeded in driving the family back into the relative security of the Pecos Valley. With the land unoccupied, their grant claim was abandoned.[5] However, the attraction of the dangerous but extremely desirable prairie meadows did not abate, and would-be colonists from San Miguel and the other nearby settlements continued to venture forth in the summer from their mountain-protected valleys to take advantage of the fine pasturage on the plains.

The settlers of San Miguel were among those who coveted the acres that C. de Baca had been forced to abandon. Keeping a wary lookout for Indians, some herdsmen were already pasturing their animals in the summertime on this land. Its year-round occupation would help alleviate the increasing poverty of the growing population, which could no longer be sustained by animals and crops restricted to the confines of the Pecos River valley. Therefore, in 1831, when the community had swelled to more than 2,000 as a second generation continued to add pressure on the existing resources, the parish priest at San Miguel, José Francisco Leyba, drafted a lengthy manifesto in which he proposed a way of ameliorating not only the lives of his own impoverished parishioners but also those in other New Mexican communities. At the same time his proposal addressed the need to improve the safety of the territory's frontier.[6]

Father Leyba's manifesto pointed out the scarcity of resources in the already occupied settlements and the abundance of available land in the valleys of the tributaries of the Pecos River to the northeast, if the dangers of their exposed location could be overcome. He then suggested a means of colonization through the application of the recently passed Ley de Vagos, or vagrant law. Article 14 of this statute declared that destitute persons could participate in settling grant lands in lieu of the other two options in the legislation: going to prison or being drafted into the military.

The document Father Leyba sent to Santa Fe outlining this sensible strategy advocated government support in the form of oxen, hoes, axes, and other tools that would be needed if the settlers were to succeed in building homes and farming the land. A commission of government officials reviewed his proposal favorably and subsequently recommended that the political chief should remit to the Supreme Government a copy of Father Leyba's proposed project, so that the necessary monies would be made available to carry it out. The commission further instructed the political chief to use "his utmost energy in acquiring the support of the *alcaldes* in the territory to establish a tribunal for vagrants as prescribed by law." [7]

In 1832 José Ulibarrí, the constitutional justice, and other local officials drafted a proclamation along the same lines as Father Leyba's, urging the emigration of some members of the community to the northeastern sector of the New Mexican territory. Three years later a petition advanced by San Miguel del Bado residents Juan de Dios Maese, Manuel Archuleta, Manuel Durán, and José Antonio Casaus on behalf of themselves and 32 other men to occupy the grant that had been abandoned by C. de Baca was approved by the municipal council and ratified by the governor. Following this important legal achievement, the 36 men from San Miguel ventured forth to claim in common the 500,000 acres they called Las Vegas Grandes.[8] At the same time, members of other nearby communities applied to the officials in Santa Fe for the right to join the original Las Vegas grantees. As a result, an additional 118 settlers were included among the recipients of the community land grant. One of these was Miguel Romero y Baca, the man destined to become the fledgling settlement's de facto leader and first *patrón*.

The settlers' first step was the selection of a town site. Water was a primary consideration, and the place they chose was at the point where the Gallinas River, a seemingly inconsequential tributary of the Pecos, flows out of a deep, narrow canyon before reaching the flat, grassy land at the western margin the Great Plains. They named their settlement Nuestra Señora de los Dolores de Las Vegas. In this way they combined the name of their patron saint, Our Lady of Sorrows, with their most important economic asset: the vast grasslands they had been eyeing for several years with mixed desire and trepidation.

Even though they faced a scarcity of oxen and tools and still lived in fear of Indian depredations and kidnappings, the settlers managed to retain their land, and by 1838 they had succeeded in forming a permanent community. Like the colonists of all the other Hispanic farming communities in the high desert of rural Northern

New Mexico, where agriculture is impossible without irrigation, the Las Vegas settlers' immediate priority was a system of water management. The rainfall and snowmelt from the nearby mountains furnished the small but reliable Gallinas with a sufficient flow to meet their needs, but in order to distribute the water to their fields, the settlers had to divert it into an *acequia madre.* Therefore, before they could occupy the land they faced the arduous task of digging this long, embanked "mother ditch." Perpendicular to it they dug subsidiary ditches to serve as irrigation runnels. The engineering of this system required that the *acequia madre* be built at a slightly higher elevation than the river so as to allow it to receive water from upstream; the runoff, if there was any after it had been successively channeled into the settlers' fields, would then return to the river at a point downstream. A series of *trampas*, or traps, controlled the sequential release of water. In Las Vegas you can still see portions of the original acequia madre and its trampas, although several stretches now flow through culverts beneath paved streets.

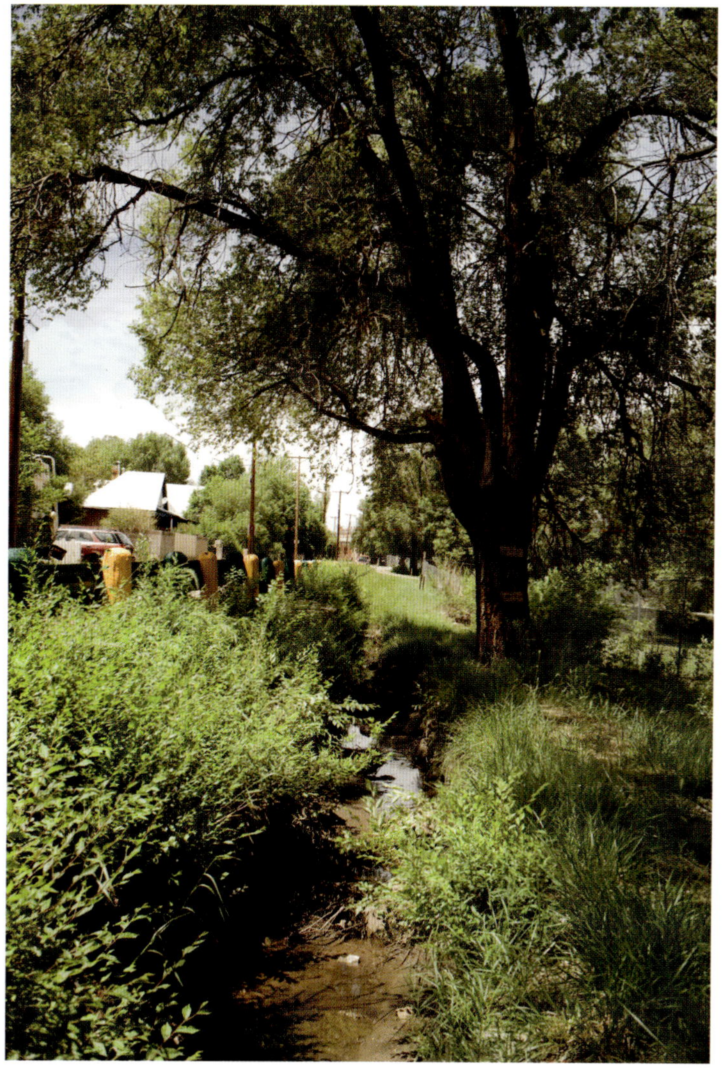

Acequia Madre, Rio de Gallinas

The part of the Las Vegas grant set aside for the town was parceled into *solares*, or house lots, around a central plaza. This layout was according to the 1680 Laws of the Indies (*Recopilación de las leyes de los reinos de Indias*), the prescribed royal town-planning model adopted from Roman law.[9] Construction of the original church of Nuestra Señora de Dolores, which stood opposite the west side of the plaza, was begun immediately. The rest of the border of this central rectangle was soon defined by a wall of contiguous one-story adobe houses. Entrance from the outside was constricted, with only two openings that in times of danger could be barricaded after herders had driven their livestock into this protective enclosure.

To the east of the plaza and its adjacent street grid were the acequia-irrigated fields running in long narrow strips from the river toward the *crestón*, the ridge flanking the western edge of the town, and from its east bank to a series of low-rising hills. Each family received somewhere between 100 and 250 *varas* of river frontage, a vara being approximately 33 inches. The crestón, which served as a source of firewood and timber, was communal land like the grazing land to the east. With an alcalde appointed by the territorial government of New Mexico to oversee the orderly disposition of land and a *mayordomo*, or acequia supervisor, in charge of water allocation, Las Vegas became a self-sufficient and self-governing community under Mexican law.

Using family wealth supplied by the Delgado gold mines near Dolores, New Mexico, Miguel Romero established himself as an early and prosperous Santa Fe Trail shipper. He and his wife, Josepha Delgado, took up permanent residence in Las Vegas in 1838, and in 1851 they moved their large family to a sprawling compound that Miguel built on the northeast corner of the plaza. Influential in establishing law and order, Romero donated the land just north of their home to the town and contributed to the construction of a courthouse and jail on the site.

As the richest and most powerful family in San Miguel County, Romero and his five sons held the reins of political power well into the twentieth century. Eugenio, the second oldest son, succeeded his father as patrón, and as civic leaders, he and his brothers—Trinidad, Hilario, Benigno, and Margarito—and grandsons—Secundio and Cleofes—ran the Republican Party machine for several decades. The Romeros reinforced their unopposed political leadership with various charitable undertakings and the numerous public benefits that they bestowed on the town. Along with their mercantile activities, law enforcement was the Romero family business, and through the years one family member or another was elected sheriff. In these ways the family maintained its power, even as New Mexico became a United States territory and then a state of the union. Thus their influence extended over the period when Las Vegas was transformed from a small settlement of subsistence farmers and Santa Fe Trail traders into one of the most important cities in the American West.[10]

The Army of the West

The first historical event that spurred the transformation of Las Vegas occurred on August 14, 1846, when the 1,700 troops commanded by General Stephen Watts Kearny (1794–1848), head of what was grandly dubbed the United States Army of the West, encamped a mile outside the town. The following day, as women and children were sent to hiding places on the slopes of the crestón, Kearny arrived, mounted a ladder to the roof of alcalde Juan de Dios Maese's house on the north side of the plaza and announced to the 150 men gathered below that New Mexico was now a territory of the United States, assuring them at the same time, "We come amongst you as friends—not as enemies; as protectors—not as conquerors." Mixing promise with threat, he went on to say that "those who remain peaceably at home, attending to their crops and their herds, shall be protected by me in their property, their persons, and their religion. . . . But listen! He who promises to be quiet, and is found in arms against me, I will hang."[11] Before the mostly non-English-speaking Mexicans gathered in the plaza, Kearny then made the alcalde swear an oath of allegiance, after which the general rejoined his troops for the final march into Santa Fe. There they discovered that the Mexican governor, Manuel Armijo, had fled the city. Kearny could therefore claim that New Mexico was now a territory of the United States.

Less than six weeks later, Kearny departed for California, where the war against Mexico continued. The young subordinate commanders left behind to maintain order found themselves in frequent pursuit of Indian horse raiders. Whether rightly or wrongly, they assumed that Mexicans were implicated in these thefts. During the next few months friction mounted as horses were lost, stolen, and recaptured by all parties alike. Although the exact circumstances leading to one particularly unfortunate incident remain unclear, on July 6, 1847, in reprisal for the murder of three Missouri Volunteers who had disappeared in the San Augustín valley a few days earlier in search of lost horses, the officer in command of the Las Vegas regiment Kearny had left behind gathered his forces and marched to a high ridge above the village that lay at its head. There his men opened fire with a 12-pound mountain howitzer, killing ten of the hapless folk below. After rounding up fifty prisoners, the troops went on to steal chickens, hogs, and grain before reducing the sandstone and adobe dwellings and barns to rubble. Six of the captured men from the village were charged with the murder of the soldiers. Pronounced guilty by a military tribunal, they were taken to Santa Fe, placed on a gallows that had been erected behind the Palace of the Governors, given the last rites, and executed. More than merely retribution, their hanging was intended as a sign to other Mexicans who, not having acquiesced to the American takeover, were stirring up rebellion throughout the territory.

A more stable and disciplined military presence was subsequently established in 1851, when the U.S. Army built Fort Union in order to protect the mule trains going in both directions along the Santa Fe Trail. Previously, eastward-bound wool, fur, and silver traders had returned west with mostly empty wagons. Now westward-bound caravans transported military supplies as well as mining tools, ranching implements, groceries, household wares, and calico for the growing population of New Mexico. Thus, because of its favorable location adjacent to the immense, grass-rich Mora and San Miguel land grants and its ready market for eastern merchandise, Las Vegas was by the second half of the nineteenth century more than able to sustain its own two-way regional trade economy independent of the Santa Fe connection with the Camino Real. Before long its population had surpassed that of the capital.

The First Jewish Merchants

At the time of its founding, Las Vegas's growth and future prosperity were already ensured by the presence of the Santa Fe Trail. William Becknell had correctly surmised that the trail's traffic would greatly multiply as the Anglo-American homesteaders, miners, merchants, and soldiers who were part of the country's westward expansion continued to populate the area. In meeting their needs, the merchants who plied the trail would find profitable new markets.

Following the political upheavals of 1848 in Europe, many young German Jews, wishing to avoid military conscription and aware of the new mercantile opportunities along the American frontier, crossed the Atlantic and then the vast sea of grass to seek their fortunes in the burgeoning West. A number of French-Canadians, whose forebears had prospered trapping beaver and other mammals abundantly populating the streambeds and forests of Northern New Mexico, also settled in locations where proximity to the trail was economically advantageous. At the same time, prominent Hispanic families who were traders in gold, silver, wool, and hides also began to send caravans to Missouri. The commerce of the prairie that would bring wealth to many New Mexicans had begun.

As the importance of the trail increased, Las Vegas prospered and grew significantly. By the 1850s its population had leapt from 900 to more than 1,500, and by 1860 it stood at 2,500. Moreover, the U.S. Army forts that had been established to protect the trail from Indian raids needed supplies, and Las Vegas was the logical distribution point for such military outposts as Fort Union, Fort Bascom, Fort Sumner, and Fort Stanton. In order to be near the area's principal transportation center, merchants from other parts of the territory located their outlets, warehouses, and granaries in Las Vegas. New Mexican raw materials, notably wool, hides, and livestock, constituted an important part of eastward-moving freight.

Wealthy Hispanic families built large homes and trading establishments around the plaza. They were joined by Anglo merchants who set up businesses as well as by Jews who also became important beneficiaries of trail commerce. Hermann von Grolman, a Hessian, was the first Jewish merchant to establish himself in Las Vegas. Other Jewish traders followed, some of whom opened branches in Las Vegas in order to expand the mercantile operations they had established elsewhere. Among these were the Spiegelberg brothers from Santa Fe and the Jaffa brothers from Trinidad, Colorado. Samuel Kohn, Moses Friedman and his two sons, and Isidor Stern and his partner, Marcus Zuckerberg, also founded mercantile houses in Las Vegas. Joseph and Emmanuel Rosenwald from Bavaria were among the most successful of this first group of Jewish traders to settle permanently in Las Vegas. In 1877, after their original place of business burned, they built a large wool warehouse (the now-vacant Navajo Textiles building) on the southeast corner of the plaza.

Among the influx of enterprising Jews was Charles Ilfeld, a native of Homburg von der Hohe in Prussia. In 1865, at the age of eighteen, Ilfeld sailed from Hamburg and, soon after his arrival in New York, traveled to Missouri where he joined an ox-wagon train bound for Santa Fe, a trip of ninety days. From Santa Fe he made his way north to Taos where he became the business associate of fur trader Adolph Letcher.

However, the remoteness of Taos from the trail caused the two men to relocate to Las Vegas, a boomtown-in-the-making. Subsequently Ilfeld bought out Letcher's interest in the business, and as his company flourished, his brothers Louis and Noa came over from Germany to join him. In 1874, Charles married Adele Nordhaus, the daughter of Rabbi Jacob Nordhaus of Paderhorn. Her brother Max soon followed her to Las Vegas, and in 1878 he became Ilfeld's business associate.

The arrival of the Atchison, Topeka and Santa Fe Railroad on July 4, 1879, immediately made freight transportation by wagon obsolete. By this time Santa Fe had been eclipsed by Las Vegas as a trading center. Because of the easier grade through the Galisteo Basin, the railroad bypassed Santa Fe altogether, leaving it with only a spur track from the nearest stop at Lamy. Las Vegas thus became New Mexico's primary shipping center, the nexus of a wide regional rail network. Grain and lumber from Mora and San Miguel counties, along with wool, hides, and metals from the Pecos and Mesilla valleys, provided rich commercial opportunities. Coupled with the possibility of shipments in much greater bulk, Las Vegas was poised for expansion, and for the next thirty years it enjoyed an era of great prosperity as the wool capital of the United States. Throughout this period, its Jewish community played an especially prominent role in its economic life and growth, and as members of the affluent merchant community, they were instrumental in making Las Vegas the most important and the handsomest city in New Mexico.

Two Towns

Although the coming of the railroad in 1879 marked the birth of East Las Vegas, or New Town, the Ilfelds, Rosenwalds, and other members of the first generation of Jewish merchants in Las Vegas continued to live and operate their businesses in Old Town beside the plaza alongside their Hispanic counterparts. At first believing that the train depot would be located near the plaza, other merchants had started to further commercialize its perimeter. Several of the old adobe structures surrounding it, including ones owned by James Broadwell and the Romero, Perea, and Gonzales families, were remodeled in what would become known as Territorial style. Their pitched roofs, brick trim, squared-off columns, and classicized moldings framing large windows defined this New Mexican version of the Greek Revival. With security no longer an issue, the plaza's unbroken perimeter wall of adobe structures, which had previously served as a fortification in times of danger, was breached at all four corners.

The original adobe Our Lady of Sorrows Church was replaced with a new church one block west of its original site on the plaza. Signaling the American Catholic Church's determination to impose a European form of Catholicism on Hispanic New Mexico, New Mexico's powerful archbishop, Jean-Baptiste Lamy, influenced the design of the new church in the provincial Gothic Revival style. Constructed of

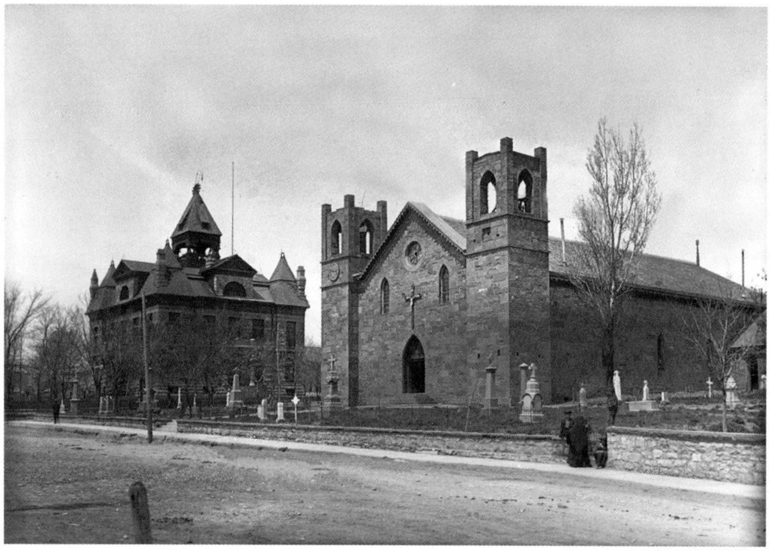

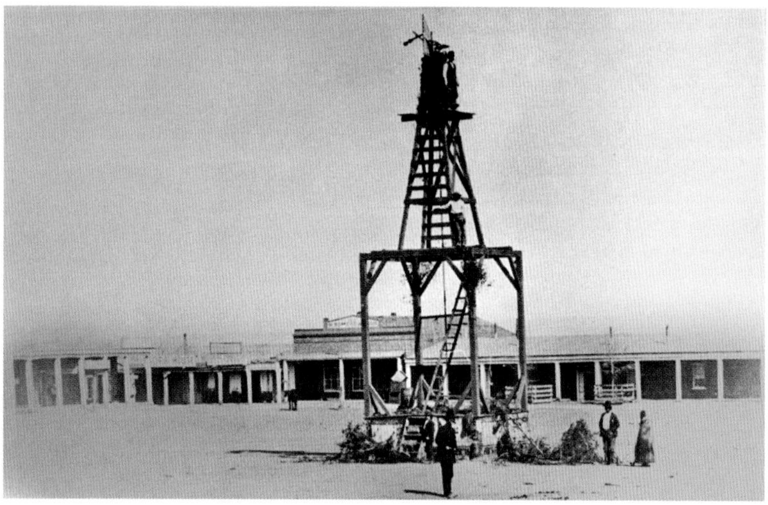

reddish sandstone ashlar blocks, it has twin bell towers and for many years was the most impressive church in New Mexico, after the Basilica of Saint Francis in Santa Fe.

In order to profit from the additional new construction generated by the town's growing prosperity, John Whitlock, along with James Broadwell and John Sease, set up a sawmill north of town where the forested slopes of the Gallinas Canyon provide abundant timber. To carry lumber into town and create a thoroughfare for the increasing traffic from that direction, a road was built, extending from the northwest corner of the plaza to the village of Hot Springs, later known as Montezuma.

In the 1880s Las Vegas was, like other Western boomtowns, a magnet for outlaws as well as for new settlers seeking opportunity in a rapidly expanding part of the country. There were gambling houses and saloons that also served as commercial dance halls. After an unsuccessful attempt was made to harness power from a windmill constructed in the plaza in 1876, its derrick found another use as grim instrument of rough justice, serving for a few years as a forty-foot-high gallows for the perpetrators of armed robbery, murder, and other crimes. Posses and vigilantes did their best to quell the continual violence, but even minor quarrels sometimes ended in gunfire. As examples, hot-headed Doc Holliday killed a man named Mike Gordon for yelling at a saloon girl, and William H. Bonney (Billy the Kid) was among the outlaws Lincoln County sheriff Pat Garrett captured and jailed in Las Vegas.

A decade later, Vicente Silva, proprietor of the round-the-clock Imperial Saloon, became the leader of a ring of cattle rustlers and horse thieves. Known as La Gavilla de Silva, or Silva's gang, its members acted like Mafiosi, murdering on Silva's orders those he had accused of betrayal. Thus was Patricio Maes given a mock trial, found guilty, and hanged from the bridge at the Gallinas River crossing during a blizzard in 1892. The following year Silva participated in the ambush and murder of his brother-in-law Gabriel Sandoval, alleging that Sandoval had double-crossed him. A few

Our Lady of Sorrows Church and Courthouse, c. 1915, by Jesse Nusbaum. Courtesy Palace of the Governors.

Windmill gallows, c. 1880, by J. N. Furlong.

months later he induced his wife Telésfora to bring money from the saloon to his hideout at Manuel Gonzales y Baca's ranch beside the Sapello River. Upon her arrival he stabbed her to death, presumably with the intention of leaving Las Vegas and living elsewhere with his mistress. His henchmen, who had been paid ten dollars to participate in Telésfora's murder, were waiting outside. Perhaps with a plan to abscond with the money, they proceeded to shoot Silva and hastily bury both bodies in a nearby arroyo.[12]

In spite of gunslingers, brawlers, and criminals, the civilizing of Las Vegas continued. At the same time that the area around the plaza and along Bridge Street was being reshaped in the early 1880s, a spruce new town was rising on the other side of the river. The railroad company's previously prepared plat now materialized in a grid of streets lined with houses and commercial buildings. A variety of professional services came into existence, and emporiums and specialty stores were opened to cater to the needs of the growing population of Anglo-American residents. A city directory published in 1882 lists eight attorneys, two architects, two banks, eight billiard halls, five barbers, four cigar and tobacco shops, four confectioners, four druggists, three dentists, twenty general merchandise stores, thirteen hotels, five hardware stores, six millinery shops, two newspapers, seven physicians and surgeons, and eight real estate and insurance agents.

What emerges is a portrait of a prosperous Midwestern-style town located cheek by jowl with the original Hispanic settlement. Although the area around the plaza retained a good deal of its commercial importance, most of the new enterprises and professional offices gravitated to the second business center growing up around Douglas and Sixth streets near the railroad. The widening disparity in the importance of the two sides of town was made official in 1888 with the incorporation of East Las Vegas as a separate municipality, making it officially a "city," as opposed to West Las Vegas's status as a "town." This act served to confirm the lasting division that even consolidation into a unified system of governance nearly a century later did not entirely erase.

First National Bank building, 2012

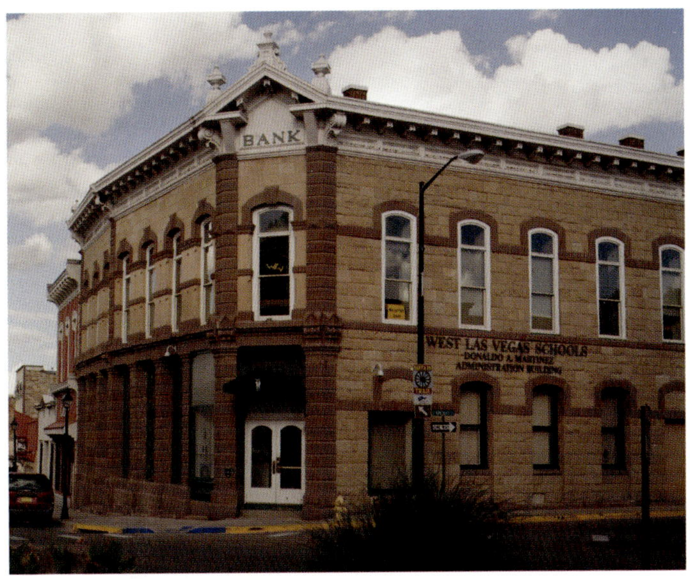

Nevertheless, Old Town's commercial importance was not immediately eclipsed, as testified by the distinguished Victorian-style buildings that were constructed around it.[13] At the juncture of Bridge Street and the plaza, the First National Bank was erected between 1880 and 1886. With a corner entrance topped by a broken pediment, it was the successor to the private bank founded on the site in 1876 by Jefferson, Joshua, and Frederick A. Raynolds from Ohio.[14] In 1881, diagonally opposite on the northwest corner of the plaza, Don Benigno Romero built the red brick Plaza Hotel. Its cast iron columns, window pediments, and ornamented cornice lent the plaza's perimeter the same kind of architectural character as that of the principal business districts of other proud and prosperous late-nineteenth-century American cities.

The following year Charles Ilfeld demonstrated his faith in Old Town's continuation as an important economic nucleus by replacing the adobe structure on the north side of the plaza where he had set up his dry goods business in 1867 with a handsome three-story masonry building of Italianate design. In 1890 he added an adjacent companion building, also faced with brownstone. The Ilfeld Emporium (now part of the renovated Plaza Hotel) has a lower story with large store windows set between square stone columns and two upper stories. In the basement, groceries, liquor, and hardware were sold; on the first floor dry goods; on the second millinery and dresses; and on the third carpeting.[15] Ilfeld was at this point no longer catering simply to the existing regional population and the United States military but to the influx of Anglo-American residents in Las Vegas well as customers throughout the

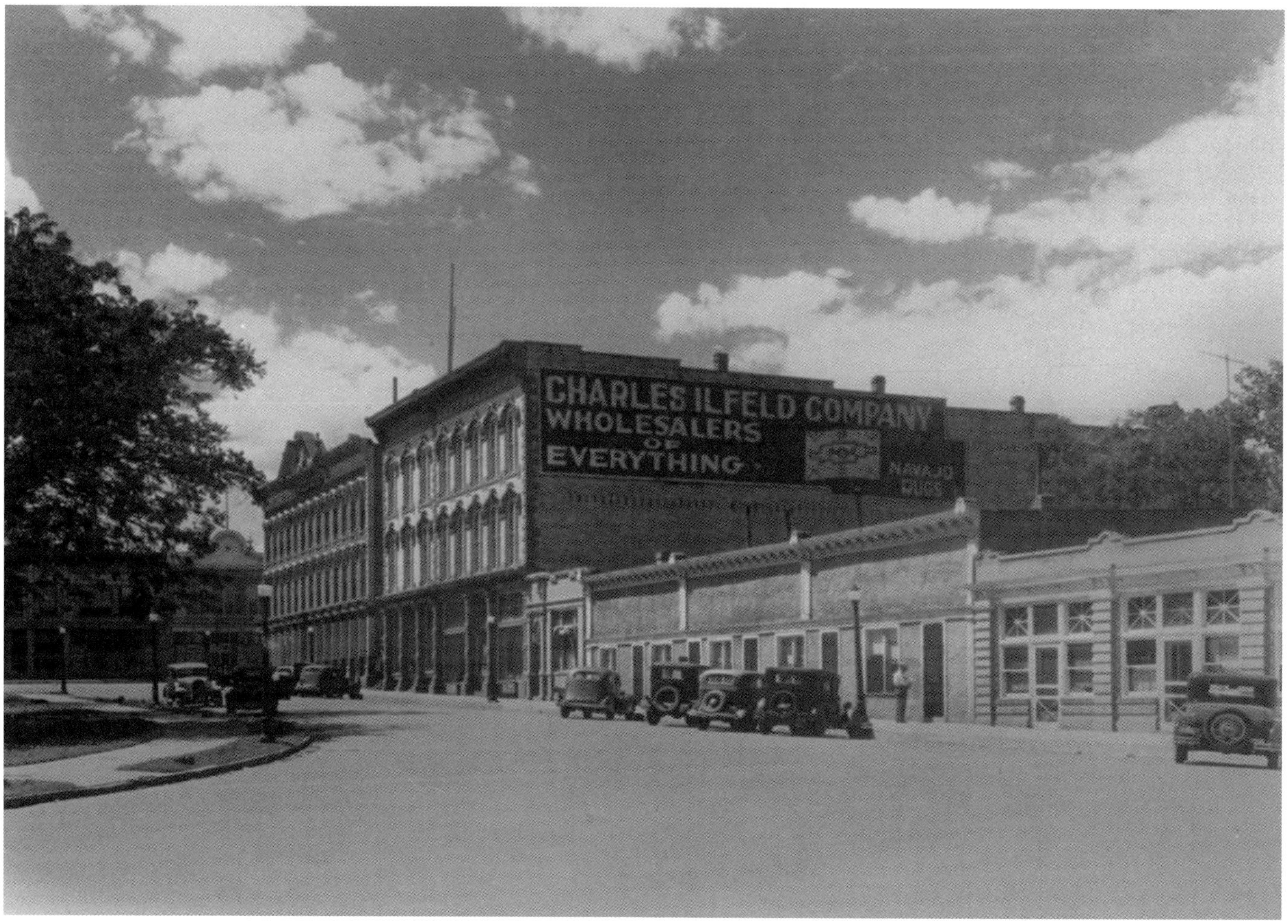

Ilfeld Emporium and Plaza Hotel, 1920s. Courtesy Las Vegas City Museum.

rest of New Mexico. The firm, moreover, also served in a banking capacity, financing much of the state's commerce.

Ilfeld's new building and the hotel with a ballroom and well-appointed rooms for traveling salesmen helped the other three sides of the plaza attract entrepreneurs who built similarly substantial and architecturally significant structures on this side of town. Once there was no more need for its use as a place for unloading trail wagons, the plaza was made into a park worthy of its improved surroundings. The new horse-drawn trolley line encircling it reconfigured the rectangular shape as an oval. Instead of the windmill gallows, there was a bandstand in the center, and radial walks, shade trees, and cast-iron benches made it an agreeable spot for social encounters in the daytime and a pleasant setting for concerts in the evening. Beginning in 1888, the Fourth of July was celebrated with a parade from New Town across the bridge into Old Town, ending at the plaza. Hispanic residents asserted their own cultural identity by extending the traditional American holiday into three days of fiestas. In 1910 the plaza was redesigned in the Romantic style with curving paths and irregularly scattered trees. A new bandstand was built at this time.

Plaza park, c. 1884, by T. G. Merwin. Courtesy Palace of the Governors..

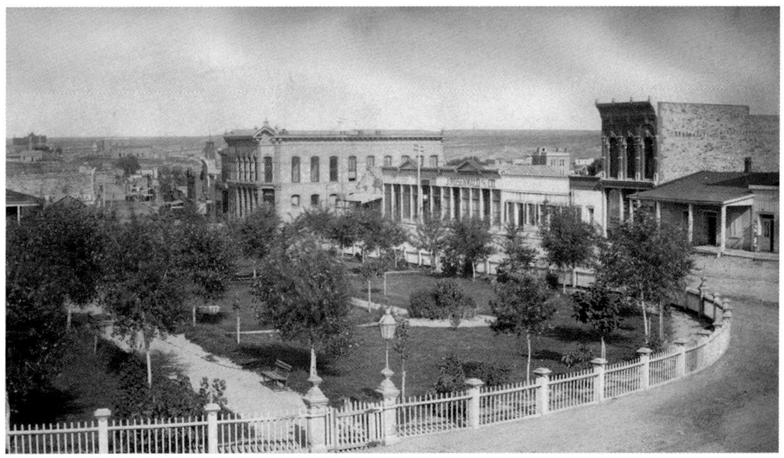

Casteñeda Hotel, c. 1900. Courtsy Las Vegas City Museum.

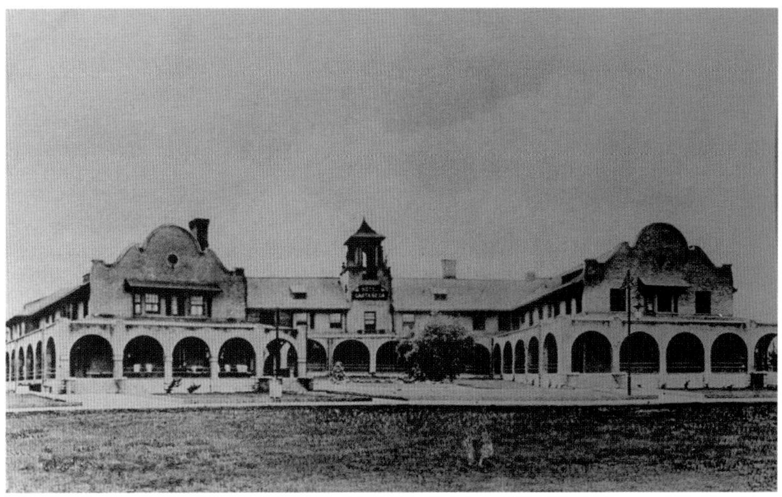

The residential sector of New Town reflected the prosperity of Las Vegas's merchants, bankers, doctors, and lawyers. Their legacy lies in the impressive Victorian and Italianate houses and the mansions built in a neoclassical style derived from the 1893 World's Columbian Exposition in Chicago. These, together with early twentieth-century Arts and Crafts brick homes with ample front porches, still line Sixth, Seventh, and Eighth streets to the north of National Avenue.

East of Grand between Railroad Avenue and the tracks, the railroad company built a train station and the large Castañeda Hotel next to it. Two commission houses, Otero, Seller & Co. and Browne and Manzanares, which received goods and also made loans to sheep growers and other suppliers, were located nearby, one on either side of the station. The ends facing the tracks served as warehouses, and the rest of these large buildings functioned as retail outlets.

By way of explanation, commission houses like Otero, Seller & Co. and Browne and Manzanares were among the mercantile adjuncts that typically followed train construction crews, creating their businesses at the temporary shipping stations located at the furthest point where the line happened to be. As the tracks moved forward, the hastily built commission houses were dismantled, rolled along the freshly laid rails, and reconstructed at the next terminal site. In the cases of Otero, Seller & Co. and Browne and Manzanares, when the wooden buildings these firms erected in Las Vegas burned in 1880, they were quickly rebuilt of brick, signifying that the town, now a rail hub, would remain their place of operations.

Along Railroad Avenue, saloons, billiard halls, stores, hotels, bakeries, and an assay office soon sprang up. Several of the merchants who had also been following the railroad construction crews, opening trading outlets in the little towns that had mushroomed along the train route, now established themselves permanently in Las Vegas. Several of the large, architecturally distinguished warehouses they built are now considered landmarks. Not surprisingly, this area was also a red-light district.

As all this development suggests, although the Union Pacific had already built the first transcontinental line, the Atchison, Topeka and Santa Fe remained the preferred route for shipping cargo, and Las Vegas was the principal freight depot in the American Southwest. Since it was a division headquarters of the railroad, the company built a nine-stall roundhouse for mechanical repairs near the train station. A hospital was constructed for the now-numerous company employees, as was a timber-preserving enterprise where railroad ties were treated with creosote.

Entrepreneurs quickly took advantage of the business opportunities the railroad opened up. Soon after its arrival Eugenio Romero set up a logging operation on the communal woodlands of the crestón and sold lumber milled from the cut timber to the railroad for ties and bridges. In1882 George Ludemann, a Jewish immigrant from Holstein, established a wool-scouring plant. Because of the ease of obtaining iron from mines in Colorado, in 1881 J. C. Adlon built a foundry. Rail shipments of machinery as well as raw materials enabled local manufacture of carriages, wagons, implements, and other utilitarian items. Businesses began to export goods to towns throughout the territory where the railroad had built spur lines, and several merchants expanded their operations to other burgeoning cities of the West. For example, the Charles Ilfeld Company opened branches in Albuquerque, Raton, and Durango, Colorado, and built warehouses in smaller places—Farmington, Gallup, Santa Rosa, and Magdalena in New Mexico and Trinidad in Colorado. Elsewhere the firm established country stores.

The railroad thrived as a passenger line, as well. In 1882 the company realized the opportunity to make Las Vegas a resort destination by laying down a spur from the eastern end of Bridge Street to the village of Montezuma in the Gallinas Canyon. At the spot next to the river where the geothermal springs rise to the surface it built a large wooden resort hotel called the Montezuma. The hotel burned down in 1884, and the following

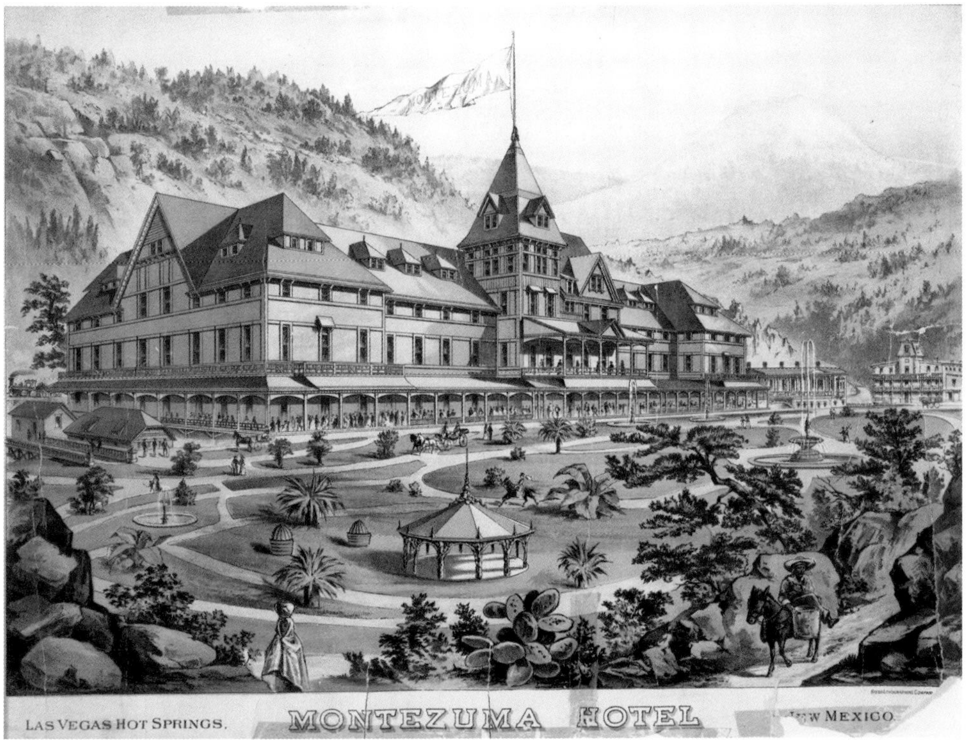

Second Montezuma Hotel. Courtesy Palace of the Governors.

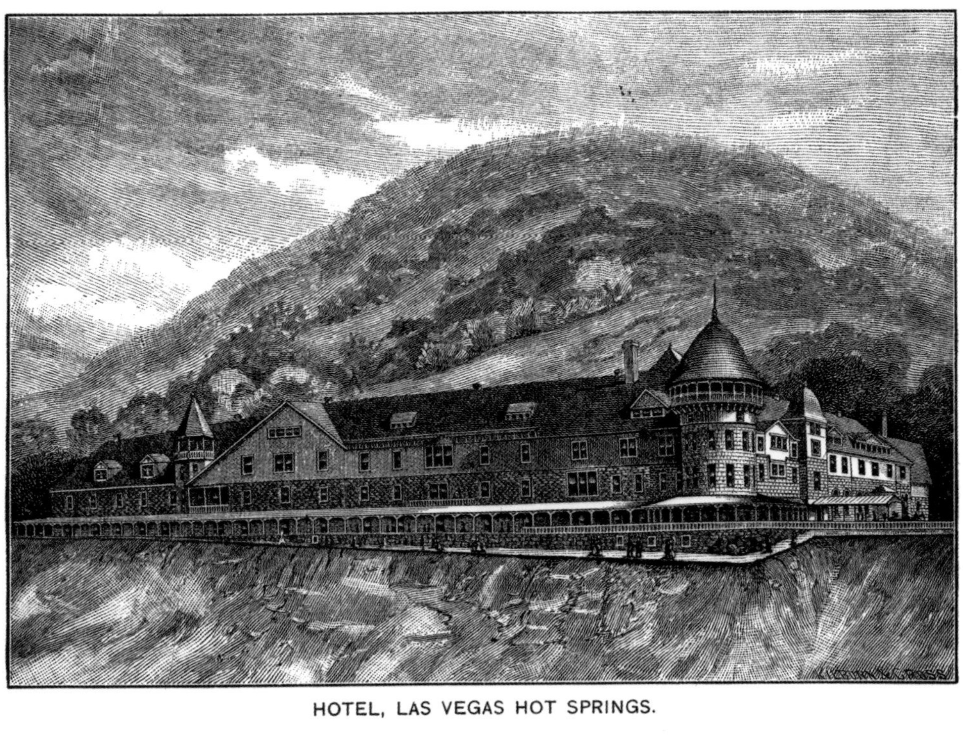

HOTEL, LAS VEGAS HOT SPRINGS.

Third Montezuma Hotel. Courtesy Palace of the Governors.

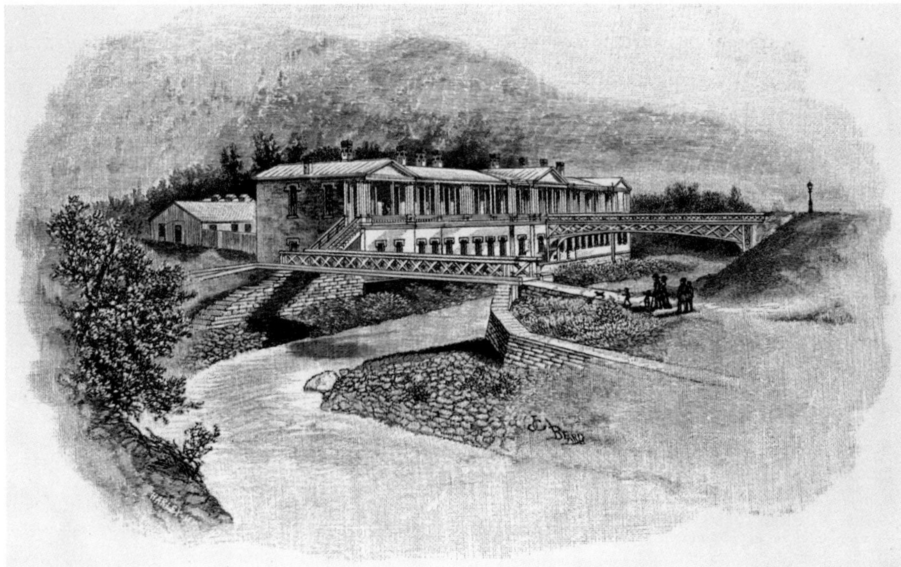

Bath house, Hot Springs. Courtesy Palace of the Governors.

year its successor was also destroyed by fire. Undeterred, in 1886 the company built the large, turreted Queen Anne brick "castle" higher up on the slope overlooking the hot springs. Designed by the distinguished Chicago architectural firm of Burnham and Root, it remains a prominent Las Vegas landmark. Here vacationers from the East came to enjoy the climate, scenery, and the twenty stone-lined outdoor springs. There was also a two-story stone bathhouse with a pool and fourteen steam rooms.

Like the Castañeda Hotel next to the train station, the Montezuma Hotel was operated by the Fred Harvey Company. Staffed by Harvey Girls, for several years it served as a popular tourist destination for well-to-do midwesterners and easterners. But its success did not last. By the beginning of the twentieth century, recreational attractions in other scenic locales throughout the Southwest and Far West and newer hotels along additional transcontinental passenger lines, plus the allure of Yellowstone and other more recently created national parks, reduced the area's desirability as a tourist destination. Although passenger service was still routed through Las Vegas, the Montezuma's appeal as a fashionable resort waned.

Forced to close in 1893 when the Atchison, Topeka and Santa Fe went bankrupt, the hotel continued to operate during the summer for another ten years. However, in spite of the existence of the hot springs and the hiking and fishing opportunities to be found in this scenic corner of Northern New Mexico, it never regained profitability, which led to its permanent closure in 1903 and sale by the railroad in 1905. After a series of reuses over the years, in 1982 it became the United World College-USA, part of a consortium of institutions in thirteen countries that offer an International Baccalaureate degree to precollege students from all over the world.[16]

Languishing as the city's white elephant, the empty hotel symbolized the beginning of Las Vegas's decline as a business community. The loss of jobs and supply businesses associated with the waning appeal of the Montezuma and other establishments catering to tourists and traveling salesmen sparked numerous mostly unsuccessful entrepreneurial initiatives. The Las Vegas Driving Park and Fair Association raised subscriptions to build a racetrack, grandstand, and athletic field three miles north of town. In 1905 and 1906 horse races, Indian dances, a baseball tournament, rodeo events, and races by volunteer firemen were held, but probably due to the poor commercial return, along with the demise of the electric trolley line the following year, this scheme was abandoned.

Agricultural development was tried as another economic avenue when, shortly after the legislature established a board of trustees for the Las Vegas Land Grant in 1903, its members began investigating the possibility of developing an irrigation project on a portion of the grant. To accomplish this, a dam would have to be constructed to impound water from the Gallinas River. The water could then be dispersed through a network of canals to irrigate thousands of acres of adjacent land. Farmers were to be given the opportunity to purchase parcels through loans made by the irrigation corporation. Such a scheme was not unique to Las Vegas. For a time speculation by corporate investors in irrigation projects such as this one was common in other dry parts of the country. Because of the large expense of civil engineering and the slow process of attracting buyers, however, most did not succeed. But in this case, the land-grant trustees invited the United States Bureau of Reclamation to undertake the proposed project, and the bureau's engineers determined that, with a $572,000 investment, it was feasible to irrigate 10,000 acres.

Unfortunately, the trustees were not able to sell enough land to cover this sum, and as a result, in 1908 the Bureau withdrew its support. Rather than give up at this point, however, they decided to think even bigger. In 1909 they entered into a contract with D. A. Camfield of Colorado—known at the time as the Western Irrigation King—to construct a dam on a site about five miles north of Las Vegas, which would impound enough water diverted from the Gallinas to irrigate between 30,000 and 40,000 acres of land. The New Mexico State Engineer denied the trustees' application on behalf of Camfield after determining that it had been superseded by that of another water rights speculator. While litigation progressed, Camfield began an embankment of dirt, but he ran out of funds and had to relinquish his contract in 1912. In 1916 another investor, R. C. Storrie of San Francisco, was hired to finish the dam. With its completion five years later, Storrie sold his interest in the project, leaving behind his name on the dam, the lake that it impounds, and the state park that now surrounds it.

The new owner formed the Las Vegas Land and Water Company, whose manager, Thomas W. Conway, was successful in luring prospective land buyers from the Midwest, many of them World War I veterans. Most had limited experience farming in a high desert environment, but with Conway's coaching in the production of such cool-weather vegetables as lettuce, peas, carrots, and cauliflower, they succeeded in producing crops. Unfortunately, fickle weather, high transportation costs to distant urban markets, and debt payments destroyed their agricultural profits, and following a devastating hail storm in 1927 most of the farmers gave up and moved away.[17]

While the Storrie irrigation project was getting under way, other entrepreneurial ideas continued to sprout. In 1912 local sports enthusiasts launched an effort to make Las Vegas the national capital of boxing. Funds were raised when promoter Jack Curley agreed to bring the heavyweight champion Jack Johnson and contender Jim Flynn, who was then emerging as "the great white hope," to Las Vegas. Dissension in the state legislature and governor's office over the brutality of the sport, a dispute with the contractor who was building a stadium for spectators, late snows hampering the training of the contenders who were already in residence in Las Vegas, and cancellation by the railroad of special trains for out-of-town ticket holders undermined chances for the event's economic success. The sponsors' dreams sank further after Johnson taunted and then mauled his opponent in the eighth round, causing the fight to be stopped.

The year after what was later dubbed "Boxing's Greatest Fiasco," the Commercial Club invited the silent movie writer, director, and actor Romaine Fielding to make Las Vegas a location for filmmaking. Cecilio Rosenwald started the Las Vegas Amusements Company, and he and his brother backed Fielding, who proceeded to produce several thrillers. These included *The Rattlesnake,* the story of a young Mexican and his rival in love, and *The Golden God*, a sensational movie about a labor revolution for which Fielding hired 5,000 extras and spent $50,000 on a cavalry and artillery scene. Two years following Fielding's departure, Tom Mix set up a motion picture lot in the town and directed a number of pioneering westerns there.

These less-than-successful attempts at economic reinvention by means of private enterprise notwithstanding, Las Vegas was far from moribund. Opportunities for regional trading still existed, families felt rooted, and institutions had been put in place that gave Las Vegas substantial staying power. Town leaders would continue to enhance its physical and civic infrastructure.

Cultural Development and Institutional Growth

The Jewish merchants, whose families intermarried and grew to form an affluent community, were instrumental in the betterment of Las Vegas. Because this wealthy and civic-minded segment of the population came from a European background rich in music and other performing arts, it helped foster an active cultural life in Las Vegas, which furthered the transformation of the town's appearance into an impressive cityscape with such distinguished works of architecture as the Masonic Lodge on Douglas Avenue and the Ilfeld Auditorium, later incorporated into the campus of Highlands University.

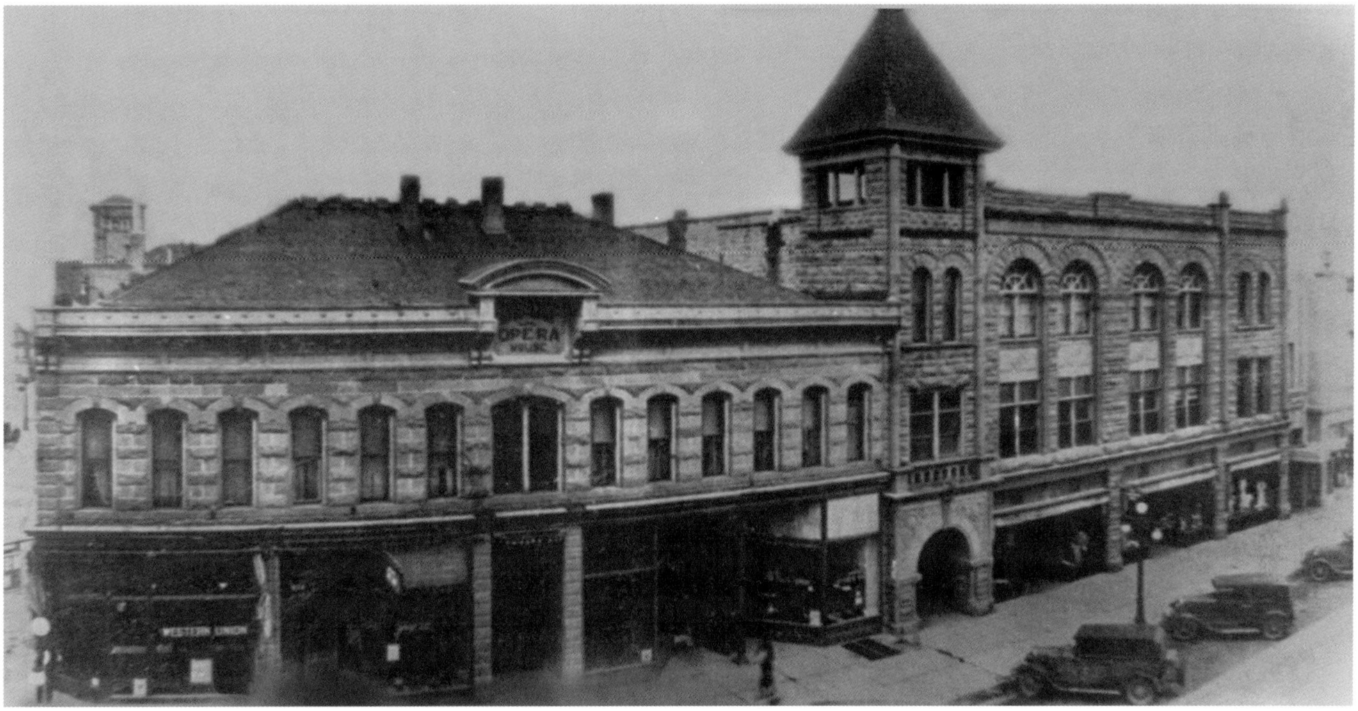

Duncan Opera House and Masonic Lodge, c. 1920s. Courtesy Las Vegas City Museum.

Anglo-Americans also helped build Las Vegas into a place of note, founding several Protestant churches and instituting a number of medical services. Eight town physicians organized the Las Vegas Medical Society in 1881, and the Ladies' Relief Society, representing members of various local churches, opened a small hospital where they served as volunteer nurses. In 1891 the territorial legislature appropriated funds to build the New Mexico Insane Asylum—later known as the State Hospital—on land donated by Benigno Romero just below the crestón. When it opened its doors two years later, 40 patients were admitted. With the subsequent addition of a 110-room wing, it housed more than 100 patients in 1902. This number had increased to 700 by 1935 and to 1,000 by 1953. In 1911 the Relief Society, staffed with ten physicians, incorporated as the Las Vegas Hospital. A Young Men's Christian Association was started in 1900, and a number of other civic, commercial, and social organizations came into being not long thereafter.

Due to its high altitude and dry climate, convalescence in Northern New Mexico was considered a sound therapy for tuberculosis. The Plaza Hotel catered to many tubercular guests and even organized the One Lung Club as a means of providing them with social pastimes. A more institutional approach to treating patients with the disease began when Dr. Francis A. Atkins advertised the benefits of Las Vegas as a site for a sanitarium. As a result, the Sisters of Charity from St. Louis, Missouri, and Leavenworth, Kansas, came west to staff

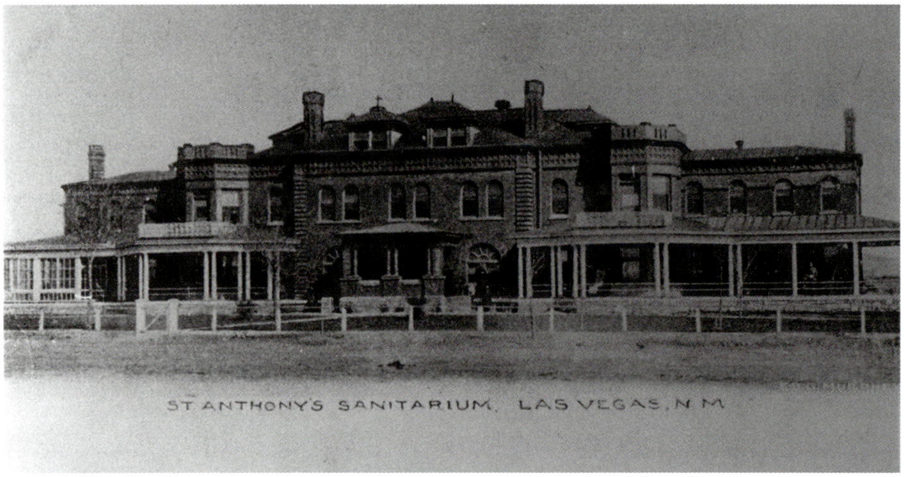

St. Anthony's Sanitarium. Courtesy Las Vegas City Museum.

St. Anthony's Sanitarium when this fine brick building, occupying an entire block on Eighth Street, was completed in 1897. In 1900 another physician, Dr. F. W. Seward, came out from New York and converted Don Trinidad Romero's former mansion into a sanitarium. In 1905, after working with Dr. Seward for a few years, Dr. William T. Brown left to found a sanitarium in Valmora, not far from Fort Union. Under the subsequent direction of his son-in-law, Carl H. Gellenthien, this institution was destined to become one of the premier pulmonary medical facilities in the country.

Because of its status as a city with its own independent school district, East Las Vegas was able to float municipal bonds for the construction of a public elementary school on Douglas Street. Subsequent bond issues funded three more school buildings, which by 1932 accommodated twelve grades with a total of over 1,200 students. Finding trained teachers and administrators was no problem, thanks to the founding in 1893 of the New Mexico Normal School, the predecessor of today's Highlands University. Located on the hill above the east bank of the Gallinas, Normal Hall, built of rusticated local sandstone in the Romanesque style, opened its doors three years later.

The portrait of Las Vegas that emerges during these years is that of a thriving Western city comprising a citizenry devoted to culture, education, and the provision of health care and social and legal services. This, however, was only part of the story. Las Vegas's ethnic conflicts, based on discrimination and injustice, create a darker side to the picture.

Patrones, Peones, and Rough Justice

As the Anglos and Jews experienced rising economic success along with the Hispanic *ricos* with whom they formed the upper echelon of Las Vegas society, the gap between rich and poor widened. Mitigating the status of the have-nots was the patrón system, which worked in the following manner. Patrones—the Romeros and other important Hispanic families—distributed favors, gifts, and jobs to the poor, creating a bond in which the price of patronage by the former was unconditional loyalty on the part of the latter. Once the territorial government was established and the male citizenry was enfranchised according to the United States Constitution, patrones could readily use their power to influence voters. The political consequences were such that for a long period in the history of Las Vegas, these wealthy patrones, who were large landholders with vested interests in the mercantile trade and the construction of the railroad and New Town, aligned themselves with Anglo interests. Members of the Republican Party for the most part, they easily swayed the Hispanic populace to vote according to their instructions.

In spite of the patrones' ability to achieve allegiance and obedience while manipulating the system to their own benefit, the rights of the poorer members of the population with regard to the use of the land became an overriding issue. Theirs was a grievance based on a particular historical injustice. The original community land grant from the Mexican government to the thirty-six families from San Miguel del Bado who had settled Las Vegas, along with grants to other settlers throughout New Mexico, were mandated to remain in perpetuity by the Treaty of Guadalupe Hidalgo of 1848, which marked the end of the Mexican War. However, much as the Hispanic settlers had appropriated the grazing lands of the western fringe of the Great Plains and the mineral, timber, and game resources of the adjacent mountains from the Native American inhabitants, their descendants were in turn systematically dispossessed as increasing numbers of Anglo-Americans moved into the territory. The flagrant infringement of the provision of the Treaty of Guadalupe Hidalgo guaranteeing the inviolability of all prior land grants thus became a source of profound bitterness.[18]

The land grant story is tangled. When New Mexico's territorial government was established in 1848, it was apparent that if the provision of the Treaty of Guadalupe Hidalgo honoring the original grants by the Mexican government were set aside, undeeded portions of New Mexico would—as was the case with open lands in other U.S. territories—become federal property. As such, they could be surveyed and sold, providing a welcome source of revenue for the federal government. In addition, the Homestead Act of 1862 legislated the freehold settlement of 160-acre parcels, provided that claimants would make certain minimal specified improvements, grow crops, and show proof of residency for a five-year period. Land speculators immediately found loopholes in the law, and therefore, in addition to fostering the agrarian settlement of the West, the Homestead Act inadvertently served investors seeking to form land companies for large-scale ranching operations. With its broad expanses of grassland, the Las Vegas grant was especially attractive to those seeking to subdivide and fence off certain areas as private ranches for sheep- and cattle-raising. Investors were determined to take possession of these lands whether by outright purchase or by claims, generally fraudulent, under the Homestead Act.

The federal government did little to confirm Hispanic ownership of these rich communal lands. This laissez-faire attitude paved the way in New Mexico for chicanery on the part of lawyers and land grabbers who saw how American survey-based property laws could be used to disenfranchise Hispanic owners of rights in the *ejido*, or common land. Prominent among these predators was the lawyer Thomas Benton Catron, the principal in a pool of investors known as the Santa Fe Ring, which controlled the economic life as well as the political and judicial machinery in the recently formed territory. The ring included the surveyor general of New Mexico, whose sole mandate was to subdivide the country into 640-acre sections. Handicapped by his circumscribed authority and lack of staff, the surveyor general was thus unable to perform the necessary job of first surveying the original Hispanic land grants protected under the Treaty of Guadalupe de Hidalgo. The never-surveyed Mexican land-grant boundary lines thus remained vague, advantaging the Anglo land investors who sought in various unscrupulous ways to shrink them as much as possible in order to give legitimacy to their claims.

Although the Las Vegas grant was not immediately diminished in the same wholesale way as other northern New Mexican community grants, including that of neighboring Mora, poor Hispanics who depended on access to its resources felt increasingly victimized as their grazing, water, and timber rights continued to dwindle. Along with the inhabitants of their sister communities in the nearby small river valleys, they deplored the steady erosion of large portions of their communal lands. To make matters worse, as their subsistence existence began to collapse, these heirs of the original Las Vegas land grantees were unable to obtain other than menial jobs within the new capitalist economy. For what hired work they were given, they were paid lower wages than their Anglo counterparts. In Las Vegas, such overt discrimination against Hispanics became common after 1879 with the birth of New Town and the concurrent publication of its daily newspaper, the *Las Vegas Optic*. In its pages the editor, Russell Kistler, aired his virulent prejudice against Hispanics with appalling frequency, maintaining that *"mexicanos"* were basically lazy and genuinely preferred a nonmaterialistic, technologically primitive lifestyle. "Give a Mexican a peck of beans and a string of red peppers, and he is thoroughly contented, nor will he work while a particle of either remains," he opined.[19]

Moreover, because so many Hispanics at that time did not speak English, they were essentially powerless to protest in court, where, in any case, their suits would have been adjudicated by Anglo judges. Education was obviously essential if they were to attempt to defend their land rights. In this, they were helped by the fact that public schools were becoming a growing necessity for Las Vegas's rapidly expanding population. Large landowners resisted public education in part because it meant the imposition of a property tax. However, by the 1870s public elementary schools had joined existing parochial schools in bringing the advantages of classroom instruction in English to a growing number of Hispanic children.[20] Increasing literacy and the ability to speak the official language of the territory fostered greater political awareness and skills.

Anger over Anglo land appropriation continued to fester within the Hispanic community. The Spanish-language newspaper *La Voz del Pueblo* advocated a political movement that would "do everything in its power to assist in the advancement and development of the native people."[21] Above all, this meant supporting those who sought to resist ranchers seeking to obtain titles to portions of the communal grant. The leadership of this resistance was assumed by the Herrera brothers, Juan José, Pablo, and Nicanor. The eldest, Juan José, called El Capitán because of his rank in the Union Army during the Civil War, considered himself a loyal citizen of the United States and wished to see the wrongs of his people addressed through the existing judicial system. From a political perspective he saw that a strategy of Anglo alliance would increase the chances for the success of his cause. To accomplish this, he recruited a large number of Hispanics to join the recently formed New Mexican chapter of the Knights of Labor. As it turned out, these proponents of workers' rights were basically disposed toward the view that the Las Vegas land grant was, like the unsettled lands in the other territories, the property of the federal government and therefore open to homesteaders. At the same time, both sides saw the advantage to be gained by strength in numbers in such matters as demanding better working conditions and pay from the railroad company. Adding political strength to their cause, Herrera was instrumental in the Knights' success in forming a third party, the populist El Partido del Pueblo Unido, which could nominate candidates for election to public office.

As fellow owners of large parcels of fenced land for cattle and sheep operations and exploiters of the timber resources of the ejido, wealthy Hispanics such as the Romeros, who were also profiting from Las Vegas's mercantile success, did not at first seek to defend the interests of their dispossessed Nuevo Mexicano neighbors. In advancing their own economic well-being, they sided with the town's conservative Republican Party business elite. Those protesting the whittling away of the ejido and the restricting of access to water and communal grazing land were therefore hampered in achieving sufficient power to gain redress of their grievances.

Further east, the range wars had bred a militant group known as White Caps because of the face-concealing hoods worn by these night raiders. In New Mexico their counterparts became known as Gorras Blancas. Herrera, now dubious of the efficacy of working within the system, joined his brothers, who were already recruiting men from the outlying villages for a series of clandestine assaults on the ranchers fencing in the commons. The principal tactics of the Gorras Blancas were the cutting of barbed wire fences, the burning of crops, farm equipment, sawmills, and haystacks, and the destruction of railroad bridges and timber ties. They did not discriminate between their Anglo and Hispanic foes in this regard. Their numbers quickly grew, and in March 1890, some 300 masked riders appeared in town and posted a manifesto stating their determination to protect the rights of all people and especially the poor. They were adamant in demanding an end to land thievery and partisan politics, declaring that if the persecution and mistreatment continued at the whim of the politicos, retribution would be the perpetrators' reward.

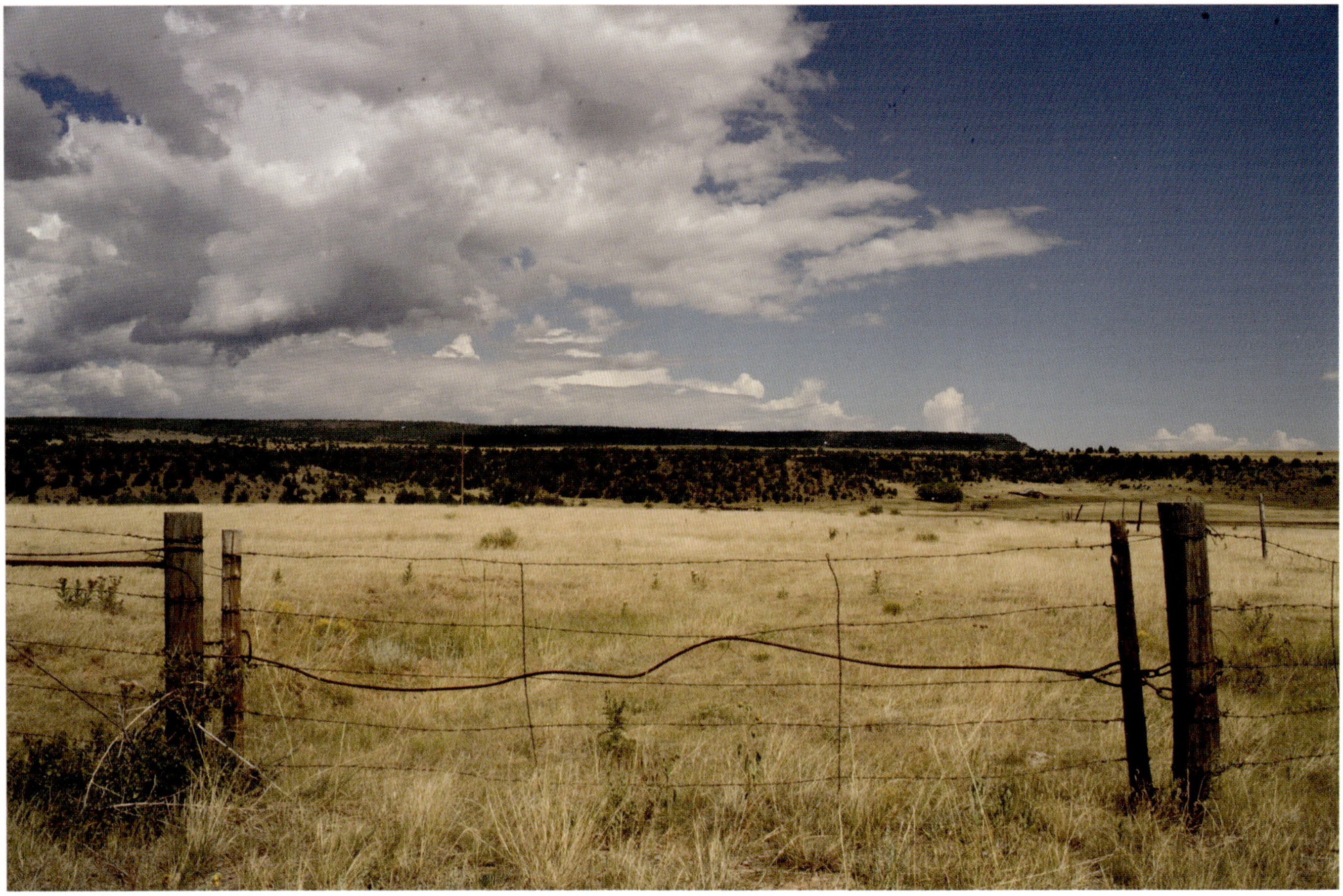

The Ejido, 2010

Thanks in significant measure to the Partido del Pueblo Unido's growing political strength, Congress passed a bill in 1891 creating the United States Court of Private Land Claims to adjudicate cases in the western territories acquired at the end of the Mexican War. Although the portions of the original Las Vegas grant located in the mountain-enfolded valleys formed by tributaries of the Pecos River—lands that were not ideal for grazing large herds—remained in the common ownership of the residents of their villages, the better part of the grant was sold large parcel by large parcel until the ejido had become what it is today, a series of contiguous fenced ranches. As what was left of the original half-million-acre grant was further whittled away, it dwindled to a negligible remnant, which is now governed by a board of trustees appointed by the county court.[22] Thus the fate of the Las Vegas land grant shows in microcosm how the "winning of the West" by Anglo-Americans came at the cost the displacement of poorer Hispanics as well as native populations.

Hispanismo and Highlands University

The wresting of political control of East Las Vegas by Hispanics beginning in the 1970s altered the social and political landscape of the town. The determination of Hispanic power brokers today to maintain control of the Democratic Party machinery in San Miguel County, and with it the selection of those running for elected office, is intensified by lingering grievances over the past treatment of Hispanics as second-class citizens. Not surprisingly, present-day Hispanic political hegemony has had the effect of making some Las Vegas Anglos feel that they are permanent outsiders no matter how long they have been residents.

Highlands University played a major role in Las Vegas's political transformation. By the 1960s it had grown from its normal school beginnings to become a liberal arts institution modeled on colleges in the East. Its student body was drawn from within New Mexico and out of state. Thomas Donnelly, the president of Highlands at this time, expanded the campus from 28 acres to 278 acres and built twenty-eight new buildings.

Toward the end of the decade, the Vietnam War and civil rights protests, which were causes of student unrest throughout the rest of the country, provided the climate for radical change in the nature of the university. But these broader issues were ancillary to more locally focused grievances. A student group known as the Spanish-American Student Organization (SASO) began to agitate with aggressive force. SASO members claimed that Highlands' traditional humanities and sciences curriculum, lack of minority faculty and administrators, and admissions preference for out-of-state students and athletes were evidence of Hispanic oppression. Inspired by the recent inclusion of black studies in college and university curriculums elsewhere, SASO agitated for more courses emphasizing the Hispanic experience. Beset by this turmoil within the institution, Donnelly resigned in 1970.

The agitation at Highlands was something more than a student movement. Unlike other places where student protests were opposed by civil authorities, in Las Vegas the university became the lever for the political transformation of the entire town. Capturing control of the university was simply a first step in replacing Anglo dominance with Hispanic power. Masterminding this metamorphosis was Democratic party boss and district attorney of San Miguel County, Donaldo "Tiny" Martinez, who directed the student protest at Highlands from the table where he presided over his lieutenants at "Mama" Lucy Lopez's restaurant overlooking the plaza. Mama Lucy was in sympathy with Martinez's call for Donnelly's ouster and the appointment of a Hispanic president, and her son Jesus, a Highlands student at the time, was one of the principal leaders within SASO.

Jesus Lopez and his fellow SASO members were backed by militants within the Chicano movement, known as El Movimiento or La Reconquista, which had targeted Highlands as the intellectual center of its multipronged agenda for redressing various forms of discrimination. The Chicano movement's New Mexican agenda inevitably sought to focus on historic Hispanic grievances concerning land rights. Helping to lay the ground for this renewed struggle over the abrogation of the Treaty of Guadalupe Hidalgo, Reies López Tijerina, a charismatic Assembly of God missionary from Texas, had earlier come to Northern New Mexico. Here he had found a cause worthy of his formidable abilities as an inspirational leader.

In 1963 Tijerina, or El Tigre, as he was dubbed in the press, formed the Alianza Federal de Mercedes Libres, an organization dedicated to recruiting young Hispanics and enflaming them with a sense of injustice over their lost lands. Tijerina was arrested, jailed, and subsequently acquitted after his 1967 Alianza raid on the courthouse in the northern New Mexican town of Tierra Amarilla. Invited to Highlands to speak in 1968, he was instrumental in the political development of SASO and its eventual success in taking over the Student Senate. Many Las Vegans were sympathetic, and Father James T. Burke of Our Lady of Sorrows gave SASO members the use of the church's press for printing leaflets.

Following Donnelly's resignation, the New Mexico Highlands University Board of Regents picked Dr. Charles Graham as president, a choice that prompted further SASO protest and occupation of the administration building. Although the takeover was nonviolent, Dr. Graham, who understandably felt intimidated, declined the job. The dissidents stepped up their level of civil disobedience during the interim presidency of Dr. Ralph Carlisle Smith. To defuse the tense situation at Highlands, the governor appointed a new Board of Regents. Two of the five members were Hispanic, and Father Burke was counted among the other three. Following this ethnic realignment, the board hired Dr. Francisco Angel as Highlands' first Hispanic president.

During his tenure from 1971 to 1975, with funding from Title III and Title IV of the federal Equal Opportunity Act, Dr. Angel was able to recruit a number of Hispanic faculty members and initiate a Chicano Studies program and bilingual education. However, his changes were not sufficiently far-reaching for radical members of the movement. Pedro Rodriguez, the first director of Chicano Studies at Highlands, took his students to Mexico in order to teach them how to paint in the manner of the great Mexican muralists Diego Rivera and José Clemente Orozco. Between 1971 and 1973 he and the students expressed their ideals by painting six murals on campus buildings, which a few years later would become a source of heated controversy. Even at the time, their depiction of conquistadores as aggressive invaders of Native American lands distressed those Hispanics who were proud of their Spanish descent. Other antiimperialist images, including heroic portraits of Che Guevara, proclaimed their radical agenda. One mural that many people found particularly offensive contained a caricature of Dr. Angel as a pig.

At this point the militant Chicanos, whose agenda was determined by the principles of the Texas-based Raza Unida Party, urged SASO members to cast aside their "pure Spanish ancestral fantasy." The organization was renamed CASO, with the "C" for Chicano substituting for the "S" of Spanish-American. On September 25, 1973, CASO demanded President Angel's resignation and staged a seven-hour sit-in. Betita Martínez fueled the Chicanos' La Raza agenda in *El Grito del Norte*, the Marxist newspaper she published in Española. Militants, angered by what they perceived to be the passive role of the Catholic Church in terms of education, formed an organization called Montezumos Unidos, which tried to turn the old Montezuma Hotel into an alternative school with a more ethnically focused curriculum than that of the local public and parochial schools.

Determined to succeed in politically reconstructing Las Vegas as a Hispanic-dominated town, Tiny Martinez lent support and direction to these confrontational politics, which included picketing, legal action, and sometimes violence. He encouraged the walkout at the East Las Vegas High School in protest of the appointment of an Anglo district superintendent. As chairman of the Democratic Party of San Miguel County, he perfected the patrón system of local government, dispensing favors and building a political machine that would cause the Anglo residents of East Las Vegas henceforth to bow to Hispanic political control of the entire town.

Dr. John Aragon, who was appointed by the governor to succeed Angel, served as Highlands president for ten years. During the next decade under his successor, Gilbert Sanchez, the campus got a face-lift. The week after he took office in 1985 the controversial murals were painted over. Several buildings were subsequently renovated and the grounds beautified. Before Sanchez left office, Highlands was perceived as having completed another transition, this time from an ethnic-studies-driven university in turmoil to a mainstream provincial institution with a career-oriented curriculum. At the same time, Las Vegas remained a Hispanic-ruled community.

Moving on and Getting by

Although certain social benefits came out of the turbulent 1960s and 1970s, the economy of Las Vegas, which was already in distress, suffered greatly as it completed a transition from private-sector entrepreneurship to a system based primarily on government support. As early as the 1950s Las Vegas had lost the majority of its Jewish population; only a few of their old mercantile operations remained in business locally, and the Ivy League–educated younger generation had begun to find career opportunities elsewhere. Moreover, by the 1970s, because of its role in Mexican drug traffic, Las Vegas had earned the pejorative moniker Smack City. Its difficult and still-incomplete recovery did not begin until the 1980s.

The town's long decline can be summarized as follows. Along with the opening of alternative rail lines, which stimulated the economies of other regions, the invention of synthetic fibers left New Mexican sheep growers and wool traders with only a fraction of their former market. No longer a major transportation hub or mercantile center with a prosperous middle class, and with no more manufacturing jobs and no need for railroad train repairmen, Las Vegas's days as a busy commercial center with a solid job base were over by the mid-twentieth century. The permissiveness of the sixties and seventies and the rise of Las Vegas as a center for the distribution of drugs coming from Mexico hastened the departure of the remaining Jewish merchants and their descendants. Robberies multiplied, stores closed, and warehouses were emptied. As residents moved elsewhere, many of the town's fine old mansions fell into disrepair. Its survival was now almost entirely dependent on federal and state monies. As a result, following a descending scale of numerical ranking, today the majority of employees are found at the New Mexico Behavioral Health Institute (still known as the State Hospital), the two public school districts, Highlands University, the district office of the State Highway Department, the City of Las Vegas, and Luna Community College (formerly Luna Vocational-Technical Institute). Not surprisingly, the dispensation of jobs in these public institutions is still the currency of political patronage, and appointments to government offices and institutions are now accepted as one of the prerogatives of public office. In short, money and jobs rather than liberal ideals drive San Miguel County's overwhelmingly Democratic Party politics to a large extent.

The evidence of decline is writ large on the face of the town. Although some of the boarded-up warehouses and retail establishments have been bought and renovated by new owners, there is still an air of desuetude to other parts of the once-vibrant commercial streetscape. The history of the former 1890 Rosenwald warehouse on the southeast corner of the plaza symbolizes Las Vegas's economic shift, its empty, hulking presence a reminder of how many historic buildings were abandoned during the town's extended period of economic stagnation. By the mid-1940s, a decade after its mercantile use had ceased, it was a shirt factory, and after that it became the JayVal Factory for the manufacture of parachutes, an enterprise that employed approximately 300 women. From the 1960s until the 1980s it was occupied by Navajo Textiles, a trading-post-style operation. Since then the historic building has stood vacant and boarded up. Because the present owner will neither occupy nor sell it, the kinds of renovation improvements that have recently been made by the investors and small-business proprietors who have bought up other vacant buildings around the plaza have not occurred here.

One should not for this reason despair about Las Vegas's future. It is important to look at the half-full as well as the half-empty glass. History is ongoing, and there are signs that a town renaissance may indeed be under way. As we shall see in the following chapters the lives of many, though not all, of the current residents are satisfying and full. Las Vegas is still a place of community pride and, something increasingly rare in today's mobile society, the home of a large population whose surnames are the same as those of the town's founders. Their roots run deep in its soil.

Two ethnic differences distinguish Northern New Mexico from the rest of the United States. One is the strong indigenous culture of the Pueblo peoples whose ancestors settled along the Rio Grande and the Pecos River around nine hundred years ago. The other is the deep-rootedness of the descendants of the Spanish conquerors and colonial settlers. Long after 1821, when Anglo-American merchants from Missouri came across the Plains to the upper end of the Camino Real, and continuing to the present day, their ancestral Spanish has retained parity with English as the language of the region.

Deep Roots

In Northern New Mexico, heritage and ancestry are points of pride. The Spanish spoken here is sometimes said to sound archaic because of the settlers' long isolation at the northernmost reaches of the Spanish Empire. Here people do not have to hire genealogists or visit ancestry.com on the Web to draw their family trees; some, in fact, can recite their genealogy six generations back from the present. Their pride is in part the pride of the impoverished, inasmuch as the Anglo occupation of New Mexico signaled the end of their wealth in land, leaving them merely their dignity along with an abiding sense of cultural ownership of place. But poverty is relative; as teachers, servicemen, artists, tradesmen, restaurant owners, mechanics, politicians, and government employees over the years, most, though not all, Las Vegas Hispanics have decent livelihoods.

Almost invariably when I spoke with members of old Las Vegas families, the conversation became genealogical. As in the halls of a palace or lordly mansion, portraits of ancestors frequently adorn living room walls. Mostly enlarged photographs, they are evidence of the importance of family within Hispanic culture, as well as the connection of certain families to this particular place—a sense of belonging by birthright.

ELBA C. DE BACA

Elba C. de Baca was born on Taos Street in Las Vegas in 1918 and died in 2010 on her family ranch fifteen miles outside Las Vegas. Because of her reputation as a regional folklorist and author of several booklets on the stories and customs of the past, a couple of years before her death I went to see her and her sister Carmen, the last two then remaining of eleven siblings.

As we talked in Carmen's living room, Elba explained her ancestry. Like many old-time residents of Northern New Mexico, her family has an illustrious genealogy dating back to the time of the conquistadores. Her forebears arrived in the company of Don Juan de Oñate, the seventeenth-century governor of Santa Fe, and she was a descendant of Luis María C. de Baca, the original Las Vegas land grantee. "My great grandfather's grandfather was given an enormous amount of land—really, miles and miles," she said. "Besides raising cattle, he was a trader and befriended a lot of French trappers." She insisted, however, that her ancestors were not related the legendary sixteenth-century Spanish explorer Álvar Núñez Cabeza de Vaca. "The movie that was made about him and how he was the first white man to enter the Southwest—that sort of thing gives me a pain in the chest. No one even knows whether or not he had any children. But Luis did, which is how there came to be so many Bacas all over this place."

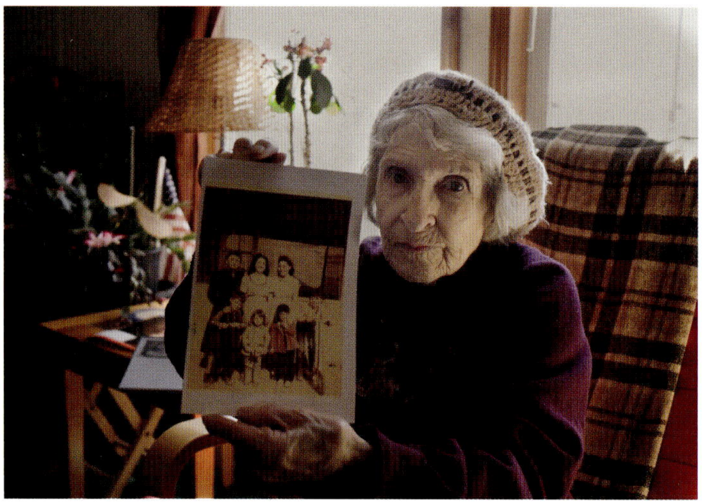

Elba C. de Baca

On the opposite wall, surrounding a framed Cabeza de Vaca coat of arms, were portrait photographs of her father, Florencio (1881–1966), her grandfather Manuel (1853–1915), her mother, Juanita (1887–1984), who belonged to the prominent Gallegos family, and other relatives. Each face sparked a story. "That's my mother and dad when they were married in 1905, and that's my dad in the military uniform. He wanted to go off to war in Cuba with Teddy Roosevelt, but his father said no. Instead, he sent him to New Mexico Military Institute, and although he never served in the army, his three sons did." Another picture showed the dignified face of a handsome, silver-haired man wearing rimless glasses and a bow tie. This was Ezequiel C. de Baca. She remarked, "He was a Democrat who got elected New Mexico's lieutenant governor in 1912, the year it became a state, which was something you wouldn't expect, since all the powerful politicians were Republicans in those days. Then in 1917 he became governor. Unfortunately, he died only forty-nine days after taking office, but he was still able to get the legislature to do some important things during that time."

I later found out that Ezequiel C. de Baca is indeed a legend in New Mexican politics. He is admired today for having stood firm against the powerful Republican politicians whose economic interests ran counter to those of the rural poor. He spoke for Nuevo Mexicanos in need of bilingual education and protection for their communal land grant at a time when it was being whittled away and fenced off by Anglo ranchers. Remarkably, during his very brief tenure as governor he was able to get introduced in the legislature some of the reform laws for which he had long fought as an educator, journalist for *La Voz del Pueblo*, and member of the Caballeros de Labor (Knights of Labor).

Elba held up for me a picture of herself and her siblings: "There's Flossie and Mary, who was twelve years older than me. Mary had so many proposals, you can't believe. She turned them down in order to help our parents. She started teaching at eighteen and didn't marry until she was twenty-five." Elba herself taught for over twenty-five years, mostly in the one-room schoolhouses that formerly provided rural New Mexican children with the only education most of them would ever have. World War II brought her generation into contact with the outside world. "Here's my brother who was killed," she said, pointing to the family photo in her hand, "and then there was my younger brother, who enlisted when he was only seventeen, and he came out without a scratch." Other men in the family have subsequently served in Korea, Vietnam, and Iraq.

I made a mental note of the fact that the U.S. military has always attracted many in Las Vegas and the rest of New Mexico. One explanation, in addition to patriotism, may be that in a state lacking a vigorous private-sector economy, most of the available jobs are derived from the state or federal government. As in the case of Las Vegas's public institutions, the armed services provide an opportunity to make a living and gain a retirement pension.

Like her aunt Fabiola C. de Baca Gilbert, whose many books gathered the recipes, folklore, and agricultural practices of her traditional Northern New Mexico villages, Elba became a folklorist and was often asked to speak in public. She is the author of a booklet titled *Legends of a Hermit,* a compilation of one-page vignettes. Some are straightforward bits of local history, but most are tales having to do with the supernatural in which one of the protagonists is an apparition who turns out to be a disturbed spirit or the devil and is intended to be recognized by some wrongdoer as an admonitory presence. In one, a tiny lady dressed in black and wearing a lace mantilla is seen at night hurrying through the corridors of the Public Employment Retirement Association (P.E.R.A.) Building in Santa Fe, which was constructed on the site of an old cemetery. The author wonders, "Who is the mysterious black-clad figure from another world? Is she unhappy because her remains were moved to another location? Or, if they were not removed, is she haunting the building because it was built over her bones?"

In another fable, a man whose nickname is Sopitas owns a bar and a large dance hall. He serves liquor on Good Friday, and despite his wife's urging him not to hold the usual Friday and Saturday dances since it is a day of prayer and meditation, Sopitas carries on business as usual. The punishment for his transgression: At the end of the evening a well-dressed stranger appears at the bar and orders a glass of whiskey. Looking up from the cash register where he is counting his money, Sopitas notices that the man has horns, a tail, and hooves, whereupon he falls into a dead faint. When his wife comes and tries to revive him, he screams that he has seen Satan himself, his horns, his hooves, and his tail, and smelled his reek of sulphur. The story concludes: "The poor man was in shock for a long time. He sold everything and he and his wife moved away."

Such supernatural tales are time-honored staples of Hispanic folklore, ghost stories that were often used in former days as disciplinary aids by parents who wanted to proscribe certain kinds of behavior. The continuing popularity of *Bless Me, Ultima,* by Rudolfo Anaya, a story of a *curandera* whose healing powers are pitted against the evil black magic practiced by three *brujas*, or witches, as she leads Antonio, the young protagonist, to reconcile conflicting moral forces in his life, is evidence of the attraction this form of literature holds for the world at large.[2] Elba C. de Baca's spirit is probably too serene to cause her to wander abroad after death. Nowadays, however, in Las Vegas she is herself something of a legend.

LUIS MARTINEZ

Luis Martinez has lived for three quarters of a century on the Gallinas land grant, where his roots go back four generations. "I've never been anywhere else except for when I was in the military," he told me when I went to visit him.

The Martinez house sits on the canyon hillside in the tiny village of Gallinas, overlooking the upper reaches of the Gallinas River. Luis's great-grandfather was one of the settlers who ventured forth from San Miguel del Bado in the 1830s to establish the town of Las Vegas and colonize the nearby valleys of the eastern edge of the Sangre de Cristos, also part of the Las Vegas communal land grant. "They found a lot of prairie chickens here, so that's why they named the place Gallinas," he told me. "They'd been coming up in the summers to pasture their cattle, but the Navajos would steal all their animals and crops. Then after the land grant was made they all got together and ran the Indians out so they could settle down for the whole year here. They started farming then. My grandpa was born and lived here until he died around 1910. My mom was born here in 1900 and then me in 1936. Now there are my four sons, who were all born here, too."

I wanted to know what it was like growing up in this remote corner of Northern New Mexico. "Well," Martinez replied, "I only went to school till I was eight. I got in a fight and broke Gilbert Padilla's nose, so they threw me out. All I had was third grade. I learned a little more how to read and write in the service. After I left school my dad had me work with the old-timers cutting timber. Then when I was seventeen I wanted to go into the military. I was underage, and my mom didn't want me to go, but one day when I took her into Vegas to buy groceries, I persuaded her to go with me to the recruitment office and give permission. I was only away for a couple of years when I hurt my back and got discharged. After that I came home and worked in construction till 1959 when I started helping my dad doing odds and ends on one of the ranches he was taking care of up here. In 1963 I bought my first sawmill. I've been a lumberjack ever since then until five or six years ago, and now my boys have taken over." Pointing out the window, he added, "We've got two sawmills in back there, and a couple of years ago the boys bought a new mill and a wood splitter with a conveyor."

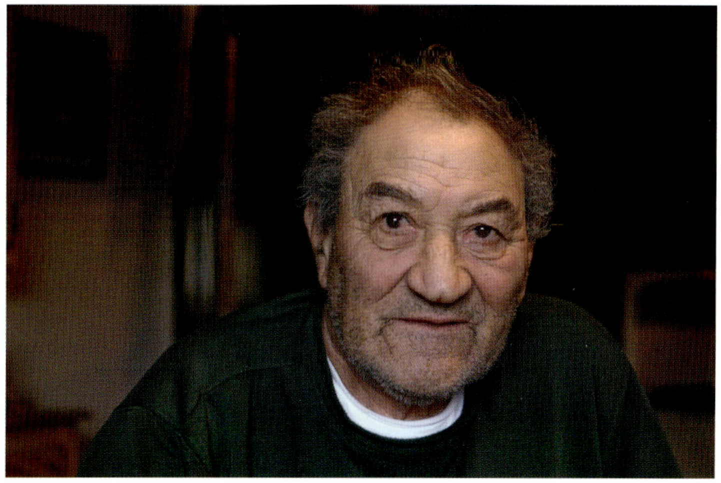

Luis Martinez

I continued asking Martinez questions about his life and what this place was like when he was growing up. "When I was a boy horses were my main love," he replied. "The old-timers would turn the mares loose and they would colt, so we had about eighty head of mustangs. I'd run like crazy after them all day until I could rope some. Then we'd bring them down here, break them in, and sell them as harness horses for four or five dollars."

A boy in those days was not too young to do regular work. "Back when I was ten years old," Martinez said, "my dad would put me in a wagon with a load of wood, and I'd take it down to the village of Montezuma. I'd also go up to the land grant with him to cut trees. Then we would peel them, load the posts at night, and deliver them to the railroad. They were used to brace the mines, and the railroad shipped them to Colorado and all over. We also chopped down trees to make vigas, and we cut railroad ties."

Looking down toward the river where Martinez's fields lie along the valley bottom, I inquired about the family's current ranching and farming activities. "Oh, right now we run fifty cows and two bulls," he replied. "We grow hay in that field over there, which is what we use to feed the cows in the winter. In the summer we drive them up to pasture on the hill over there," he said pointing to the opposite ridge. "Up here behind the house my grandpa ran 500 goats back in the thirties. Everything was open then because of the grazing; now it's all gone back to trees. There was a corral for the milk goats. We put the dry goats in a separate corral and used the milk goats to make cheese. My mom had a big garden over there, and you would not believe the size of the carrots; some were four inches around. We had turnips and red beets; she would plant a little of everything. My dad grew corn in the field down below, and my grandpa had fruit trees on the other side of the river. The years have changed things so badly. The whole canyon was planted back in my grandpa's time. Then around 1935 the United States Forest Service claimed a lot of the land. There were also private individuals who wanted to buy ranches in the canyon. We had no papers or anything; everything was just word of mouth, so there was nothing we could do to hold onto the land that was ours."

But the Martinezes fared better than their neighbors overall. According to Luis, "When they wanted to take away the Martinez grant, which was our part of the original Gallinas grant, my grandpa brought Judge Armijo up here and talked about how we had always had the right to it. He was real close to the judge, so we got to keep our part of the grant land, what is in the valley and 80 acres this side of the cattle guard. The only designated grants left within the original Las Vegas communal land grant now are the Martinez grant of 3,000 acres and the Vigil grant, which is 3,049. We finally got our papers in 1952. Judge Armijo sold the rest of the land for twenty-five dollars an acre.[3] Now the kids whose families used to live on those properties have all gone away to other places like Albuquerque, and I'm the oldest member of the Lower Gallinas Land Grant Association."

Staying on in the canyon, Martinez made a living in a variety of ways. "You might call me a jack-of-all-trades," he said. "Besides buying the sawmill after I came back from the military, I went down to Albuquerque and bought a welder. I used to do a lot of welding, but the metal got in my blood, an electrical charge of some kind maybe. After I was laid up in the hospital for a while, I got better and went back to welding until I got sick again. Besides running cattle, I've worked on road construction here in the upper canyon and helped take care of the properties people have bought in the valley, baling their hay, clearing trees, fencing pastures, and so forth."

Technology as well as government regulations regarding land use have altered the old way of life, and, as is true elsewhere, ranching and farming have become mechanized in New Mexico. "Horses aren't used to round up cattle or pull wagons anymore," Martinez remarked. "Everything is done with four-wheelers now. We have nine horses, but we haven't used them for eight years. Now the cows are used to the four-wheelers. They hear the noise of the motor and just come up to where we are to get their feed." In addition to their cattle, the family raises a herd of goats: "We pen them up in the part of the property that once belonged to my grandpa." With regard to crops, he said, "We don't grow much anymore because the coons come and bother us. But one of my boys made a garden a couple of years back, and the corn grew real big. We also had pumpkins, cucumbers, and other things, but the summers are so short up here and when the freeze comes early everything gets ruined. We plant wheat and oats now, but if the weather turns cold too soon, the ice gets on them and everything gets burned. Right now we're having a drought, so the water is not running in the acequia and we can't irrigate the fields."

The mainstay of the family economy is still timber. "There are regulations as to where we can cut trees, and the timber we take from the grant land can only be for personal use," Martinez explained. "The wood we sell has to come from the Forest Service land, and they charge us ten dollars for every cord we haul away. We cut and split the wood and sell the cord for $100 in Las Vegas or $150 in Santa Fe."

Martinez's eldest son, Paul, is a self-employed cabinetmaker, but Ken, Marty, and Peter continue in their father's footsteps. Their cousins who live next door sometimes help. At Martinez's suggestion, I walked out back with Peter, who showed me the new mechanized equipment that makes cutting and splitting firewood a lot easier. Near the big pile of cordwood waiting to be sold was a stack of long logs, the trunks of recently felled ponderosa pine trees. Peter demonstrated the way the new hydraulic mill stripped one of these of bark and squared off its circumference at the same time the conveyer belt and rollers passed it across the blade that cut it into planks of specified widths.

Looking around, I took in the view. In the foreground next to the new sawmill and log splitter was the old sawmill, some milled lumber, a stack of vigas, some storage sheds, and several obsolete pieces of equipment including an ancient Mack truck. In the middle ground was the valley with a corral containing an array of "four-wheelers" in various states of repair, the fields beside the acequia, and the forested ridge on the other side of the river. In the background looming against the sky was the granite mass of Hermit's Peak. For the Martinez family the scene is probably too familiar to be remarkable; for me it was a thrilling landscape uniting human use and nature, past and present, and the ordinary with the sublime.

I went back inside to say goodbye to Luis. "I don't know what would have become of me if I hadn't punched Gilbert and had gone on and gotten an education," he said as I was leaving. "You'd probably have a Ph.D. now," I joked. "But I do have a Ph.D.," he responded in a flash. "It stands for Post Hole Digger!"

Martinez Sawmill operation

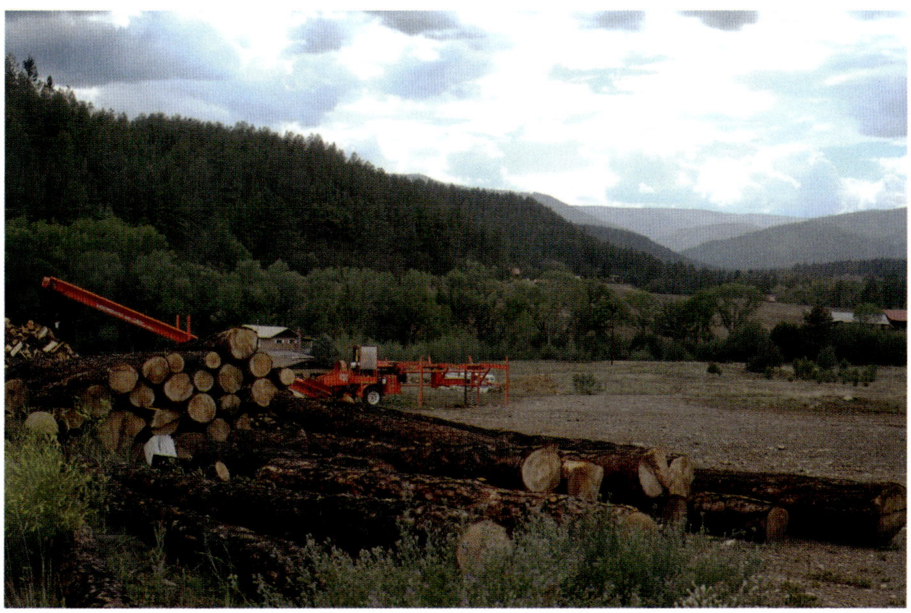

ANSELMO ARELLANO

To delve deeper into Las Vegas's past, I went to see Anselmo Arellano, a retired history professor. A native of Springer, a railroad town and the Colfax County seat sixty-eight miles north of Las Vegas, Arellano entered Highlands University in 1962. After receiving his bachelor's degree, he left for California, where he taught ethnic studies, Spanish, and literature at Fresno State College. After earning his Ph.D. at the University of New Mexico, he returned to Highlands during the turbulent period of the Chicano movement to help develop an ethnic studies curriculum. At this point he decided to settle permanently in Las Vegas, where he could alternately pursue an academic career and his work in rural community development programs in Northern New Mexico. Retired since 2001, he now lives with his wife in a comfortable single-story house on Washington Street.

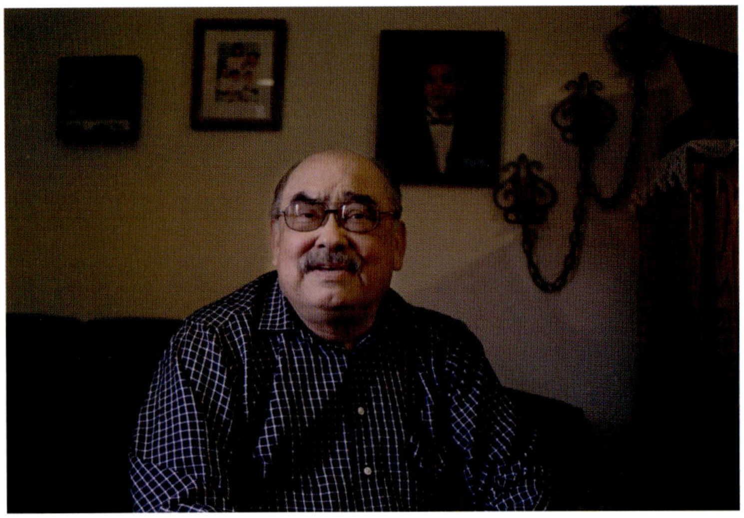

Anselmo Arellano

Arellano's ancestry, like Elba C. de Baca's, is illustrious. While hers can be traced back to Luis C. de Baca, who obtained his vast land grant from the newly established Mexican government in 1821, Arellano has recorded a genealogy that stems from seventeenth-century forebears who were granted by the Spanish crown an even larger holding comprised of what is now northeastern New Mexico. Before the Colfax County wars in the late nineteenth century deprived them of much of this land, their heirs owned large flocks of sheep.

Ancestral portraits are grouped on the living room walls of the Arellanos' home. The family, whose name derives from their native community in the Basque country of northern Spain, arrived in New Spain in the wake of Cortés's conquest of Montezuma's Aztec empire. Several generations later Capitán Cristóbal Arellano came to New Mexico as a twenty-four-year-old soldier in the company of Don Diego de Vargas, the conquistador who repossessed the territory twelve years after the Pueblo Revolt of 1680.

The most striking ancestral portrait in the room is a large photograph of Arellano's grandfather, Don José Manuel Arellano (1861–1944), a prominent Colfax County politician and poet. As a retired historian who can nimbly name all his forebears back to Capitán Cristóbal, Arellano has become the family archivist. While we were talking he excused himself to go into the next room to fetch an old ledger book whose pages are covered with verses written in faded ink by a hand displaying the elegant penmanship of a bygone generation. These were the poems of José Manuel Arellano, which Anselmo has transcribed and collected in a spiral-bound booklet titled *Poesia y baladas de mi pueblo.* Many are political in nature, with such titles as "Elecciones y facciones," "Partido Republicano," and "Amigo Demócrata." Others deal with the sadness of death, the graduation of a daughter, the advice of a grandmother, the admiration of a friend, and similar subjects relating to José Manuel Arellano's life and time and place in the world.

To help me in my research, Arellano lent me a copy of his doctoral dissertation, a history of Las Vegas, which recounts its early settlement by the emigrants from San Miguel del Bado, their descendants' unfortunate loss of the communal lands previously granted by the Mexican government, and how the Gorras Blancas fought the chicanery of Anglo politicians, lawyers, and complicit judges in the territorial courts over the issue of land ownership. It is a narrative without rancor, but one that makes clear that Anglo-American settlement of the Hispanic land-grant patrimony was no more legitimate than the Spanish conquest of the lands of the Native Americans. Well substantiated by archival documents, it is a valuable source for anyone seeking a fresh perspective on western history.

Business Interests

To understand more fully the extent of Hispanic loss and Anglo-American gain during this turbulent period in United States history, I realized that I needed to visit the former ejido, those vast grasslands blanketing much of San Miguel and Mora counties to the north and east of Las Vegas. Here I would learn about the relationship between this huge grazing range and the emigrant entrepreneurs who propelled the westward-moving American economy during the time when Las Vegas was a railroad hub and the nexus of a vital trade between manufacturers of goods in the East and stockmen and woolgrowers in the West.

NED AMES

To see one of the great ranches carved out of the Mora land grant, which is contiguous with the original Las Vegas land grant, I visited my friend Ned Ames while he and his wife, Jane Sokolow, were making their annual summer visit to the Fort Union Ranch. Ames is the current president of the Fort Union Land and Grazing Company, the stockholding entity composed of the 134 heirs of the remaining 95,325 acres of ranchland bought in 1885 by easterners General Benjamin F. Butler and his son-in-law General Adelbert Ames.

The story of the Butler-Ames purchase illustrates how a communal land grant could be converted into property for sale through the machinations of a conniving lawyer in league with a syndicate of investors. In the case of the Fort Union Ranch that lawyer was Thomas Benton Catron, the principal in the rapacious pool of investors known as the Santa Fe Ring. Not surprisingly, Catron maintained close relations with the surveyor general of New Mexico, whose primary responsibility was to extend the federal public land survey system dividing the country into sections of

640 acres. This opened the door for outside claimants, and since lawyers like Catron were able to control the manner in which overlapping claims were adjusted, vast amounts of grant land were transferred to new owners, including himself.

It is fair to say that Butler and Ames, who were easterners with more important business matters to attend to, were not involved other than as long-distance investors in the nefarious activities of the Santa Fe Ring. When offered an opportunity to buy land in 1885, however, they acquired a large section of the Mora Grant. In addition to this purchase, Butler was able to buy a portion of Catron's interests, although a long dispute regarding payment was not resolved until 1895 when Ames and Catron agreed to a property division at the 36th Parallel. Catron was left with 250,000 acres, and Butler took clear claim to 350,000 acres, of which 143,000 acres were identified and eventually fenced. As a coda to the story, Catron was elected to the United States Senate when New Mexico became a state in 1912, and on February 22, 1916, as the result of a partition suit from which the Union Land and Grazing Company was held exempt, the unallocated lands of the Mora grant were sold at the courthouse door, thereby depriving the remaining descendants of the original grantees of their rights to all but a fraction of their ancestral commons.

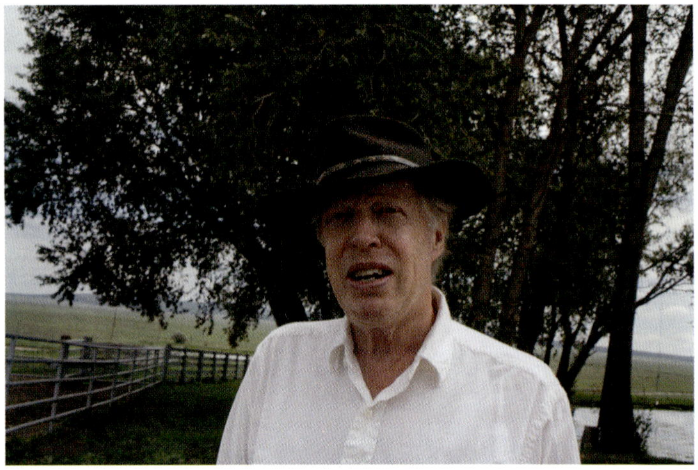

Ned Ames

Fort Union Ranch was for many years regarded simply as a remote business holding of the Butler-Ames family, and for the first half of the twentieth century it was managed by an agent, Edward B. Wheeler. Following his tenure, Andrew Marshall, Jr., and his wife, Peggy, became the first family members to live on the ranch and actively oversee the affairs of Union Land and Grazing Company, which Marshall did until 1981. Wheeler had been approached by the National Park Service in 1939 regarding the sale of the small portion of the property occupied by the ruins of Fort Union, but it was not until 1954 that Marshall completed negotiations on behalf of the company. As part of the agreement conveying 721 acres (exclusive of mineral rights) to the federal government for the establishment of Fort Union National Monument, the ranch received the benefit of a paved access road to the historic fort.

During their 2008 sojourn, Ames and his wife invited me to spend a day with them at the ranch. When I arrived they were just unsaddling horses they had ridden that morning into one of the many beautiful canyons of the Turkey Mountains. As we bounced along ranch roads in a pickup truck, we spotted elk as well as cattle grazing in the rolling grassland that stretched before us. Pulling to a stop on a rise where there is a campfire ring, we got out and took in the vast, 360-degree horizon. It is a stirring panorama. Here you can see what the Santa Fe Trail wagoneers, merchants, and travelers saw as they rolled toward Fort Union: Hermit's Peak, other adjacent peaks and ridges of the Sangre de Cristos, and in the dim distance Santa Fe Baldy and the mountains around Taos, all part of the great topographic wall that delineates the western edge of the Great Plains.

Many people do not realize that there is no single track marking the Santa Fe Trail. This is true along its length all the way back to Missouri, since new ruts were carved when caravans veered from the well-established parts of the trail as their leaders sought more direct routes or better places to ford rivers. On Fort Union Ranch, however, the tracks of the converging Northern and Cimarron branches of the trail created something resembling a highway, which can be read today as a broad depression, a sunken swath of grass. Ames asked if I would like to take a walk along the wheel ruts, pointing out as we did so the banks of eroded soil on either side that marked their width.

As the fort came into view, I tried to imagine the caravans on the last leg of their journey to Santa Fe. Mercantile ventures were still fraught with peril, for as wagon traffic across the Plains increased, there were not only more temptations for horse thieves and cattle rustlers, but also continuing warfare between Native Americans and Anglo-Americans. Still, the profit motive prevailed over danger, and the wheels rolled on, creating these visible lines in the grass. Later, the Plains

Fort Union ruins

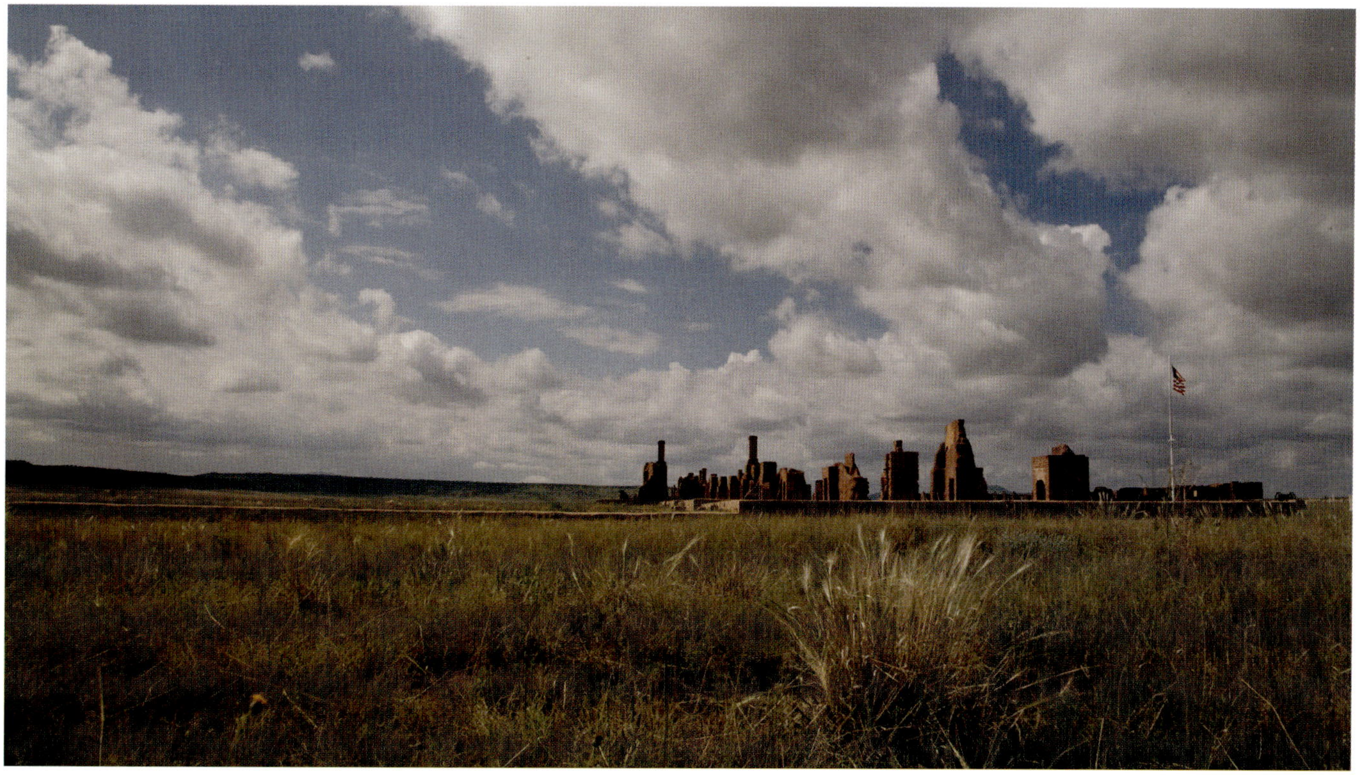

Indians were subdued and Fort Union decommissioned; then, with the coming of the railroad and the opportunity to ship live cattle as well as hides and wool to eastern cities, these same grasslands were no longer flecked with the curved white canvas tops of prairie schooners. Too arid for farming, they were as ideal as ever for grazing, but now the old ejidos of the Las Vegas and Mora land grants had been supplanted by Fort Union Ranch and other large cattle- and sheep-grazing operations.

DANIEL T. "BUD" KELLY, JR.

The building of the railroad greatly facilitated shipping wool, livestock, hides, and pelts to textile mills, stockyards, leather manufacturers, and furriers. Conversely, the growing market in the West for such products as dry goods, groceries, hardware, barrel whiskey, and farming, mining, and hauling equipment gave rise to commission houses. Serving as middlemen in the transfer of raw materials and merchandise, these businesses were profitable operations. Charging commission fees for their services on both ends—generally around 2.5 percent—they also functioned to some extent as banks.

To learn more about this important aspect of Las Vegas's old rail-based economy, I met one day with Daniel T. Kelly, Jr., better known as "Bud," the last head of Gross, Kelly & Company, the now-defunct successor firm of Otero, Sellar & Company. As we talked in the comfortable home on Palace Avenue in Santa Fe that was originally owned by his grandmother, Kelly recounted the story of his grandfathers' emigration to the West. "My paternal grandfather, Harry W. Kelly, and my maternal grandfather, Jacob Gross—that's not a Jewish name, by the way, although it sounds like one—worked for Otero, Sellar & Company, a firm that set up temporary businesses at railheads along the route of the train line. It's all here in the book my father wrote," he added, handing me *The Buffalo Head* by Daniel T. Kelly.[4] "You can borrow it if you like."

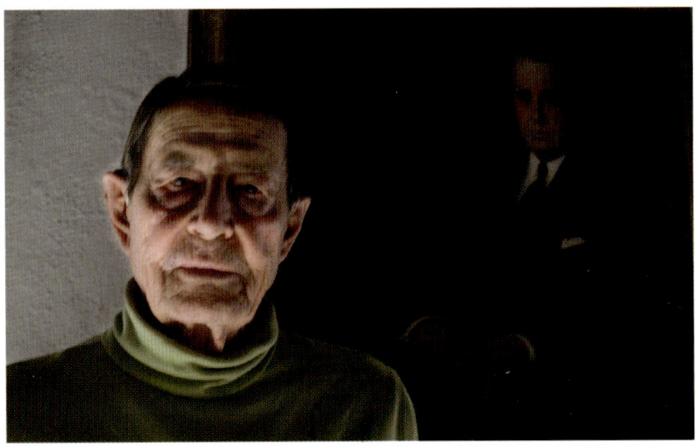

Daniel T. Kelly, Jr.

When I started to read the book I learned that "the mercantile companies became traveling companions, so to speak, of the railroads as they pushed their way across the country from one boom terminal to the next." Kelly, Sr., then describes the activities of the firm that had been founded in 1867 in Leavenworth, Kansas, by Miguel Antonio Otero and John Sellar and the role it and other commission houses played in the post–Civil War industrial era when tracks were being laid to link eastern cities with the western frontier: "Sometimes copper and silver ore from the mines of Arizona and Mexico were brought in by the freighters to pay for the necessities supplied by the merchant. Often no money exchanged hands; business was carried on by simple barter, or by credit and debit on the bookkeeper's ledger." He describes the appearance of the temporary towns where the commission houses set up business until it was time to move on to the next location. Across from the railroad station there would be a main street lined with a couple of blacksmith shops, a makeshift hotel, a row of flimsy frame dwellings, and of course, saloons and dance halls "with their inevitable quotas of fancy ladies who wore calico Mother Hubbards more often than silk and satin."

These provisional settlements left little behind: "As the railroad completed track westward it was not only the men and their families that moved. The existing town site was abandoned, and actual buildings were picked up and transported to the next place. Only the cellar holes and the cemeteries were left behind as the warehouses were sawed into sections and small frame buildings loaded on flatcars. In the new town all segments were reassembled, and the mobile community [remained in that spot] until it was time to move again. Some towns lasted a few months, some as long as four years. Only a few survived the boom to become permanent."[5]

When the railroad got to Kit Carson, Colorado, rather than take their commission house north with the Kansas and Pacific, Otero, Sellar & Company decided to follow the Atchison, Topeka and Santa Fe southward. It was when the company was headquartered in Granada, Colorado, in 1873 that Miguel Otero, the senior partner, hired Harry Kelly as a "commission house boy." Kelly, then fifteen, had recently gotten in trouble and been expelled from school in Leavenworth, Kansas.

In 1876 the company moved to La Junta, Colorado, and by the following year it was situated in El Moro, Colorado, where young Kelly survived a bout of typhoid fever. In 1879 he found himself in Otero, New Mexico, the next settlement established by the railroad and named in honor of the firm's founder, who was known by his honorific as Don Miguel. That same year the railroad reached Las Vegas. Inasmuch as there were several existing mercantile establishments surrounding the old plaza, many people thought the tracks would be laid in proximity to this already-thriving center of trade. However, the railroad company, already equipped with a plat for an entire new town, located them one mile to the east on the other side of the Gallinas River. Obviously East Las Vegas was intended from the beginning to be an important hub rather than a temporary railhead settlement. For that reason Otero, Sellar & Company decided to make it their permanent headquarters. This time the firm built their trackside commission house of brick instead of wood.

Continuing his father's story of the firm's establishment, transformation, and growth in Las Vegas, Bud Kelly said, "At the time Otero and Sellar arrived, Jacob Gross, a native of Baltimore who was later to become my grandfather's partner as well as my maternal grandfather, was a senior employee. In 1881, when the ownership of the firm changed, it was renamed Gross Blackwell & Company. Gross, who was about fourteen years older than my grandfather, Harry Kelly, was a senior stockholder, and my grandfather was a junior stockholder. My grandfather Gross had married a debutante from St. Louis; however, after four or five years of living in Las

Vegas, she said she couldn't stand it, so they went back east and raised their children in St. Louis. My grandfather Kelly became the managing partner of the firm, but my grandfather Gross was still a major shareholder in the company. He would come out in the summertime and bring the whole family. In 1902 they changed the name of the firm to Gross, Kelly & Company. Later they acquired the other Las Vegas commission house, Browne & Manzanares, which was beside the tracks next to them."

Going on with his story, Kelly said, "My Kelly grandparents stayed in Las Vegas, and after my father was born in 1886 they built a big house on the corner of Sixth and Columbia. When he married my mother, it turned out that she didn't like living in Las Vegas any more than my Gross grandmother did, so they moved over here to Santa Fe. By that time, the firm had set up branches in several parts of New Mexico, and my father, who graduated from Harvard in 1908, was put in charge of the Santa Fe branch."

Gross, Kelly & Company prospered not only through its mercantile business, which had branches throughout the state of New Mexico, but also through the company's livestock, wool, and timber operations. Kelly said, "On a routine basis the company would purchase a large number of New Mexico lambs and ship them to Colorado and Nebraska ranches to be fattened. Because of our holdings I became familiar with most of the state. I was sent off to prep school and Harvard, and altogether I had a very interesting, culturally rich bringing-up period. I could have stayed in the East, but Northern New Mexico is a magnet, and I never wanted to live anywhere else."

I asked Kelly to describe his boyhood memories of Las Vegas, which he visited frequently when the family gathered at his grandparents' mansion on Sixth Street. Pulling out a photograph of a gracious Victorian home with wide verandas, he reminisced: "It was a wonderful house. The entrance was on Sixth, which had trolley lines back then. I remember sitting on the porch watching the Cowboys Reunion parades. Behind the house was my grandfather's garage and the help quarters. There was Petra, their maid, and Marcella, their cook. Petra and Marcella were still in their teens when they came down from Rociada to work for my grandparents. McDaniel was my grandfather's driver and factotum. On the south side of the main house was the tennis court. At Christmastime, my parents would drive us over in their touring car with isinglass windows and drop us off. Then they would head back to Santa Fe, which for them was where the action was. But for my older brother and sister and me, it was just magical. My grandparents had Christmas trees, Santa Claus, turkeys, everything."

Kelly continued to recount the story of his carefree, adventurous youth: "Once, when I was around twelve I biked all the way over from Santa Fe to see my grandparents in Las Vegas. When I was a bit older, I'd ride horseback over the mountains to the ranches outside of Las Vegas where I had a lot of friends like the Davises in Sapello. There was a good deal of horsing around. I was only a teenager, and the

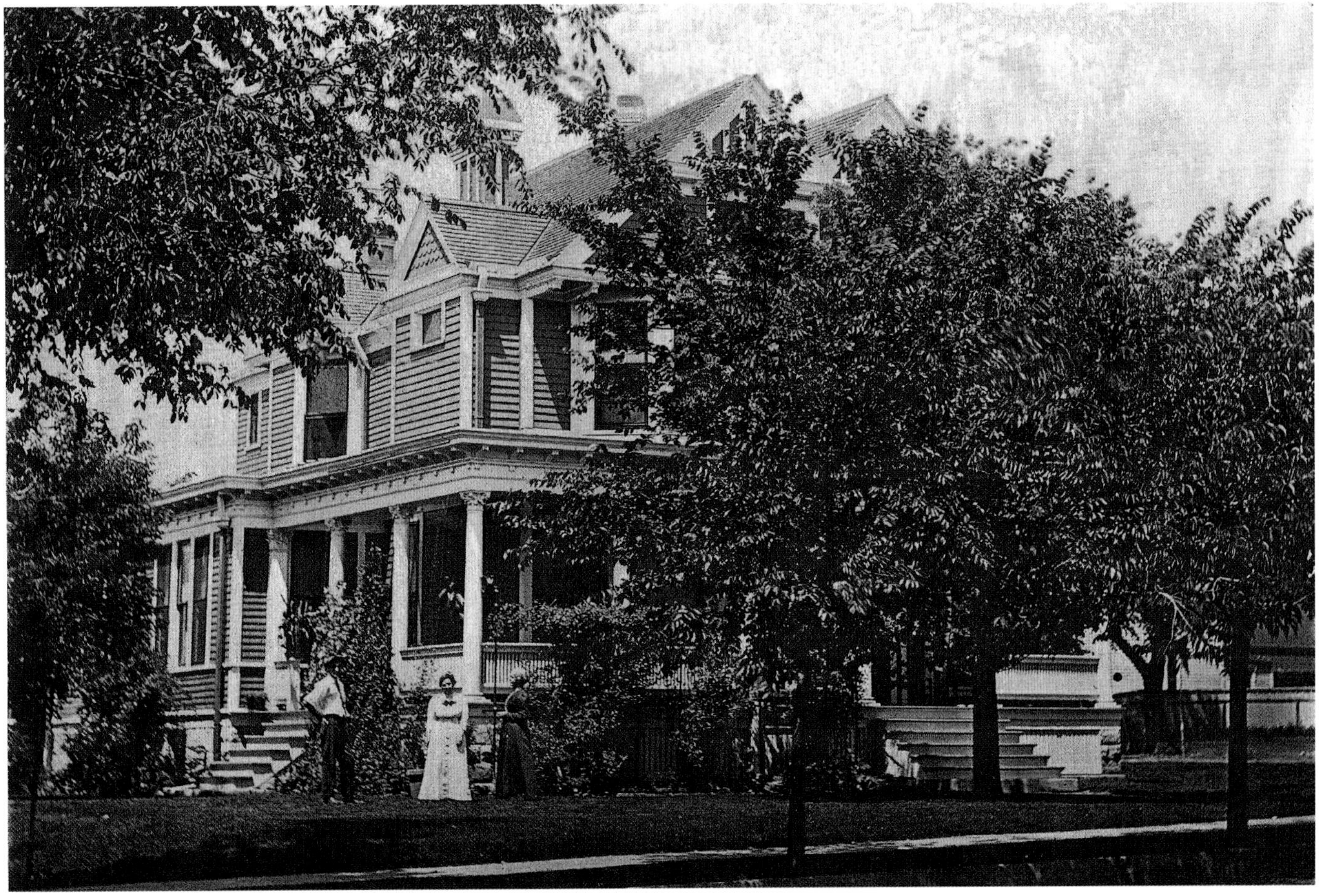

Harry Kelly House, c. 1900. Courtesy of Daniel T. Kelly.

Davis bunch were in their late twenties. They took me along to some pretty hot parties where there was a lot of drinking. By that time the Duncan Opera House was no longer used for theatrical performances but had become bar and a dance hall."

Kelly was a good horseman. He said, "I was what is called a drugstore cowboy. I knew how to rope and ride but was never hired as a hand because I didn't do enough of it." Reminiscing further, he told me, "Our ranch supplied remounts for the National Guard training at Camp Luna, and I remember the officers coming down to buy them. Some of the horses were just halter-broken. When they picked out a bunch of these green ranch horses and mounted them for the first time, you can imagine how terrified the animals were and how they reacted to a saddle and rider equipped with a scabbard, rifle, saber, picket rope, and canteen."

Kelly remarked, "I would have loved to be a rancher." Instead, when he got out of the army in 1946, he went to the Harvard Business School to prepare himself to succeed his father as president of Gross, Kelly & Company. Before being recalled to serve in the U.S. Army in 1951 during the Korean War, he was frequently in and out of Las Vegas learning the family business, which he took over following his father's retirement ini 1954.

In order to see firsthand the sites he had discussed, I asked Kelly if he would accompany me to Las Vegas and tour the town and its environs with me. A few months later, just after he celebrated his ninety-first birthday, we made the trip. Our first stop was at the old Gross, Kelly commission house next to the train station, now the property of Public Service Company of New Mexico. Designed by the firm of Rapp and Rapp, it is a handsome building with arched windows and an upper-story loggia graced with white Ionic columns. Pointing to the second floor rooms behind the loggia, Kelly said, "That's where the commission house boys stayed."

Walking around to the side, he called my attention to a rectangular one-story building directly across the tracks. "That was originally our wool-scouring plant," he said. "Later it was a door-and-window manufacturing facility. We bought our wood from the timber producers nearby. After we ceased manufacturing, we still carried on a furniture-carving business. Although the building was pretty much vacant by the time I was a young man apprenticing to run Gross, Kelly, the boiler was still in operation, so when I stayed over, that is where I'd sleep and where I would take a shower. My friends from Santa Fe would visit me sometimes, and we would have fun fussing around with the old machinery."

The narrow weedy strip running alongside the commission house parallel to the existing tracks had once had rails where trains pulled up to load and unload raw materials and goods. Pointing to the area beyond the loading dock where we were standing, Kelly said, "Our warehouse for wool and hides was down there. When we cleaned it out there were still some old buffalo skins.

Walking back to the car, we looked across the parking lot at the boarded up Castañeda Hotel. "I remember what the Castañeda was like when I was a kid and went there with my grandparents," he reminisced. "With all the Harvey Girls dressed up in their white uniforms, it was a pretty snappy spot. The railroad also ran the Montezuma Hotel up at the hot springs, and there were big social events there."

Crossing Grand Avenue, we paused opposite Lincoln Park to look at the offices of the *Optic.* Kelly remarked, "Back in my grandparents' day, Hub Kane was editor.[6] He was married to my Aunt Helen, so I always knew him as Uncle Hub." As we approached the corner of National Avenue and Sixth Street, where the Immaculate Conception Church stands, he told me to turn. As I pulled to a stop beside the Carnegie Library, he informed me that the building across the street next to the church, now the rectory and church offices, was once the Kane home.

We walked over and stood in the empty church parking lot. Kelly pointed to the far end where Petra and Marcella's quarters were still standing alongside the garage that once had housed the car in which McDaniel had chauffeured his grandfather to work. On the vacant asphalt surrounding us, he made site-specific in words the photograph he had previously shown me: "Here was the end of the house, here was the lawn, and over there were the tennis courts. That's where the trolley line ran in front along Sixth and here is where we would sit on the porch and watch the Rough Riders Rodeo Parade going by." When I asked him how the church had acquired the property, he answered, "In 1933, a year after my grandfather died, when my grandmother decided to move to Santa Fe, she gave it to the Catholic Church. Sometime after the war in the 1940s ICC moved from its original site down the street and built the present church in its current location. They used our house next door at first for various purposes but later tore it down to create more parking."

I suggested that we travel out of town to look at some of the ranches that had played such an important part in Kelly's early life. As we drove north on Highway 518 past a string of fast-food stands and chain stores he said, "None of this was here when I was growing up." Just beyond Walmart, he asked me to pull the car over to the shoulder of the road. Pointing east beyond the railroad tracks, he told me, "Here is where we leased 60,000 acres for our summer pasture."

The road began to rise as we approached what had been the Davis Ranch near Sapello. "Look over to the left," Kelly directed. "We called that the Bonita pasture. It was a detached portion of the ranch. They raised purebred Herefords." On the other side of the road, he drew my attention to a lane lined with cottonwoods leading to what was once the Davis ranch house, saying, "That's where I spent a lot of time. They treated me almost as a member of the family, and their son, who was also called Bud, became like a big brother to me."

Near the top of the rise overlooking the Sapello River valley we turned off the highway onto a dirt road beside which stood one of the small adobe Catholic churches that dot rural Northern New Mexico at frequent intervals. Some, like this one, are situated in picturesque isolation, having been built in places where travel distances between villages were too great for farmers to otherwise attend church. Kelly remarked, "Here is where I would go to mass on Sundays when I was staying on the Davis ranch. Mr. Davis would bring me over and hand me a silver dollar, saying to be sure and give it to the priest. I don't know how those rural priests got by in those days; they were so poverty-stricken."

As we were driving through a ponderosa pine forest, Kelly said, "When I was about twelve I spent the summer at the Mossimann ranch, which was at the head of Sapello Canyon. This was the ranch where most of the logs for our timber operation came from. I remember how Old Man Mossimann would heat up water on a wood stove, pour it in a big round tub, and make me take a bath on Saturdays."

At Mora we stopped for lunch at the Mad Cow and Calf Cafe. Fortified with cheese enchiladas, we continued north a few miles to the tiny village of Cleveland, named after President Grover Cleveland. "Here is where we'd take the road up to Rio La Casa," said Kelly. "That was where the Daniels Ranch was. After the Second World War when I was back in New Mexico, we'd go up there sometimes for house parties."

Having promised earlier to tell me the story of how he had proposed to his wife, he now recounted, "Jeanne was a pretty New York girl whom I had met while she was visiting in Santa Fe shortly after I returned from the war. In 1948 our friendship blossomed, and later when I was in New York on business and again when I was serving a recall tour of duty in Korea, I would see her. After returning to the U.S. in 1953, I asked her to join me at a house party at the Daniels Ranch, which was being given by my cousin Mary Ellis Kane. On Sunday we went to church in Mora, and during Mass I was struck with spiritual guidance and decided that the time had come for me to pop the question. I did, and she accepted my proposal. But I told her that to test her fitness to be my wife she'd have to clean a trout!" The future Mrs. Kelly obviously passed the test, and on November 23, 1953, the couple were married in New York City.

Living in Santa Fe and presiding over the company as his father's successor, Kelly soon realized that, with the advent of long-distance trucking, the era of rail freighting was waning. This shift in the means of bulk transportation meant that there was no longer a role for commission houses like Gross, Kelly. In addition, the number of family shareholders who wanted increased dividends made it difficult to run the other parts of the business profitably. In 1954, therefore, when a Texas firm made an offer to buy the company, Kelly decided that the time had come to liquidate. Looking back, he concluded, "I can't say I have any regrets. I have had a wonderful life. I feel privileged to have been born in this place and time."

EDITHA BARTLEY

Northwest of Sapello on the edge of the Santa Fe National Forest is Rociada, another hamlet tucked into one of the tributary river canyons of Northern New Mexico. Today the area is best known for its adjacency to Pendaries Village, a resort community carved out of the original 5,000-acre Pendaries Ranch established in 1875 by Jean Pendaries from Gascony, one of several French settlers who came to Northern New Mexico as wool and timber traders and sheep ranchers. Nearby is the Gascon Ranch, home of Editha Bartley. The ranch's history and Bartley's life story are tied to the sanitarium founded in 1904 by her grandfather, Dr. William T. Brown, in Valmora, near the town of Watrous on the Mora River a few miles north of Fort Union. Bartley's mother, who was Brown's daughter, married Carl Gellenthien, another physician who had come to Valmora as a patient, or "lunger," as they were called in those days. Gellenthien, who subsequently gained prominence as one of the leading pulmonary specialists in the country, succeeded Brown as medical director. Thus, Bartley and her brother grew up on the premises of the sanitarium.

Valmora Sanitarium was originally funded by several large industrial companies in Chicago following Dr. Brown's persuasive advocacy of sending tubercular employees to New Mexico to be cured. Under Gellenthien's administration, the sanitarium became famous throughout the country. In 1920, Brown, who had an entrepreneurial streak, decided to purchase the Gascon Ranch and turn it into a retreat for artists, friends, and paying guests. The original dude ranch of 400 acres later grew to 4,000 as the family continued to buy contiguous properties as they came up for sale. With his son-in-law in charge of the sanitarium, Brown was able to devote his energies to the ranch. He bought draft horses, established a cattle operation, built a sawmill, and introduced the first Hereford bulls into that part of the country as well as the first registered Jersey and Holstein cows. He also sold modern farm equipment and was a trader in Native American crafts. It is not surprising therefore that the walls in Bartley's house are hung with Navajo rugs and lined with shelves displaying Pueblo pottery.

A woman of cheerful pluck and abundant energy, Bartley, with the help of her son John, still operates the sawmill, raises livestock, and rents the rustic cabins beside the pasture below her house to summer guests. As we sat on one of the comfortable sofas in her light-filled living room facing the surrounding mountains and the valley below, she told me, "We don't do major timber cutting. We weed our forest and sell Christmas trees, milled boards, and firewood. Our motto is 'Eat beef, build and burn with wood.' " She now writes a column for the *Las Vegas Optic,* which has something of the "here's-what's-on-my-mind-today" flavor of a blog.

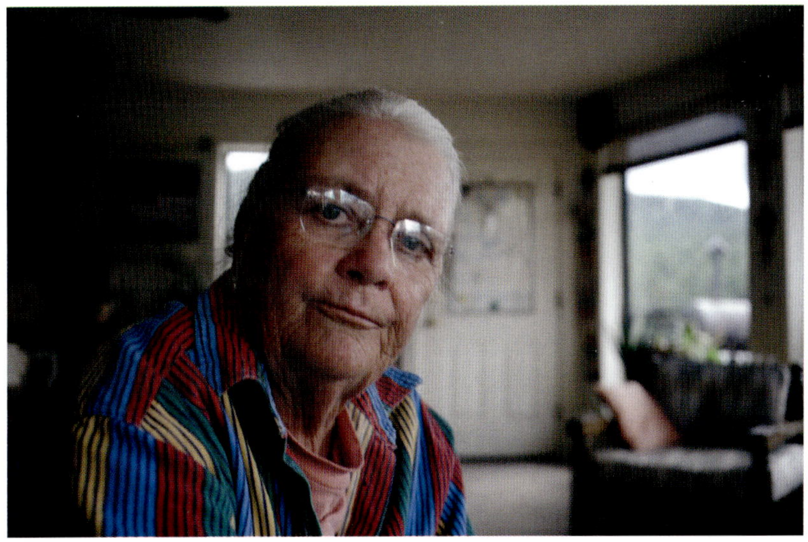

Editha Bartley

When I admired her collection of museum-quality Indian pottery, Bartley said, "Practically everything here came from Valmora after my brother and I sold the sanitarium in 1991 two years after my father died. We had a big two-day auction of all the furnishings. There were ten thousand items for sale. My dad continued his medical practice up until the end, but after tuberculosis began to be treated with streptomycin and other drugs, only a couple of patients stayed on in a hospice-type situation since there was nowhere for them to go. Bill McKay, the owner of Rancho Valmora, a school and treatment facility for adolescents with emotional and behavioral problems, bought the place from us. Selling it to him was just the right thing to do and the right use for the buildings. Sometimes when I go over to visit there, he shows me how he left the gold lettering on the operating room where I was born."

I asked Bartley to describe the Valmora of her youth. "My dad invented something called heliotherapy, and you would see patients holding mirrors up to direct the sun's rays into their throats. Those were the days of tobacco, and smoking and chewing in moderation were permitted, but strict rules were imposed on spitting. You could only spit in your spit cup or in one of the large spittoons that were provided for that purpose." With regard to the effect Valmora had on the surrounding community, she said, "For one thing, it provided jobs for a lot of people around Mora. The doctors were Anglos, but the caretakers were almost all Hispanics." As young children, she and her brother were home-schooled. "We took correspondence courses," she explained. "One of the patients' wives would serve as our tutor. I got ahead of myself by two years, so I was eleven when I started high school in Las Vegas." Reflecting back, she remarked, "One of the beautiful things about growing up in Valmora was we had to work when we got to a responsible age. We were postal employees, took inventory in the store, my brother waited tables, we milked the cows."

Bartley is more worldly than these biographical details would indicate. Because her father was a pioneer in developing new medical protocols for the treatment of tuberculosis beyond the traditional therapies—a dry sunny climate, plenty of rest, good food, and an optimistic attitude—he was a celebrity in the field. The epitaph on his gravestone reads, "He Came a Lunger, He Left a Legacy." Looking back on her life with much the same sense of good fortune as Bud Kelly, she said, "I feel I've had the best of both worlds. My father's fame took us to New York, where I camped out at the Waldorf, and I got to go to places like San Francisco and Chicago when I was growing up." Gazing out the window at her pastures and the spruce and ponderosa pine trees climbing the slopes of the Sangre de Cristos, she concluded, "And then I have always had all this."

At the Jewish Cemetery

LOUISE TAICHERT

The impressive headstones of Montefiore Cemetery on the slope of the crestón are almost the only remaining evidence of the Jewish population that was once the commercial backbone of Las Vegas. One would expect that, with practically no Jews in residence nowadays, it would be overgrown with weeds. Such is not the case. Although the rock wall surrounding it has been vandalized and pieces of it carried away as building material, the cemetery has been well maintained since Marvin Taichert, a member of a once-prominent Las Vegas Jewish merchant family, started the Montefiore Cemetery Association in 1993. Today there is a permanent caretaker, Ted Herburger, and the association organizes an annual cleanup day when surviving children and grandchildren come back to Las Vegas to tend the graves of their deceased relatives.

Two years before her death in 2010 I met Marvin Taichert's cousin, Louise Taichert, a retired psychiatrist who lived in Santa Fe. One day, before driving around town to visit scenes of Dr. Taichert's childhood and Montefiore Cemetery, where her parents and other members of the Las Vegas's former Jewish community are buried, we ate lunch at the Plaza Hotel. Over Cobb salad, Dr. Taichert recounted her family history.

One of the last of the Jewish merchants to immigrate to Las Vegas, her father, Joseph Taichert, the youngest of five orphan boys, came in 1904 seeking a cure for his tuberculosis as well as the same kind of commercial opportunity other Jews had earlier sought in the West. He started out as houseboy at the El Porvenir dude ranch at the head of the Gallinas Canyon, and according to Dr. Taichert, "When he realized that he could make a living selling pelts, he started trapping for beaver, bear, anything he could find up there. So when I was growing up I used to see all sorts of animal traps. Now it makes me sad and sick to think about all those poor animals."

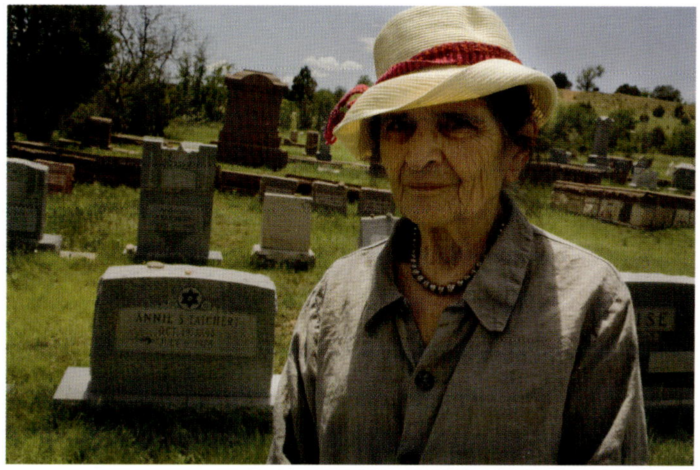

Louise Taichert

The fur trade was just the beginning of Joe Taichert's business career. With his brother Milton, who became a prominent civic leader in Las Vegas, he opened the Taichert Haberdashery. Although they became successful merchants, the Taicherts remained traders as well. Louise remembers, "This was big sheep country before synthetic fibers killed off the wool industry. In addition to being a fur trader, my father bought wool and hides, and because of this he used to take me with him to the ranches out in the country around Mora where he did business. He could pick up a lamb and tell you what it weighed to an ounce. After it had been shorn, he would grade and store the wool and then ship it to the mills in New Hampshire. The hides he bought were sent to tanneries in Mexico."

Las Vegas Jews practiced Reform Judaism, and they never saw themselves as a separate segment of the town's population. Dr. Taichert said, "Whether they were Jewish or non-Jewish, early settlers intermarried with the Spanish-American community and became identified with the town. They didn't remain German. My best friend was Patty Sanchez, whose grandfather was Jewish. The Kahn brothers, who owned a fine hotel in Mora, married two Hispanic sisters. I still have their recipe for chile sauce. There was no ethnic division in those days. Rather, it was an economic divide between a rich class and a poor class."

After lunch we paused to look at the historic Ilfeld Building, now an annex of the renovated Plaza Hotel. Dr. Taichert reminisced, "This was the Ilfeld Emporium. They had everything, I mean *everything*. I have fond memories of going there with my parents to shop. Charles Ilfeld was one of the earliest people to start trading in Indian jewelry. I bought my first concho belt there." Her other Ilfeld family recollections are just as vivid. "Mrs. Herman Ilfeld was a Christian Scientist and also

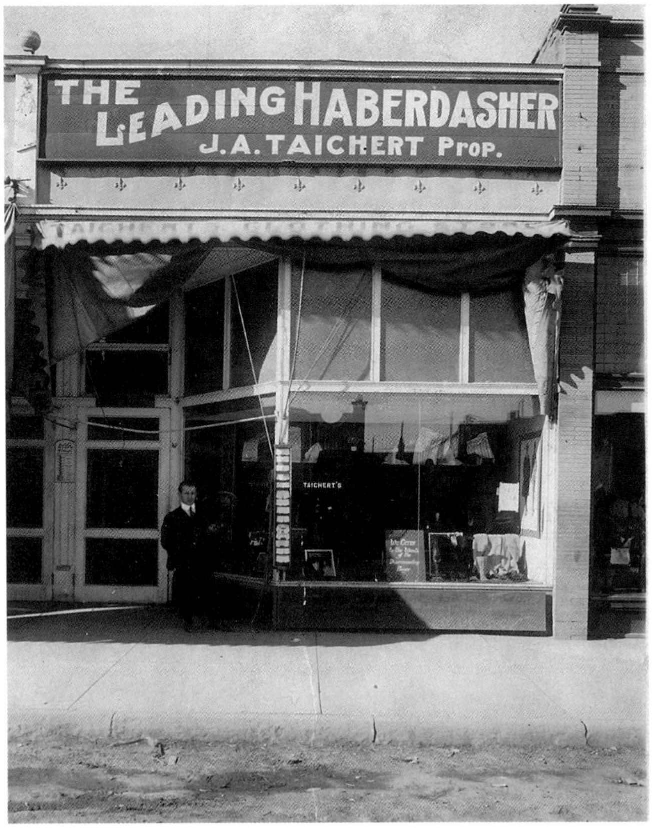

Taichert Haberdashery

loved animals. She and my mother were probably the only members of the Las Vegas Humane Society. The Ilfelds had a beautiful swimming pool, which she drained so she could have some place to put the stray dogs. Her daughter Charlotte is now a hundred years old and lives in Beverly Hills. Her brother Bill was a wonderful jeweler. Arthur Ilfeld and his wife, Bessie, lived next door to us, and the Herman Ilfelds lived on Seventh Street across from my aunt and uncle."

As we drove slowly up and down the streets of New Town, almost every house between Fourth and Eighth streets summoned a memory. Pointing to a large red stone mansion on Fourth Street, Dr. Taichert informed me, "New Mexico Supreme Court Justice Sig Noble lived there. Mrs. Noble was my Girl Scout leader, and I played with their daughter." We paused in front of 1036 Seventh Street, a big brick structure with a spacious front porch, which had been her uncle Milton's house. She then pointed out the Terr house directly across the street at 1037. "They were a Jewish family from Michigan. He was a doctor who wanted to find a better climate. They had four children who were younger than me, and our families were always very close. Mrs. Terr is still alive and must be up in her nineties now. I should go see her the next time I'm over here."

In the same block on Seventh Street as the Terr house is the beautiful Georgian Revival Herman Ilfeld mansion of red brick with a portico supported by Corinthian columns, the jewel of Las Vegas's North New Town Historic District. Moving on to Eighth, we passed 1026, a charming white house with a picket fence in front, where the Taicherts' dentist, Dr. Paul Henry, once lived. "Stop here," she said in front of 1045, her own childhood home. While we stood on the sidewalk, she gave me an imaginary tour of the interior from the basement, where preserves were stored, to the attic, where the maid slept. Through her sharp mind's eye I saw the downstairs hall where the piano used to be before turning right and going through a pair of sliding doors to the parquet-floored living room. Leaving the living room, we entered the formal dining room and then the pantry and kitchen. Upstairs in the back of the house we fancied ourselves in her bedroom.

Back in the car, we moved on down the street at a slow crawl as Dr. Taichert continued to recite, house by house, the names of the former owners. At 1053 Eighth Street, next door to her own home, was the Arthur Ilfeld house, an imposing Jacobean Revival–style mansion with steep roof gables. "We ended up owning and renting it out," she said, "because it was going to be sold to a mortician and made into a funeral home." We paused in front of 1210, a large pink Victorian house. Here I learned that Mrs. Graham, after she was widowed and forced to take in sewing had made all of Dr. Taichert's dresses, including a tennis dress "because no one sold women's tennis clothes in those days."

Commercial Las Vegas produced another series of fond recollections. At the boarded-up Castañeda Hotel, she said, "I used to play dress-up with Betsy Hayward, the manager's daughter. My parents would take us there for Sunday dinner. It was a special ritual. The food was very elegant, and we were waited on by Harvey Girls. We would also go up the Gallinas Canyon to El Porvenir, and sometimes we would have dinner at the Montezuma Hotel. I learned to swim in the enclosed swimming pool at the hot springs there." In the winter she would go skating on the ponds above the hot springs, which in those days were still being harvested for ice. One of the many Las Vegans who remember happy teenage hours spent with friends at Murphy's Drug Store on Douglas and Sixth, she said, "They had a soda fountain, and for a nickel you'd get a chocolate ice: milk, chocolate syrup, and ice cubes."

In the same block as Murphy's, Dr. Taichert pointed out the building that formerly housed the Taichert Haberdashery. After that she showed me the warehouse that Joseph and Milton Taichert bought in 1916 to store wool, hides, and furs, a handsome building in the block next to the river where National Avenue becomes Bridge Street. Looking up, I could make out the faded lettering that had been painted long ago near the top of one of the brick side walls: "Raw Furs / R. A. Taichert & Co. Compradores de Pieles Crudas y Lanas y Pagamos Dinero al Contado." After that we drove over to Twelfth Street and paused in front of the warehouse that the Taichert brothers bought in 1936. A fine purple-brown sandstone building, it is now listed on the State Register of Cultural Properties, as is the warehouse on National. The Taicherts' mercantile business continued until 1971, when both these buildings were sold.

Joseph Taichert House

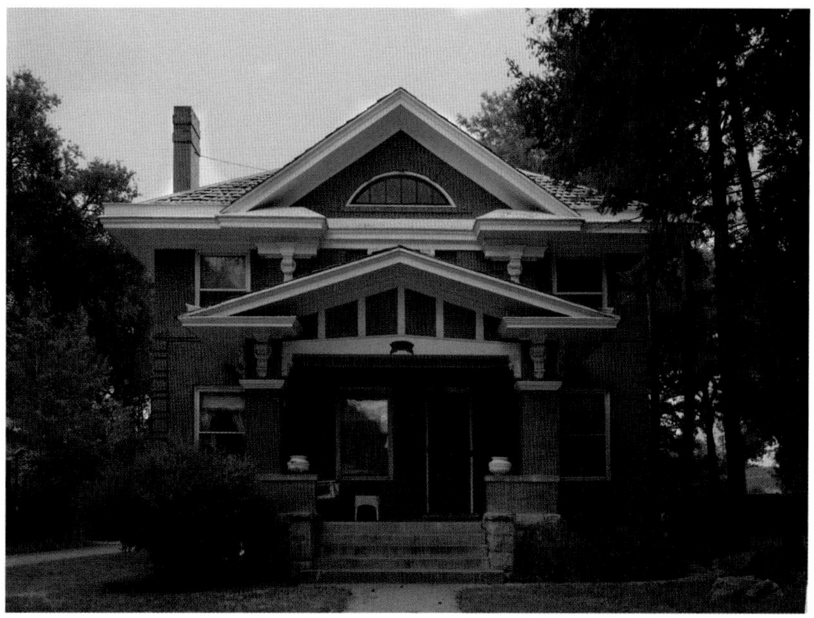

By then, Dr. Taichert and the rest of her generation of Las Vegas Jews were pursuing successful professional careers elsewhere. When I asked her how she had decided to become a physician, she replied that she had been encouraged by Dr. Harold Mortimer, the family doctor, who had wanted her to come back and practice with him in Las Vegas. After hearing her describe the two summers when she had worked as a medical extern at the State Hospital, I thought it was remarkable that she had persevered in her medical education. "It was," she said, "a truly horrific experience. They used to do prefrontal lobotomies on hard-to-manage patients. You would see the mentally retarded in diapers sitting on the cement floor where they would get hosed off periodically. Before giving shock treatments they would gag patients and put something between their teeth to keep them from biting their tongues. The head of the hospital was a proctologist, not a psychologist. It was truly dreadful. It upset me so badly I would come home for lunch and just sit there and cry."

Nevertheless, she persisted in her ambition to become a doctor and applied to medical school after graduating in 1947 from the University of California, Berkeley. There was no medical school in New Mexico at that time, and World War II veterans were being given preference over other applicants, especially women, so her plans were temporarily thwarted. However, after getting a physiology degree she was admitted to the University of Colorado medical school. At this point, our conversation jumped ahead more than half a century to 2004 when, after closing their practices in San Francisco, she and her husband, Stanley Feldman, also a doctor, retired to Santa Fe, where they already maintained a second home.

Our last stop of the day was Montefiore Cemetery. As with the houses in town, each monument prompted an association with the past. But here, in addition to the people whose homes we had visited through Dr. Taichert's powers of recollection, lie other family friends who lived in Mora and Springer, Jewish merchants with whom the Taichert brothers did business. Their gravestones summoned up recollections of numerous trips to these outlying communities with her father. "There was then, of course, no Interstate 25, and the dirt roads made for very rough going. Mother dreaded these outings. We always had a plank in the car in case we got stuck. We also took a shovel and a 12 gauge shotgun with us." Standing before her family's plot, I noticed a fresh granite slab with the inscription "Stanley Feldman, 1914–2004." Thinking of her recently deceased husband, Louise quickly wiped away a tear and said abruptly, "Let's go now."

After I learned from Dr. Taichert's son, John Feldman, a rabbi in Albuquerque, that she had died on February 27, 2010, I went back to Montefiore Cemetery to pay my respects at her gravesite. It was still covered with fresh dirt, and a circle of carefully arranged *matzevah* stones marked the spot where her inscribed granite plaque would be the next time the dispersed Jewish community visited the cemetery for its annual cleanup day. When I returned in July 2011, it had been installed; however, about fifty headstones throughout the cemetery had been smashed and toppled by vandals. When I spoke with Rabbi Feldman by telephone about this, he said that he agreed with the Las Vegas police that the desecration was not a hate crime, as some people surmised it to have been. "It's really part of a statewide economic problem," he said. "With no job prospects, juveniles have nothing better to do."

When I asked him to reflect on the possibility of a turnaround for Las Vegas, he replied, "The town will never be the same as it was for the people who are buried in the cemetery. There really is nothing on the horizon for Las Vegas, and it is a shame when I think of what this place was like back in the 1940s when there was still a mixed Hispanic and Anglo-Jewish business elite who established hospitals and supported a substantial cultural and economic infrastructure. Now that's all gone, and there doesn't seem to be a lot of hope at the moment that the town's well-being will return anytime soon."

At the time we spoke, repair to the desecrated cemetery was already under way. Adding further testimony to the power of place, even in the face of civic decline, Rabbi Feldman said, "I'll be at Montefiore, too, some day—for a long, long time," confirming the strength of the hold Las Vegas has on so many of its Jewish sons and daughters, even after they have lived the greater part of their lives elsewhere.

THE TERR FAMILY

The summer after Dr. Taichert died I decided to make the call on Mildred Terr that she would not now be able to make. Pulling my car to a stop at 1037 Eighth Street, I saw the large red brick house with a wide bungalow-style porch that she had pointed out on our earlier visit. Lewis Terr came out to greet me and took me inside to meet his mother. There I also found his sister Nancy and her husband, Robert Behrendt, who had driven up from their home in Albuquerque that day.

At ninety-two Mildred Terr still bears evidence of the beautiful woman she was in the 1940s photograph Lewis later showed me. Reminiscing about the Taicherts, she said, "The first day we came to town, which was July 4, 1958, they invited us over for a backyard picnic. After that we became very, very close. They were Jewish, and we were Jewish, so that was a bond from the start." Nancy picked up the conversation at this point, adding bits of anecdotal detail about her family's Taichert neighbors. "Mrs. Taichert's house was so clean you could eat off the floor. She drove a white Corvair—she was a terrible driver—and she always kept open cardboard boxes on the floor of the backseat for you to put your feet in so the car would stay clean."

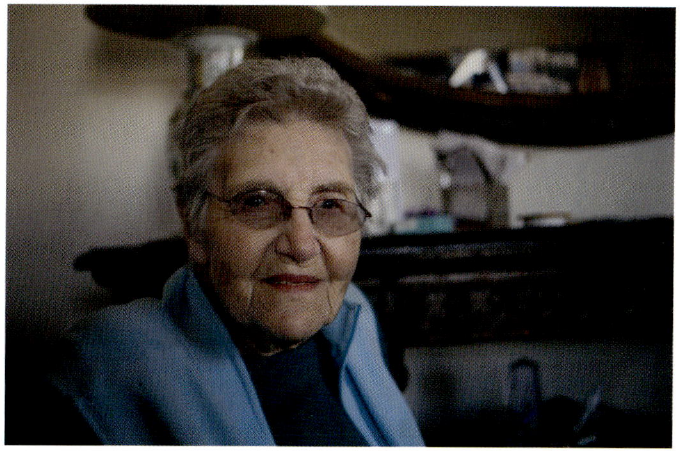

Mildred Terr

With my prompting, Nancy then went on to describe what it was like to be a Jew in Las Vegas during the years she was growing up. "We were pretty assimilated into the town. We were a community, but being Jewish was really more like being part of a book club. Only when some outsider came in and said something nasty about Jews did we feel any sense of discrimination. Yes, we lit candles every Friday, knew some Yiddish, and went for High Holidays, but Chanukah was not a big deal, and we always had a Christmas tree. None of the Jewish families were kosher, and we really didn't feel like outsiders. Milton Taichert was the perfect example of that: he spoke Spanish, and like most of the other Jews in town, he was a Mason. It wasn't so much that we felt different as that we were mutually supportive."

About the social and cultural duality of the town, Nancy Terr observed, "When I started first grade, half the class didn't speak English, and since Hispanic kids weren't allowed to speak Spanish, we were each given a buddy. They learned English that way, and I learned some Spanish, of course. There was still a lot of racial tension between East and West in those days. But I didn't experience it as much as some of the others. In the first place, Dad was everybody's doctor; he treated patients on both sides of town. I remember going to Mama Lucy's restaurant on the plaza in West Las Vegas as a kid, where I was especially welcome because she was my father's patient. Then, since I played the bassoon and there was no bassoonist at West Las Vegas High School, I would go over and be part of their band whenever they needed me. I think it was for those reasons that I was never harassed."

It was obvious that Mrs. Terr was tired, so the Terr siblings and I went out to sit on the front porch to continue our conversation. How pleasant, I thought, to be looking out at a street lined with trees and sidewalks where people walked by and waved hello to you—a throwback to an era that New Urbanist architects and planners are now seeking to replicate in their designed communities. Nancy said, "One thing that can't be discounted: we always walked everywhere. Downtown was just a few blocks away." Lewis then painted a picture of what that part of Las Vegas was like then: "My father's office was on University Street just behind Taichert's Haberdashery on Douglas. In those days every single building downtown had a store, and you could see how the place was thriving. There were four big department stores besides Taichert's: Montgomery Ward, J. C. Penney, Gamble's, and J. J. Newberry. There were real drug-store soda fountains: Murphy's and Western. There was a Greyhound bus stop and two banks, the First National Bank, which is still there, and the Bank of Las Vegas, which was torn down. It was next to the Duncan Opera House, which was also torn down."

I asked them when things had begun to change. Nancy said, "Just before I graduated from high school in 1971. There started to be so many drugs in this town. That's when people started to call Las Vegas Smack City. Everyone knew someone who had died of an overdose. One store after another got robbed. You could see them closing all along on Bridge, National, and Douglas. The town simply fell to pieces. My dad had his car stolen. He stayed on because of his medical practice, but most of the merchants just folded their businesses. Besides that, except for the Taicherts, the Jewish community was dying off."

Speaking of the town today, Lewis said, "even though the place is economically depressed, you don't feel any real insecurity. People aren't desperate to leave;

they really are attached to the area. There is something that is okay about the town, some kind of vibe about it. I know it has a bad reputation and that some people still consider it borderline and are afraid to come over here. But that's a false impression. It really is safe. Sure, you see the outpatients from the mental hospital walking around, but nobody gets worked up about that." What he does find irksome is the general deterioration of the physical fabric of Las Vegas. "I know this sounds politically incorrect," he admitted, "but it truly is a cultural thing. This part of town is just different now that so many Hispanics live on the east side. The aesthetic thing is just not a priority. If you are local and want to put up a doublewide in your back yard, the building department won't say anything about it. On the other hand, if you come in from the outside and start fixing up one of the old Victorian houses and making it beautiful again, they are all over you."

I asked Lewis to sum up what Las Vegas means to him personally. "Boy, why am I here?" he answered. "I suppose at this point, I feel more connected to Las Vegas than to anywhere else. It's a strangely compelling place. I can be sitting out here on the porch, people come along, I know who at least half of them are, they remember me. It's the same when you go to Walmart; you can barely get out of the store without having a conversation with someone you know. It's like that for everybody. This is a real community."

ROBERT NORDHAUS

The Nordhaus family has retained its tie with Las Vegas because of the quiet beauty and good fishing at Trout Springs, the 1,000-acre family compound in the Gallinas Canyon purchased in the 1880s by Max Nordhaus, brother-in-law and business partner of Charles Ilfeld. I drove up one summer day to meet with Robert Nordhaus shortly after he and his wife Jean had arrived there for a week's vacation. Upon my arrival, I found myself in an idyllic forested retreat overlooking the Gallinas River at the point where it is joined by the stream flowing from the springs for which the property is named. The main house and the remaining buildings nearby—a large house for visiting family members and friends, a nearby stone house for other Nordhaus relatives, and down the hill a Prohibition-era dance hall and a second large house with a wide wrap-around porch—have a pleasing architectural rusticity. I took a deep breath of pine-scented fresh air before we walked inside.

Robert Nordhaus

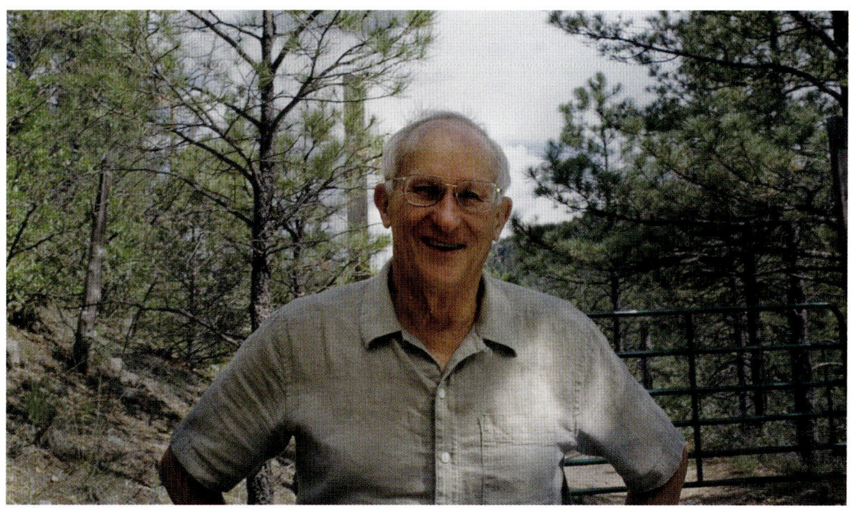

Nordhaus grew up in Albuquerque, where his grandfather moved in 1912 when that city became the headquarters of the Ilfeld-Nordhaus family business, but his parents took him and his siblings to Trout Springs every summer. Over lunch on the veranda overlooking the Gallinas Valley with Hermit's Peak in the distance, he told me some of his family's history. "Much of the business was done through credit. Merchants, and my grandfather in particular, would extend credit to ranchers. His firm was a bank as much as a mercantile operation. If you think about it, Las Vegas was as alien a place to an urban German Jew as anywhere on earth, but he was a very good businessman, and all the customers got along with him. He never spoke English without a German accent; however, according to my father, his Spanish was flawless." Explaining the transformation of Las Vegas's Jewish population over the years, he said, "There weren't any traders in my father's generation; they were mostly professionals. All of them were highly educated. My father and his sisters were sent to Eastern universities: he went to Yale and Yale Law School, and his sister went to Smith. He loved New Mexico, so after he got his law degree he moved back to Albuquerque and ran an Indian law practice and various family businesses. He did a bit of everything, including developing a ski area, but a trader like his father he was not. I followed in his footsteps and graduated from Yale Law School in 1963, which is where I met Jean, who was getting her Ph.D. in German. When I was young I was eager to leave New Mexico, and after I graduated I set up my practice in Washington, D.C., where we still live. But Trout Springs allows us to have an ongoing connection with a part of world where I would come with my parents as a child. I really look forward to being in this place once a year."

When I asked Nordhaus what he thought about the town of Las Vegas today, he replied, "I have a strong attachment to the place because that's where my ancestors lived, but now I'm afraid it is has become an impoverished and somewhat dysfunctional community. The generation of old merchant Jews had mostly died off by the 1970s and their children had all left. After that there was very little private enterprise, and the town became economically stagnant, with only government jobs to keep it alive." He continued, "Most of the population today does not have an appreciation or interest in the town's colorful past and sees little value in maintaining the buildings or restoring its architectural heritage. On the positive side, none of the old mansions have been torn down or disfigured by remodeling, and a few are being fixed up by people, mostly from the outside, who appreciate their fine architecture and structural soundness. In an overall sense, though, Las Vegas—for those of us who saw it in its former glory—is a bit like walking around the ruins of ancient Rome."

There are some who would argue with Robert Nordhaus's rather bleak assessment of Las Vegas's current state. They see the local historic preservation movement and the growth of a modest tourist industry as harbingers of the town's economic revival. However, because of the difficulty of raising sufficient capital to restore the dilapidated commercial buildings, success has been elusive. There is also an undercurrent of resistance to outsiders' visions for Las Vegas's future that militates against change. Nevertheless, the sound of carpenters' hammers coming from the deteriorated buildings around the plaza and along Bridge Street is a sign that this part of town is coming back to life.

Las Vegas's renaissance dreams, moreover, go beyond economic redevelopment and architectural preservation. The town's proposed revival as an arts community offers a vision of cultural self-renewal. Such renewal, however, is tempered by antipathy to the nonlocal, and a majority of Las Vegans prefer a small-town, do-it-ourselves approach to the kind of sophisticated cultural scene they find in nearby Santa Fe.

Historic Restoration

Many outside visitors seeing Las Vegas for the first time are impressed with the sheer number of handsome nineteenth- and early twentieth-century commercial buildings and fine old homes. Why, they wonder, hasn't this impressive concentration of historic architecture become the basis for a thriving tourist economy?

One can rightly make the case that too many places trick out their pasts to such a degree that they assume a theme-park aspect. By that logic Las Vegas is admirable for eschewing such self-commodification. But a surplus of abandoned buildings is not a good thing. Fortunately, opportunities to avoid excessive architectural ingratiation while also achieving economic benefits from the adaptive reuse of some of these handsome historic structures have in fact been realized, resulting in significant, albeit tenuous, change.

WILLIAM "WID" SLICK

Wid Slick, an entrepreneur from Texas, and his former wife Katherine, known as Kak, who has served as a trustee of the National Trust for Historic Preservation and as the director of the New Mexico State Historic Preservation Office, were in the vanguard of Las Vegas's most recent attempt at renewal. In association with eighteen other investors, the Slicks undertook the restoration of the Plaza Hotel in 1982, exactly one hundred years after Don Benigno Romero built it.

The hotel's interior décor is in keeping with its late-nineteenth-century architecture. The lobby, which has the appearance of an old-fashion parlor, once boasted a Steinway piano ordered from New York at the turn of the twentieth century by José Albino Baca, a prosperous local sheep rancher. The bar is named Byron T's Saloon after Byron T. Mills, a former owner of the hotel. An important figure in New Mexico history, Mills served as mayor and territorial representative in Congress. His self-esteem was such that he had the wide commercial thoroughfare on the northern edge of town named Mills Avenue. More important as far as hotel staff and guests are concerned, Byron T. is the hotel's resident ghost, whose eerie footsteps are sometimes heard in 310, his favorite room in the hotel.

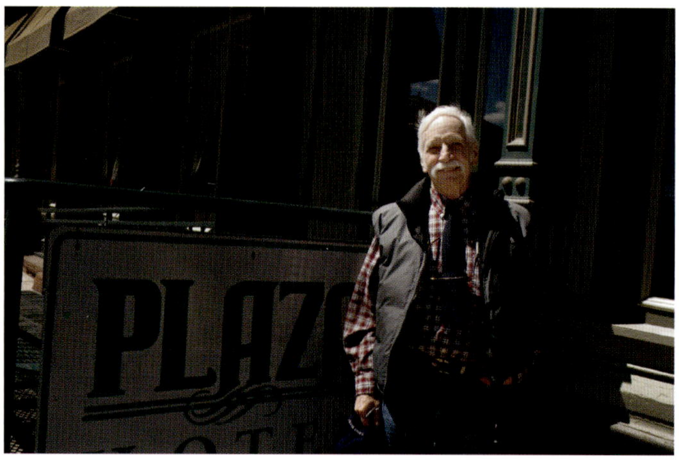

Wid Slick

The Plaza Hotel is the linchpin of the Las Vegas Plaza Historical District and is listed on the New Mexico State Register of Cultural Properties, as well as on the National Register of Historic Places. When I first met with Slick in 2009 over breakfast at the Plaza, he was filled with optimistic vision. During our conversation it was clear that he saw the hotel and the jobs it creates as one prong of the town's economic recovery. At the same time, he maintained that Las Vegas's potential for redevelopment was much greater than the tourist business that could be stimulated by the restoration of the hotel and the historic buildings around it. "We could have a power plant based on energy from wind, solar, and biomass," he said. "Look at the timberland all around us. Think of the logging jobs and how we could manufacture flooring and building blocks made from compressed wood." He said that he wanted Alta Vista, the recently built regional hospital on Legion Drive on the northern outskirts of town, to be managed as a for-profit institution by a private corporation and that he would like to see Highlands University's enrollment grow through an aggressive recruitment program that would attract students by offering a tuition-free freshman year. He thought, moreover, that

Las Vegas was ideally situated for pharmaceutical companies. He also advocated incentives in the form of bank loans and tax breaks to link the preservation of the town's old buildings to economic growth. He felt that Las Vegas could capitalize on the market for assisted-living facilities for seniors and suggested converting some of the downtown real estate into housing. "Look at it this way," he concluded. "Las Vegas is in a regional position to attract more population. Right now ours remains at 14,000 while there is growth in the rest of the country and the region. It just doesn't have to stay that way."

In spite of his earlier talk about being involved in promoting a larger sphere of economic development, after Slick enlarged the Plaza Hotel by buying and renovating the vacant Ilfeld Emporium building next door, his primary focus became its day-to-day operation. Unfortunately, the well-appointed rooms intended to attract tourists and the new ballroom, which is an ideal venue for conferences, parties, and various town events, was not as profitable as he had hoped. The bank loan to finance these improvements had been negotiated when lending rates were at their height before the mortgage crisis in 2008 and this unforeseen bad timing, coupled with the slow-down in recreational travel, led to default and foreclosure in 2012.

Thinking about this turn of events, I considered the fact that this Texas real estate developer had chosen to stay in Las Vegas for the past thirty years in spite of more profitable business opportunities to be found elsewhere. Such attachment to place suggests that he has had a more compelling reason than would be the case if he were simply trying to make his investment in the renovation of a historic hotel pay off. When I next saw him I said that I wondered what had originally attracted him to Las Vegas and why, given its apparent economic stagnation and the longstanding prejudice on the part of some of the townspeople against outsiders—especially outsiders from Texas—he had gone ahead and expanded the hotel and, for all intents and purposes, had established himself in Las Vegas for good.

He replied, "My wife and I were first here on a vacation in 1979. The following year we came back to go hiking. It was a memorable trip. We stopped at the hot springs and lay there soaking in one of the pools. When we looked up at the beautiful mountains all around us, we knew we had fallen in love with this place. We were bitching and moaning about living in Dallas. I was only interested in preservation development, and my business partner at the time and I had gone our separate ways. When Kak and I found out that this old hotel was for sale, we decided that buying and renovating it might not be such a bad idea. Then we started talking about what a great place this would be to raise our son. Originally I thought of staying here as a ten-year proposition. Every two years or so we would think about moving, but I had gotten involved with various civic associations and, by the time I had been here for twenty years, I knew I didn't want to go someplace else. When Kak decided that she did want to leave and carry on her historic preservation interests elsewhere, we divorced."

Like almost everyone else I have spoken with, Slick likes Las Vegas pretty much the way it is today—an unsophisticated small town. "I'm in love with the plaza with its beautiful trees," he said. "It hasn't become overrun with tourists like the one in Santa Fe. Right now I do not have any intention to move away and start over someplace else." What apparently motivated Slick to invest in Las Vegas's future in the first place was not simply the restoration of the old hotel but rather the overall revival of the entire area around the plaza and along Bridge Street. When I asked him to explain his role in the turnaround of this part of town, he said that after settling in Las Vegas back in 1982 he had formed a limited general partnership called La Plaza Vieja, a syndicate of building owners seeking the means to restore the numerous derelict historic buildings, many of which stood empty and boarded up. In the then robust economy, he was successful in obtaining investment financing for the consortium, and the current suitability of most of these formerly deteriorating structures for offices, shops, studios, galleries, and other small businesses is due in no small measure to the partnership. Remarkably, before it dissolved in 2009, the efforts of La Plaza Vieja resulted in the restoration of eleven buildings and a reduction of the area's vacancy rate from 75 percent to 25 percent. Slick's loss of the hotel is thus made more lamentable by the fact that without his early vision and ability to spark this significant turnaround, Las Vegas's economic doldrums would be even more dire than they are today.

RAY VALDEZ

According to Ray Valdez, a community organizer Slick worked with in Dallas before coming to Las Vegas, "Wid had a vision when he came here, and it was much different from that of your typical developer. Instead of simply viewing the renovation of the Plaza Hotel as a business opportunity for himself and a syndicate of outside investors, he saw the revitalization of all of Old Town as a project that should be spearheaded by local building owners. That's why he created La Plaza Vieja. He knew that because I was Hispanic and had a strong background in community consensus building I could help him bring the townspeople and owners of the buildings on board. As you might imagine in a place as closed as Las Vegas, they were really wary about working with an outsider.

To induce Valdez to join him in the La Plaza Vieja enterprise, Slick sent him to Las Vegas to become acquainted with the mayor, the chief of police, the presidents of Highlands University and Luna Community College, and other town leaders. "I really fell in love with the place," he told me when I went to see him in his home on South Pacific Street two blocks west of the plaza. "I had recently gone back to school and graduated from North Texas State College in Denton with a degree in sociology and anthropology, and here was a chance to do what I was good at doing as well as meet two of my other life objectives: to live in a small town and build my own house."

That Valdez is an expert builder as well as a woodworker is evident when you enter his home. It is one of the few remaining long, street-side, one-story adobe family compounds in Las Vegas. In spite of its obvious historic character, the exterior is unprepossessing. Previously, in fact, when I passed by it on my way in and out of town, I had thought it was abandoned. Inside, however, the beautiful hand-finished antique furniture and cabinetry, products of Valdez's expert craftsmanship, are evidence of his desire to put down roots, a commitment to place that has deepened over time. His taking up permanent residence in Las Vegas thirty years ago was reinforced by his marriage to a woman from Villanueva, a small town on the Pecos River just beyond the town's mother community of San Miguel del Bado.

"The house was built in 1869," he said. "It had this wing added in 1932 when it was a grocery store. Before I bought it in 1985 for $21,000, I had no idea that there was a house in back. Pointing to some beautifully finished oak shelving for dinnerware, he laughed, "Now I work for my wife. I also own seven other houses that I have restored myself, and the rents on them provide a decent retirement income."

After we sat down in the once-dark adobe room that is now a light-filled sun porch, Valdez told me about his early days in Las Vegas and how he had gone about his work as a community organizer for La Plaza Vieja.

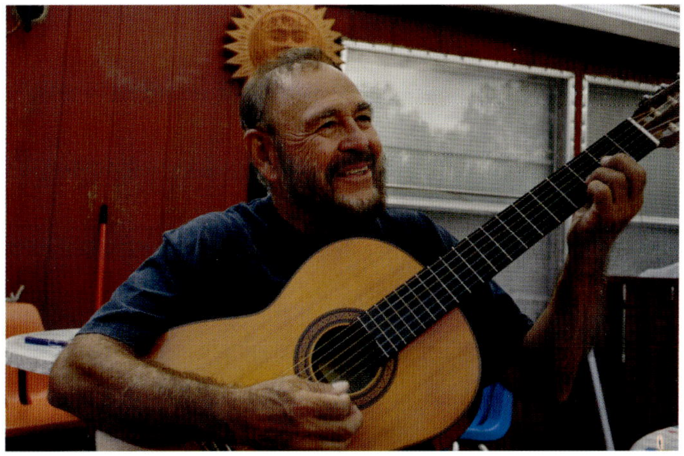

Sam Valdez

"Wid said it was up to me to sell the project. He was clear about the fact that this was basically real estate development but that we were going to do things a bit differently. He wanted the local people to remain building owners. We figured that there were 200,000 square feet of developable space in the buildings around the plaza and along Bridge Street and that we needed to get a critical mass of at least 50,000 square feet in order to move forward. That meant between fifteen and twenty buildings. My job was to explain to the building owners how the partnership could work in their interest. If they would deed the buildings to La Plaza Vieja, we would help them capitalize their renovations and then return the ownership of the buildings to them after a period of fifteen years. As general partners, they were on the board, so they all had a say in how things were done. But still it wasn't easy. The banks were standoffish, as you might imagine. At that time historic preservation was still in its infancy, and the bankers didn't get it, especially since we were talking about West Las Vegas, which was a redlined part of town."

Valdez gives a great deal of credit for the success of La Plaza Vieja to Kak Slick. "We didn't get along at first," he confided. "She thought I was just a Mexican Texan who drank and chased women, and I thought of her at first as an uppity Anglo woman, but we came to respect one another and what each of us was doing." His biggest battle was overcoming the resistance to change on the part of the Hispanic community. "We chose the buildings we wanted to see restored according to their historic and architectural importance, as well as their location and the willingness of the owners to work with us. I tried to build consensus with such organizations as the Chamber of Commerce, the Fiestas Committee, the Kiwanis, the Citizens Committee for Historic Preservation. Everyone knows everyone here because they are all related, and everything is intertwined. I had a great time. One of the best things I did was to create a curriculum in the business school at Highlands. This was Wid's idea. He is, as I said, a real visionary, and he sees the need to train people for the leisure and hospitality industry. This is the kind of job base the town needs to develop. Of course, what we need most now is for the next generation to move into leadership positions, and that will take some training, too."

In addition to his open, engaging personality and the fact that he is Hispanic, Valdez's musicianship has led to his acceptance by the community as someone other than a Texas outsider. He plays the guitar and likes to jam with other local musicians in impromptu gatherings. On the evening of the day we met he invited me to go with him to the house of his friend Benny Gallegos, where the two men played in harmony as Valdez sang soulful Spanish ballads and such popular tunes of the 1940s as "Stardust" and "Blue Moon." We sat outdoors, and though the moon was not blue, it was full. The field beside the bosky border of the Gallegos property next to the acequia madre and the river was filled with old cars, including an impeccably restored turquoise green vintage Nash Rambler. As I sank into this pleasant time warp, it was easy to see how Valdez had fallen in love with Las Vegas.

ELMO BACA

Elmo Baca, another member of Slick's Plaza Vieja team, is a native Las Vegan. He grew up west of Grand Avenue near Lincoln Park on Tilden Street in one of the houses that had been built for railroad workers in the town's heyday as a transportation hub. "There was a pretty rough element of teenage gang members on the other side of the tracks that would cross over, and you had to watch out for these pachucos when you were playing in the park, but otherwise it was a safe neighborhood," he said. "There was a tight social fabric, and I would play street games such as kick the can with the other kids in the evening. I used to ride my bike on the brick sidewalks in our neighborhood and everywhere throughout New Town. I remember Murphy's and Western Drug Store as well as Taichert's, which was still being run like an old-fashioned haberdashery, with shirts folded up in beautiful hardwood cabinets and a smell like lavender and mothballs throughout the store. My mom worked at Montgomery Ward on Douglas Street. That part of Las Vegas was my world. I rarely went over the river into Old Town. There was a psychological barrier in those days, and it just didn't seem accessible, even for a Hispanic boy like myself. But we did sneak down to the Gallinas riverbank to play. Near the Independence Street bridge where Farmway Feed is, next to the river it was all overgrown and felt like the jungle to us. You could make up adventures for yourself—like exploring the West or going to

Africa. Sometimes our play was about myths and legends, such as the one of La Llorona. That made the part of the river beneath the Bridge Street bridge very scary."[1]

Following his graduation from Robertson High School in 1971, Baca went off to Yale. "It was a very exciting, dynamic time, and I wanted to see for myself what was happening. It was more a desire to go out into the world than to escape Las Vegas. When I came back in 1976 after college, the two towns had been consolidated, and there was a changed perception. I had majored in architecture, and I started to appreciate the wonderful buildings in Old Town. Then I met Rhuea Pearce, who had restored one of the old adobes on South Pacific Street. She was really the person who started the historic preservation movement in Las Vegas. She got Fidel "Chief" Gonzales, the first mayor after consolidation, to create the Design Review Board, which she then chaired. I worked as an architectural advisor with her, Bob Mishler, Luis Olivas, John Gavahan, and Diana Stein, all of whom were instrumental in getting historic preservation launched in Las Vegas. I was able to form relationships with the New Mexico State Historic Preservation Division, which had just been established, and through the National Park Service's National Register of Historic Places program we got a grant to survey the buildings in Las Vegas and determine which ones were the most architecturally significant. I worked with Ellen Threinen, an architectural consultant, who wrote the report that defined the town's six historic districts."[2]

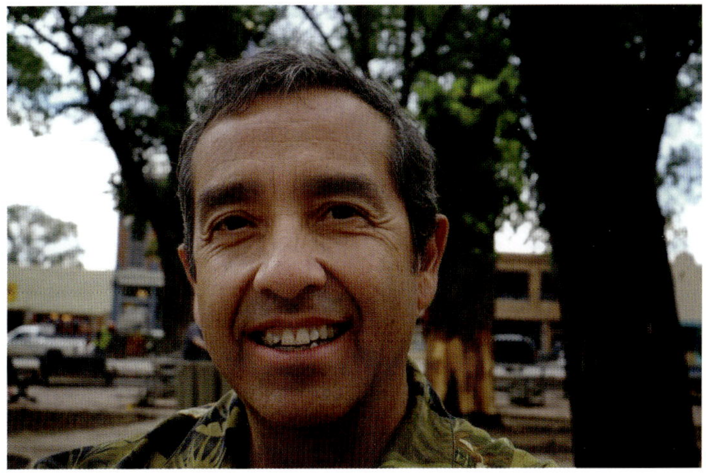

Elmo Baca

Baca is a film buff, and during the five years he spent after Yale working on historic preservation in Las Vegas, he was one of five partners who showed art films at the then-vacant Kiva, the Art Deco movie theater on Bridge Street. "We put on all the Truffaut and other French New Wave films, old Humphrey Bogart movies like *Casablanca,* the Beatles' *Yellow Submarine*—that sort thing. We called ourselves the Kivites, and it was a fabulous time for me. But I thought I ought to go back East and get my master's degree at the Graduate School of Architecture, Planning, and Preservation at Columbia, which I did in 1981. I had no money and no job when I got there, so I answered an ad that Cinema Five had put in the *New York Times*. Pretty soon I was managing two of the company's twelve premier art-movie theaters on the East Side of New York. It was a dream job for me and I didn't want to leave the city after I finished my coursework at Columbia in 1983. But then I got a call from Wid. He told me about how he was trying to start La Plaza Vieja and said, 'I need you to come back to Las Vegas.' He knew that this town was my Achilles heel. I really thought his vision to rehabilitate Old Town was a grand and noble thing to do, and so, much as I hated to leave New York, I decided to come back. I had to. This is my place—absolutely. And that's why I am still here. And, strangely, that's why Wid is still here. It has become his place too."

For two years after coming home to Las Vegas, Baca worked with Slick, Ray Valdez, Tim Goodwin, and Rosemary Forray to assemble the key buildings La Plaza Vieja needed as a critical mass. With the $2.3 million in capital that Slick had raised—$1 million in tax credits, $630,000 in a federal HUD grant, and $670,000 in conventional bank loans to investors—the bulk of the organization's rehabilitation occurred between 1985 and 1988. Baca himself, along with his late father, Manuel, and his mother, Emma, was one of the general partners in La Plaza Vieja, and he remains the owner of the Baca Building located on Bridge Street next to Estella's Café. He maintains, "When you think about it, it was an unbelievable community development project, and we were more or less successful, especially in light of the fact that the banks were not that helpful and the financial community acted like it really wanted to stymie urban development. There was also the Hispanic old guard, who were skeptical of what we were doing. However, some of them, particularly the rancher and philanthropist Antonio Sanchez and the former Old Town mayor Ernie Olivas, both of whom are now deceased, supported the investment we were making in this part of town."

Following the time spent working to establish La Plaza Vieja, Baca became active in historic preservation at the state and national level. He supported the legislation that established New Mexico as part of the National Trust for Historic Preservation's Main Street downtown revitalization program, and between 1994 and 1999 he served as its director. Two years later, following a year spent as a fellow at the American Academy in Rome, he became director of the Historic Preservation Division of New Mexico and the administrator of the state's historic preservation program and policy. Not surprisingly, in 2005 he was instrumental in getting Las Vegas designated a Main Street community under the aegis of the National Trust for Historic Preservation.[3]

In Las Vegas and elsewhere preserving the past is necessarily linked to improving the present and envisioning the future. In 2006 Baca started Quixote Productions, a consulting firm that specializes in economic development with an arts and culture focus. Understandably, movie theaters are part of his definition of arts and culture, as well as being central to his notion of what constitutes a vital downtown. "There are very few businesses that can draw five hundred people in one night," he explained to me. "That's why a movie theater is so powerful. If you have one in your town, it can be magical in a way that the quadruplex in the mall never can. Las Vegas is fortunate to have two historic movie houses, the Kiva and the SERF, as well as the Fort Union Drive-In, a great old representative of a dying breed."

In 2007 Baca helped write the enabling legislation to create the New Mexico Arts and Culture District Program under the aegis of the state's economic development department. The program's mission is to promote "place-based community economic development rooted in a community's dynamic arts and cultural

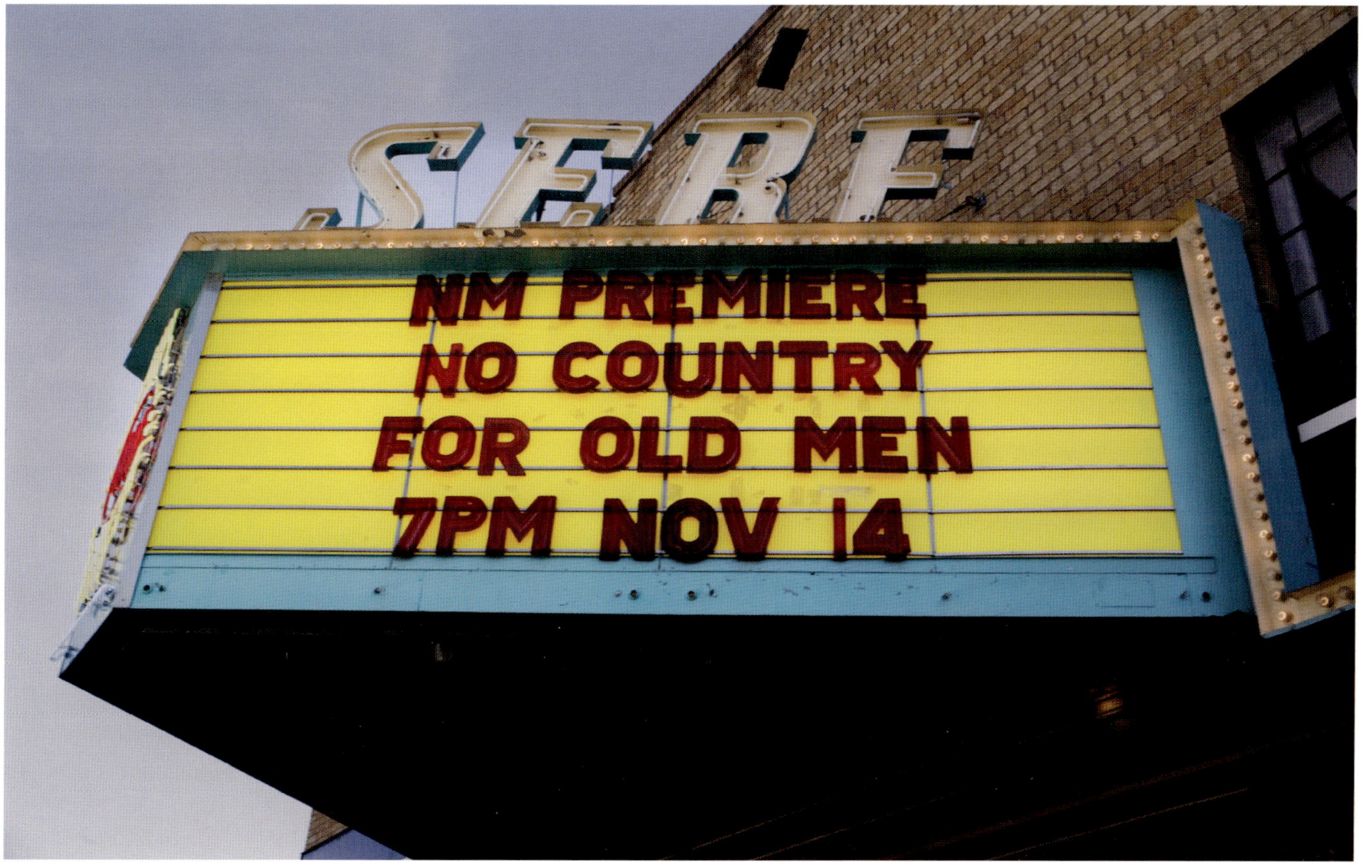

SERF Movie Theater

environment"—a way of saying that there should be funding for facilities and support for artists, artisans, and craftspeople living and working in designated parts of cities throughout the state. He then helped Las Vegas MainStreet, the conduit for state funding, to form a steering committee to spearhead the town's successful application to create an Arts and Culture District in Las Vegas.[4] The committee's members included representatives from the Las Vegas Arts Council, the Citizens Committee for Historic Preservation, the Economic Development Corporation, United World College, Highlands University, Luna Community College, and Las Vegas MainStreet.

The program was slow to get off the ground. According to Baca, "Part of the problem is that we are working here with a lot of older leaders and, along with this boomer generation, we need new blood, young locals and artists in their late twenties and thirties." A significant challenge, however, is the traditional one of who wields power when it comes to controlling policy and how monies get spent. In Las Vegas this has taken the form of an unfortunate clash between MainStreet officers and Roy Montibon, formerly the chairman of the steering committee and principal author of the document SPACE—Strategic Plan for an Arts and Culture Environment—a manifesto outlining how the arts could serve as the linchpin for the town's revitalization. Baca maintains that the goals put forth in the plan were instrumental in getting a one-square-mile area of Las Vegas designated by the state as a local Arts and Culture District.[5]

In spite of Montibon's abrupt and angry resignation from the steering committee, Baca has not ceased moving forward with his own vision for Las Vegas's revival. His background in historic preservation and urban planning along with his knowledge of government funding sources are strong assets. His current efforts include the creation of a new plaza park on Douglas Street opposite the Spic & Span. He is also working to enhance the linear park along the route of the railroad's old spur beside the eastern bank of the Gallinas going north to Montezuma. He envisions the first section, which is adjacent to the park's entrance at the beginning of National Avenue, as a sculpture garden. "This is something that might bring Roy back to the table," he told me with sincere hope. "He still has a lot to offer."

Community Visions

ROY MONTIBON

An artist and owner of a consulting company whose stated mission is "Shaping Vision, Context & Experience," Roy Montibon moved to Las Vegas with his wife Julie Tumblety in 2006 because he felt that his own life goals were congruent with what he believed to be the town's arts-and-culture-driven renaissance. Indeed, he came because he saw an opportunity to be a primary driver of that renaissance.

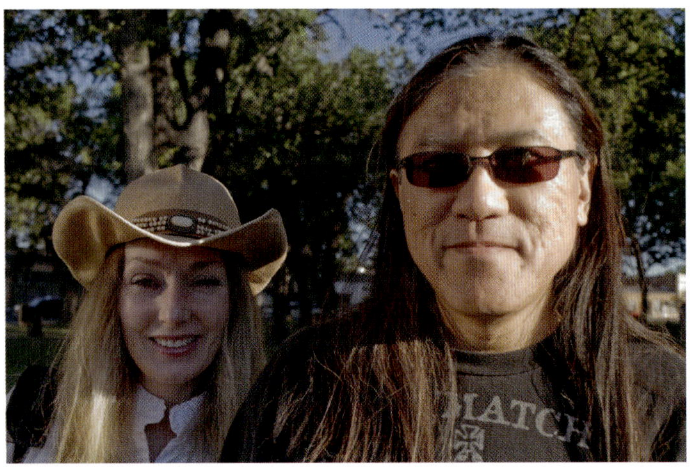

Julie Tumblety and Roy Montibon

A look at Montibon's website biography reveals that he got his start as a professional artist when he was teenager custom-painting Harleys and hot rods. Since graduating from Pasadena's Art Center College of Design, his career "has encompassed design, animation, art direction, creative direction, and business strategy and technology development; and has taken many forms—as consultant, corporate executive, entrepreneur, educator, community organizer and arts advocate."The first time we met I asked the obvious question of why he had chosen to leave Los Angeles and

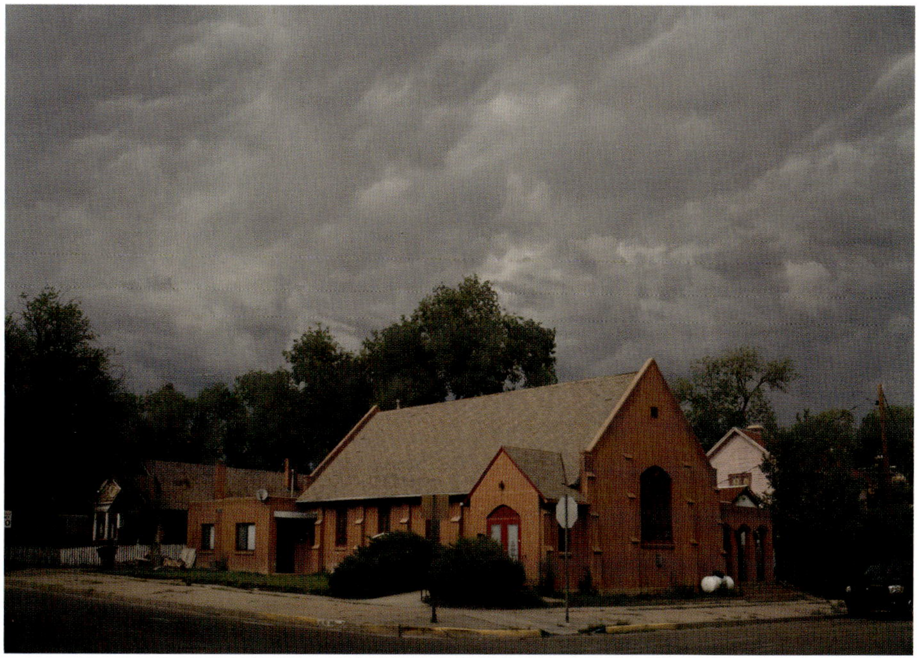

Montibon Residence

relocate in Las Vegas. "We spent two years doing research before we moved here," he replied. "And we moved here for a reason. This place has certain resources: three colleges with arts programs and an incredible stock of gorgeous historic buildings plus tremendous natural beauty and some of the cleanest air in the U.S. Las Vegas has an authenticity that has largely been lost in small towns across the country. That is something we are very interested in preserving and protecting. But we're not just interested in keeping the history of the place alive. We want to see Las Vegas become an arts-and-culture town." Echoing the general local consensus, he quickly added, "Don't imagine that we want to be like Santa Fe. We don't want to see this place have its character obliterated. We don't want it to become like Colorado Springs, Sedona, or Prescott either. We also don't want generic sprawl, and we need to keep Walmart and Starbucks from destroying the economic vitality of downtown."

Montibon and Tumblety live in a former Baptist church built in 1918 at the corner of Seventh and Columbia Streets. Roy's mother, Rita, whose last name is simply the letter *T*, resides with them. Her living quarters and studio, where she paints abstract works, is the parish house next to the lofty sanctuary space that Roy and Julie have turned into their home. Julie is a mixed-media photographer and collage artist, while Roy characterizes himself as a postdigital mixed-media artist. His website states that his work is based on "haunting photographic images, often modified and treated by drawing, painting, silk-screening, folding, tearing and/or burning." He abjures a linear design process in favor of a more organic approach he calls "Design as Discovery" and asserts, somewhat opaquely, that his work "is focused on the mythic, mimetic, and spatial sources of culture; its development, evolution and fragmentation; and the subsequent rise and dissemination of discrete and recombinant micro-cultures." Before he put it up for sale recently, one half of the 5,000-square-foot building he purchased in 2009 on Bridge Street served as a gallery, which he named the Royal Mastodon Society, a space for exhibitions of the work of other artists as well as a venue for various events and programs he sponsored.

Because of his work as a community arts advocate and organizer, Montibon's own career as an artist was forced to take a backseat. As chairman of the SPACE drafting committee, he created a document that articulated a lofty vision for the town's future. If somewhat short on practical steps for implementation, it lacked nothing in the way of hortatory prose projecting an exciting scenario calling for the branding of Las Vegas as "a unique Arts City." According to Montibon, this desired destiny would come about through "developing a comprehensive networking database, plus a live scene where talented people (including patrons and investors) can meet spontaneously." Such activity would automatically "kick the Arts and Culture initiative up to a higher, self-perpetuating 'growth' level."

Montibon's SPACE document was, in effect, the case statement that resulted in the 2007 designation of Las Vegas as a New Mexico MainStreet subsidiary; further, it was endorsed by the New Mexico Economic Development Department, as well as by representatives of the Las Vegas Chamber of Commerce, the Citizens Committee for Historic Preservation, and other community organizations and business owners. But predictably, working within the context of layered governmental authority proved difficult for Montibon, a situation complicated by the fact that the funding for the Arts and Culture District was administered by Las Vegas MainStreet. Although it incorporated the Arts and Cultural District's goals to sponsor the creation of art studios, art supply stores, galleries, design studios, performance venues, and other related businesses into its mission, Las Vegas MainStreet's larger commercial revitalization objectives encompassed a broader and more economically oriented agenda. Thus, for MainStreet, Montibon's more arts-focused approach had to be considered within the context of promoting the growth of other types of small businesses and the consequent employment opportunities and tax revenues this would provide.

Nor were the defined boundaries of Las Vegas MainStreet and the Arts and Culture District coterminous. The official Main Street Corridor consists of the Railroad District and the town's the two commercial districts—one on the east side of town around Douglas Avenue and Sixth Street and the other encompassing the length of Bridge Street and the area around the plaza. As envisioned by Montibon, the boundaries of the Arts and Culture District, although defined in fact, were intentionally imprecise. Indeed, he conceived of it essentially as a sphere of influence, and as such in his mind it had no precisely defined geographical limits. As grandly promulgated in the SPACE text, it was the key to making Las Vegas "the epicenter of creative activity for the entire surrounding region—its energy radiating outward, with artistic centers beyond the city limits radiating creative energy back in."

This misalignment of fundamentally compatible goals and spheres of activity inevitably created a divergence of opinion regarding the implementation the SPACE agenda. But that was only later. In the beginning there was a good deal of enthusiasm within the local business community and among historic preservationists for Montibon's desire to "transform the energy of Las Vegas from a sleepy and somewhat gritty town drifting through its twilight years . . . towards a talent-driven, dynamic arts destination." The beauty of the place itself would help guarantee a turnaround. Extolling the regional scenery in the language of a vacation advertisement, he wrote, "One feels like a khaki-clad naturalist on a National Geographic Special while observing thousands of migrating birds congregating on Crane Lake in November. Dropping into the Mora Valley via Ledoux at sunset feels like one is entering Brigadoon . . . pinch yourself to make sure it's real. And one wouldn't be too surprised to suddenly hear Julie Andrews on one's car stereo, singing, "The Sound of Music" while cruising towards Pendaries. South of town, the drive from Ribera to Villanueva State Park is one to savor. *No matter which way you go, the area surrounding Las Vegas is drop dead gorgeous.*" Even in acknowledging Las Vegas's unsavory side, Montibon optimistically asserted that "every problem is an opportunity to get creative." He offered as an example the notion that the capture of packs of roving dogs could be documented as a work of digital video art or provide the narrative for a children's book written as "a cautionary tale regarding the importance of being responsible for animals in one's care."

Understandably, there was considerable dissatisfaction on Montibon's part when he perceived that state grant money was being directed in ways he could not control. As the chairman of the Arts and Culture Steering Committee charged with developing an independent not-for-profit corporation to help sustain the program, he was particularly incensed when the Las Vegas MainStreet board opted to apply a $20,000 foundation grant for the development of the Arts and Culture District to the support of its underfunded administrative staff. The rationale for this was the belief that, in the absence of perceived progress on the part of the Arts and Culture Steering Committee to develop a realistic strategic plan, MainStreet officials should assume direct administrative responsibility for the program. The ensuing battle between Las Vegas MainStreet and Montibon grew acrimonious after an ill-advised remark directed toward Montibon by one of the attendees at a MainStreet board meeting. Furious, he e-mailed a diatribe detailing his grievances to a number of state officials. When it became clear that the director of New Mexico MainStreet supported its Las Vegas MainStreet subsidiary in the quarrel, Montibon wrote a letter of resignation from the steering committee, which he subsequently made public in the *Las Vegas Optic*.

When I asked Montibon about the blowup, he replied in an e-mail, "MainStreet just sees economic development of the core as what is important. It's a Chamber of Commerce perspective. They want to do things like trashcans, park benches, and signage, and that's not the same thing as encouraging people to make art and set up arts-related businesses. I think artists and creative types really don't need a community development organization like MainStreet. As an artist and community activist, I have always battled against injustice, racism, exploitation and plain old small-mindedness whenever I have run across it, sometimes to my great personal detriment, as was the case with New Mexico State MainStreet, Las Vegas MainStreet, and the State Arts and Culture District."

But Montibon is clearly not one to give up on a vision, particularly one that he has committed himself to with enormous passion. He therefore decided to form what he calls an independent community arts network. To give continuity to the ideals he had espoused as the author of the 2007 SPACE document, he branded the new entity with the same acronym, only this time it stands for Special Projects in Arts, Culture, and Education. He firmly believes that education focused on development of artisanal and mechanical trades is a key to reforming delinquent teenagers. Therefore, the primary mission of the new organization consists of mentoring the town's youth population in ways that tap its creative potential. "Why do kids get angry, drop out?" he asked rhetorically one day when I stopped by to talk about SPACE in its new incarnation. "If they're getting gang tattoos and going to jail, who is going to hire them? They may not be able to go to Harvard, but they can get a creative education. Whether it turns out to be custom painting motorcycles, building furniture, or making jewelry, arts education is fundamental in providing you with the kinds of skills that will give your life direction whether you end up becoming an artist or not."

Montibon's prescription for stemming the steep high-school dropout rate in Las Vegas is based on his own experience growing up in a tough neighborhood in Los Angeles. In our conversation, he characterized himself as "a wild and rebellious juvenile delinquent who barely attended high school," adding that "I was determined 'to live free or die.' To me the words 'liberty and justice for all' were not just a political slogan. Through community arts programs, I was able to develop confidence and competence and become an entrepreneur." Even menial jobs were a step up the ladder: "When I was in high school, I worked for minimum wage cleaning toilets, so I know what low-paying service jobs are all about. Having that job, I was able to go to arts school in Pasadena. The trick is to make that kind of thing transitional, to think of it as some kind of internship. Working in hotels, for instance, you get exposure to business operations. Every kind of job and every creative activity is a form of problem-solving. That's what learning is."

One of the first acts of Montibon's new SPACE organization has been to provide sponsorship, if not financial aid, for two young men, Adam Caldwell and Aaron Juarros, who have recently set up a silk-screening business on Bridge Street in order to support their personal careers as artists—in Caldwell's case as a textile designer and in Juarros's as a sculptor in metal. Montibon is especially proud of the outcome of a graffiti art exhibition he mounted in his former Mastodon Society space on Bridge Street. "We showed work by Zak Lujan and Brian Marquez, two high-school dropouts, and three of their paintings sold to buyers, one from Chicago, one from Amsterdam, and another from Oakland. Now these former teenage outlaws are making legitimate art and see that they have a future. They have both earned their GEDs. Brian is studying filmmaking and videography and Zak is thinking of maybe going to college and majoring in art. You see, we're a group of creative people helping each other do great things—educational work, community development, starting businesses."

It is not clear whether Roy and Julie Montibon and Rita T will remain in Las Vegas if Roy's dream of creating a community dedicated to the arts does not materialize on a scale commensurate with his ambition, but for now he appears to be enjoying his role as a disaffected polemicist who has not given up. Although it does not appear likely at the moment, perhaps at some point in the future he will make peace with his former MainStreet colleagues in order to gain the necessary support to fully realize the original SPACE mission of making the arts a contextual component of broad-scale community revitalization.

MIGUEL ANGEL AND GEORGINA ORTEGA

Miguel Angel believes in a grassroots, ground-up approach that strongly favors Hispanic self-renewal over efforts promoted by outsiders. He and his wife, Georgina Ortega, a former migrant worker and activist in the Chicano movement, disparage Anglo restoration of the historic East Las Vegas homes as an inauthentic form of town regeneration. *Gentrification* is for them a pejorative term. In contrast, Miguel's loving rehabilitation of the adobe compound on Church Street between Taos and Bernalillo streets, which his family has owned since 1865 when the property was deeded to his Civil War–veteran great-grandfather, is for them an example of cultural reclamation.

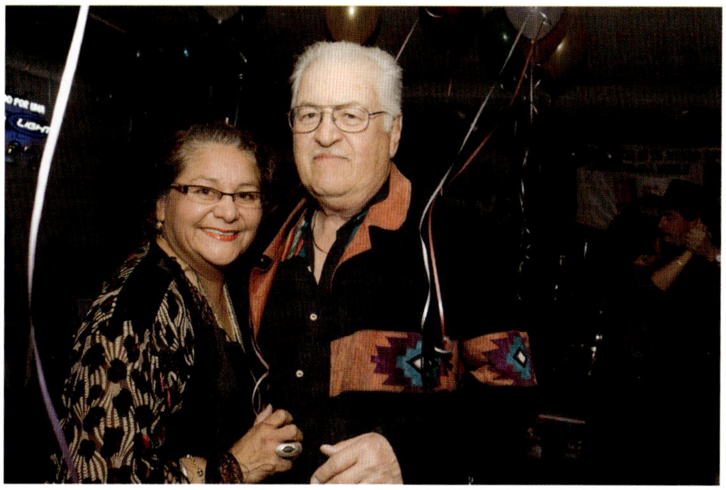

Georgina Ortega and Miguel Angel

When I arrived there and parked in the placita, Angel, who was carrying a platter of barbecued pork ribs, waved hello and invited me into the house. We sat down at the checkered oilcloth-covered table in the kitchen, its viga-supported ceiling and cabinets faced with lacquered split-aspen *latillas* of a warm deep-amber color. This is clearly the hospitality center of the house, a place where friends frequently gather for meals prepared by Angel, who evidently enjoys cooking. Like many other West Las Vegas adobes, this home, which has served four generations of the same family, had been allowed to fall into near ruin when Angel decided to live in it and restore as much of its original character as possible.

Pointing to where the coffeemaker sits in one corner of the kitchen counter, he said, "That's where I was born. This used to be a bedroom. My mom, who is ninety-six, was born in that corner over there. My grandfather was born in the next room." His family's prolonged attachment to place, however, does not mean that Angel has spent his whole life in Las Vegas. After his mother remarried and he was finishing his first year at Highlands University following graduation from West Las Vegas High School, he moved with her and his stepfather to Santa Clara, California, where both parents had jobs as teachers. He completed his college education at the University of California, Berkeley before going on to teach Chicano studies there and in several other California schools for the next thirty-two years.

Coming of age at the height of the Chicano movement, he became a political activist, organizing strikes and walkouts as well as shaping his curriculum in Chicano studies to go beyond ethnicity and reflect solidarity with all working-class people. He maintains that the underlying theme of all his courses was that capitalism is a brutal system. He remains an ardent admirer of Che Guevara; in the back room off the kitchen he showed me a *nicho*—a small recess in an adobe wall in which a statuette of a saint is traditionally placed. This one contains Alberto Korda's famous *Guerrillero Heroico* portrait of Guevara, which Angel has enshrined with votive candles.

Angel, who has traveled to Cuba several times, is proud to count himself a friend of Fidel Castro, and a photograph of the two men hangs over the kitchen table. Mixing the ideals of grassroots economic betterment with advocacy of Hispanic economic self-sufficiency, he is an apostle of Castro's brand of economic socialism based on the elimination of capitalist material values. To increase the solidarity of Northern New Mexico and Cuba, Angel worked with a sister-city association that coupled Las Vegas with the town of Banes in the Holguín Province of Cuba.

Being an activist rather than a politician, he said that he sees no point in trying to work with government officials on his agenda for Las Vegas, maintaining that politicians are all in favor of a capitalist form of economic development, especially the avaricious ones looking for kickbacks. Bypassing the system, he has formed a small not-for-profit volunteer organization called Casa de Cultura, of which he is the director. Its mission is "to foster trust and cohesion among diverse ethnic and social groups by participating in educational and cultural affairs." In addition to promoting Hispanic pride and a Marxist brand of Latinismo, its program is a practical one designed to take advantage of Cuba's free medical education system by sending young people from Northern New Mexico there to be trained as doctors, with the requirement that they return and work in underserved communities.

Georgina Angel's ideology is animated by the principles of César Chávez. She and her nine brothers and sisters all worked in the fields of California as migrant workers. "We picked prunes, grapes, oranges, apples, garlic, onions, potatoes, cabbage," she said one day when we sat talking. "Do you want me to go on?" Georgina now applies her well-honed skills as a labor organizer to various civic ends. She was the primary force for obtaining a temporary waiver from the buildings department for the one-night use of the SERF movie theater (it had been closed because of building-code violations) for the New Mexico premier of *No Country for Old Men*. Although there were major-city premieres of this scary Coen Brothers' film, the producers funded the event in Las Vegas as a way of thanking the town for its hospitality during the time the film was being shot there. The fact that no actors or studio luminaries would be in attendance didn't seem to matter. Georgina took charge of obtaining permits and overseeing the spruce-up of the deteriorating abandoned theater on Douglas Street for the occasion. At the shindig held at Joe's Ringside Bar after the screening, she and Miguel danced among a crowd of townspeople, both Anglo and Hispanic, who turned out for the festive postpremiere banquet.

On the day I first visited their home, Georgina was in the process of organizing the reclamation of King Stadium, an outdoor amphitheater originally built at Camp Luna as an equestrian ring for the U.S. Cavalry. "I'll take you over," she offered and we drove to the site behind the former military base that is now Luna Community College. "This is going to be for the people, not for the rich," she declared. "We're planning on doing things here like star-gazing events and other kinds of free entertainment."

Georgina's militant populism is echoed by Miguel. "What we don't need," he told me, "is any more W-Ms! They don't have these kind of stores in Cuba. There money goes to social needs: free universal education and free universal health care. It's a lie what these capitalist developers say about the advantages of big outside corporations coming in and providing lots of jobs. The jobs are the lowest-paying ones, and there are no benefits. We don't want to be like Santa Fe. We don't need large supermarkets to put our local grocery stores out of business. We need to develop a *local* economy based on our traditional agrarian values."

He called my attention to a vacant corner at the south end of his property next to a white house where his grandparents use to live: "Over there is where we have started a community garden." Then, pointing to the area just beyond, he said, "That is where there is an acequia running off the acequia madre; we used to call it the *acequia de manteca*—the lard ditch—because of all the pigs people raised around here. Whenever they butchered a hog, we kids were all put to work. We had to soak the skin and scrape off all the hairs so it could be turned into leather. Then when we were finished, we were given a big bowl of green chile stew with bits of pork in it as our payment." Remembering the platter sitting on the counter, he said, "Here, would you'd like to try some of this pig?" as he handed me plate with a generous portion of the pork ribs he had brought into the house on my arrival, along with a helping of incredibly hot but savory chile sauce.

Stressing the need to resurrect the authentic nature of Las Vegas's bygone days, he continued to disparage what has happened to Santa Fe since "the tourism and culture industries got hold of it." Moreover, he has little interest in seeing his town's population increased by Anglos taking residence and restoring the historic homes in East Las Vegas. "Rich people come in and say, 'This is a nice place to live.' They have the money and start to fix up old houses. This pushes up land values and property taxes. Pretty soon the Hispanics have nowhere to go and must live in trailer homes outside the city."

Angel is currently working with some of the nearby land-grant communities on a program to reestablish a market for the kind of winter wheat that does particularly well in Northern New Mexico. Not surprisingly, he sees this as an ideal crop to export to Cuba. At the same time he wants to reinvigorate food production for local consumption. Remembering how his mother taught classes in the now-passé field of home economics, he said he would like to revive those kinds of courses in the secondary-school curriculum. "We should be teaching kids how to cook healthy meals, how to garden, how to fix a house," he said, before going on to expound on the importance of language instruction as one of the cornerstones of cultural reconstitution. In this regard he maintained that Las Vegas public education is generally deficient and too inclined toward mainstream cultural assimilation. He said he believes that teaching Spanish is important for children who are at risk of losing their ancestors' mother tongue and that foreign-language instruction shouldn't be parochial: "We are global Latinos united with other working-class people with whom we need to communicate."

Religion, politics, and water are the keys—along with the importance of family—to understanding the nature of Las Vegas. Catholicism, the bedrock of Hispanic civilization in Northern New Mexico, undergirds much of the town's communal life. Politics—not grassroots politics characterized by plural leadership but power politics based on the individual authority of a political boss, or patrón—has been a major force since the time of Las Vegas's founding. Finally, the lifeblood of any community is water, and its paucity in Northern New Mexico has fostered both cooperation and contention. Needless to say, these elements—a traditional form of faith, an entrenched system of governance, and issues regarding water supply and water rights—have influenced social behavior and economic opportunity in numerous ways.

The Blood of Christ

The name of the mountains in Northern New Mexico, Sangre de Cristo, or Blood of Christ, is a reminder that the Spanish conquest was accomplished in the name of the Catholic religion. Even more distinctively than the Irish and Italian Catholics who have imprinted urban neighborhoods in places like Boston, New York, and Chicago with their churches, parochial schools, and saint's-day traditions, the Catholics of Northern New Mexico have defined the character of their part of the world with faith-based rituals and celebrations that are deeply embedded in community life. In accounting for this, one must remember that Catholicism here was not introduced into an existing Protestant society. Carried north by Franciscan, Dominican, and Jesuit missionary friars and priests, it has been the dominant religion of northern New Mexican culture since the beginning of the seventeenth century.

Every land-grant village, including Las Vegas, began with the building of a church. Further, in this isolated northern fringe of empire, Catholicism assumed an unusual degree of fervor. A lay Catholic organization, the Brothers of the Pious Fraternity of Our Father Jesus the Nazarene— known as Penitentes because of their belief in atonement through suffering—engaged in such practices as self-flagellation and realistic reenactments of Christ's crucifixion. In addition, the *hermanos* offered assistance to the poor and needy as well as spiritual succor to residents in the scattered isolated villages where itinerant priests could conduct services only occasionally. The Penitente moradas, or meeting houses, a number of which remain in Northern New Mexico today, are decorated with carved wooden statues of saints (santos), and devotional paintings (retablos). In spite of attempts to suppress this auxiliary Catholic presence in the past, the church now coexists peacefully with the brotherhood.

More than a common cultural inheritance, Catholicism remains a fundamental component of Northern New Mexico's identity. For many Las Vegans the Mass offers vital spiritual sustenance. It is, moreover, woven into the ordinary fabric of existence, and baptism, confirmation, baccalaureate, wedding, and funeral masses are important family events attended by numerous relatives and friends.

FATHER JOHN BRASHER

If Catholicism is central to the life of Las Vegas, Our Lady of Sorrows, the foundational church of the town, remains at the center of many of its residents' lives. Father John Brasher is a busy priest. He told me when we talked together one day that he averages two or three funerals a week, commenting, "The Lord likes Las Vegas. Otherwise, why would he call them all?"

When I asked Father Brasher why he had decided to become a priest, he summarized his life history. "I was born in Washington, D.C., and grew up in Albuquerque and have lived in New Mexico for most of my life. I was in library science for a while, but then I found out that the 'Boss' had another plan for my life. I've served in various parishes all over this part of the state. I like the small towns of New Mexico, and I've lived in a lot of them, Questa for four years and Springer for six, which is about the norm for the Archbishop to have you be in one place."[1]

Father John Brasher

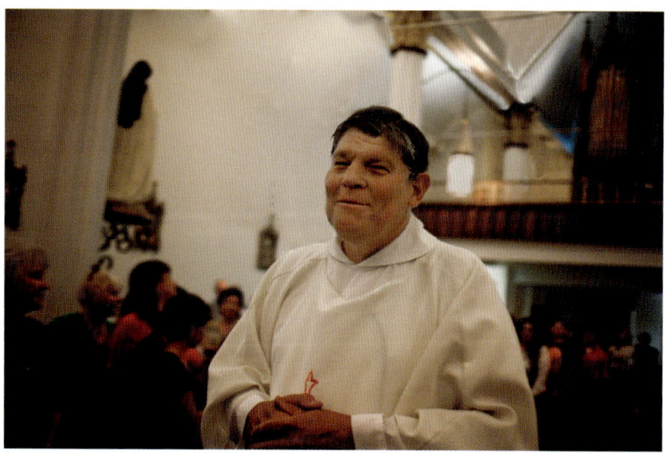

According to Father Brasher, a priest has to believe that his life is directed from on high. At the same time, he tends to be unceremonious and relaxed in his priestly role. "The funeral director Billy Rogers and I tease each other sometimes," he said. "One day we had a large funeral, and the family was grieving and the girls were all crying. I had to go back to the house and get something, and when I returned to the sacristy, Billy was on his cell phone at one end of casket, saying, 'Yes, yes, he's here now.' When he hung up phone, he turned to me and said, 'Father, that was the Lord saying to get this show on the road!' "

In addition to his regular clerical duties, Father Brasher conducts masses for various communal events. In 2008 I went to the coronation Mass held in the church preceding the three days of fiestas, for which the Fourth of July Parade is the kickoff. Royalty—the queens and princesses from Taos, Española, and Santa Fe—were in attendance. This was an occasion for the priest to deliver a homily. Addressing the gathering of young people, he said, "This country is going to be more realistic and responsible because of people like you *reinas*, *princesas*, and escorts. Your culture is an instrument whereby you can help others. It is the tiny things you do like dancing with an elderly woman that touch a life you don't even know you are touching. Your gentlemanly and womanly behavior is part of the richness of this culture, and your participation in it is your gift to the Lord."

"It's the human touch that is so important," he remarked when we spoke later. "Sure, there are bad kids in this town, but I encourage them to stay straight." When I asked him about the recent pederasty scandals in the Church worldwide, he advocated the same kind of suasion. "You have to go case by case by case. Imagine the confrontation between Peter and Christ after Peter denied the Lord! If the Lord could forgive people after their shenanigans, there's hope for the rest of us who haven't exactly stepped that close to the edge. Forgiveness is important. Forgiving doesn't mean condoning. You have to help someone do better and grant the offender the right to his own humanity. It's not easy, but reconciliation and allowing the man to go back to doing the Lord's work without blemish is what is more important in the end."

He then explained to me why the Church is so vital in the life of the community. "You know, in a town of our size there are not so many social, health, or other kinds of facilities, so we must fill other needs besides religious ones. I am blessed that I have some good deacons and parishioners to help me. And sometimes Father George Salazar, the priest at Immaculate Conception Church, and I cover for each other. But we have to joke about crossing the *río*." Echoing many other Las Vegans I have spoken with from both sides of the divided town, he added, "You know, Las Vegas is still very much two communities."

FATHER GEORGE SALAZAR

When I went to see Father George Salazar at Immaculate Conception Church on Sixth Street in East Las Vegas, he seconded Father Brasher's comment about the one-but-two character of Las Vegas, adding, "For Hispanics the river was never really a division because so many have always lived on this side as well as in Old Town. Our church over here was built as the Anglo, English-speaking church in 1885, but it was attended by the Hispanics in this parish from the beginning. Nevertheless, East and West were still two separate communities. Over here were the professionals and businessmen. That was the part that was Anglo. Along with the Jewish merchants, they lived on Sixth, Seventh, and Eighth streets in the beautiful mansions. But Fourth

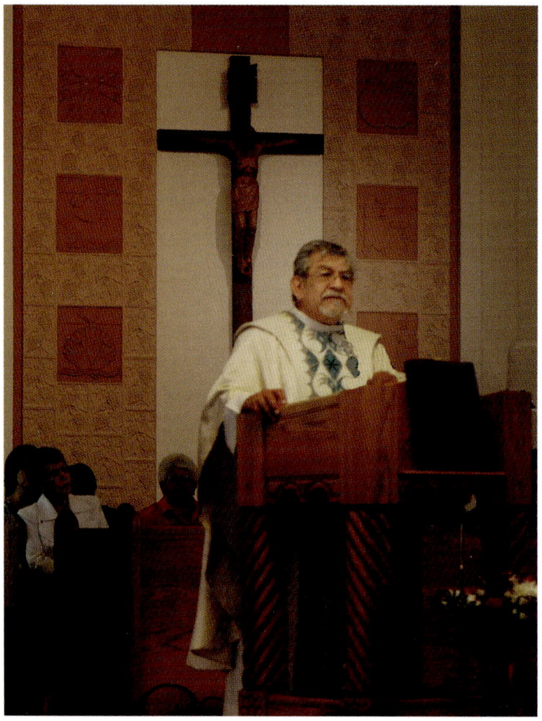

Father George Salazar

and Fifth streets and all along Grand and on the other side of the railroad was the Hispanic community living in adobes. In these areas the streets weren't paved and there were no streetlights."

He then explained how social differences accentuated the separation of cultures. "The people who came in after the railroad had puritan values and didn't understand why we were different. The Temperance League didn't like the fact that there were bars with gambling rooms in back. The railroad district was really a part of the Wild West. We liked our booze and still do. My grandfather always had wine on the table. Near the train station was the red-light district for the men who came in on the railroad and stayed overnight. The Anglos complained about that, too. We were just two different cultures."

Father George's childhood exemplifies the warm intimacy of extended family that is such an important part of Hispanic culture, an aspect of life that is especially glowing in the memories of those born at the time when home, neighborhood, and Church were the entire, emotionally sufficient boundaries of community. "I was born in 1940 and grew up on Grand Avenue near the roundhouse where the Pizza Hut parking lot now is," he told me. "The people in our part of New Town, which was the warehouse district, were poor, but over on the other side of the tracks were the poorest of the poor. The difference wasn't anything you talked about; you just knew it was there. We were still all one in the eyes of God. There were little grocery stores on every block and, of course, lots of kids in the neighborhood. All the adults, whether they were relatives or not, had authority over us. Our parish church was where Allsup's now is. We lived in such a Catholic environment that if we were at Mount Calvary cemetery to bury someone we were told we couldn't even look over at the Jewish cemetery next to it. But if you were making your first communion or on some other important occasion and when you needed new clothes instead of hand-me-downs, you went to Taichert's Haberdashery or one of the other Jewish stores."

Unlike Father Brasher, who received his call to the ministry as a young adult, Father Salazar knew from childhood that he wanted to be a priest. "We always prayed and recited the rosary in our home. My family was very religious and my father would never let us be late for Mass. One day when I was seven I was in Mass with my mother. I tugged at her sleeve and told her I had something important to tell her. She wouldn't listen and said that I should look at the altar and pay attention to the sacrament. I finally got her to listen to me after church when she was about to take my brother and me to get an ice cream cone. 'I am going to be a priest,' I told her. She looked me in the eyes and nodded. As we started to cross the street to the ice cream parlor, I insisted that I go home instead; I wanted to tell my grandmother right away. I remember it to this day. She was sitting in the kitchen rolling a cigarette. When she saw that what I had to say was important, she put the tobacco back in the can and said, '*Siéntate.*' I sat down and said, 'Today at Mass I didn't hear any voices, I didn't have any vision, I just knew I am going to be a priest.' She embraced me so closely I could hear her heart beating. After that I went to the Castle school (the predecessor of the East Las Vegas public school) until eighth grade, and then I started seminary. I spent four years at the College of Santa Fe and another four years with the Benedictines in Missouri. After that I became ordained. I still remember that day—May 13, 1967—like it was yesterday. Before my ordination was to take place I went up to the cemetery in San Antonio, or Upper Town as some people call it, with my dad to tell my grandmother, who had recently died. The soil was still mounded on top of her grave, but while we stood there I watched it slowly sink into the earth. I could imagine her saying to me: 'God waited. Now my bones can rest.' "

I wanted to know what going to school in Las Vegas was like when Father Salazar was a boy. "I only spoke Spanish when I first went to school." he said. "My grandmother never learned English, and Spanish was all we spoke at home. But Miss Martinez said that we were not allowed to speak a word of Spanish in school and had to learn English. I told my mother I wouldn't go back to school the next day, but she made me return. After that, even though she didn't speak English very well herself, my mother never said another word to us in Spanish at home."

Although Father Salazar did not seem troubled in this regard, as we spoke about the changes in the Church since Vatican II, I realized that for him there was another language shift that had been more difficult to accommodate. He remarked, "I was ordained in 1967 right after Vatican II. That meant that we had to begin saying Mass in the vernacular. It was really traumatic for us, especially for the older priests. I had calluses on my knees because we had always knelt for all our prayers, but hearing them in Latin even if you were following along in English or in Spanish was so beautiful. The liturgy seemed more emotional and the mystery more powerful. When things changed, it was like a bunch of cut flowers. They were still beautiful, but there were no roots anymore. We felt that we had lost our pious tradition and sense of community and family. It was like doing away with Thanksgiving or some other American holiday. There is still sacredness in the liturgy, but it requires more for me to feel it now, so I have to find that sacredness inside of me."

MARGARET SANCHEZ

Like other older Hispanic residents who have invited me into their homes, Margaret Sanchez lives surrounded by portraits and wedding pictures on the walls, tables, and shelves in her house on South Pacific Street in West Las Vegas. Each of these evokes a personal memory or a story about her ancestors. The house itself is a historical document of the lives of her grandparents and parents as well as of her own life. Her grandfather built it shortly after he married her grandmother. Pointing to one wall of the living room where we were sitting, Sanchez said, "That room next to us is where my grandmother used to have a grocery store, but it became a bedroom when my kids were growing up." Indicating another room toward the back of the house, she said, "There is where I was born. In those days we spoke mostly Spanish. It was like the old, old conquistadores' Spanish. When I went to Puerto Rico with my former husband who was in the army, they spoke a way different kind of Spanish from what I spoke, and the people there would laugh when they heard me."

Intermixed with the family photographs throughout the house is Sanchez's own large collection of statues of saints, inherited from her grandmother. "This one is Saint Theresa," she told me, "and over here is a crèche given to my grandmother by the Christian Brothers when she worked at their school.[2] The Baby Jesus was broken somehow, which is probably why they told her she could have it," she said as she went to fetch a plaster Christ Child dressed in swaddling clothes from the next room. "You can see, though, that it's too big for the crèche, so then somebody gave her this other one that fits just right."

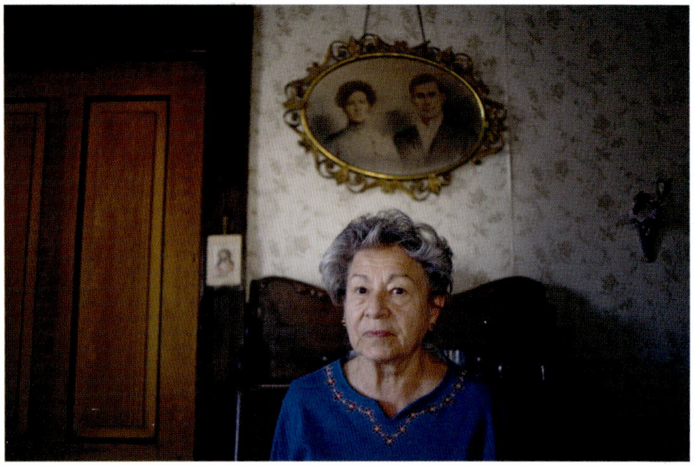

Margaret Sanchez

Sanchez told me that her great-grandfather, who was a driver on the Santa Fe Trail, traded some land he owned for indulgences granted by Archbishop Jean-Baptiste Lamy. "In those days," she said, "they encouraged you to buy them in order to get into Heaven." In this instance, church funds from the sale of indulgences were no doubt used for the building of the Basilica of St. Francis in Santa Fe, the cathedral church of the archdiocese of New Mexico, and for its adornment with images of saints like those found in Archbishop Lamy's native France. Here and elsewhere throughout the archdiocese he insisted on removing the "primitive" holy images by untrained artists, replacing them with European-style statues and paintings. According to Sanchez, "He made everybody get rid of those old santos. He didn't like the fact that the people themselves made them. He said they were ugly. People would hide them, and now look, they are works of art!"

One of Lamy's first actions in addition to banning indigenous religious art was to suppress the Penitentes. His strictures drove them to practice in secrecy. "My aunt who just died was married to one," Sanchez told me. "Here they are no longer into extremes anymore, but they used to reenact the Crucifixion on Good Friday. You had to volunteer. If you did not get taken down from the cross before you died, the brothers took your shoes and placed them outside the door of your family. That was the sign. My grandfather told me how sometimes when he and my grandmother would go for rides they would spot a group of men all bound up. They had ropes wound all around them. The Church could not accept that, which is why they would cover their faces just like members of the Ku Klux Klan whenever they went about town. But everybody knew who they were by the way they walked."

Margaret said that her sons, who are "real churchy people" like herself, had considered becoming Penitentes. With a laugh, she added, "I told them they would have to learn to pray in Spanish and that probably stopped them. The reason my boys pray in English is because their father insisted that they learn that language first, which is what he didn't do when he was young." According to her, "Father Brasher doesn't pray the Stations of the Cross; he lets the *hermanos* do it. And I have put down in writing that I want them to sing at my funeral."

The subject of the Penitentes brought a new topic into our conversation: the hermit of Hermit's Peak, a religious ascetic who wandered into Gallinas Canyon in 1863. He was considered a curandero, and the Las Vegas townsfolk were thankful for his healing powers and medicinal herbs. Sanchez told me that, in addition to the hut built for him on the ridge top by a brotherhood of his followers organized by Margarito Romero, he had a cave in a box canyon just south of Las Vegas. "My grandfather said that he would come to town and that people would follow him. He was, you know, an Italian nobleman who left home to become a hermit. Just like a good athlete, you have to be obsessed to do something, and I guess hermits must be obsessed. He used to preach, and the priests didn't like that. My godmother knew the hermit and had a picture of him. Every December 4 he would make bonfires on the mountain in honor of the Virgin of Guadalupe. He told the people to look for the bonfires and that if they didn't see them they would find him dead."

When Margaret is laid to rest it will be in Mount Calvary Cemetery. In Northern New Mexico death is perceived as a family reunion among the living, the recently deceased, and those who have previously passed on. Most of the gravesites are fenced plots with such surnames as Trujillo, Romero, Roybal, Montoya, Ortiz, Sanchez, Gonzales, and Abreu prominently displayed on a single large marker with family members' Christian names inscribed on smaller adjacent headstones. Concrete slabs typically cover the ground beneath which the bodies lie, and these slabs serve as platforms for such tributes of devoted remembrance as plastic flowers forming the letters MOM or DAD. Some gravesites have shrines decorated with crosses and figures of saints, particularly the popular Virgin of Guadalupe, protector of Hispanic people throughout what was once the Mexican empire. Grave markers frequently have inset photos, and many bear inscriptions testifying to the virtues of the loved one. Plaster figurines of cherubs and saints are common funerary decor. Seasonal offerings such as Christmas wreaths or Easter eggs lie at the foot of the headstone along with plastic toys for a deceased child commemorated as "our little angel." Lovingly tended by family members who make a special point of weeding and cleaning the plots on All Souls Day and Memorial Day, Mount Calvary appears as a colorful landscape tapestry of communal remembrance spread out upon the east flank of the crestón.

LA MANGA

One Sunday, at the invitation of Lorraine Gallegos and her brother Benigno Ortega, I attended Mass on the feast day of Santo Niño de Atocha—the Christ Child known for succoring those in distress—in the village of La Manga, a hamlet located in the valley of the Tecolote, a tributary stream of the Gallinas flowing through one of the canyons outside Las Vegas. As is the case with other small towns in this part of Northern New Mexico, there is no full-time priest. However, since the churches are still the symbolic heart of each remnant rural community, they are reconsecrated annually on the feast day of their particular patron saint. On such occasions, it is the responsibility of an itinerant priest assigned by the Santa Fe archdiocese to come and offer Mass. These events are also the occasion of family reunions at a big *comida*, a communal feast held after the procession around the church at the end of the service, and relatives often drive long distances to be there with one another.

I realized as I wandered around the camposanto encircling the church before the service that everyone I met was related and that their surnames were the same as those inscribed on the headstones. The portrait photographs embedded in many of

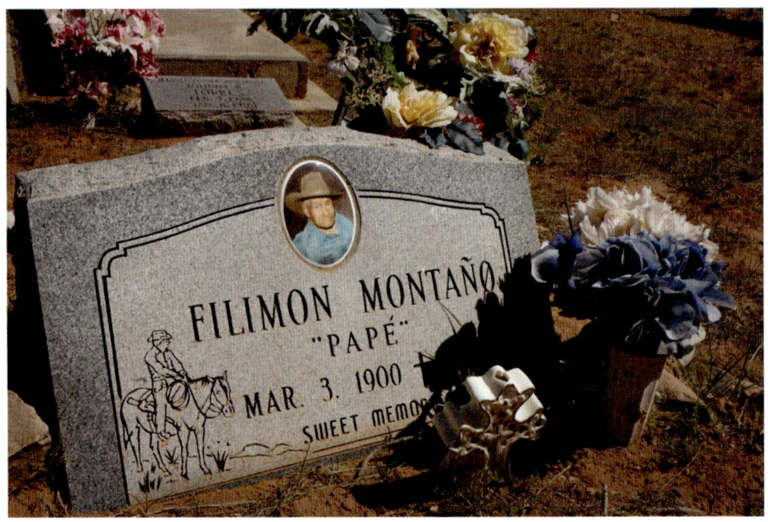

Camposanto, La Manga

these gave the deceased a palpable reality, as did the addition of nicknames to their Christian names. The one that particularly struck me was "Granny Bingo." Her handsome granite marker bore beneath her oval-famed photograph an incised winning bingo card on one side and Santo Niño de Atocha on the other. A woman who saw me photographing it explained that it commemorated her grandmother, who had gotten her moniker because of her passion for the game: "There was never a day she didn't want to play bingo!"

The church bell was rung, and we all squeezed into the sanctuary. I stood in the back next to the overflow group of people crowding around the door. To one side of the altar was a carved and painted wooden figure of Santo Niño de Atocha as a seated child holding a basket in one hand and in the other a staff to which was attached a flask. This particular santo is intended to represent Christ as a pilgrim boy, the Holy Child who brought food and water to the Christian prisoners incarcerated by the Moors in the town of Atocha in Spain. A popular saint in New Mexico, the Niño de Atocha is considered an intercessor for the cure of dire diseases and injuries. Lorraine Gallegos told me that the statue is the church's patron and namesake because her ancestor Juan Bautista Ortega had prayed to Santo Niño de Atocha that if he was cured of a terrible, life-threatening growth on his neck he would build a church in his honor on the 360 acres of land he owned in La Manga.

Mass was said by Monsignor Cipio Salas, a retired priest who is now a busy itinerant clergyman on call for occasions such as this. As my Protestant tongue stumbled over the Catholic litany, the rest of the church was filled with a united chorus of firmly ingrained responses. Certain parts of the service were punctuated with guitar bursts and singing. Instead of preaching a full sermon, Monsignor Cipio discoursed anecdotally on his fifty-year career as a parish priest, dwelling with obvious pleasure on the numerous gratifications he had experienced serving his scattered Northern New Mexico flock. He also remarked how much he was looking forward to the imminent gratification of the comida. Then he presented the Host and poured wine and water into the chalice, reciting Christ's words at the Last Supper.

After everyone had taken Communion and before returning for the conclusion of the Mass, there was a procession around the church, with the litter-borne Santo Niño de Atocha preceded by a crucifix carried by a nine-year-old boy and the church banner by a girl of about the same age. Monsignor Cipio brought up the rear, busily pressing the button of his digital camera. At the finish of the procession, people crowded back into the church. After the priest blessed us and gave the benediction, we drove up the hill to Stella and Benigno Ortega's house, where several long tables filled a barn-size, open-sided room. Although a long buffet line had formed, the lids remained on the steam dishes containing chile, beans, enchiladas, posole, *calabacitas,* rice, and macaroni until the Monsignor, having packed up his traveling box of Eucharist articles, arrived to say grace, whereupon we all proceeded to heap our plates and fall to with relish.

Patrones and Politicians

In Las Vegas the system of Old World feudalism linking lords and serfs was carried over into the patrón system whereby wealthy and powerful dons protected and assisted their poorer neighbors. Vestiges of this tradition have lasted down to the present day. The patrón's quid pro quo for favors bestowed is loyalty and votes. Followers are rewarded; foes are punished. Everybody understands this simple rule. It is fair to say that the patrón's power has been the primary economic engine of Hispanic Las Vegas as well as the political force that eventually brought the town's long period of Anglo-American hegemony to an end.

Donaldo "Tiny" Martinez (1924–2005) is generally acknowledged as the last of Las Vegas's all-powerful patrones. Ruling from a permanently reserved table in "Mama" Lucy Lopez's restaurant, this long-reigning Democratic Party boss was responsible more than anyone else for what might be called the re-Hispanization of Las Vegas in the late 1960s and early 1970s. To gain an understanding of this powerul figure, and the workings of the patrón system in general, I went to see Mama Lucy's son, Jesus Lopez.

JESUS LOPEZ

Familiarly known as Jesse, Jesus Lopez was born in Las Vegas in 1951. More than just an observer of the patrón system at work, he is the quintessential Las Vegas insider. I started our conversation by asking him to tell me about Tiny Martinez, a subject he warmed to immediately. "He was one of the great sons of New Mexico. He was among the first to really start championing the cause of Hispanic people," he replied. "At the rosary before the funeral Mass, I delivered his eulogy, and if I read it to you, you'll see what a great man he was." Pulling a document from his files, he read it to me with well-honed elocutionary skill and sincere emotion: "More than a great and learned attorney, Tiny was a courageous attorney. Fast and furious, that was Tiny. He would take cases for no fee. People loved Tiny, but he also had fierce enemies." The speech went on to intricately detail the great patrón's many victories, beginning with his success in overturning Anglo political leadership in Las Vegas and San Miguel County and his pivotal role in transforming Highlands University into a Hispanic-run institution.

I wanted to know more about Martinez's particular political genius and how he had amassed power. This inevitably led to a discussion of the patrón system. Waxing eloquent once more, Lopez said, "The patrón system was a special and unique ingredient in Hispanic culture. It was inculcated into our being over the course of centuries, and it was a good system. Remember, in New Mexico we go back to 1598 when Juan de Oñate arrived and established the Spanish presence here—that was before Jamestown. However, most of us were not conquistadores. We were of humble origins, though noble always. But we were uneducated and poor, except for some families who, because of accidents of birth and education, were landed gentry. They were the ones who ended up with the wealth." He then went on to describe how isolated this part of New Mexico was, unlike the rest of the Spanish Empire to the south: "Las Vegas had only a slender thread of contact with the outside world, because of the Santa Fe Trail. But people forgot that there was this little enclave that was part of the Spanish Empire, and later Mexico. This abandoned colony was sundered completely from its mother country in 1846 when we became a United States territory. So what happened? There was essentially no government. The local community naturally began to follow the man who seemed to know what the hell he was doing. People like the Romeros became the first patrones in this area. In effect, they formed a dynasty, passing on power from one generation to the next. They had the best houses; they were educated. They were therefore the ones who emerged as the leaders of a very humble people who were for the most part uneducated. The Romero brothers were incredible. If any monument should be built, it should be to them. They ran the whole show! Were they good? Yes! They were benevolent in the finest sense of the word. Did they use their benevolence to stay in power? Yes, yes! Did the people love them? Yes! Could they count on the people to deliver the votes? Yes! It was just a beautiful system. It started with Miguel Romero, who was born in 1797 and was one of the first settlers of the Las Vegas land grant, and the dynasty lasted until the death of his grandson Secundino Romero in 1929."

Lopez continued to explain how the system worked: "Before charities, before public welfare, all you had were patrones. Like the Jews in Las Vegas, the Romeros were big in the mercantile business. Margarito Romero would bring in scores of wagonloads to the plaza—dry goods, food, all kinds of merchandise. This was all for the people; that was the welfare system of the day. Everyone would line up in orderly fashion and they would take what they needed. The Romeros were very good. I have not read or heard anyone besmirching their name. They maintained their humility, and the people followed them."

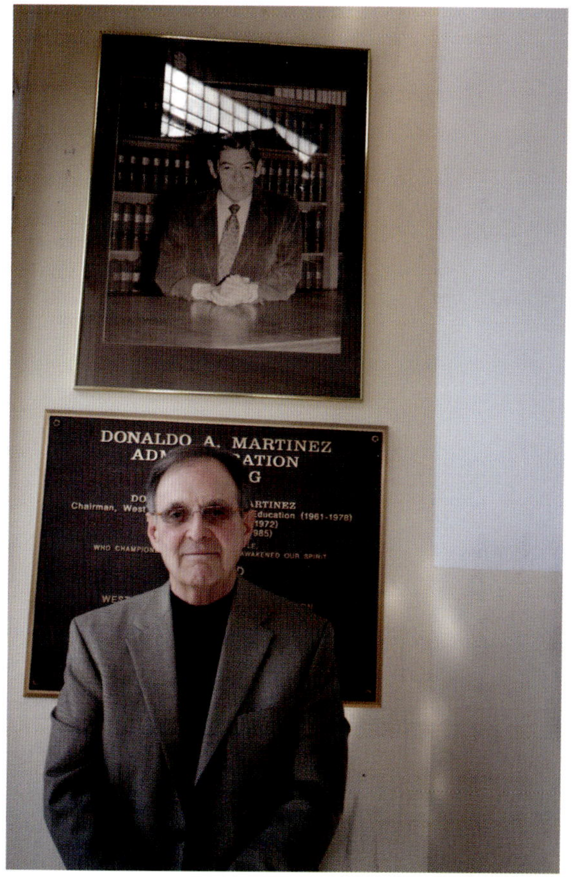

Jesus Lopez with portrait of Donaldo "Tiny" Martinez

Lopez told me that the power of these early patrones was unassailable, even after the rules of the game grew more complicated with the United States' annexation of New Mexico as a territory in 1846. "The Romeros and other wealthy families were able to send their children east to school or have them tutored privately. Now it became the role of these better-educated Hispanics to defend the interests of their people, particularly with regard to the land transactions that had begun eating away the original community grant our thirty-six first settlers received from the Mexican government that was formed after we got our independence from Spain. A legal education was an enormous asset in fighting in court and also in politics. Public office became a pillar of power. Before the Great Depression, most Hispanics were Republicans, which was the progressive party at that time." He then proceeded to explain how the system worked: "All your courthouse offices were controlled by the Romeros. The sheriff was always a Romero. All your jobs were connected to their ranches, their farming lands, their hotels. They were called Dons, which is a mark of respect, of distinction. Don Eugenio or any of the other four brothers would just say we are going to do this, word would go out, and that's how people knew who to vote for."

After 1912, when New Mexico became a state, the patrones were still a political force to be reckoned with, no matter which party was in office. Lopez recounted, "When the Romero brothers ruled, the governor at the time simply asked, 'What do you want to have to help the Las Vegas economy?' The answer was the State Hospital, which was the pet project of Don Benigno, who also built the Plaza Hotel. The hospital has provided us with at least a thousand jobs at any given time for almost a century. Earlier it was the Romeros who donated the land for the Insane Asylum, which was the predecessor of the hospital. They said, 'We need jobs for the community.' And so they went about making that happen. Isn't that beautiful?"

In Las Vegas political power and family connections are inseparable, and dueling for power within families was not uncommon. According to Lopez, "Lorenzo Delgado became Secundino Romero's heir apparent in the 1920s. He was tutored by the Romero cousins and uncles. Delgado died young in the early 1930s, however, and it was his brother-in-law, Luis Armijo, who had studied law and spoke English fluently, who ended up becoming the patrón during the time between the Romero dynasty and Tiny's reign." Lopez continued, "Times had started to change, and Armijo had neither the wealth nor the extended family to command the unrivaled influence of the Romeros, but he did rule with an iron fist, and incredible as it may seem today, he did this from the bench while sitting as our longest-serving district judge."

Hailed in a *Las Vegas Optic* front-page obituary as "The Last Patrón," Tiny Martinez was Judge Armijo's immediate successor. He was district attorney in San Miguel County for sixteen years, chairman of the West Las Vegas school board for eighteen years, and state district judge for six years. In addition, he was longtime chairman of the county's Democratic Party and served one term as a state representative. "With all these political offices," Lopez said, "his power was as great as that of Judge Armijo. However, he used it for very different purposes. He was ultraliberal and antiestablishment. A patrón cut from a very different cloth, he simply flipped the system on its head and supported the interests of the common people."

Martinez's strongest ally in wielding his uncontested power was Jesus's mother, Lucy Lopez, a renowned cook, restaurateur and warm, nurturing presence with the endearing sobriquet "Mama." Her death in 1994, like Martinez's twelve years later, warranted a banner headline: "Las Vegas Mourns the Death of Mama Lucy." During his reign as patrón, a table was permanently reserved for Tiny at Mama Lucy's restaurant. Lopez explained how it became the town's political power center: "This is where Tiny and his 'gang' met every day and discussed their various strategies for running Las Vegas and the rest of San Miguel County. If you want a physical picture, they are all seated around a table. His underlings were also brilliant;

some were scholars and well educated. But you knew immediately who the main guy was. It was Tiny, who was always seated in the middle with everyone facing him. Never mind that it all looks informal: beer cans, liquor, and of course my mother's food. You could sense that everybody was obedient in the best sense of the word; they just respected him so much. It's simply like this: Tiny was the one everyone went to for advice and succor. Of course, they all talked sunup to sundown, and I was there day and night, taking everything in firsthand."

But the restaurant served another purpose besides politics. "I'll tell you what many say my mother did," Lopez exclaimed, "They said Mama Lucy brought down the 'Tortilla Curtain!' That's what we used to call it, the division between Anglo East Las Vegas and Hispanic West Las Vegas. She was such a damn good cook, and she had such a warm personality. Everyone loved her. In those days, West Las Vegas and East Las Vegas were entirely separate: two mayors, two city councils, two school districts, two fire departments, two everything. The Anglos in East Las Vegas would seldom venture across the bridge. Old Town was the Hispanic side, and that was considered by a lot of Anglos as foreign territory. They were honestly afraid to cross the bridge and venture into this part of town. But my mother's food was wonderful, and little by little they began to come over to eat in the restaurant. In the 1950s families from all over the country would send their kids to college here. They'd hear about my mom's restaurant, and pretty soon she was boarding them, giving them two meals a day. You'd see two hundred kids walking up Bridge Street from Highlands University and across the park to my mom's. They loved her food, and more important, they loved her. It was the strangest amalgamation: Tiny the militant and all these Anglos under the same roof. Of course, everyone was fascinated to get a glimpse of Tiny. So that's how the 'Tortilla Curtain' came down. Only a special person could have done that, and that's because she had the best political skills in the world. She knew how to make people feel special. That's what successful politicians do, make everyone feel special—and, take my word for it, my mom was a successful politician in her own right with a lot of influence throughout New Mexico and even in Washington. In fact, although she never held public office, in 1990 she was inducted into the New Mexico Democratic Party Hall of Fame."

I asked Lopez to tell me about the Chicano movement in Las Vegas and how student radicalism at Highlands played a role in the way Martinez had engineered the transition from Anglo political domination to a town under virtually complete Hispanic political control after 1970. "I am not sure about the extent to which the Chicano movement was responsible for the change," he replied. "I believe that the liberal attitude of the Kennedys and the Civil Rights movement under Martin Luther King, which was in the air, helped, but I don't know that it was a catalyst. The Chicano movement made us feel that what we were doing was okay, that we were not out of step, but it was really Tiny's altruism and brilliance that was the moving force. We did little without his advice, and he would seize the moment. When the paramilitary Brown Berets came to town, he told them they could camp out at West Las Vegas High School. He was criticized, however, when he let them raise the Mexican flag and fly the U.S. flag upside down beneath it."

Lopez went on to say that back in the late 1940s, well before student radicalism was a factor, Tiny had agitated for the hiring of a Hispanic president and more Hispanic faculty members at Highlands. "Remember," he told me, "The Anglos ran that place lock, stock, and barrel. They wouldn't even let us be secretaries or clerks. Hispanics were allowed to enroll because they needed us for their numbers—that's all. But Tiny had much more in mind than just turning Highlands into a Hispanic-run institution. He stands above everyone in transforming this town so that Hispanics could again be in charge of their destiny, and that's why he remains one of the most important men in the history of Las Vegas."

The beginning of the transformation of Highlands coincided with the consolidation of Las Vegas into a single municipality. Lopez confided, "No one thought that was possible, but Tiny was the first one to defy the notion that East Las Vegas was always going to be controlled by Anglos. Until then there had been only one token Hispanic on the East Las Vegas school board, and the East Las Vegas City Council was pretty much the same. Tiny worked hard to transform both so that Hispanics could participate and have a role, but consolidation was never part of his agenda. That was done on the initiative of the state legislature. Tiny didn't want us to be part of East Las Vegas; he just wanted to loosen the Anglo stranglehold on the east side. However, eventually he accepted consolidation on the condition that there be a referendum. It did pass overwhelmingly, perhaps because people thought by that time the Hispanic community would exert its authority, which we had in sheer numbers." According to Lopez, things tended to work out well after consolidation, although Martinez had a falling out with the first mayor, Fidel "Chief" Gonzales, because he thought Gonzales was too politically accommodating toward Anglos and not working fast enough to assert Hispanic control over the newly consolidated city.

Explaining how events leading to the appointment of the university's first Hispanic president had unfolded, he said, "First, when Bruce King was running for governor in 1970 and sought Tiny's support, Tiny asked only one thing in return, that King appoint a majority of Hispanics to the Highlands Board of Regents. King kept his promise, which led to the appointment of the first Hispanic university president in the United States, Dr. Frank Angel. Tiny could have asked Governor King for anything, but he didn't ask for anything for himself or his friends—it was for his people."

Lopez proceeded to relate what happened during the years following Martinez's reign as the patrón of Las Vegas. "Well," he said, "his power really didn't exactly end, but he just gradually lost the total control he once had. You know, Tiny would tell me that it was a very stressful business being patrón. Every day people came to see him about this thing or the other, and few people ran for office without his permission. But a younger generation was coming into its own, and they began to question his complete authority over the way things were run. By the 1980s it was just time for him to step aside, but even then he still continued to make important decisions on behalf of the people."

I broached the subject of Tiny's successor and told Lopez that most people said that Martinez's role as patrón was transferred to him. "You know," he replied, "my dad died when I was eleven, and Tiny was always my surrogate father. I literally grew up at his knee. It was natural therefore that I would learn from him, and that he would trust and confide in me. With his blessing I became an important political figure here and held many positions through the years. Everybody knew that Tiny was my counselor and mentor, and I did my best to be a good and honest leader. People may tell you I succeeded Tiny as patrón, but I don't think so. Tiny was surely the last patrón, although many people did look to me for advice and support, and I hope I filled this role well."

Lopez still has an important say in the political life of Las Vegas. At the same time, with his infallible memory for names and dates, he has another outlet for his proficient communication skills, that of New Mexico historian. His weekly "Nuestra Historia" column in the *Las Vegas Optic* has a wide following, as does his talk show on the local radio station KFUN. Although he can deliver historical facts about the town with dispassionate authority, for him Las Vegas's past is something deeply personal as well. "Remember," he told me, "for thirty years my parents operated the Plaza Hotel and Restaurant and after that my mother ran her famous Mama Lucy's on the opposite side of the plaza. All the time I was growing up, the plaza was my front yard. It was my playground. When I look around Old Town today I can see all of its history as well as my own, everywhere, all about me."

I was fortunate to experience the plaza and the buildings surrounding it through Lopez's eyes one day when we took a walk. In the same way that Louise Taichert had repopulated East Las Vegas for me with the ghosts of her girlhood, he unfolded Old Town's history amid a rich trove of boyhood memories as we stopped every few feet. Behind the Plaza Hotel he pointed to some empty parking lots. "This block was entirely covered with Ilfeld warehouses," he remarked. "There was one big brick warehouse on the westernmost side of the block and over here a huge frame structure for wool storage. I used to go into them and play around when I was a boy. Then at the end of the block is where the Romeros built the first courthouse and jail. Although Miguel Romero wasn't among the 36 settlers who obtained the original land grant, he was one of the 118 grantees who were deeded land a month later. I think of him as the real founding father of this town. Nobody else but Don Miguel had any money. That's because the Romero family was involved with gold mining before he came here."

We had turned the corner and were standing at the northeast corner of the plaza. "Look here," he said, gesturing to embrace half the block. "Don Miguel built his hacienda right on this spot. It had a big courtyard, or placita, in the middle and an orchard and gardens running down to the river. Later his sons constructed great mansions, which were also near the plaza. Before it burned down I knew the one his oldest son, Trinidad, built alongside the acequia on South Gonzales Street very well. It was big and beautiful inside and had white columns in front. We always called it the Ilfeld mansion because Charles and Adele Ilfeld had bought it from Trinidad Romero when Trinidad built an even bigger mansion out in Romeroville."

On the north side of Bridge Street where it runs into the plaza stands the Romero Block, built in 1919 by Don Miguel Romero's grandsons, Cleofes and Secundino. According to Lopez, during Secundino's years as patrón, he was the most formidable of the Romeros. "He ran the Republican Party, he selected all the state officials, and San Miguel County was called 'Sec's empire.' Cleofes's son, also named Cleofes, was called Cokey, and I knew him well in my childhood. He ran the place as a sundries store, and the beautiful soda fountain that is still there is where I would come in the fifties. He and his family lived upstairs. His daughter Arabella was, and still is, one of my dear friends. Because we

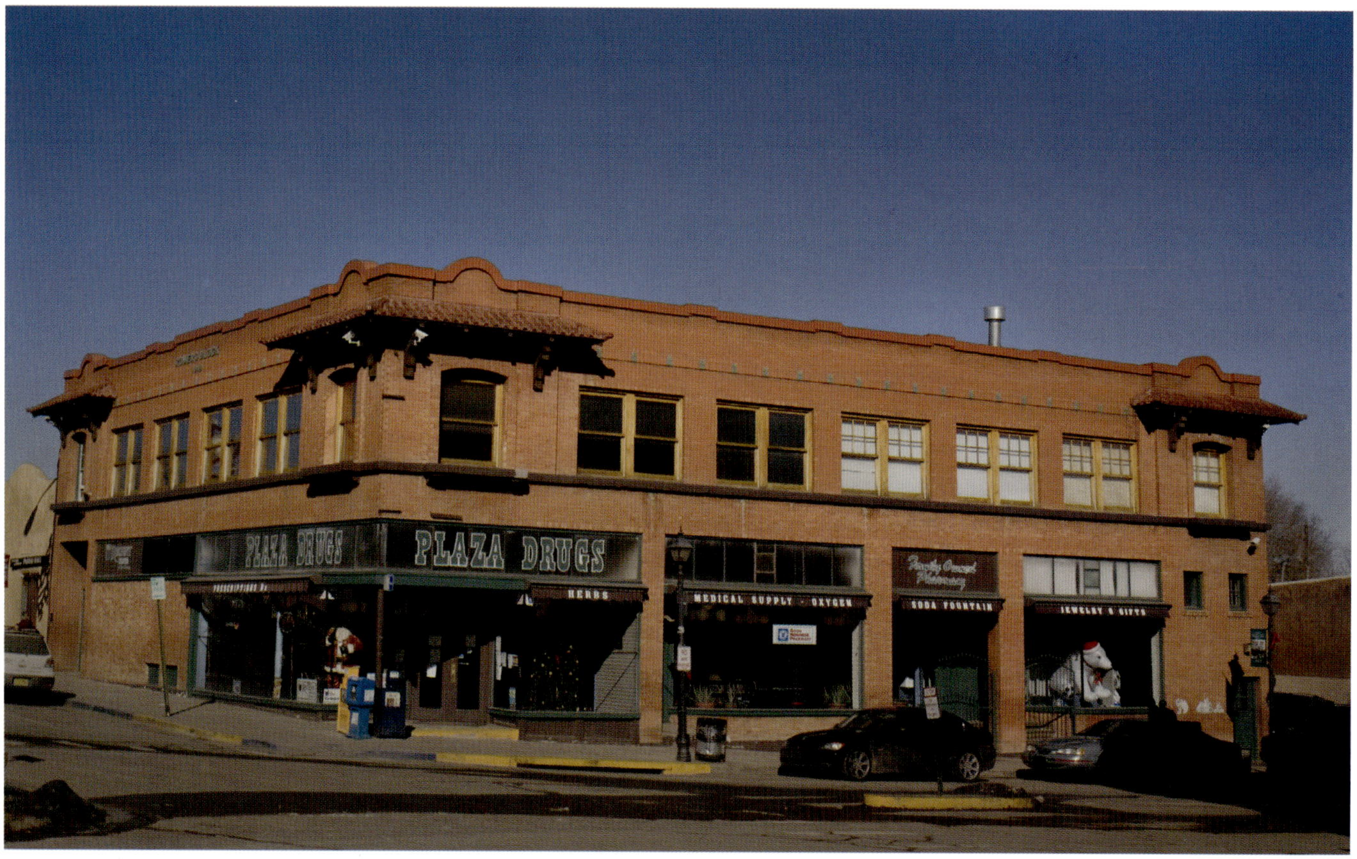

Romero Block

played in the plaza when we were kids, she and I would say that we had the best front yard in town."

On the opposite side of Bridge Street we admired the handsome corner structure built as the First National Bank by the Raynolds bothers, Jefferson and Joshua. Lopez explained, "They got here just ahead of the railroad and built their first bank on the west side of the plaza. They were followers of the railroad, the kind of guys who wanted to get there first and start a bank in whatever town the train was going to come to next. They built this in 1880 as their permanent place of business. Isn't it a beautiful building?" Pointing above my head, he said, "Look up, see the letters on the side of the building just above the first floor." I read, "Donaldo Martinez West Las Vegas School District Administration building." Lopez said, "I'm so glad that in 1993, after Tiny had retired from the political scene, and well before he died in 2006, I was chairman of the West school board and was able to get the building named for him. Taking me inside the door, he pointed to a plaque beneath a photograph of his mentor and said, "Read what I wrote and put on it." I studied the words on the plaque:

In honor of Donaldo Tiny Martinez
Chairman, West Las Vegas Board of Education (1961–1978)
District Attorney (1957–1972)
District Judge (1979–1985)
Leader of His People
Who Championed Our Causes
And Awakened Our Spirit

"He 'championed our causes and awakened our spirit.'— Isn't that beautiful?"

Moving up the block on the south side of the plaza, we paused in front of the imposing derelict building with the sign "Navajo Textiles." Lopez told me that this was originally the Rosenwald store and warehouse. "Emmanuel and his brother Joseph, who were from Bavaria, came here in the late 1850s. They were among the very first Jewish merchants in Las Vegas. You know, when you hear how some Hispanics still resent past Anglo prejudice, they don't include the Jews. Look, they settled with us here in Old Town. The Rosenwalds, Charles Ilfeld—they all spoke Spanish. Emmanuel Rosenwald even gave his son a Spanish name: Cecilio. Isn't that wonderful? The firm became Rosenwald and Son, and after his father and uncle died, Cecilio expanded into the amusement business and built the Coronado movie theater across from the firehouse in New Town."

Lopez next called my attention to the handsome stone building built in 1883 by the second Romero brother, Eugenio, father of Cleofes and Secundino. "It's called the court building, but it never was really used to try cases because the big courthouse next to Our Lady of Sorrows Church was already going up. It's been used for just about everything since then, including the Obama headquarters in the last election. Benigno, the fourth of the Romero brothers, was the one who built the Plaza Hotel, where my mother had her first restaurant until the 1960s, when we moved over to this side of the plaza. Here is where Tiny and his gang would hang out," he said, pointing to a corner of the room on the other side of the window of what had once been Mama Lucy's restaurant. "His table was over there." The next building we passed was the Victory Bar, a celebrated Las Vegas landmark and, until recently, when the owner, Rose Peña, closed it, the last of the many bars that once populated the area around the plaza and along Bridge Street. "Imagine, it's been in the Peña family since 1919!" Lopez exclaimed. "And here is where Henry Beisman, who was our town surveyor, had his business. He and his wife and their two boys made their home in the building. His son Gary, who lives outside of town, stays here part time to look after the building. And right over there before it burned down was the big two-story building where Trinidad Romero, oldest of the five Romero brothers, had his mercantile business, Romero and Son."

Crossing the street, Lopez showed me a vacant lot next to the police station. "This is one of the lost treasures of Las Vegas," he said. "Here is where Don Margarito Romero had his big store. He was the youngest of the Romero brothers. It ran the whole length of the block and up to where his huge mansion—one of the finest ever built in this town—stood across the street from the church. Then in the 1950s and 60s the store belonged to an eccentric Jewish man named Eli Stein. He lived in back but was never open for business. The place just sat there with all the old merchandise still on display. I am probably the only one who ever got to go into the old store. That's because, like everyone else, Eli loved my mom. He ate in her restaurant practically every day, and I can remember how on her birthday he would take me in the store and open up one of those dusty display cases and say, 'Pick out a present for Lucy.' I witnessed firsthand all that beautiful cutlery, china, clothing, hats, and then we'd settle on a gift for my mom. I don't know why he never opened the store again. It just stood there until the day it burned down in 1974."

As we walked along the block on the west side of the plaza, we paused in front of Plaza Antiques. My guide continued, "This is where the first church was, and after the diocese sold it, it became a shoe store and then a grocery store. After that it was rebuilt as a Territorial-style small hotel, one of several around the plaza. All my lifetime until recently it was where Tru-Parts Auto Supply was." A few doors down, as we passed a sign that said "Music Album," he remarked. "Selsa Rubio and her husband bought that building in 1947, and it's been a music store since then. She's still there." Taking a few steps further, we paused in front of the Moresque yellow-brick Veeder Building, built in 1895 and recently renovated. Attached to this building is an earlier two-story pink brick structure with a pediment and tall arched second-story windows above a ground-floor plate-glass storefront. "This was also owned by the Veeders," Lopez said. "When I was young I knew Mrs. Veeder who lived in the apartment upstairs. Her daughter, Katherine Peterson, lived next door in the old Veeder carriage house. They ran an insurance agency, and the post office was in back. When Tiny bought the building from Mrs. Veeder, it became his law office."

Before we parted that day, Lopez reasserted his belief that the old patrón system worked well in its time. Reiterating his admiration for Tiny Martinez, he concluded, "Tiny played such an important part in making Las Vegas what it is today, which so many people take for granted. He was my mentor and role model, and I am proud to say that. I have always tried to follow in his footsteps, and without his example I would have never succeeded. So I persevered with my studies and became a lawyer just like Tiny, and I became district attorney just like him. For fourteen years I was chairman of the school board, as Tiny had been, and for more than a decade I was the Democratic Party chairman, as he had been. I also held all those positions at the same time, just like Tiny had done. I'm proud to say that he and I are the only ones who ever did that, and I feel proud and blessed that we were so close and that he believed in me."

Asserting that the sense of ownership of place through politics and history has been the motivating force in his life, Lopez acknowledged that times have changed. Although Tiny Martinez's legacy is still entrenched in Las Vegas, the political system that ensured allegiance to the patrón and his values is becoming a thing of the past. He told me that now that he has retired from his leadership role he has no regrets but does wonder how things will work out in the future in what he considers to be a vacuum in which no one person is in control and everyone is going in a different direction. Somewhat wistfully, he concluded, "For me, Las Vegas has been a little empty since Tiny passed away."

MARTIN SUAZO, SR. AND MARTIN SUAZO JR.

To learn more about Las Vegas politics today, I met on separate occasions with Martín Suazo, Sr., who was one of Tiny Martinez's close associates and a daily habitué at the table at Mama Lucy's where the great patrón made deals and doled out favors, and with Martín Suazo Jr., the current Democratic County Chairman for San Miguel County. Like Jesus Lopez, Suazo Sr. sees the formidable patrón as a leader of his people who amassed power through politics in the interest of justice rather than as an iron-fisted political boss wielding power for its own sake,. "You see," he told me when we were having coffee one day, "he was a civil rights person and there was a disparity here. It's not fair when you live in a society that is sixty to seventy percent Hispanic to neglect this section of the population."

Retired now, Suazo Sr., still observes the rule of obedience to the patrón. It is telling that, although Martinez was already dead, Suazo felt that he had to receive his blessing before undertaking his current mission to teach young people to shoot basketball not as a coach would teach a player on a team but as a form of individual spiritual concentration leading to self-esteem. "Tiny had originally discouraged it," he said, "but then he came to me in a dream and told me, 'Don't ever give up on what you believe is right.' "

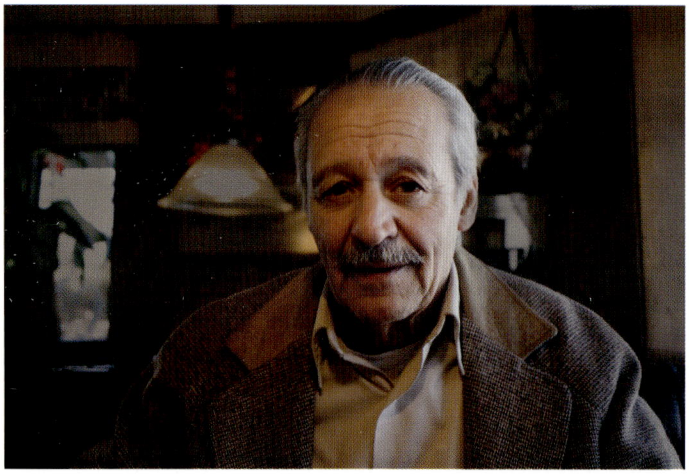

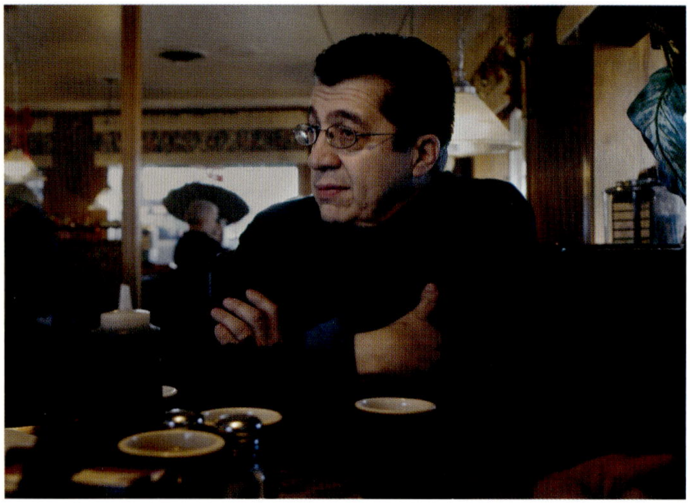

Martin Suazo, Sr.

Martin Suazo, Jr.

For the most part inactive in local politics today, Suazo Sr. still plays a role behind the scenes. But now it is Suazo Jr. who is found every morning drinking coffee at a round corner table at the Hillcrest Restaurant on Grand Avenue amid a circle of regular breakfasters. Although his position as San Miguel Democratic Party Chairman gives him prominent political stature, Suazo Jr. claims, "Mostly we just talk about sports." However, even if he does not hold sway over the six or seven men who appear there every day in the same way Tiny Martinez did when his father sat at the patrón's table at Mama Lucy's, the Hillcrest serves as a valuable listening post, and the morning meetings allow the currency of information to pay off in the process of local decision-making.

Suazo Jr. shies away from the label *patrón*. "Technically there aren't any patrones anymore," he told me one day over lunch at the Spic & Span, while at the same time claiming with assurance that the patrón system is still very much in force. He then went on to explain how the system works now. Although he is in a politically influential position, he asserted that, unlike Lopez, Tiny Martinez, Judge Armijo, or the Romeros, he did not see himself as a benevolent despot with absolute control over the electoral process and the jobs that are the rewards for personal and party loyalty. "I am more of a consensus builder," he said. "And I will get out and do anything I ask anyone else to do, you name it, whatever needs to be done to help the Democratic candidates get elected. Tiny and Jesus would never do this. Everything was behind closed doors back then, and they decided who could come talk with them. It was always the party faithful—those who had done something for them. At the same time—and this may sound self-serving—I consider myself a protector of the people just like they were and the old patrones before them. It's not that one way or the other is better; Jesus was my mentor and the one who taught me how to get it done. But things are different now. It's just that I am more inclusive, whereas Tiny and Jesus were more exclusive and rewarded just the people who were their close political allies. I know I am being criticized for letting younger people into the inner circle of the party. I still believe loyalty is important, but I like to operate somewhat differently. I'll get out and put signs in people's yards along with all the other campaign workers."

Like Lopez, Martin Suazo Jr. has a firm grasp on local political history, an asset in a place where tradition counts for a great deal. Even though circumstances have changed, the system hasn't, no matter which party is in control of San Miguel County. As is true elsewhere, politics and the state of the economy and the rules under which it operates direct the attitudes and actions of the people. The peculiarities of Northern New Mexico's history perhaps serve to make this truth more conspicuous than elsewhere. Suazo explained, "When Judge Armijo was alive, the county was still Republican, but since the New Deal work programs in the Great Depression we have been at least eighty percent Democratic. And even though our population is only 21,000 for the county, in close elections where 4,000 votes make the difference, the state politicians and presidential candidates come to us looking for support. But the most important thing is to be able to hand out jobs. Unlike in Judge Armijo's day when he could give out land from the bench to his cronies, we are now a seventy percent government-driven economy. The land grant issue is essentially dead, even though people still resent what Judge Armijio did to breach the Treaty of Guadalupe Hidalgo. But that is in the past. Today the eight hundred to a thousand jobs at the State Hospital are our mainstay in terms of employment."

I wanted to know how the patrón system works with regard to the dispensation of jobs. "In the old days," Suazo said, "The patrón could just give orders on a slip of paper, and a person would get a job. But after the State Personnel Act of 1978, everyone had to take an exam to qualify. Still, when it gets down to two or three candidates for a job, I can call up the administrator of the hospital, who is appointed by the governor, and say who should get it. But I don't just do this without listening first. Maybe a precinct chairman has a recommendation, and I will say to hire that one. In the old days patrones would sometimes lobby against someone trying to get a job. I would never do that. Jobs are too precious a commodity. If you try to punish someone for not doing things your way, you hurt a whole family."

I asked about the impact of federal programs on other forms of government employment in Las Vegas. "Have you seen all the road construction going on lately?" he replied. "That is because of the Obama Administration's American Recovery and Reinvestment Act. The Highway Department is a huge employer for us. Even though State Personnel controls those jobs, most of the Highway Department commissioners are my friends, and if somebody applies for one I can put in a good word with them. To get hired they still have to go through the personnel review process, but when it gets down to who gets the job, I can pick up the phone and call the district engineer. We also get some HUD [U.S. Department of Housing and Urban Development] monies under the Community Development Block Grants, and how these are spent is at the discretion of the state and local governments. This gives us funds for everything from water improvement projects to senior centers, and that's another source of jobs. If the chairman of this program is smart and understands how politics works in New Mexico, he will call me. But when it comes to actually handing out the jobs as in the old days of the patrones, I still stay above the fray and try to be careful of how I do things because it's not like in the past—when the patrón had complete control." When I told him that I had been talking to people who were interested in restarting the town's economy through private enterprise, he reminded me, "The real economy of Las Vegas is the Highway Department, the schools, the hospital—that's what keeps the place going." He further reminded me, "Here in Las Vegas everything is politics. It is all about who you know who can help you. That's our real business here."

Land and Water

No matter how energetically the political pot is stirred, certain fundamental realities govern human affairs more powerfully than any patrón. Water is the lifeblood of every community, and the way land is settled, used, and disputed is the essential precondition of the habitation of place. Contested water rights loom larger than ever in the political culture of all parts of the arid West as increasing development puts acute pressure on a finite resource. This is true in Las Vegas, even though, according to recent census figures. its population of around 13,700 is steadily dropping. The community derives its water supply from two principal sources: about 90 percent comes from the Gallinas River and about 10 percent from the more than fifty-year-old Taylor Well Field west of town, which only has two wells currently in operation. Repairing the other wells is prohibitive, and when the two functioning ones are pumping water, nearby domestic wells are prone to run dry. Furthermore, the hundred-year-old Peterson Dam, which theoretically impounds 200 acre-feet of water per year, is leaking at the rate of 60 million gallons annually. In times of drought when there is insufficient snowmelt or rain, Las Vegas lives even more precariously close to the edge. In addition, the Gallinas is the source of the acequia system, and those farmers who still maintain diversion ditches must continually assert their historic water rights. But for whatever purpose water is used, competing claims for the allocation of this precious and scarce commodity create a political picture of Byzantine complexity.[3]

ANDREW FELDMAN

To learn more about water issues in Las Vegas I went to see Andrew Feldman, a geologist and hydrologist who is the head of the Department of Science, Math, and Engineering Technology at Luna Community College. A native of Detroit, Feldman lived in Florida for twenty-one years, including the time he spent in graduate school at Florida State University in Tallahassee. In 2002 he accepted an offer to teach geology at Highlands, leaving in 2005 to chair his own department at Luna. Like other transplants to Northern New Mexico, he and his wife fell in love with the place for its climate, scenery, and proximity to Taos's incomparable ski slopes and the hiking trails in the Pecos Wilderness. They remodeled one of the lovely old Victorian houses on Sixth Street, and although he might be able to find better career opportunities elsewhere, for the foreseeable future they have no intention of forsaking Las Vegas and its agreeable lifestyle.

Civic involvement is another tie that binds Feldman to Las Vegas. As a member of the City Council from 2008 to 2012—incidentally, the first non-Hispanic to be elected to municipal office here in the past thirty years or so—he was able to bring his expertise to the table in the debate over solutions to the thorny political and economic issues surrounding the town's acute water problem. When we met in the summer of 2011, because of the previous year's lack of rainfall and snowmelt, the Gallinas River as well as some private wells had gone dry and Las Vegas had only a forty-day supply of water in reserve.

"The water situation is critical, and I'd say it is the Number One issue this town faces," Feldman told me as I sat across from him in his office. "Actually, jobs are the Number One issue, if we are going to stop domestic violence and drug abuse," he corrected himself, "but that's a problem that can't be solved until we secure Las Vegas's water future, which will allow us to create such things as light industry and thus more opportunities for employment."

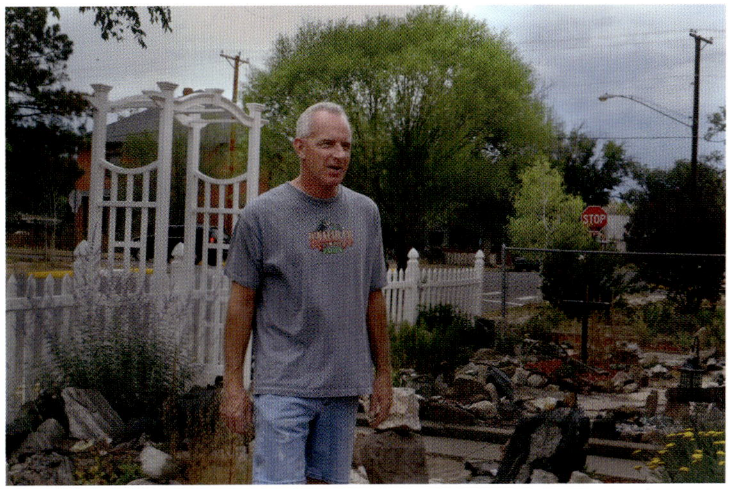

Andrew Feldman

Why, I wondered, was water an even more dire problem in Las Vegas than in other parts of the high desert of Northern New Mexico? "Come over here, and I will show you," he said, unrolling a topographical map and spreading it on a table. Pointing to Las Vegas, he traced the Gallinas corridor through the forested mountains. To the east of the forests' deep green, the rest of the map was colored tawny yellow, denoting the midcontinent expanse of almost pancake-flat land. It was clear from looking down at the map that Las Vegas sits on the line separating two great geological regions—the vast, level grasslands of the Great Plains and the high ridges, peaks, abrupt slopes, and deep valley canyons that form the southernmost end of the Rockies. "Here is what happens," Feldman explained. "The prevailing atmospheric currents move across this part of the continent from southwest to northeast. As moisture-laden air masses hit the western slopes of the Sangre de Cristos, it rains or snows but the precipitation is not carried further east to the other side of the mountains. This creates what we call a rain shadow. We get our best rain and snow storms when low-pressure systems from the Gulf of Mexico come our way, but these types of storms are pretty rare."

Drawing his finger in a circle around a small patch of map containing Las Vegas, Feldman continued, "Not only are we in the rain shadow here, but also we have a watershed of only eighty-four square miles. The situation becomes more complicated when you realize that our supply is pretty much restricted to this particular water basin since the Office of the State Engineer doesn't easily permit intrabasin transfer of water rights. This means that we can't divert water from the Mora River a few miles away because that water flows into the Canadian River, whereas the Gallinas is part of the Pecos River drainage system. We have to abide by our interstate stream compact agreements and send water to Texas. So the situation is this: We only get around eighteen inches a year of precipitation to begin with, and we can't buy or borrow water rights from outside our own watershed. On top of that, there is this arcane system of Spanish law that complicates the allocation of the water we do have.

"You've got 29,000 acre-feet[4] of 'paper' water rights and an average of only 14,000 acre-feet of river flow, so who does water really belong to? This year we will be lucky to see 7,000 acre-feet of flow, about half of the average. As a scientist I look at it as a limited resource that has to be apportioned rationally. With an approximately 50 percent loss, the acequia system is very inefficient and an outdated means of delivering agricultural water. In addition, 95 percent of the *parcientes*—people with water rights and property along the acequias—don't grow anything and therefore don't need the water for crops like their ancestors did. Nowhere else in the country do you have the kind of water law that is governed by seniority, with priority being determined by historical compacts rather than by current needs. The supply of water from our main source, the Gallinas, to the 14,000 people who live in Las Vegas is therefore restricted by the politics of the acequia owners and state water rights law."

To meet Las Vegas's near-desperate need for water, other sources besides the Gallinas need to be tapped, but that supply is also limited. Feldman explained how the strata of sedimentary rocks covering some parts of the Precambrian bedrock of the region were insufficient in thickness to serve as an adequate aquifer. Being uncertain, precipitation often fails to adequately recharge the groundwater supply contained within these strata. Nevertheless, in certain parts of the region where groundwater does exist, municipal wells have been drilled, and homeowners not connected to city water mains must, of course, dig private wells. With continuing drought, the level of subsurface water has dropped by 350 feet in the past few years, and it is feared that the several city-owned wells in the area just southwest of town may run dry. "The aquifers in the region are not extensive, and the lack of precipitation limits recharge," Feldman reiterated. "You can see the crystalline bedrock sticking up at the surface everywhere you look in the mountains, and these are not aquifer rocks. Overall it's a pretty complicated geology."

Storrie Lake[5] impounds about 22,000 acre-feet of diverted water from the Gallinas. The city pays what Feldman and others consider an exorbitant amount of money to the Storrie Project Water User's Association (SPWUA) to store the 500 acre-feet of water that the city is allowed to bring back into the Gallinas to feed the municipal water system. The SPWUA irrigates land and provides water to the Las

Vegas National Wildlife Refuge. The New Mexico Department of Energy, Minerals and Natural Resources holds a lease on the 1,100-acre lake surface and 82 acres of surrounding parkland. During high river flows, the excess water is diverted to keep Storrie Lake level as a reservoir and recreational water body. Again compounding the situation is New Mexico's historic prior appropriation doctrine. When river flows are low, there is a continuous battle between those with acequia water rights and those who see the city's system as endangered by anything that siphons off the limited water supply. The acequia owners all along the Gallinas claim senior water rights, contending that they should not be deprived of their share by the city, whose water rights are legally junior to theirs. Litigation and mediated negotiation have yet to resolve this issue, which has been festering since 1958.

What, I asked, must be done if Las Vegas is to survive long-term drought? "Well, there are options," said Feldman, "but they all have their drawbacks. First, you can drill for water in sandstone with gypsum in it, but then you would have to desalinate the water because of its high calcium sulfate content. Getting rid of the salts is expensive, since you'd need a five-to-ten-million-dollar desalinization plant that would only net us about 200,000 gallons a day, less than one-sixth of daily use. Besides that, you'd have to have a twenty-five-acre pond to dry out the rejected brine. Even if you sold the 25,000 pounds of gypsum you can extract from every million gallons of water processed, you'd have to build a rail spur to ship it. Another option we are looking at is reclaiming effluent water from the sewage treatment plant through reverse osmosis. We are using gray-water effluent now on parks and the municipal golf course, but as far as making it potable you have to consider the 'yuck' factor. Still, this is being done around the world and is a viable option in my opinion. Conservation is our most important strategy at the moment. We are now under Stage Four water restrictions. People need to realize that we are in a midlatitude arid steppe climate, and they just shouldn't be growing grass lawns. Instead we should all be xeriscaping, using drought-tolerant native plants."

Feldman agreed when I remarked how hard it seemed to bring about change in Las Vegas. "It's a political issue as well as a water issue," he said. "There is a certain mentality among some folks here, and they do not want to see the town change or grow. As long as they can get by, they would rather see no change. We cannot handle a large increase in population due to the water issue, but we can have economic growth. The patrón system may be losing its power, but it's still a factor. The town is changing, of course, but very slowly. Las Vegas is a perfect place for historical and ecological tourism as well as other enterprises that would use very little water. Some light industry would be feasible, including certain kinds of parts manufacturing and also the fabrication of forest products that made use of our timber resources. But there is not very much entrepreneurship from within the community. Many people are afraid Las Vegas will become like Santa Fe, and it's not because they don't want to be culturally sophisticated as much as they don't want to relinquish political power.

I think this, in addition to a lack of funding, explains why there has been so much neglect over the years in addressing water issues."

Although the problem may seem intractable, Feldman is one of the Las Vegans who want to continue to push the town forward toward a solution. As I was getting ready to leave, he said, "I may be crazy, but I am thinking of running for mayor next time. If our current mayor, Alfonso Ortiz, who is as committed to finding a solution to our water problem as I am, doesn't stand for re-election, I may throw my hat in the ring. I'm probably the only member of the Green Party in New Mexico, but in municipal elections it doesn't matter which political party you belong to. The water issue is just too important to ignore. I started off my career in politics as a member of the Utility Advisory Committee of the city, and for the past five years I have been president of the Las Vegas Community Water Board, a nonprofit organization that a group of us formed in 2006. We're government-sanctioned but an independent grassroots entity committed to finding solutions. The water report that I was instrumental in drawing up has been put on the shelf, but slowly we are making inroads. I think people respect the fact that I have a sound perspective on the issue. There are political and economic realities that have to be faced, and even if there are no answers, we have to move forward."

When I went to see him a few months later Feldman's role in moving forward with a solution to the water situation had been stymied and he no longer had a seat on the City Council. As we sat on his front porch facing a picket-fence-enclosed rock garden made up of geological specimens he has collected over the years, he told me that he decided not to run again because he had some stress-induced health problems.[6] In addition, Ortiz, who had stood for mayoral re-election and won, was on the outs with him and had not reappointed him to the Utility Advisory Committee. He suggested that this was because of the mayor's reluctance to sign a recently enacted piece of legislation spearheaded by the Coalition for Community Rights, an organization he supports.[7]

"Before I've always moved somewhere else every ten years or so, and there is nothing tying me here now," he told me. "But I have no intentions of leaving Las Vegas at the moment. I just felt it was time to regroup after four years of political life." We discussed the remodeling project he and his wife were then engaged in, and after he had taken me inside and shown me their state-of-the-art kitchen and the closet where they plan to put stairs to the new master bedroom in the attic space above, it did indeed appear that for Feldman Las Vegas has become home.

WILLIAM GONZALES

William Gonzales is a descendant of the settlers of the San Augustín land grant in a part of the Gallinas valley downstream from Las Vegas. The San Augustín grant is a 3,600-acre subgrant of the original vast Las Vegas grant. Because of its location in one of the narrow, cliff-protected river valleys of the Sangre de Cristo Mountains, the San Augustín grant was not large enough to fall prey to the avarice of nineteenth-century Anglo investment syndicates. Instead, the tiny settlements embraced by canyon walls throughout the length of the valley have collapsed into picturesque ruin as their inhabitants have been drawn away from their old agrarian way of life by economic opportunities elsewhere. Although the San Augustín land grant is held in common by the heirs of the historic owners, they are able to sell their private holdings within it, should they desire to do so.

After returning from a twenty-year stint in the army, Gonzales and his wife, Ginny Johnson, restored a crumbling adobe house that had belonged to his uncle in the village of Lourdes at the head of the valley canyon. They reside in town, but he drives the fifteen miles to and from the ranch almost daily in order to engage in the agrarian lifestyle of his ancestors. As mayordomo of the acequia that runs though the San Augustín Valley, Gonzales supervises the schedule of sequential water allocation, as well as the ditch's annual spring cleaning when the brush and debris that have collected over the winter are removed. Ginny would like to travel more, but, having lived in several parts of the world during his time in the military, William is inclined to stay home and take care of his responsibilities as a farmer—irrigating, baling hay, tending livestock, growing vegetables and fruit trees. He is clearly a man who has wedded himself to his own piece of earth.

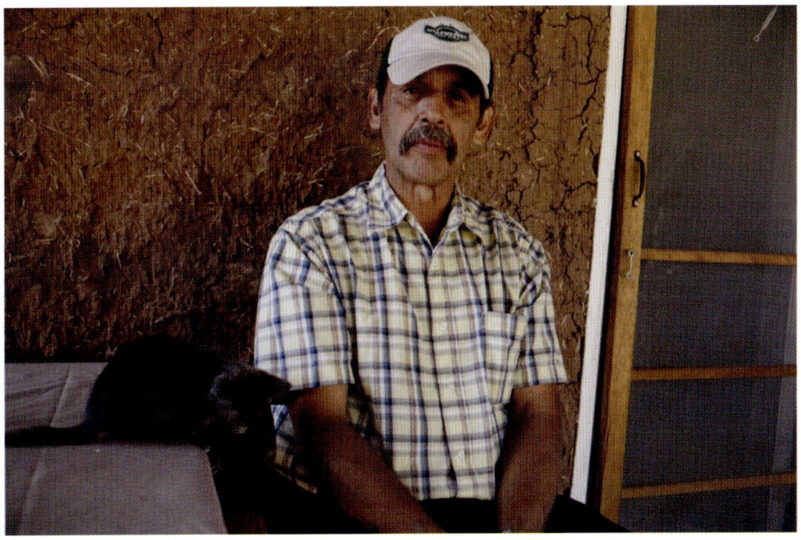

William Gonzales

As Feldman reported, although many acequias are now unused, the water rights associated with them are hotly contested. In 1988 the New Mexico Acequia Association was formed as an advocacy group to protect the autonomy and self-governance procedures of the state's 1,500 independent acequia associations, most of which were formed in Spanish colonial times. Within this parental structure, Gonzales serves as president of the Río de Las Gallinas Acequia Association, which was created in 1991 as a means of assisting the local acequia parcientes in this particular riparian corridor. When we met one day in his office in the New Mexico Legal Aid building, he pulled out a large map and showed me the acequia diversions that form a chain running alongside the Gallinas and its El Porvenir tributary from their headwaters all the way past his own acequia in the San Augustín valley to the point where the river empties into the Pecos.

Although he spends a lot of his time wrestling with legal problems, Gonzales also sees his work as an educational mission. He cares less, however, about education as a means of protesting the wrongs of the past than about proselytizing the preservation of the acequia system as a living landscape component of the town. Relying on an informed approach based on mapping and fact-collecting rather than political activism, like Feldman he speaks the language of acre-feet of water and can point to the places on the map of the Gallinas where water is diverted to the city, to Storrie Lake, and to the various acequias that tap the river. Negotiations after years of litigation between the Río de Las Gallinas Acequia Association and the city over the allocation of water from the river resulted in a tenuous agreement, but it has since fallen apart.

The drive into the San Augustín Valley is scenically thrilling. The road passes through pastures and winds around rocky ledges before it dips down to the river next to which the ruins of Lourdes are situated. For those who are romantically inclined, there is a kind of poetry in the collapsing rock walls and crumbling adobe bricks of the houses and barns. Thanks to Cornerstones, a not-for-profit organization that helps preserve the near-ruined churches of the depopulated little towns throughout Northern New Mexico, the church of San Augustín has been recently repaired and stabilized with the application of an exterior coat of plaster, which helps mitigate the surrounding aspect of desolation.

I had a chance to see the whole valley with William and Ginny one summer day. As we bounced along the rocky and rutted road in William's four-wheel-drive pickup, we passed alongside first one acequia and then another in the chain of river diversions he had pointed out earlier on the map. Sloping down from these acequias toward the river were gravity-irrigated fields, after which the canyon opened up into rangeland. Pointing up at one of the canyon ridges, Gonzales said, "That's a good place to find arrowheads. I've collected several in that spot over there when I've been out hunting. There are actually lots of Indian ruins here in the valley. This was also where buffalo liked to graze up on top and shelter down below."

Past a small meadow called Alcan del Gato we came to the remains of the little village of Concepción. Archaeologists would recognize the mounded earthen forms as places where former adobe structures had simply melted back into the earth. There were also roofless walls of several buildings in a transitional state of decomposition. One partially preserved ruin, the church, is still standing, a sign that someone has cared enough to make occasional repairs. After peering inside, we walked up the hillside above the church to a graveyard with headstones that look as if they were carved in the same labored, unskilled manner by a single hand. William was able to find the grave of one of his Gonzales ancestors before we turned and walked back to the truck.

As we followed the river, the valley continued to broaden. He named the mesas and ridges as we went along, and when he told me story after story of things he had experienced and found on each, I realized that he must have the same intimate knowledge of this valley as the vanished Indian occupants once had—a true perception of place and an ability to read a landscape in minutest detail that few people can claim anymore.

While he and Ginny were cooking dinner on another occasion when I visited them, I had a memorable walk through the village of Lourdes at dusk. The warm golden-brown adobe ruins against the backdrop of a magnificent evening sky, the quiet murmur of water in the acequia, and good country smells of animals, vegetation, and clear air spelled deep peace. For someone who can live without an Internet connection, this is a good place to be. But, of course, because of many things besides global communications—ease of transportation, cheaper food produced by industrial agriculture, K–12 public schools instead of a one-room schoolhouse, plus many other modern conveniences—it is unlikely that Lourdes will ever spring back to life again. Although William's garden, orchard, and hayfield provide an example of the kind of sustainable agriculture that is being strongly advocated today, Ginny likes to point out that there is no profit to be found in the valley of San Augustín other than her husband's contentment in being there and doing what he is doing. Nevertheless, he hopes that, even if none of his three children or other relatives return, someone will still decide to dwell on the land and bring Lourdes back to life. Because of the great natural beauty of the San Augustín valley, there are occasional offers to purchase ranches in the canyon. Still, it is doubtful that anyone will share Gonzales's willingness to undertake the manual labor necessary to perpetuate the old agrarian order of this part of the world.

Ruins, Lourdes

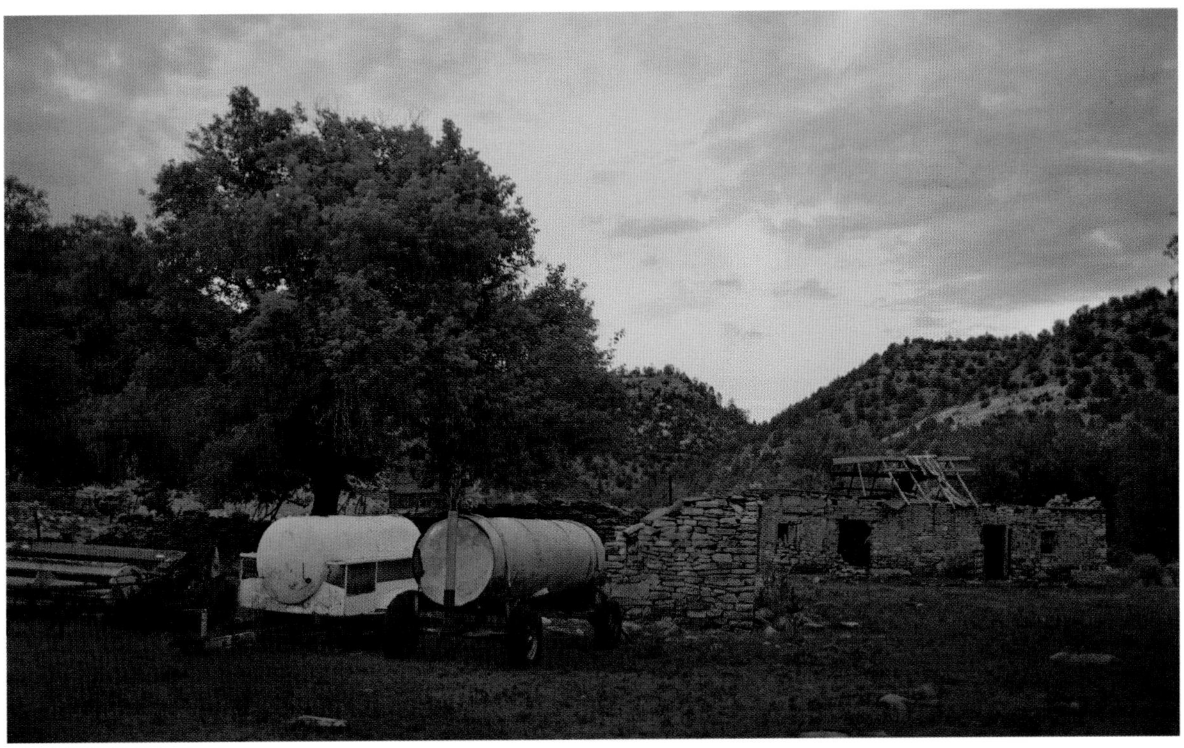

Few if any towns of comparable size have two school districts. Las Vegas does, a carryover from the days when West Las Vegas and East Las Vegas were separate municipalities. The New Mexico State Legislature periodically attempts to pass a bill to consolidate them as one, but this proposal is usually tabled because of strong local opposition. The reason for this resistance goes deeper than the obvious one: consolidation would eliminate the number of administrative jobs now available. A reminder of the persistence of old antipathies, the dual education system perpetuates, at least symbolically, the historically fraught relationship between Hispanic and Anglo residents. However, with an overall municipal population that is currently 83 percent Hispanic, the East Las Vegas side of town can hardly be considered Anglo territory anymore. Nevertheless, for some the legacy of social separation is still expressed in terms of geographic duality, and the term "crossing the bridge" remains symbolically significant.

School Days

East Las Vegas's high school is named Robertson, and West Las Vegas High School is usually referred to as "West" for short. The school colors are red and green respectively, and even among adults there is a good deal of chauvinistic sensitivity about accidentally wearing the "wrong" color to a football game, something that might be interpreted as a badge of allegiance to the opposing side. The Robertson sports teams are called Cardinals, and their counterparts in West Las Vegas are known as the Dons and Lady Dons. In contrast to the chivalric character of the West Las Vegas logo—a heraldic shield bearing a torch flanked by a man and a woman in caballero attire —the Cardinals have as their totem the profile head of a fiercely aggressive crested red bird.

In addition to regular public schools, the West Las Vegas School District includes Rio Gallinas, which is a charter school with a teaching program called Focus Learning by Doing. Villanueva Elementary School serves children who are bussed in from the small towns south of Las Vegas, and the Family Partnership, begun in the 1990s, provides off-site instruction for students at risk and others with special needs. At West Las Vegas High School the enrollment is 93 percent Hispanic, 5½ percent Anglo American, one percent African American, and one-half percent Native American.

The other school district, Las Vegas City Schools, is made up of Robertson High School, Memorial Middle School, and five elementary schools. The composition of the combined student bodies of these East Las Vegas schools is 86.5 percent Hispanic, 14 percent Anglo American, and less than half of one percent African-American. Enrollment figures show a steady drop of around 50 or more students a year over the last ten years, going from around 2,500 students to fewer than 2,000 today. To meet the people behind these facts and statistics, I set aside a few days to visit some of the town's schools and talk with several students and teachers as well as with a former elementary and middle school principal and the two district superintendents.

SHERYL MCNELLIS-MARTINEZ

I went to see Sheryl McNellis-Martinez, the superintendent of Las Vegas City Schools, a few months after her appointment to the position following a two-year period as interim superintendent. She had taken the job at a time when a series of scandals rocked the district. I had followed the revelations of these destabilizing incidents in the *Optic* and was therefore aware that they included a sports coach alleged to have ignored a particularly ugly hazing incident involving members of the Robertson High School football team, the trial of a teacher for long-term sexual relations with a student, the use of educational grant monies by an administrative staff member for personal ends, and the discovery of pornographic material on a school official's computer hard drive. However, as I sat with McNellis-Martinez in the boardroom of the district's headquarters on Douglas Street, our conversation skirted these subjects and focused instead on her vision for the future.

Sheryl McNellis-Martinez

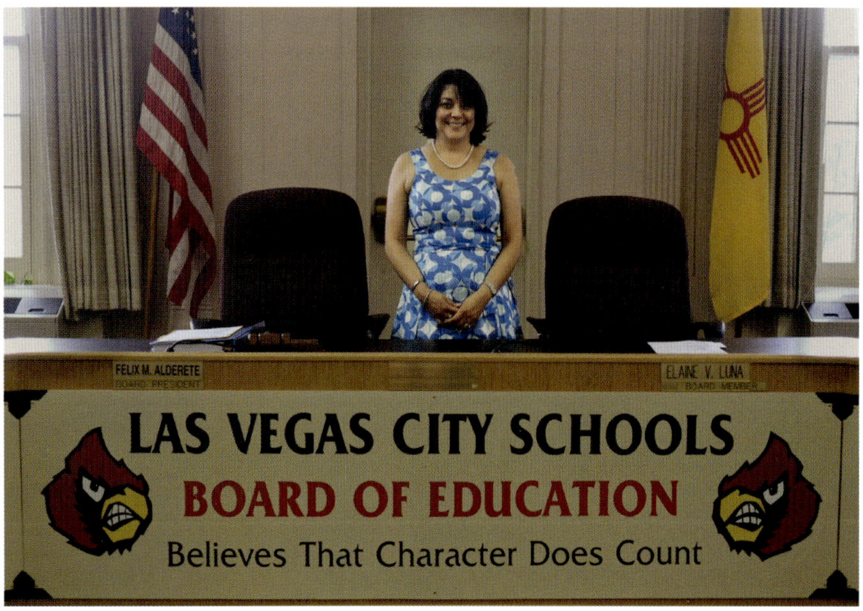

Although born in Las Vegas, McNellis-Martinez lived elsewhere while she was growing up. "I was here until I finished first grade at the Galllinas Street School," she told me. "Then, when my father was accepted in a Ph.D. program at the University of Washington, we moved to Seattle where I grew up. After high school I attended a community college and then moved to Denver where I got a summer job. When I found out that I was making money and could buy clothes and have a good time being on my own and supporting myself, I decided not to go back to school. I was hired by an insurance company to be a statistical analyst, and after that I got a job at the University of Colorado's Health Science Center. After I married my husband and moved to San Diego, where I ran a nurse-midwife clinic operated by the University of San Diego Medical School. Unfortunately, my position underwent a reclassification and I had to leave because I didn't have a college degree. By that time I was pregnant with my second child, so I took stock and decided I'd like to have a career where I could spend more time with my children and be more aware of what they were learning. Getting my degree in education was therefore an obvious choice."

By this time McNellis-Martinez's parents were living in Las Vegas, where her father was a professor and dean at Highlands University. "Because of the low cost of living here I saw that we would be able to get by on one income while I went to school," she explained. "We had every intention of going back to San Diego after three years, but that didn't happen. I ended up with the degree but not my first husband. Now I'm still here after twenty years, and I must say that I can't think of any place better to have brought up my children than in Las Vegas."

Following her graduation from Highlands, McNellis-Martinez commuted from Las Vegas forty-three miles north to Wagon Mound, where she served as a technology-network administrator and programs director for ten years. Back in Las Vegas she was assigned to be in charge of special services for students with learning disabilities and social deficiencies.

Tacitly referring to the series of scandals that had led to her current position as superintendent, she said, "I was only a couple of months into the job when the big turnaround occurred and the superintendent resigned and the school board named me as interim superintendent. They then conducted a broad search for the next year, and after they were unable to find anyone they named me interim superintendent for another year. During that time I felt I was the City Schools steward and responsible for making the district function as it should. But even though I saw what basic initiatives needed to be put in practice, it wasn't until I was offered the job of superintendent that I was able to really take ownership and start to move things at a quicker pace."

The most notable initiative McNellis-Martinez has taken to date is instituting a four-day, rather than a five-day, school week in all the district's schools. Explaining the shift, she said, "We are going to have more researched-based education as we institute instructional strategies based on the Common Core State Standards. This will give us a learning framework that allows students to transfer from one school to another with the same proficiency at each grade level. By having Fridays open we can do more teacher training directed toward learning how to integrate core requirements into the regular classroom curriculum. We will be able to have a set schedule for remedial services, and we can offer more tutoring opportunities. We will have some Friday enrichment classes with thematic instructional units, labs, and other kinds of things teachers can't provide during the other days of the week. There will be more time for the students' club activities, and the free Fridays will also allow us to have a set day for ISSD." When I inquired what the acronym stood for, she said, "In-School Suspension Detention, which is a disciplinary program for kids who have violated rules that are not so serious as to have them kicked out of school." She went on to explain that except in the case of ISSD, Friday school attendance is not mandatory, and both teachers and students have the option to stay home or use the free Fridays for such things as doctor and dentist appointments. "This will cut down on absenteeism of both teachers and students during the rest of the week," she added.

I wondered what kinds of training teachers would receive. McNellis-Martinez replied, "We need to figure out how to bring those teachers who are not qualified to go to conferences up to speed. I am not going to say I don't have any who are qualified; it's just that some teachers have not had the opportunities to hone their teaching skills or see what current research and practice says. Believe it or not, we have teachers who do not yet know how to use e-mail, Word, or PowerPoint. We want to give them a safe place where they won't be embarrassed about stepping forward and letting their peer colleagues know they don't know these kinds of things." As to how this instruction would be offered, McNellis-Martinez said with no sense of contradiction, "There is no budget for outside instruction so our tutorial workshops will be run by peer colleagues who have shown leadership and proficiency using technology."

When I mentioned that I understood that the four-day curriculum was still controversial in some quarters, McNellis-Martinez replied that it had been voted on by the school board, students, teachers, and parents and would be in effect in the coming school year. "It makes absolute sense academically and at the same time it allows us to meet budgetary challenges. Everyone on the staff—teachers and administrators—are taking a 3½ percent pay cut based on a certain number of furlough days. This way we are not forced to lay people off."

Regarding hiring practices, I said that I had been told that the school system was, along with the state hospital, a chief source of patronage opportunities. "What I have encountered thus far is some frustration with not following the political protocol in terms of employment," she replied candidly. "We are carrying a legacy, absolutely. But we have made known publicly that we have a policy that allows us to take a look at people who want to come in who are open-minded to new things."

It is too early to assess the results of the new initiatives McNellis-Martinez has set in motion. With regard to the four-day week, she admits, "We can't determine whether in the other schools who have tried this there is a statistically significant factor in student achievement, but we can say that there hasn't been a negative impact in terms of achievement scores in these places."

RUBEN CORDOVA

Dr. Ruben Cordova, the superintendent of the West Las Vegas School District, was born in Mora Country in the small village of Ojo Feliz near Wagon Mound. Though this area was isolated in his youth before Interstate 25 strung together the small rural communities of Northern New Mexico between Raton and Santa Fe, people came into Las Vegas because it was the hub of the region. "It was the place where you did your shopping," he told me as we sat in his office in the administration building at the southeast corner of the plaza. "When I realized that I could go to college, I came here to Highlands for my education degree, and later I went to the University of Colorado for my doctorate." For Cordova, however, the pull of home was strong, and he never considered living and raising a family anywhere other than the Las Vegas area.

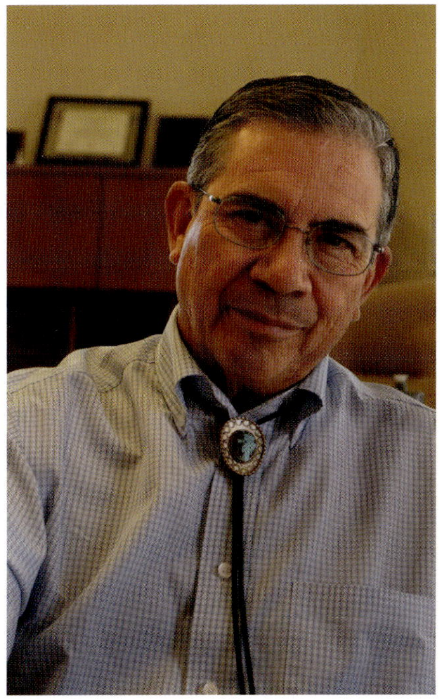

Ruben Cordova

When I went to see Cordova shortly before his resignation in 2012, I asked him to compare his district with that of East Las Vegas. He said that the latter has an advantage inasmuch as its bonding capacity is greater because there are more students living on the east side of town. "Most of the people who move in live on that side because there are more options to buy good houses," he explained. "But for the past nine years we've seen a steady decline in enrollment in both districts. People are moving away from the area to go to places where, unlike here, there has been job growth."

As I had learned from McNellis-Martinez, in addition to the drop in school population there has been a significant decrease in state appropriations to all New Mexico school districts. The two superintendents are coping with their budget deficiencies in different ways. In the case of West Las Vegas, Cordova told me, "We have taken cuts in personnel, but these are all in administration, which is a big category that includes custodians and maintenance employees as well as the people who work in office jobs." When I asked if he thought that the Las Vegas City Schools district's new policy of a four-day school week was a good idea, he replied, "I would never recommend it. Not in a town like this. I see a lot of kids whose parents have to work, and they need supervision at home, which they are not able to get even now. The schools provide supervision as well as education for kids. I see these kids out on the streets both in the daytime and at night. That is not good for them or for the community. It is not good in terms of education either."

According to Cordova, "Right now school grades are not a very popular topic. In terms of the AYP (Annual Yearly Progress) report, we are rated C and D, which is nothing to brag about. Even if we had a rating of A or B, life is getting more complex and difficult, and we need more, not less, education and the best environment for learning we can provide. Why would we want to shortchange the kids by going to a four-day week?" Regarding the optional enrichment courses that are being offered by the schools in East Las Vegas on Fridays, he said, "If you ask kids whether they would like four days or five, of course most are going to say they want to go to school four days a week. Then on the extra day a lot of them will stay home or go out on the streets and get into trouble. We shouldn't allow them to do that. That's not to say that some of our kids don't have responsible parents who would encourage them to take advantage of extracurricular classes and activities. But I am thinking about the ones who need the kind basic guidance and supervision they are not getting at home."

On the perennial topic of district consolidation, Cordova said, "There are these people who are adamantly against it because of the way they were mistreated in the past, and they have good reasons personally. They think that having more control over their children's schools means having more control over their personal destiny. This is a poor school district, and there is a danger in being subsumed by a wealthier one. Our kids offer different challenges, and we have got to be sensitive to those things in order for them to have a chance to be successful."

When I steered the conversation in the direction of specific adolescent problems, Cordova responded with candor, "We used to have a better record with teen pregnancies, but now we have reached a statistic we are not fond of. Our staff is doing what they can to assist those kids; we have a recovery course for ones who need help, and we offer courses online for those who have to stay home with their babies and can't attend school. When it comes to drugs, the principals try to identify suspicious behavior. They usually deal with the problem as best they can and only bring cases to me that are out of the ordinary. I honestly don't know if there are any less drugs being sold in Las Vegas than back when it was known as Smack City. There is also a DWI program, and along with the police we are trying to raise consciousness about that. In my experience the worst time for car accidents is around prom time."

Summing up his attitude toward Las Vegas, Cordova said, "This town is a very caring place. I love the students dearly and will do everything I can to help this district. I feel good that I have been blessed with the opportunity to work in education. That is a privilege, for which I am very grateful."

WEST LAS VEGAS HIGH SCHOOL

To get a first-hand look at the students in West Las Vegas High School, I asked Dr. Cordova if I might visit some classrooms. He directed me to the principal, Gene Parson, who designated Camille Vasquez, a senior, as my companion for the day. Her first class was chorus. When we arrived at the rehearsal stage, which was located at the back of the school cafeteria, the director, a tall, blond young woman who introduced herself as Sarah Oliver, offered me a chair.

Perhaps because New Mexico sees itself as a place with a strong heritage in art and music, the schools in Las Vegas, unlike many public schools in other parts of the country, have not had their budgets eliminated for such classes. That day the honors choir, the one in which Camille sings, was preparing for a competition in which a panel of district judges would determine whether or not these West Las Vegas High School students would go on to the state finals.

Oliver, who, I found out, had graduated from music school only the previous spring, had the unenviable job of stepping into the shoes of a much-admired predecessor who had taken West Las Vegas student choirs into the finals in several district and state competitions. She did not seem daunted, however, and her enthusiastic attitude and conducting skills appeared to have won the respect of the students. Camille, who was in the soprano section, has a lovely voice, and I was pleased to hear such clear tenor and rich baritone notes coming from her male classmates.

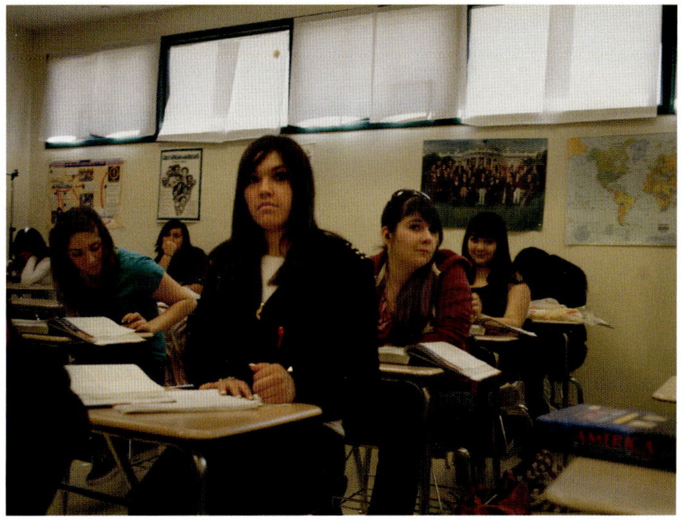

Camille Vasquez

Over lunch in the cafeteria, she and I had a chance to get better acquainted. When I asked her about her family, she told me that her mother works at the state hospital, and her father is a maintenance man at one of the schools in town and also does odd jobs. Neither parent endorses her aspirations to go away to school, "away" meaning Albuquerque, where Camille would like to attend the University of New Mexico. She said, "My dad just wants things simple. He says I should go to Luna Community College here in Las Vegas. But I've already applied and been accepted at UNM and, hopefully, I'll be able to work out my financial assistance plan. My goal is to get into a good nursing program and become a practitioner of some sort or even a doctor. I love going to school, and I really can't see myself not in school," she concluded. I told her that I strongly endorsed her aspiration for higher education, and she replied, "That's what I live for, to learn. I want to leave Las Vegas, at least for a while, and see the outside world. Once I went to Monterey, Mexico, to see my grandmother who lives there. We stayed about a week, and that's the only place I've ever been to besides around here."

The 1:30 class bell was about to ring, so I went to meet another student, Shawntell Tenorio, who had been selected by Parson to escort me to her class in plant science. I entered the classroom expecting to find students with textbooks opened to chapters covering such things as soil improvement, pests and diseases, pruning, grafting, botanical taxonomy, irrigation, and so forth. Instead, two of the boys were filling long, rectangular planting trays halfway to the top with water while one girl painted her fingernails and another busied herself applying mascara. The teacher then dispensed some small brown objects to the class. "These are Jiffy Pellets, seeds contained in compacted peat moss. You just put them in the trays of water until the plants sprout. After that you can take them outdoors and stick them in the ground," she explained. I noticed some trays under fluorescent lights at one end of the room, and sure enough there were a few threads of green sprouting from them. "What is nice about using peat pellets," the teacher added, "is that they're cheap; you can buy thirty-six of them from Walmart for $2.99."

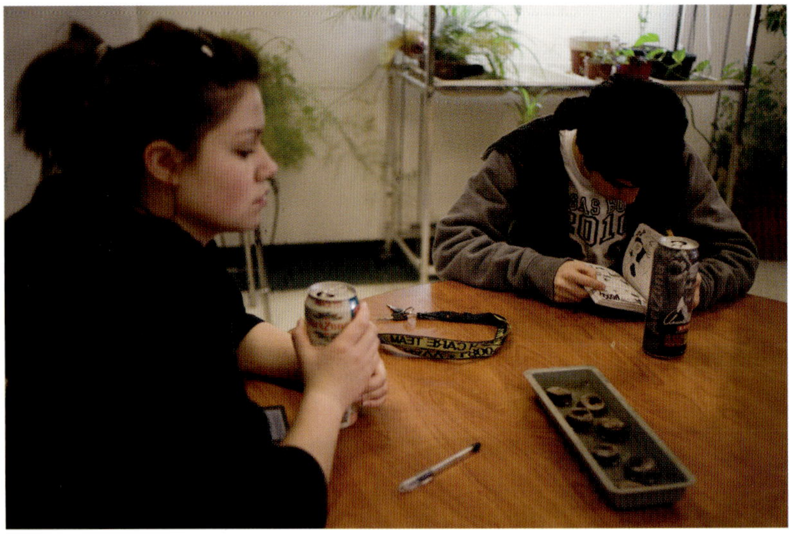

West Las Vegas High School plant science class

Excusing myself early from plant science, I went to find Camille, who had offered to take me to civics. I found an empty desk chair in the next row as she slid into hers and the teacher brought the class to order, with the exception of one boy who was asleep and a girl who was talking on her cell phone. Just as I had expected a different sort of curriculum in plant science, I was surprised to find that rather than instructing the students on comparative systems of government or the societal values embedded in the American Constitution, the Bill of Rights, Supreme Court decisions, and Congressional legislation, he was firing a series of rhetorical questions based on postulates about the Muslim world. A few of the students raised their hands and gave tentative answers. The lesson went somewhat as follows. Teacher: "Why is it okay to kill Osama Bin Laden but not Saddam Hussein?" Student: "Because Bin Laden is an outlaw and Hussein is the head of a country." Teacher: "Would you sit on a plane next to someone who was wearing a turban? You might feel uncomfortable, right?" Students: silent assent. Teacher: "How do you feel about airport security?" Students: No reply. Teacher: "They take away your liquids, right? But then there are all these shops as you go toward the gates that sell the same stuff because they want you to buy the same things that have just been confiscated."

At this point the teacher did in fact get around to discussing the Constitution: "What does it mean that the government has a responsibility to provide for the general welfare?" Answering himself, he said, "I hate April 15, but I still think that paying taxes sure beats living under a dictator. I think it's a pretty good thing to be protected by a Constitution that says I live under a law that lets me do anything I want and be protected." By this time Camille had put her head down on her desk, but the girl in front of her, who was obviously the class's independent thinker, raised her hand. "Sir, what if I don't agree with what you are saying?" The teacher replied, "That's good. You should make up your own mind. I am here sharing as much knowledge as I have, so what you are getting is just somebody's perspective. If you really want to know for yourself, you have to go and read about twenty books." With the exception of the independent thinker, most of the students appeared more bored than daunted by the challenge, and on that note class ended.

In the English class I attended with Shawntell the next day a student-teacher in the graduate education program at Highlands was in charge. The students, whose assignment was to read *Macbeth*, had their books open. "This is our Freud day," he told me as an aside, giving me a list of the psychological definitions he was handing out to the students. I had never approached Shakespeare through the lens of psychoanalysis before, but I could see some relevance to the play as I scanned the list and found such terms as "Anxiety: An intense emotional response caused by the preconscious recognition that a repressed conflict is about to emerge into consciousness"; "Coping: The process of dealing with internal or external demands that are perceived to be threatening or overwhelming"; "Emotion: A complex pattern of changes, including physiological arousal, feelings, cognitive processes, and behavioral reactions, made in response to a situation perceived to be personally significant"; "Hallucinations: False perceptions that occur in the absence of objective stimulation"; and "Phobia: A persistent and irrational fear of a specific object, activity, or situation that is excessive and unreasonable, given the reality of the threat." Only a few of the students were writing in their notebooks, and the room was filled with a genial hum of conversation. There was no teacher-led class discussion. Instead, he walked back and forth between the desks attempting to help the students with the exercise, which was to find five quotes in which applicable psychological terms could be assigned to the characters in the play. As I studied their faces I had to conclude that the comprehension quotient of the class did not seem very high, and I wondered whether an approach that stressed the dramatic qualities and action of *Macbeth* might have made Shakespeare more accessible and engaging for the students.

CHRISTINA PADILLA

After my two days of sitting in on classes at West Las Vegas High School, I wanted to visit a school in East Las Vegas. I therefore arranged to meet Christina Padilla, a sixth-grade student at Memorial Middle School and was delighted to find a pretty eleven-year-old waiting for me at the front desk when I arrived. Her next period was social studies, and after we walked down the hallway to her classroom, I took a seat in the back row. That day the students were studying the Roman Republic, an occasion for learning Roman numerals, and I watched as they diligently copied in their notebooks the X's, V's, and I's that the teacher wrote on the chalkboard, putting the Arabic numeral beside each Roman equivalent.

When the bell rang we joined the exuberant throng of children in the hallway and made our way to Christina's literature class. On the way I noticed a girl Christina's age who was pushing a baby stroller. I looked closely as she wheeled it to her seat a couple of desks in front of Christina's and saw that the infant was artificial, a life-size doll resembling a three-month-old baby. The teacher, who was having a bad bout of laryngitis that day, was nevertheless managing to conduct the class in whispers and sign language. As I watched Christina's neat handwriting move across the page, the "baby" suddenly began to cry. Quietly, the girl who was tending it picked up the doll and patted it on the back as if calming a real baby. Then she got a bottle of what looked like milk out of the pouch of the stroller and proceeded to feed it as the others kept on working. No one's head turned, and when she put the pretend infant back to rest she picked up her pencil and continued with the assignment. Soon the mechanical wailing sounded again, and she dutifully got up and changed the make-believe baby's diapers.

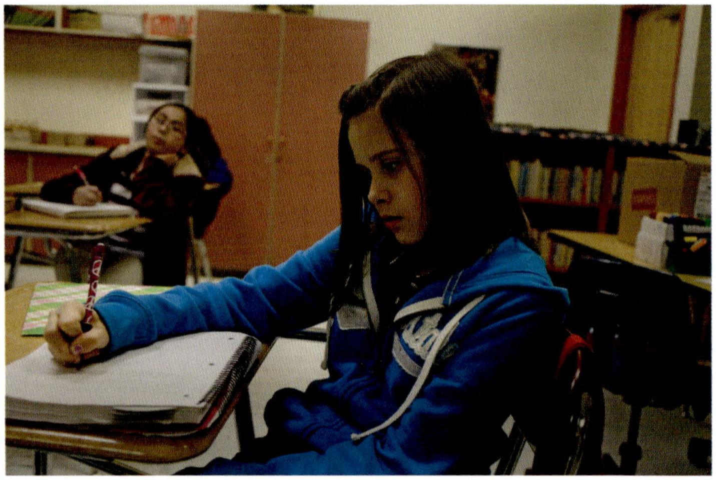

Christina Padilla

After the bell had rung, I sat down with Christina on a bench outside, and we talked about her life both at school and at home. To break the ice, I asked her the traditional question about what she wanted to be when she grew up. "I want to be an actor," she replied. "Last year I had a big role in *King Arthur's Quest*, and I really enjoyed that. But maybe a fashion designer or a chef." This led to a discussion of food. Christina praised such Northern New Mexican dishes as beans, chile, and posole; however, her attitude toward diet transcended ethnic foods. "I'm a vegan," she said, "and the only meat my family eats is buffalo because that's organic. We have a vegetable garden at home, and I help my mom and dad take care of it."

In terms of extracurricular activities, Christina said she enjoyed being in the school band and has recently taken up the bass guitar, which she plays indoors but not when the students are marching in a parade because the instrument would be unwieldy. She told me that the day before she had brought the guitar home from school, explaining, "I just sat on the couch for about three hours practicing till my mom called me to dinner." She said that she also enjoys soccer and gymnastics and—as is true of generations of Las Vegas children before her—that she likes to go ice-skating on the ponds above the Montezuma hot springs where the railroad company used to harvest ice.

Looking up from the bench where we were sitting, I noticed the district schools logo painted on the wall. It struck me that the expression of the cardinal was far more glowering, even threatening, than any bird in nature. For Christina, however, the ferocious cardinal is a friendly icon, "Our school colors are red, black, and white, and the cardinal is our school mascot. We have a lot of school pride. We have pep rallies every day before a game, and we go wild like we just met a celebrity."

Still wondering about the "baby" I had seen in her previous class, I asked Christina to explain why it appeared so normal to the students as well as the teacher for one girl to combine her class work with childcare practice. "It's so girls will know how much trouble it is to take care of a baby if they get . . . you know," she replied. I didn't say what I was thinking, which was how much her classmate appeared *not* to be annoyed by the mechanically crying infant; already she had seemed to me to be a little mother-in-the-making.

Changing the subject, I surmised, "It's too early for you to think about college, isn't it?" With surprising maturity for an eleven-year-old, she said, "Oh, I've already thought about going to Arizona or Colorado. But I want to go to Highlands for my first year before I leave home." She spoke about her mother and father with respect and affection: "I think it is good that my parents are strict and don't let me go to the movies with friends or watch television for more than an hour a day. I don't have a cell phone. I do have a Nintendo, but they won't let me play on it if I haven't done my homework and my chores. My dad was real disappointed when I got a B on my last report card. I like it that he's hard on me and says, 'We believe you can do better,' because I know how important it is to get an education, and you have to have good grades to get state aid. I have an 87 in one course now but I am getting myself back up to straight A's again."

When I asked about her other relatives, Christina said with pride that she was a Romero on her mother's side and that her grandfather, Cleofes Romero, used to own the Romero Block on the southeast corner of the plaza. "There's a lot of history in the family," she said, "which is one reason I like living here in Las Vegas."

MARTHA JOHNSEN

Martha Johnsen, who has served as a principal both in East and West Las Vegas schools, lives on Fifth Street opposite the Carnegie Library in a charming Victorian house that is filled with her large collection of Mexican folk art. As a native Las Vegan, she is herself a product of the school system as well as someone with an insider's perspective on today's students. To understand better what I had witnessed in the various classrooms I had visited as well as what Las Vegas was like when she was growing up I went to visit her after school one day.

When I asked Johnsen to describe the town of her youth, she replied, "Douglas Avenue was vibrant then. There was a record store, Murphy's Drug Store and several other ice cream parlors with soda fountains, and the SERF where I always went to the movies. Then, of course, we'd go over to the west side because of Mama Lucy's restaurant on the ground floor of the Plaza Hotel. The rest of the building was abandoned, but her place was always full of starving Highlands students, politicians, and other people who just wanted a good meal. She was a generous, heavy-set woman who served the most wonderful Mexican food."

Prompted to tell me her personal history, she said, "I graduated from Robertson in 1972. At that time the students literally didn't know what was on the other side of the bridge. It was called the Tortilla Curtain—the community was that fractured. But since my mother was Mexican and my father taught Spanish at Highlands, I was bilingual and didn't mind going over, even though some of my classmates called me a snake for crossing the river. I even dated a couple of Hispanic boys and worked for a while in the town's only bookstore, which was on Bridge Street. At that time the people who lived over here would actually ask to have their book orders mailed. But later, there was an attempt to reconcile the two halves of the city, a Hands Across the Bridge program. It paired kids together and got them to spend a day in each other's school. Today I don't think people feel that division so much. Still, the custodian at my former school in West Las Vegas won't go to see his nephew play football for Robertson."

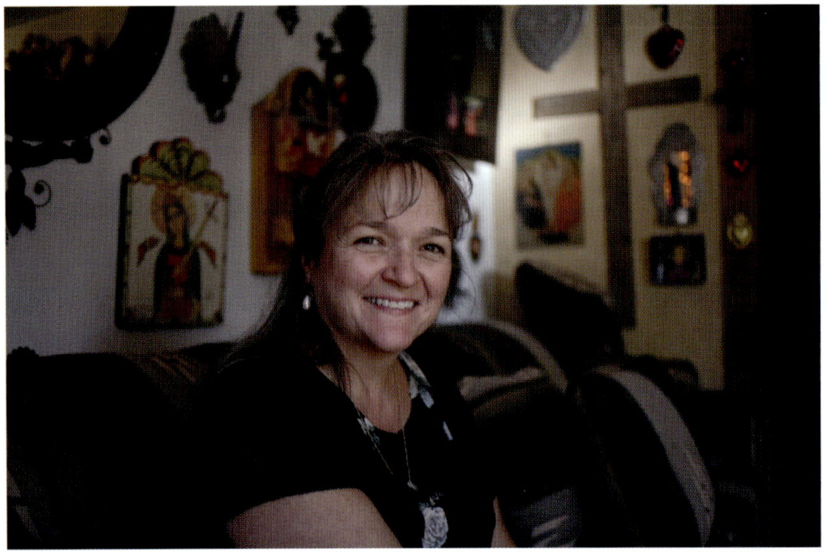

Martha Johnsen

Johnsen did not want to leave town to go to college, so she enrolled at Highlands University. Her years there coincided with the Chicano movement, a time when the school was undergoing radical change. "All the Anglo professors were literally being threatened if they didn't leave. I don't think they knew what to do with my dad because he spoke Spanish," she said "There were terrible things going on all over town. Any Anglo who was in power received violent threats. In one case, someone whose husband was on the East Las Vegas School Board had the windows of her house shot out."

After she graduated in 1979 with a degree in journalism, Johnsen worked in radio broadcasting—she still has a morning talk show on local KFUN—but her main career between 1990 and 2012 has been in education. "I tried making a living at various part-time jobs; I owned a business on Douglas Street called Cat's Meow, but that wasn't successful. My son was in kindergarten, and I taught Spanish in exchange for his tuition. Then in 1988 I went back to Highlands and got my teaching certification. After I had taught for three years I moved into administration. When a position opened up in the West Las Vegas district at the Family Partnership alternative school, which has a large population of juvenile offenders, I became principal there until I got reassigned to the North Star Elementary School where there is a dual language program. Then two years ago I got an offer to come over and work in the East Las Vegas schools. Since my responsibility would only be for elementary and middle school rather than for K–12, I thought it would make my life less complicated, but I was entirely wrong. I was put in charge of two schools, which were across the street from one another. Since I was running back and forth constantly, I bought a scooter to make it easier. Being in charge of two schools at the same time was stressful, but it was the contrast between them that really got to me. At one school there were the elite students with strong family backgrounds and supportive parents, and at the other we had our poorest children who had only one parent or grandparent taking care of them. These kids were really violent. After ten years at the Partnership, I thought I had seen everything, but I was wrong. I now saw more fights in a week than I used to see in two or three years."

When I asked Johnsen to give me examples, she replied, "There was this one boy facedown on the ground while another boy was kicking him. They were surrounded by a ring of other boys who were cheering while the boy just kept on kicking the poor kid mercilessly. Then we had another young boy who would come to school just filthy and with no buttons on his shirt. One day in the playground one of the teachers found him sobbing. He told her how hungry he was and that the night before when he had asked his mother for something to eat, she had tossed a tortilla at him across the room just as if she was throwing a Frisbee. The day-in-day-out tension, plus the fact that my mother is 101 and needs care, was just too much for me, so after twenty-two years I turned in my letter this spring."

The year before Johnsen decided to retire, McNellis-Martinez, who had just been appointed superintendent of Las Vegas City Schools, said that she would make her life easier by putting her in charge of a single elementary school. It happened to be the one in her old neighborhood on Eighth Street that she had attended as a child. "It is so different now," she lamented. You can't believe how rude kids are today. There is such a lack of courtesy and nothing that even resembles good manners. I actually saw a five-year-old give someone the finger."

As a striking exception to this bleak picture, I mentioned to Johnsen the day I had spent in the Memorial Middle School with Cristina Padilla, and we both agreed that she is a model student. When I queried her regarding the girl I had seen in class minding the programmed infant doll, she confirmed that this was in fact part of an effort to discourage teen pregnancy. "It's mostly for high school girls, so I'm surprised that this was in sixth grade. It is something like physical education, an extra-

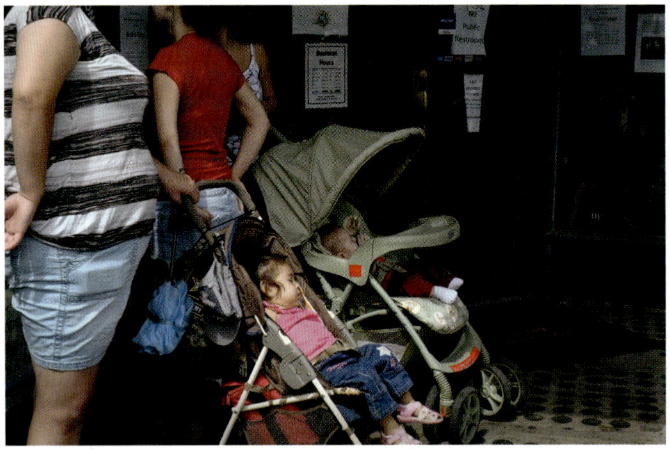

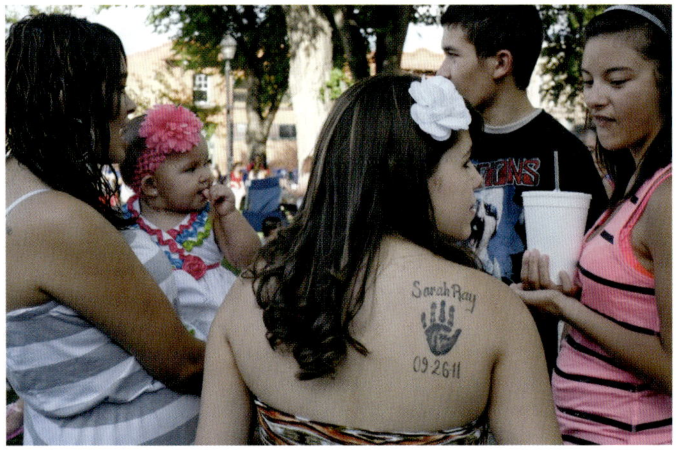

Young mothers and children

curricular course for which the students get credit. Boys as well as girls take it, and it requires that a student take responsibility for the doll they are assigned full time and not just for the hours they are in school. They have to mind it twenty-four hours a day and on weekends, which means that they bring it with them on dates, to football games, and wherever else they are going. There are computers inside the dolls that only the teachers can access, and this tells them what is going on."

When I asked her if the program had proved to be a deterrent to girls getting pregnant, Johnsen shook her head, "Not really. I can't give you actual statistics, but I'd say that, at least at the Partnership where I used to be, it was an exception for a girl not to be pregnant when she graduated from high school. It is just the norm, something that is accepted, and the parents don't disapprove. The girls think that if they get pregnant, they will be able to keep the boy, but this of course isn't true. It breaks my heart to see this sort of thing on top of all our DWI statistics." Since we were on the subject of troubled youth, I asked about Las Vegas's drug problem. "It's huge," Johnsen admitted. "I think most of the crime is drug-related. You have to realize that this is a poor, poor town, so using drugs is how the kids get their kicks."

NEW MEXICO CENTER FOR BEHAVIORAL HEALTH

As I learned from Johnsen, grade-school bullying, teen pregnancies, substance abuse, and domestic violence are common problems in Las Vegas, as in many other disadvantaged communities. Many of the young offenders in the schools are likely to become adult criminals whose unlawful acts and first-degree crimes are addressed by the police and the courts. For the most part, those who are convicted are sent to the San Miguel County Detention Center on the southwest edge of town beside I-25. However, the fact that Las Vegas is home to the New Mexico Center for Behavioral Health[1]—locally known as the State Hospital since people continue to call it by its old name—provides a provisional means of addressing some forms of deviant behavior. In cases of criminally charged persons with psychotic symptoms, they are remanded to the hospital by the district courts for a thirty-day testing period to determine upon diagnosis if they are competent to stand trial.

According to Dr. Troy Jones, the current executive director of the institution, "We are not a prison. These men are considered mentally unstable; that is the criterion for their admission, and we test carefully to ensure that only the ones who are not competent to stand trial remain here. While this is being determined, those that are minors are put in the twenty-bed CARE unit—that stands for Center for Adolescent Relationship Exploration—which is part of the Forensic Division." At the time of my conversation with Dr. Jones, eighteen adolescent boys who were deemed mentally ill and had a history of sexual offenses and substance abuse were being treated at the center.

When I asked about adult offenders, Dr. Jones said that persons with severe psychiatric symptoms are assigned to the Acute Care Unit of the Forensic Division and those who are more stable but in need of ongoing therapy are put in the Continuing Care Unit. Men convicted of pedophilia and other forms of sexual abuse are assigned to the Sexual Offender Treatment Program (STOP). The buildings where those charged with severe crimes live have bars on the windows and the area around them is fenced with chain link topped with razor wire.

HIGH SCHOOL GRADUATION

I happened to be in Las Vegas in May 2008 on the day West Las Vegas High School was holding its graduation ceremonies in the Gillie Lopez Gymnasium. In a town where all the major milestones in people's lives are celebrated by the Catholic Church, there is no agitation over school prayer, and after the band had played "The Star-Spangled Banner," Father John Brasher gave the invocation. The excitement was palpable as the senior class, clad in green robes and yellow hoods, marched into the gym, where the ceremony was being held. Along with proud relatives, children of all ages and babies in the arms of young mothers and fathers crowded the cordoned aisle next to the line of graduates. Cameras were held above the heads of people in front, ready to flash when a son, daughter, sibling, or family friend passed by. From the bleachers relatives called out joyfully as they spotted one of their own, and everywhere there were whistles, cheers, and waving hands.

In thanking her parents, brothers, and sisters, along with her best friend and her teachers, the salutatorian was overcome with tears. The commencement address grew long with the speaker's encomiums to all the members of his family, including parents, grandparents, brothers, sisters, aunts, uncles, cousins, nieces, and nephews. There was a lesson here. All had succeeded in their various jobs or careers, and not coincidentally, all were graduates of West Las Vegas High School. The speaker used the figures of a recent survey showing the correlation between education and income levels, telling the students how important education has become today, especially

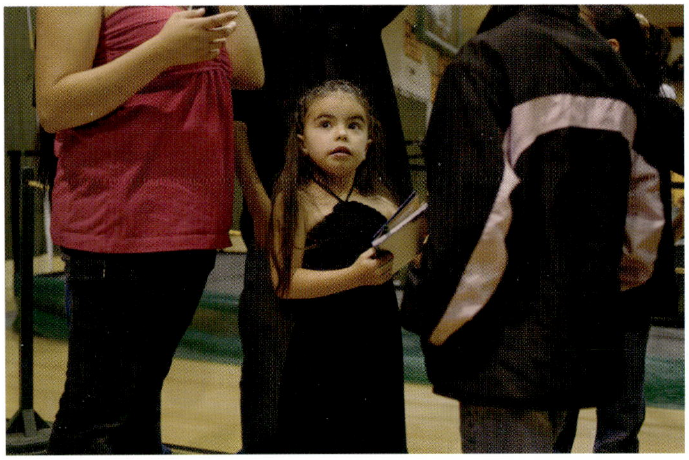 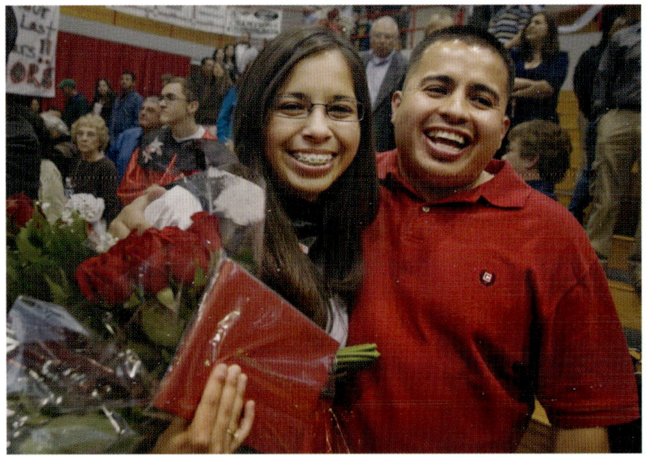

Graduation Day 2008, West Las Vegas High School

Graduation Day 2008, Robertson High School

with the price of gas approaching $4.00 a gallon. As they were handed their diplomas, each was identified as the son or daughter of this and that mother and father. Every graduate's continuing educational goal was announced. Virtually none were planning to enroll out of state, whereas a good number planned to stay in Las Vegas and attend Highlands University or Luna Community College.

College Town

HIGHLANDS UNIVERSITY

With its attractive campus just east of the Gallinas River, Highlands University owes its origins to the Normal School, built in 1893 (rechristened Normal University in 1902). Not surprisingly, for many years graduates became schoolteachers in Mora, Springer, Wagon Mound, and other small villages in Northern New Mexico. In 1941, when its curriculum had grown to include more than the courses necessary for certification in the field of education, it was renamed Highlands University. Today there are three professional schools—Education, Social Work, and Business—and two undergraduate colleges, one in Science and Mathematics and the other in the Humanities.

In the two decades following the turbulent 1970s, the university enjoyed a period of stabilizing progress as radicalism gave way to realism. Unfortunately, the tenure of politico Manny Aragon between 2004 and 2006 marked a time of presidential ineptitude. Faculty members and staff brought legal actions on the grounds of discrimination and unlawful discharge, and the American Association of University Professors placed Highlands on its censure list. However, since 2007 when the current president, Jim Fries, a former chemistry professor and experienced academic administrator, took office, this stigma has been removed. The institutional research office (a data-collecting operation critical to accreditation) and the career services office, both of which had been dismantled under Aragon, have been reinstated, enrollment is up, a new student center is in the process of being built, and a strategic plan, as well as a campus master plan, is in place. Seeking a perspective on Highlands history and the tenor of life in Las Vegas over half a century ago, I was fortunate to find someone who has been connected in one way or another with the university since well before his days as an undergraduate.

LEVEO V. SANCHEZ

The son of a mother who was a Highlands graduate and one of the first two New Mexico Hispanic faculty members hired by the university, Leveo Sanchez served for twenty-three years on the board of the New Mexico Highlands University Foundation, the not-for-profit arm that raises private capital for projects not funded by the state. Appointed a member of the Board of Regents in 2008, he continues to participate actively in the affairs of the institution. His love for his mother and pride in her accomplishments, which were remarkable for her time and place in American society, is such that his personal business card has on it a photograph of the two of them taken when he was a young man. I was impressed when he told me his life story, which in fact was hers, too.

A widow from the time of Leveo's birth, Victoria Sanchez taught school in many small northern New Mexican towns, including Lamy, where her son was born, and Nambé, where he attended elementary school before they moved to Las Vegas when he was ready to enter seventh grade. "There the classroom was separated in half, with two rows of Anglos on one side of the room and two rows of Hispanics on the other," he told me. "That was because Hispanic kids had to improve their English in order to catch up in their reading and writing ability. At school socials we never danced with Anglo girls, since that just wasn't done in Las Vegas. The only thing that brought Hispanic and Anglo boys together was sports, but after practice we'd go our separate ways."

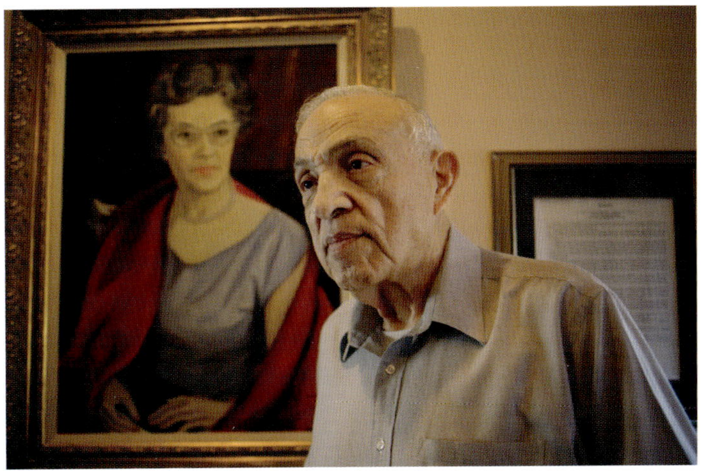

Leveo V. Sanchez

In 1946 Sanchez and his mother moved to Guatemala, where, under the sponsorship of the Rockefeller Inter-American Education Foundation, she was a leading member of a group of five educators who started a normal school to train rural teachers. Before continuing her career in Latin America, however, she returned with her son to Las Vegas in order for him to complete high school. Following his graduation in 1948, Sanchez enrolled at Highlands. His undergraduate career was interrupted in 1951 when he enlisted in the military to serve in the Korean War. During the second half of his stint he was as an officer in an all-black detachment stationed in western France. Returning to Highlands at the beginning of 1954, he completed his college education, graduating in the spring of that year.

I asked Sanchez to tell me what Highlands was like back then. "Well," he replied, "this was just at the end of the period when the school had experienced a large influx of returning World War II veterans who enrolled because of the GI Bill. They were from various parts of the United States—Pennsylvania, Iowa, New York, Texas, all over—and this really gave the university a large Anglo student body. Also, throughout the 1950s you still had numerous students, Anglos for the most part, coming from eastern New Mexico and the western part of Texas. There were also many Hispanics and Native Americans on the GI Bill at Highlands. Having so many veterans brought a level of maturity to the student body. During this time the president of the university, Edward Eyring, recruited several excellent new professors. Unfortunately, few of the GIs who graduated from Highlands stayed on in Las Vegas, but the next president, Thomas Donnelly, who was in office from 1952 until 1970, continued to build the university into a widely respected institution for the arts and sciences as well as education and business administration. This made Highlands attractive to students from other states besides New Mexico. President Donnelly was responsible for greatly expanding its size and improving the appearance of the campus. He renovated several buildings and constructed others, including the library, which was later named for him because of his many accomplishments. After Donnelly left, Highlands was transformed from a primarily liberal arts institution into one that was much more focused on Hispanic studies. It was the time of the Brown Berets and there was a good deal of agitation, so it was inevitable that the president following him would be a Hispanic, which turned out to be Frank Angel, whom I knew well because he was my Cub Scout master when I was a boy."

Since Sanchez had also known Tiny Martinez personally, I wanted to hear what he thought of the political boss's role in masterminding the sea change in the ethos of both the university and Las Vegas. "In 1948 when I was a freshman," he said, "Tiny, who was three years ahead of me and a vet, ran for president of the student body at Highlands. He just walked away with the election. You could say that this was the beginning of his political career and the seed of his later support of the Spanish American Student Organization at Highlands, or SASO as it was known, and the Chicanos who wanted fundamental changes in the administration and curriculum. Then, after he graduated from Highlands, he went off to Georgetown University in Washington, D.C., where he obtained his law degree. I attended George Washington University, where I earned a masters degree in foreign relations, but after that our lives ended up very differently."

Sanchez's career has included both public service and private entrepreneurship. His curriculum vitae is impressive. During the Johnson Administration, he served as deputy director of the Peace Corps for Latin America. Later he was director of the U.S. Office of Economic Opportunity for the Mid-Atlantic Region and director of the U.S. Office of Institutional Development for the Latin American Bureau of the Agency for International Development (AID). In 1969 he founded and chaired Development Associates, an international and domestic consulting firm specializing in social and economic development. In 1974 he started the Hemisphere National Bank in Washington, D.C., and served as its chairman until the bank was sold in 1981. Not surprisingly, he has been on many boards of directors, including those of the Smithsonian Institution and the National Hispanic Chamber of Commerce. His success in business allows him to live in a large hilltop home in Santa Fe and engage in several philanthropic activities, the latest of which is the founding of the Leveo Sanchez Summer Institute at Highlands, a remedial program in reading and writing designed to reduce the university's freshman drop-out rate.

It is from this perspective that he commented, "I never understood why Tiny decided to come back to Las Vegas and become a patrón when he could have been so much more and done some of the same kinds of things I have done, working for our people at another level. When I would come back, I'd ask him, 'Why did you do that? I have things going on all over the world, and you could have operated in that same arena.' But he really liked having all that power, even on a small scale."

We went on to speak about the decline in the commercial economy of Las Vegas. "Oh, you should have seen it back in the days when I was in school. Remember that Camp Luna, which is now a community college, probably had about two to three thousand servicemen stationed there during World War II. The GIs shopped in Las Vegas, and this provided a solid retail market for the merchants. We still had Taichert Haberdashery and Hoffman & Grabarth Department Store on Douglas Street, and there was a Montgomery Ward, a J. C. Penney, and a Kress Five & Dime. Now there is only Walmart, and it is out on the highway and not in the old downtown business district."

As Sanchez and his wife Patricia walked me through the high-ceilinged living room and dining room of their beautiful home, which is named Villa Victoria after his mother, he pointed out the portrait of this sternly handsome and determined woman, whom he credits as the primary force in shaping his life. "Because of my mother and her accomplishments as a highly successful Hispanic woman, I got a larger perspective on the world," he said. "Thanks to her, I lived for eight years in Latin America. During the forty-six years I was in Washington D.C., it was a great thing for me to maintain my tie with Las Vegas. I think you can say that I still think of Las Vegas as my real home."

LUPITA GONZALES

I first met Lupita Gonzales when we were both attending a music-and-dance performance in the plaza. Striking up a conversation while patting her little dog Chien, I learned that she had grown up in Gallup, New Mexico, graduated from Highlands in 1968, taught school for eleven years in Wagon Mound, married a man from there, and returned to Las Vegas with him and their two children in 1979 when he accepted a job as district superintendent of the Storrie Lake Headquarters of New Mexico State Forestry Division. After that she had continued her teaching career in both West Las Vegas High School and Robertson High School until her recent retirement, which now gives her time to write a series of "Senior Profiles" and a periodic column called "Dulce y Amargo"—Sweet and Bitter—for the *Optic*.

Later, when we had become better acquainted, she invited me to continue our conversation in her home, which is in San José, the rural village immediately south of Las Vegas. Sitting in her kitchen with its expansive views of the surrounding landscape and the large pine trees her late husband had planted around their house, I asked her about her experiences when she was a student at Highlands. "I was there at the time things began to get militant," she replied. "The Raza Unida people came in from California and found a little niche for themselves at the old Montezuma Hotel, which was then a seminary for Mexican boys who were here in this country studying to be priests since the church in Mexico had outlawed seminaries. Things just escalated with the formation of SASO, which got renamed CASO when the Chicanos came in and said that it was more important to have a name signifying a pan-Latino heritage rather than one that applied just to descendants of the Spanish conquistadores with their European genetic origins. If you were a Hispanic and didn't fall in line with them, they called you a *vendido*, a sell-out."

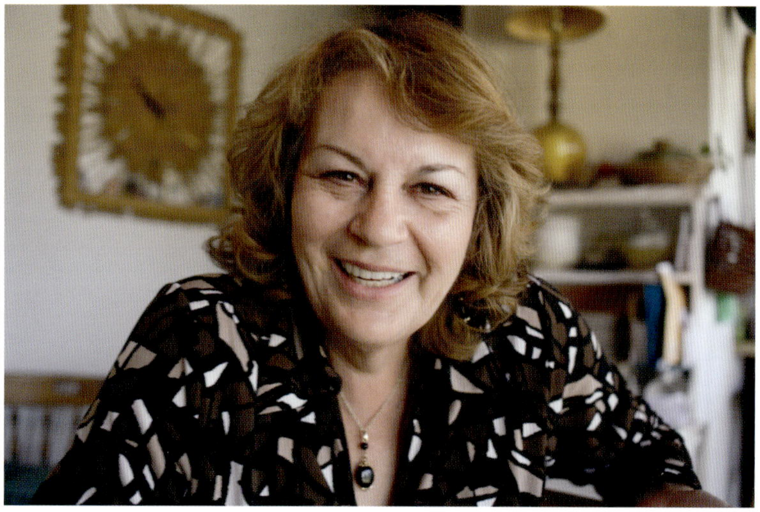

Lupita Gonzales

Gonzales remarked with candor, "I've seen that instead of keeping its strong status, Highlands has declined and become pretty much of a commuter university. There is no longer a sense of its being a college community. Back in the early sixties it was like a big family, and the kids got along in spite of their ethnic differences. At that time there were students from all parts of the country, as well as Hawaii and Japan. But because of the violence in the seventies, parents didn't want to send their daughters to Highlands anymore. The whole quality of campus life changed then and was never the same again. All the camaraderie fell apart. Even before that, however, there was another lesser kind of tension. It had to do with who were insiders and who were outsiders in the town. This resulted in all sorts of silly rivalry. At dances, for instance, there was a funny edge; on one side of the room there would be all the students from Las Vegas and on the other the rest of us from other places. You could see the girls' eyes shooting darts at us when 'their' men would come over and ask us to dance. Still, back then it was a great place to go to school."

Recalling the darker side of student life at that time, Gonzales said, "The militancy of the La Raza people was warranted to an extent, and they were right in saying that there was discrimination against Hispanics on the part of some of the faculty. I remember an incident that happened to me in my senior year. I had a double major in English and modern languages and had turned in a paper at the end of the semester. I was worried when I didn't get the paper back with my grade, and nobody would tell me why. Then my roommate, who was a student aide in the English department, said something about it to the professor and was told, 'No Hispanic can write like that!' Though the teacher had absolutely no proof, I was accused of plagiarism, and the department head said, 'I have to stand behind my teachers.' I was given an F, and that was that. It was something that shouldn't have happened, but even then I felt that you don't solve problems with fire bombs but by getting an education and finding the kind of job that allows you to do something about this kind of prejudice."

I suggested that the politics of Tiny Martinez and the Mama Lucy gang had been to a significant degree responsible for the things she had witnessed going on at Highlands during her student days. Gonzales confirmed what I had been told before: "Tiny and Mama Lucy were a real power and had their following among the kids at Highlands. They tried to recruit me. We had been told that it was unsafe to cross over the bridge to the west side, and I found it weird when one girl came to the dorm where I lived and invited me to go with her to Mama Lucy's. I was just a sixteen-year-old starry-eyed kid, and Mama Lucy, who was this nice little old lady, brought me a beer. That's as far as it went. I was in school to get an education and never got involved with politics.

I asked Gonzales what her overall impression of Las Vegas as a place was now. She replied, "It has always been very polarized. Hispanic Las Vegans either explicitly or implicitly give people the idea that this is their town, they don't want changes, and they like it the way it is. It's just an old idea whose time has passed, but somehow the notion of separation into two towns still rises to the surface. Including the time I was a teacher in Wagon Mound, I've lived here fifty years more or less, and they still consider me an outsider. I hope my column and the profiles I write for the *Optic* may be changing that perception."

LUNA COMMUNITY COLLEGE

Luna Community College occupies the site of Camp Luna, the World War I training ground for the New Mexico National Guard. Its name commemorates Maximiliano Luna, who was the Speaker of the House of Representatives for the Territory of New Mexico in 1899, a captain of the Rough Riders, and a first lieutenant of the 34th U.S. Volunteer Infantry during World War I. Luna has been a vocational training institution since 1967, with satellite campuses in Springer and Santa Rosa. Its stated mission is "to prepare students for employment through a broad range of vocational, technical, and professional education programs." Students who have not yet graduated from high school are offered preparatory classes that will enable them to receive the GED, or high school equivalency diploma.

Designated a community college in 2000, Luna offers a broader curriculum than when it was solely a vocational institution. According to the 2012 catalog, it grants degrees in media communications, teacher education, life science, electronics engineering technology, equine science, fire science, military studies, general agriculture, sports performance, and video game design and development. At the same time, it offers courses that lead to certificates in several trade-related fields, including automotive repair, barbering, building technology, business accounting, collision repair technology, cosmetology, culinary arts, furniture and cabinet-making, practical nursing, and welding technology. Degree candidates must take General Education core courses in basic science, math, engineering, English composition, and the humanities.

SAM VIGIL

I received a good background education in the history of Luna Community College when I had breakfast at the Spic & Span Restaurant one morning with Sam Vigil, the former president who, during his twenty-five-year tenure, was instrumental in overseeing the broadening of the institution's curriculum from one that was solely vocational to one that also provides courses of a nontechnical nature. Vigil was born and raised in Las Vegas. After attending parochial schools in West Las Vegas, he enrolled in the high school run by Highlands University as a learning laboratory for its normal-school students. Remembered for its academic excellence, it was, in Vigil's opinion, "almost equivalent to a top prep school today."

Sam Vigil

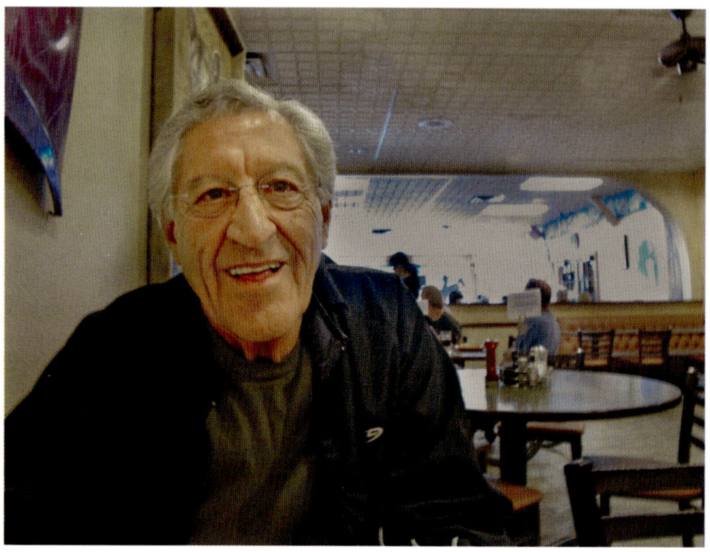

Like many other Las Vegas youths, upon graduating from high school, Vigil went into the military. After serving in the Korean War and in Japan from 1951 until 1953, he was eligible for the GI Bill, which allowed him to enroll at Highlands; there he majored in psychology and the social sciences. Following a period of teaching at the West Las Vegas High School, in 1964 he was picked by President Donnelly to become an administrator at Highlands. He therefore witnessed first-hand the period of turmoil when the civil rights movement was beginning to alter the tenor of campus life and the nature of Highlands as a small liberal arts college. In his words, "it was a time when the institution was in a constant state of chaos and flux."

Turning to the history of Luna, he explained its initial affiliation with Highlands as the university's vocational branch. The origin of this arrangement was a practical one. In 1945 many of the returning World War II veterans who were eligible for the GI Bill did not have high school degrees and other necessary qualifications for enrollment as undergraduates. Luna at that time was being decommissioned as an Army Air Transport base, and as such it provided Highlands with a ready-made auxiliary campus for vocational training. Later, however, when government funding through the GI Bill ceased, the university was forced to discontinue the program. For Vigil, whose experience as a teacher at West Las Vegas High School had given him a keen appreciation of the need for vocational education, the federal Job Corps program, established in 1964 as part of President Johnson's War on Poverty, provided what appeared to be an opportunity to revive Luna for this purpose. "The old military base at Luna was abandoned and just sitting there," he told me. "Here was a potential for something in Las Vegas, something that would really affect economic development in the town." However, the Job Corps' primary focus was on black youths in large cities, and it was not until Vigil's appointment by President Clinton to the twenty-four-person Hispanic Education Commission, along with his election to the New Mexico State Legislature, that he was able to exert the political force needed to revive vocational education in Las Vegas. "Since we already had a history," he explained, "we were able to get the state legislature to create the Luna Vocational Technical Institution, which was designed to help the kids from four local districts—West Las Vegas, East Las Vegas, Santa Rosa, and Mora. The principal of the West Las Vegas High School became the first director at Luna, and shortly after that the superintendent of the Santa Rosa district became the first person to hold the title of president. It was still just an adult postsecondary education institution when I came in as president in 1975 after it had been in operation five years."

Vigil's mission as president was to reshape the curriculum of Luna Vocational Technical Institution into one that fit the concept of a community college. To do this he had to overhaul the old military facilities in order to create classrooms and dormitories. When I asked how the funding for this capital reconstruction had been obtained, he replied, "We could do that because after my election as a representative in the state legislature in 1970, I served on the Education and Appropriation committees and managed to get friends there to support my efforts to get state money." As a member of the legislature, Vigil was able to further his vision of "starting training in specialized trades and at the same time hiring PhDs and people with master's degrees who could teach general education courses." He remarked, "I was able to connect with associations throughout the country who were trying to develop the concept of self-governed public-private technical institutions with independent boards of governors. I took my staff with me to meetings. Consequently, they were able to help me in bringing Luna to a new educational level."

When I asked about what Vigil thought of the present state of Luna, he replied, "The appointment of administrators has unfortunately become politicized. There is a lot more of the patronage thing. Politics are always present when you are running an institution, but the direction it takes depends on the people who are in office at the time."

PETE CAMPOS

The current president of Luna, Pete Campos, a native Las Vegan, is a prominent political leader in New Mexico. When we met at the college one day during his campaign for reelection as a state senator, he explained that, according to Luna's charter of governance by a city-appointed board of trustees, he could simultaneously occupy both elected office and his current position. It was clear from our conversation that Campos's principal aims are to fuse a broad regional agenda of community development with education. More than once as we spoke, he reiterated the tenets of his Website statement: "I have always encouraged empowering and involving people in shaping our future. Our collective success depends on the understanding of our diverse state and the treasures it holds. To achieve this, I live by the following, 'the more we learn and share with each other, the better we all become'."

Later, I listened to his song "El Corrido de Senador Pedro Campos"—The Ballad of Senator Pete Campos—on a CD that a campaign supporter gave me. Its verses, sung by Campos to guitar accompaniment, exhort the voters in five counties—Mora, Torrance, Santa Fe, Guadalupe, and San Miguel—to recognize the virtues of an exemplary Christian family man and educator with several advanced degrees and political experience who has gained fame by advancing the will of God and serving the people with honesty and competence. In our conversation he spoke with practiced passion some of the same words, which he amplified with significant biographical details. Ticking off the offices he has held in addition to state senator and mayor of Santa Rosa—president of the Chamber of Commerce, president of the Tourist Bureau, Grand Knight of the Knights of Columbus, and a recently appointed deacon of the Archdiocese in Santa Fe—he said, "I got involved in political life because I had it in my heart to serve the people. I am in my twenty-second year as state senator now because, even though I haven't been the favorite every time I have run, the people know I have the energy and heart to continue to help the entire region to develop."

Pete Campos

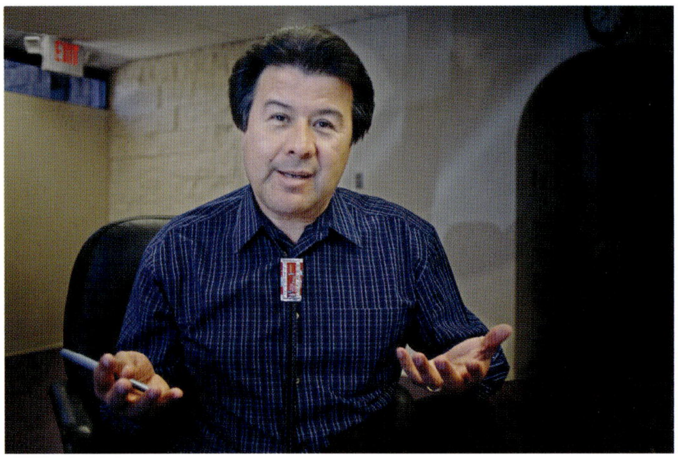

Success in this regard naturally translates into government appropriations, and Campos is proud of the fact that in the last two legislative sessions he has been instrumental in getting bills passed allocating approximately $52 million to Las Vegas. These appropriations include $36 million for the Behavioral Health Institute's long-term care unit, $8 million for a new state police headquarters, $6 million to remodel and repurpose the building once owned by the Las Vegas Trolley Company, and $4 million for increasing and enhancing the run-down buildings housing Luna's vocational courses.

Campos believes in the importance of rebuilding Luna's vocational curriculum, which was sidelined during the period when the institution was seeking accreditation as a community college. "Now we are going to be strong in both vocational studies and the humanities," he emphasized. "We are essentially a self-help economy here in rural New Mexico, and we have to provide the students who come to us with such skills as agricultural management, welding, and carpentry as well as the automotive knowledge that will allow them to become mechanics or insurance adjusters. In order to do these things, it's also necessary to have them become proficient in math and reading, which is why we make certain core courses mandatory in these certificate programs. It's important to provide an educational opportunity for everyone, because lifelong learning is key."

When I asked how the college deals with troubled youths within this educational context, Campos replied optimistically, "It's not easy, but I've spent thirty years counseling young people how to overcome social ills like poor family life, drugs, and violent behavior. It's our job to help these young people go out into the world of work with self-esteem and the necessary skills to be economically productive. We can never ever give up on any individual. When they decide to change their life, we'll be there with open arms. For those who want help, we'll find ways to assist them, and when the door opens, they will realize that they are the only ones who can take care of themselves. In the last analysis, it is about community. The bottom line is we have to have hope, support each other, use available resources, make each other's life better."

GARY MARTINEZ

To gain an understanding of how Luna Community College prepares students to join the workforce, I went to see Gary Martinez, Director of Vocational Education. He told me that Luna's original purpose as a vocational training school had diminished during the years it was building up its community college curriculum but that today vocational education has made a comeback due to new funding and President Campos's agenda of reinstituting trades-related courses. He emphasized the importance of certification as a means to getting a job these days. "Credentials are important now," he told me. "Even the family-owned shops need to have licenses if the banks are going to lend them money, so you have to teach students both technical skills and an understanding of the law."

When I asked if I could visit one of the classes in session that morning, Martinez agreed and drove me over to the welding shop, a big building with the appear-

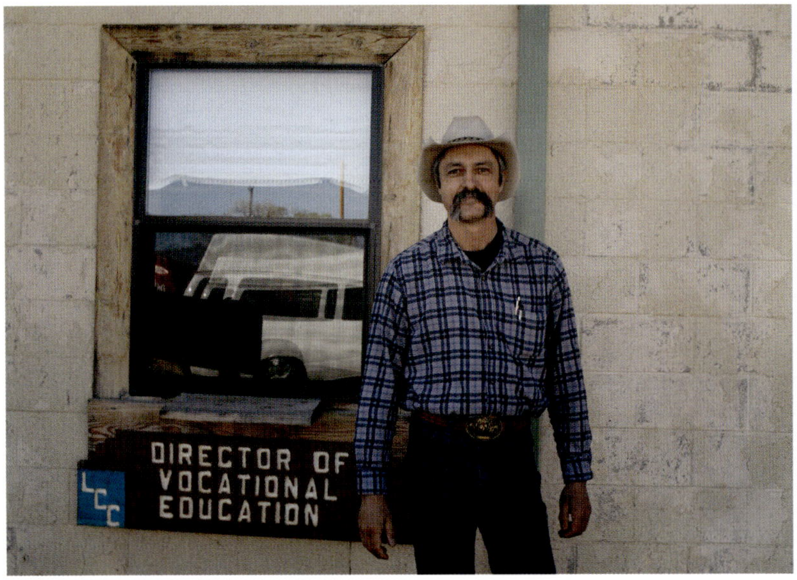

Gary Martinez

ance of airplane hangar, where he introduced me to Cory Moore, the instructor. After we had shaken hands, I asked what kinds of jobs the students would have when they graduated. Moore replied, "A lot of things are being done with robotics these days, but they still need human welders. For instance, they could work for the oil industry or in mining. We teach nonindustrial courses such as blacksmithing as well. We also offer instruction to sculptors and other kinds of hobbyists."

As I watched a student cutting a plate of steel with an acetylene torch, Moore discussed the importance of safety. "In the industry, if you can't work safe, you are out of a job. There are stringent federal regulations. As an example, there is a five-thousand-dollar fine if acetylene and oxygen bottles are left exposed. We have a constant danger of fire in here, so this equipment has to be removed and locked up in a separate airtight room when it is not in use."

Luna now has a mandatory crossover curriculum whereby vocational students are required to take certain core courses on the other side of the campus. Moore explained the educational value of the humanities, math, and science to his vocational students. "They have to have basic reading skills in order to understand technical manuals and specifications. To figure out measurements, read blueprints, and learn how to draft they need math," he said. He added, "They may not see the relevance of what they learn in the classroom, but then they get back over to this side of the campus where I help them make sense of it. People learn best by doing, not just reading about how to do it. It's important that our students see the connection between the two."

UNITED WORLD COLLEGE

In addition to Luna Community College and Highlands University, Las Vegas is the home of the United World College-USA, which is part of part of an international federation of thirteen upper-level secondary schools whose educational mission is to foster world peace and justice by bringing together from many nations young people who will learn together in an atmosphere of multi-cultural mutual respect. With an international enrollment of 200 students ages seventeen to nineteen (the equivalent of high school seniors and college freshmen) from more than eighty countries, the United World College in Las Vegas is equivalent to an advanced preparatory school for boarding students. Since 1982 when business tycoon, art collector, and philanthropist Armand Hammer purchased the old Montezuma hot springs resort hotel and its surrounding property as a campus for UWC, it has graduated over 2,500 students from more than one hundred countries.

To enter the lofty dining room of "the castle," as it is called locally, one would not suspect the checkered history of the place during the half century of slow decay following its sale by the railroad. Its resurrection is due in no small part to another philanthropist, mutual-fund investor Shelby Davis, whose gift to renovate the castle is a visible token of his extraordinary largesse to the college. Indeed, many of the students are there by virtue of funding from the Shelby Davis Scholarship Program. Moreover, through direct gifts to participating institutions of higher learning—Middlebury, Wellesley, Princeton, Stanford, St. John's, Colby, and College of the Atlantic, among a growing list in the United States and abroad—the Davis United World Scholars Program provides need-based financial aid to successful UWC applicants. The scholarship program also benefits students graduating from other United World Colleges besides United World College-USA, with a total of more than eighty international educational institutions receiving grants from this source.

Because they are aware that, if admitted, their opportunity to continue their education at a prestigious undergraduate institution is assured, most of the students I have talked with on my visits to the campus display a sense of being exceptionally lucky. They feel fortunate for other reasons as well, since they share with students at the best boarding schools in America such things as excellent teachers, a beautiful campus, good athletic facilities, after-class activities in several creative arts, and comfortable dormitories. For most, the fact that they have undergone a highly competitive selection process before being placed in this enviable situation fosters a cheerful willingness to perform their required community service jobs, such as working at a homeless shelter or assisted-living center in Las Vegas. For all of these reasons, I gained the impression that when they go out into the world most UWC graduates sincerely desire to make a social contribution commensurate with the school's philosophy of repaying privilege with service to humankind.

SARA PARCERO LEITES

Perhaps no UWC graduate exemplifies this commitment to the public good better than Sara Parcero Leites, member of the Class of 2011, whom I encountered one day when I went to see what was going on at the college. Her classes were just over for the day, and she had time to talk. We sat outside in the warm autumn sunshine on a rise overlooking the playing field, where other students were getting up an impromptu game of soccer. With a ready smile and eyes that looked straight into mine, the young woman from Spain told me the story of how she came to be at UWC. "My daddy is a masseuse, and he told me about this girl who was studying at the UWC in Hong Kong. On the 27th of July in 2007 I met her, and she told me this amazing story about how you could get a free education for two years in the U.S. By the time she was finished, I was ready to apply. In my year, there were 600 applicants for 10 UWC scholarships being offered by the selection committee in Spain. They chose 50 of the applicants to go to Madrid for two days of interviews, and I was in that group. Then they said that I was one of 18 chosen for a final interview. That's how I met the King of Spain. Two days later they called me and said that I had been accepted. I could hardly believe it. When they asked me which UWC I wanted to attend I said my first choice was the one in the U.S. I was only sixteen at the time and my friends all thought I was crazy to leave home, but my family really stood behind me. Then when I got here it was like I was on this bus going nowhere, until all of a sudden I saw the castle up on the hill, and it was just so impressive."

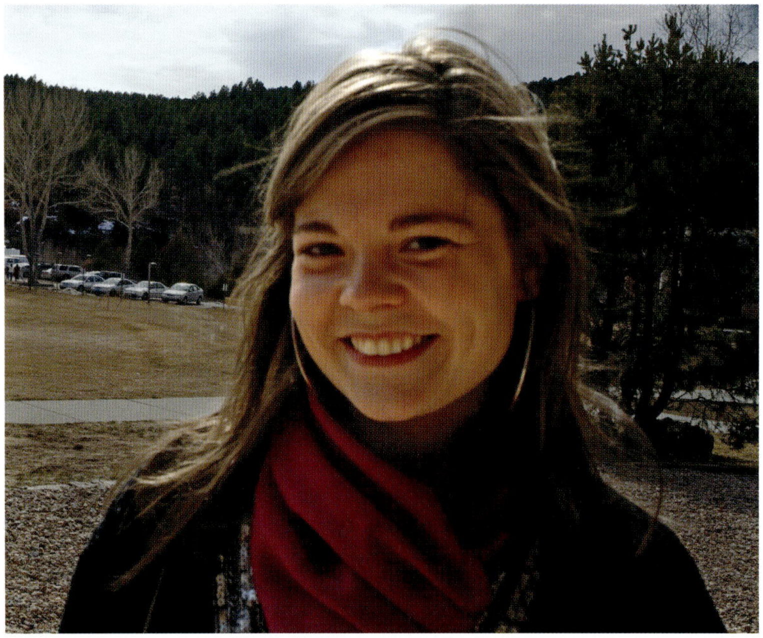

Sara Parcero Leites

Sara's English is so fluent and idiomatic that I assumed she had mastered the language before she came to America. I was wrong. "I couldn't speak any English," she told me. "I would just smile, nod, say thank you, thank you, yes, yes. At home I had studied English and was pretty good in grammar, but since no one spoke it and all the American movies are translated into Spanish, at first I had no idea what the teachers were saying. In history class we were studying Russia, and I couldn't even understand that the professor was talking about a *country*!"

Sara is by nature a humanitarian. "Back home I was involved with the Red Cross and many different projects," she said. "My family lives in a quiet town on the coast near the border between Spain and Portugal. We don't have a lot of poor people, and there are no gypsies like in Madrid. My friends think poverty only exists in movies and newspapers and that there is no need to try to help. At UWC, everyone wants to do something. I said, 'Here is my chance! I can do something,' and I signed up for a program called 'No More Deaths.'" She then explained how she and some other students had gone to a Mexican border town to bring beans and water to an encampment of destitute people living in the midst of drug wars and illegal-immigrant detention. "When I saw all those kids, all those faces," she exclaimed, "they didn't want us to be there to bring thousands of dollars or build buildings. They just wanted attention. I met this nine-year-old girl named Sofía who had to take care of her brothers and sisters. I could speak Spanish, of course, and she told me I was the first person who would listen to her. I thought she was very brave to take care of the children. She was teaching them with love. She said she wanted to go to school and study and have a better life. It really hit me when I thought, oh my God, I have education, good clothes, and water to drink, but there is really no difference between us."

Since northern New Mexican communities such as Las Vegas are no longer isolated ethnic enclaves and everyone today speaks the dominant language of the rest of the country, the present generation of Hispanic children often do not learn Spanish at home. When she was at UNC one of Sara's activities, therefore, was tutoring for two hours a week at Los Niños Elementary School. She also worked with elderly people with mental problems in the New Mexico Behavioral Health Center. About this experince she commented with compassion, "In Spain we don't have this sort of thing. Your relatives take care of you. It's terrible here when no one visits these old people and they have to spend Christmas alone. I hear their stories, listen to them. It's very intense." She was also involved with a soup kitchen run by the Methodist Church. When the Las Vegas Health Department tried to close it because of poor sanitary conditions, Sara and her fellow volunteers swung into action. Enthusiatically she recalled how they worked for ten hours on Saturday to get the place cleaned and repainted by Monday. Summing up her attitude toward social service, she added, "Volunteer: I really love that word *volunteer*!"

At the time we spoke, Sara had sent college applications to Brown, Yale, Dartmouth, Macalaster, Colby, and Trinity. "I'll be the first person in my family to get a college education," she told me. "My mom only had three years of school. We're from a small fishing town, and when I was little she worked from six in the morning until ten at night arranging and selling seafood. Then she opened her own business. I was always helping my dad. We did a lot of cooking together. They are very supportive of what I am doing and tell me to follow my dream." When I asked Sara exactly what that dream was, not surprisingly she replied, "International relations. I want to go to many places and help as many people as possible. I want to be a diplomat. That's why I decided to leave home a year and a half ago. If you just stay in your comfort zone, you don't see what is happening in the rest of the world. UWC is all about bonds and connections. If we all work together we really can make a difference."

The persistent local refrain "We don't want to be like Santa Fe" is a Las Vegan shorthand expression of disdain for sophisticated imported culture as opposed to homegrown art and entertainment. One positive side of this bias is the several possibilities local artists and craftsmen have for displaying their work in shops and galleries. Another is the numerous opportunities community members, including students, have to perform in amateur theatricals and musicales. The 727-seat Ilfeld Auditorium serves a variety of functions including concerts, plays, movie screenings, Highlands graduations, and the annual Miss Las Vegas pageant. The most prominent outdoor entertainment space in Las Vegas is the Old Town plaza, which perpetuates the time-honored Hispanic tradition of serving as both an informal social center and a venue for a variety of events including fiestas, weddings, and motorcycle rallies. On the other side of town every summer the Las Vegas Arts Council sponsors the People's Faire in the park surrounding the Carnegie Library. Here artisans and food vendors set up booths, and local and regional performing artists, including traditional dancers, singers, mariachi performers, DJs, and live bands entertain bystanders.

Arts and Crafts

The beauty of Northern New Mexico has always inspired artists, and the carving and painting of santos has been a tradition over three centuries. Along with their Native American neighbors, Nuevo Mexicanos have excelled in a variety of crafts such as weaving, jewelry-making, woodworking, and silversmithing. Connected now more closely than in previous generations with American popular culture, Las Vegas artists display both hip and traditional kinds of talent, as I discovered when I talked with a graffiti artist, a mural artist, a painter, a tattoo artist, a santero, and two shopkeepers on Bridge Street.

ZAK LUJAN

In the 1980s Keith Haring, Jean-Michel Basquiat, and other New York graffitists emerged from the underground to become the darlings of the art world. In Las Vegas Zak Lujan, a twenty-year-old graffiti artist who paints murals that have the same unstructured spontaneity, cartooning draftsmanship, and complexity of line and color, is a locally recognized talent. We talked at length one day when I was having lunch at Estella's, the popular Bridge Street café that was started by his grandmother in the 1950s and is now owned and operated by his mother, Adelita Lujan.

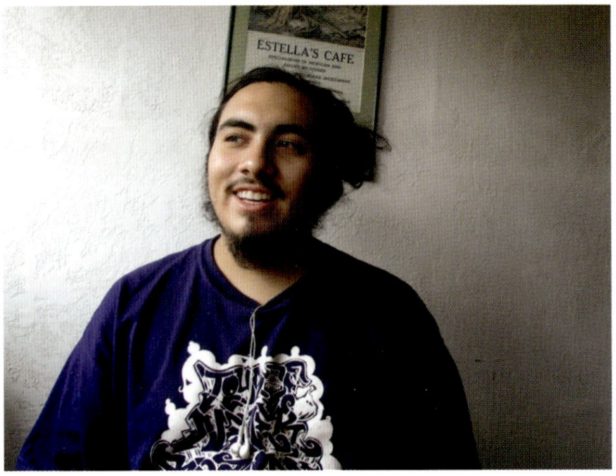

Zak Lujan

Zak's work first caught my attention as I was peering one day at a mural on the understructure of the bridge spanning the Gallinas River. It has since been painted over, as has a much larger mural just outside of town near exit 343 on Interstate 25, which formerly covered the entire side of a corrugated-steel storage building. When I expressed my admiration for the graphic freedom of its large-scale, loopy lines and the vibrancy of its colors, Zak said, "Yeah, that one was pretty cool."

Zak, who is savvy about the culture of graffiti and its place in recent art history, helped me appreciate the distinction between a graffiti writer and a graffiti artist. The former does tagging—the surreptitious "autographing" of walls with the graffitist's logo. The latter may include a tag but only as a signature for a mural of complex artistic intention. However, crossing over from the street to the gallery as some graffitists have done is something Zak finds troubling: "People say, 'You are super talented. Why do you just paint walls?' But I'm a graffiti writer as well as a graffiti artist, and I don't just want to paint on canvas. The street is a basic part of who I am and what I do. I rarely do plain one- or two-color graffiti in Vegas. I'll do shows and commissioned art pieces on walls here, but when I go out and write it's in other places like Taos, Española, Santa Fe, and Denver. You get addicted to it. When you do a piece of street graffiti, it's like it's just you."

Zak finds inspiration in what other graffiti artists are doing elsewhere and keeps track of the styles associated with different cities: "As opposed to LA, where graffiti is really cool right now, in New York, which was huge in the seventies, it has kind of calmed down, and the great artists like 'Taki 183,' 'Tracy 161,' and 'Dondi,' who used to paint subway cars and stuff, are all gone. Cities have different kinds of styles. In Chicago you get real flavorful graffiti." When I asked why, he said, "Brown people's graffiti just has more flavor somehow." Zak contradicted me when I remarked that there weren't many female graffiti artists. "Eyelash is a real good artist," he said. "And Miss Bond is famous and does her stuff on the street. Usually chicks are more artsy. Some are fast and some are slow, but most of them take more time than guys." As for himself, he said, "Right now I am into Rastafarianism, and

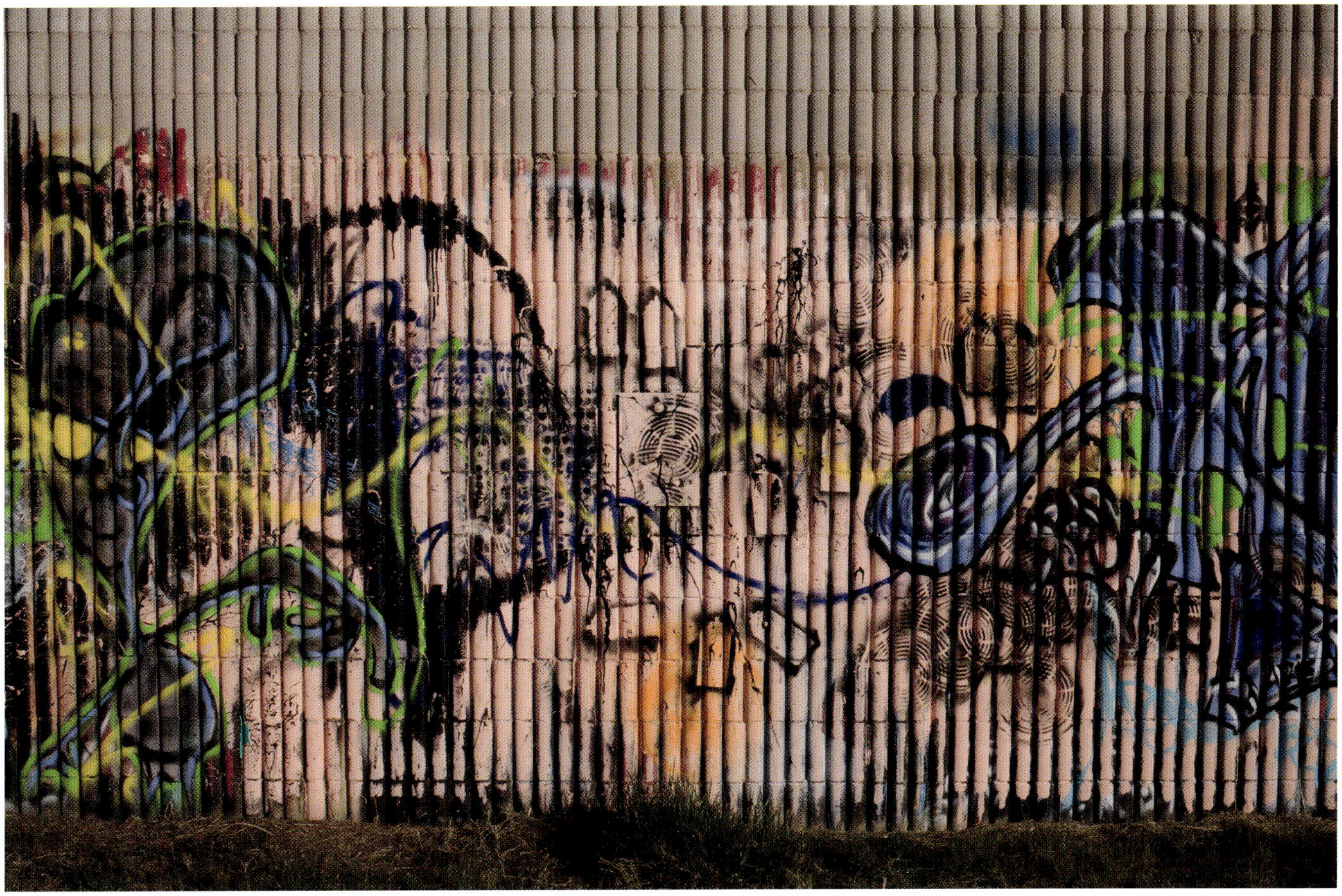

Zak Lujan, graffiti mural, 2010

that affects my work." Regarding his hometown: "In Vegas, street graffiti is not super huge, and there isn't much variety. You see the same tags. There are only four people including me in Vegas who are really known."

When I asked him why he had decided to do graffiti in the first place, Zak explained, "My dad is a musician, and all his friends are artists. It's like if you grew up around someone who was into sports, you'd become a jock. I used to draw a lot when I was a kid, and I guess I was meant to be an artist. Graffiti is like skateboarding, hip-hop, break dancing, rapping, DJ. They are all part of street culture. I've been skating these streets all my life. In Vegas you get totally different vibes skateboarding than in big urban places like Chicago, LA, or New York, especially at nighttime when there are no cars and you own the street. I love to skate, and skateboarding was my inspiration to start doing graffiti. A bunch of us used to skate at an old abandoned factory outside of town, and when I saw this really cool piece of graffiti on the side of the building I thought, 'I can do that.' We did the wall over there, and then we did three or four more. I was like fourteen, and my friend Brian was fifteen. When you are young and you start doing graffiti, you don't think anything is going to happen to you. But then we got busted. The punishment was I had to write an essay about what I thought about graffiti. Basically I just wrote what they wanted. I still loved doing graffiti, and when I discovered my tag, which is TUK, Brian and I did a few little missions." I wanted to know if TUK was some kind of acronym, and Zak said, "Yeah. It stands for 'The Unseen King.' But now I have a different tag, KAZ, which is my name spelled backwards. Most tags are short, usually just three letters, but sometimes I like to use KAZSTER."

He then went on to explain how he had made the transition from miscreant to respected creator of public art. "First there was this lady from California named Birdie who used to live here. She already had some graffiti on one of the sides of her house, and she asked me and Brian to go ahead and paint the rest of the wall. We also did a piece in an alley over by Robertson High School. And then I won this contest to do the big mural out by the highway on the abandoned car wash place where they now just store pieces of equipment. Most of the time I work really fast, but big pieces like that with background color take longer because the paint has to dry before you can go on to the next layer. But it was a fun time because I got to hang out with my family, who all came out to help."

I wanted to know more about the kind of materials Zak used and how he obtained them. "I don't like to use acrylic too much," he said. "You can't finish as fast as with a spray can where in two minutes I am already done if I'm just doing a three-letter tag. Sometimes I get my spray paints online. Molotow is a good company, and I like the Montana brand a lot. They are big and have good colors.[1] Kryon is a good brand, but they have cans where you can't take off the nozzles. With Montana you can get special caps, for instance one that gives you a real thin line." When it comes to shopping in person, he said, "I like to go over to Red House, a head shop in Santa Fe that has smokes and weird stuff. I've been going there forever now, and they are happy when I come in because they know they are going to get a big paint order." Zak said that when he got ready to do a large piece, he needed to purchase safety items as well: caps, gloves, and dust masks, remarking sensibly, "As I get older I have to be more careful about respiratory problems, because I know some guys who at thirty just like die."

According to him, graffiti is social and hierarchical: "It's like a universal language. You can go anywhere, and if you're good you get respect and nobody touches you." He went on to explain, "There are different levels in being a graffiti writer. People admire a king and don't write over his work, but toys get their stuff erased. A toy is like a chump, somebody that has a style like a punk and is just playing. Sometime a toy will put his tag next to a piece by a king just to get noticed. Then there are the haters. It's a kind of psychological warfare, and they like to go and vandalize you. Sometimes the authorities come along and remove your work. My mural under the bridge got painted over that way, but I've never had a bad rep, and most of my stuff has stayed up. The people here in Vegas think of me as a kind of legend and say that Zak is just this hippie guy."

Although street art is his preferred form of expression, Zak does sometime paint on canvas and paper. Speaking of his exhibition at Roy Montibon's Royal Mastodon Society, where he sold three graffiti paintings, he said, "Roy seemed like this real nice guy; he's from LA and loves my style. My dad told me, 'Come on, you can do it.' So I brought my idea for a show to Roy, and he said, 'Sure.' " Far more exciting for Zak was the show that he and Brian organized at Blackbird, a bar that used to be on Bridge Street next to the Kiva movie theater. "Not to be cocky or anything," he claimed, "but that was one of the best shows I ever did. It was a total street show. We were painting girls, giving them a full body graphic, which looks sort of like a tattoo. They were standing in the windows, and it was really raw, definitely not a family thing. You could do the same kind of painting on guys, but they're not going to let you. It's just the best thing when you do it on girls. When I finish painting one, I think wow! You were in my zone, you have no clothes on, and you're gorgeous. Why weren't we kissing?"

A high school dropout—"I didn't get the culture of that"—Zak later earned a diploma through the GED program at Luna Community College, following which he has "done a little bit of this and that," including cooking in his mother's restaurant. He told me that he had no immediate plans to go to college but may decide at some point to get a bachelor's degree in fine art. "The professors in the art department at Highlands are nice to me," he said, "and I like to go up there and hang out. I think printmaking is one of the coolest things ever. I love wood block, etching, it's all just super fun." Besides cooking at Estella's, he sometimes does T-shirt and poster designs for the print shop that his friends Adam Caldwell and Aaron Juarros have recently opened a few doors up the street. Nevertheless, he is certain of his real calling. As I was getting ready to leave, he said, "It seems like for me graffiti has always been there. If I hadn't done that I'd probably be in jail. It has enlarged my worldview. And I'm still a skateboarder. Getting out in the street is what I like to do when I want to just chill out."

ROCK ULIBARRI

I was able to approach mural art from another perspective when I went to see Rock Ulibarri, a former teacher at the Boys Ranch, a Christian not-for-profit organization for troubled teens. These days Ulibarri is the artist in charge of implementing Miguel Angel's Casa de Cultura mural program. As he explains it, the mission of the program is to portray through art a revisionist version of northern New Mexican history emphasizing the people's rights and their struggle against dominant power structures.

We met one day at El Centro Family Health Clinic, where Casa de Cultura's first mural covers the entire wall of an inside hallway. It depicts ordinary Hispanics who were important in the settlement of the land around Las Vegas. Ulibarri began our conversation by asking me if I knew the book *A People's History of the United States: 1492 to Present* by Howard Zinn. I did not, though later I familiarized myself with it. Zinn examines U.S. history through the lens of the exploitation and subjugation of indigenous peoples. Summing up his thesis, he writes:

> Nations are not communities and never have been. The history of any country, presented as the history of a family, conceals fierce conflicts of interest (sometimes exploding, most often repressed) between conquerors and conquered, masters and slaves, capitalists and workers, dominators and dominated in race and sex. And in such a world of conflict, a world of victims and executioners, it is the job of thinking people not to be on the side of the executioners.

"I've always taught from the perspective of that book." Ulibarri told me. "That's how Miguel Angel taught. When I first met him I realized that we had read all the same books, that we thought exactly alike and were following the same path."

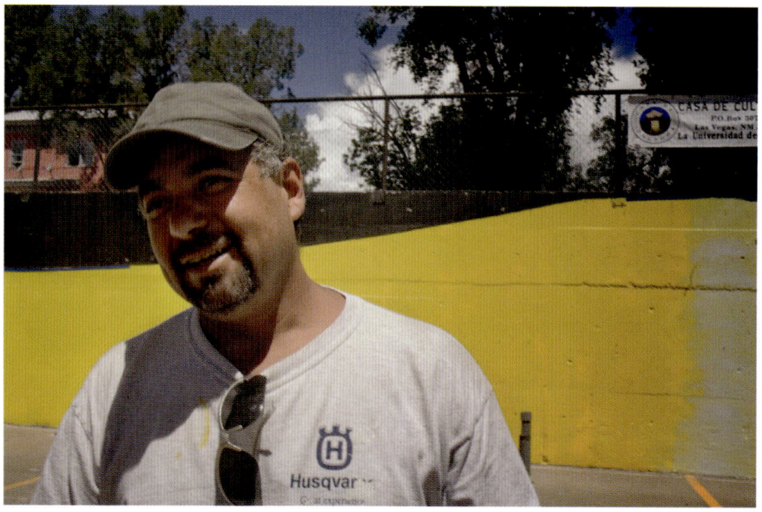

Rock Ulibarri

Community is a word that Ulibarri, like Angel, uses a lot. He explained to me how he first passes out survey forms to various community members before he starts to work on a history mural. He then incorporates their ideas into an overall design. But community participation does not stop at the planning stage inasmuch as high school students and adult volunteers are recruited to work collaboratively on the murals that Casa de Cultura sponsors.

Casa de Cultura's most recent mural covers a large concrete wall at the back of the parking lot opposite the Spic & Span Restaurant. According to Ulibarri, "It honors a lot of different struggles, individuals, and cultures from the Native American period to the European invasion to today. It will be a true community collaboration with everyone working together on all aspects of the art. The people of this town will take ownership of the mural. Everyone who works on it will be recognized in the plaque, even the graffiti taggers. They are also artists who will be expressing themselves on this wall, and because they will have ownership, you can bet this thing will be protected."

The City of Las Vegas gave Casa de Cultura $15,000 for the erection of the mural, and the organization has a contractual agreement stating that, if it is taken

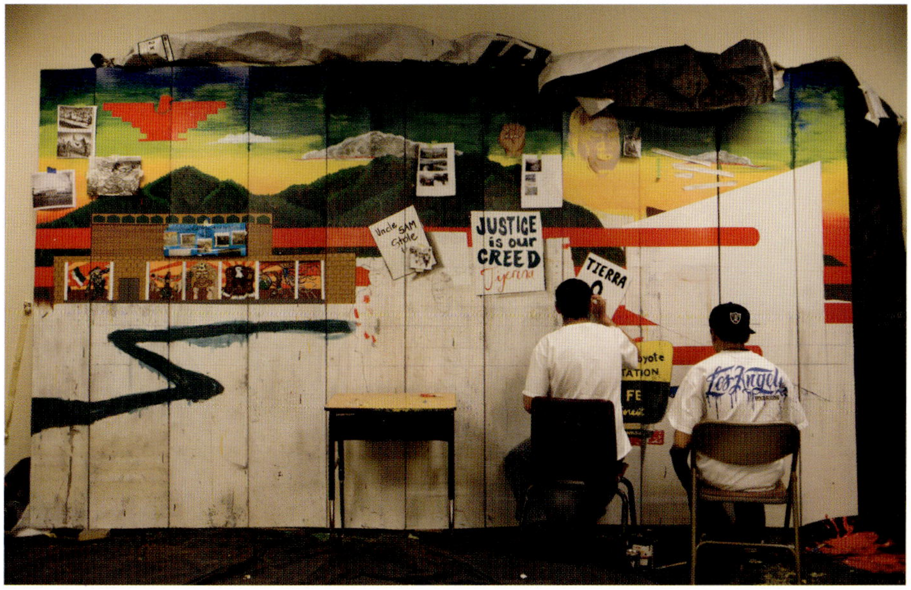

Casa de Cultura mural painters in West Las Vegas High School studio

down in the future, the city will find another location for it within thirty days. To make such contingent removal possible and in order to continue working on the mural during the cold months of the year, it was painted off-site as a series of nine panels that were later assembled as one 126-foot-long work of art. I saw it in the process of being painted when I went one day to the West Las Vegas High School, where the principal had made a large room available to Ulibarri and some students whom the art teacher had released from class to work with him. When I arrived I found them, like apprentices in the workshop of an old master, applying paint over his underdrawing.

As we walked around the room, Ulibarri explained the mural's iconography to me. "Most people don't know that it was an African—a black Moor—who was the first explorer to enter the Southwest from Mexico," he said. "His name was Estéban Dorantes, or Estevanico. He came in 1539 with Frey Marcos de Niza, who was in search of the famed Seven Cities of Cibola. What they took for a city of gold were only adobe walls, which probably looked like gold in the late afternoon sun with the light shining on the bits of mica in the adobe. Estevanico went on ahead to 'Cibola,' which turned out to be the Zuni pueblo, where he was killed by the natives. But Fray Niza went back to Mexico with tales of the fabulous wealth of Cibola. That was what lured Coronado to make his expedition the next year. No one knows why the friar had told such fantastic lies about cities built of gold and emeralds or why he came back as Coronado's guide, because all they found were the adobe pueblos of the Zuni."

Moving to the next scene, Ulibarri pointed out Don Juan de Oñate leading his 500 men up from Mexico in 1598. He explained, "This is the beginning of the land-grant system when the Spanish crown handed out huge amounts of land to certain men who came to seek gold and other riches. They brought with them the encomienda system, which meant that they would Christianize the native population and offer them protection in return for payment in the form of crops and labor. Of course, the people were not happy to have their lands invaded, their religion suppressed, having to pay tribute, and being made to offer allegiance to a king they had never heard of. So over here you see the Pueblo Revolt, the uprising in 1680 when they threw the Spanish out."

"Look," Ulibarri said, leading me to the next panel. "This is where you get Don Diego de Vargas coming back in 1692 for the Reconquest. That's why you see the conquistadores on their horses. This was the second invasion, and though some of the people around here whose ancestors came to New Mexico around that time are mad at me and don't like to see it that way, this is a people's mural and we have to be honest about what happened to the Native American population and how their way of life was again suppressed." In front of the next panel we saw two students on campstools. They were painting a scene containing the first farmers to cultivate the land. "Here we're showing the *borrego* system," he commented, explaining that *borrego* refers to sheepherding. Turning to the next wall, Ulibarri continued, "Now we come to the invasion of 1841 showing how the New Mexican militia captured an army of 300 Texans. See, we show them here in the plaza burning the Texans' proclamation claiming entitlement to New Mexico." [2]

The subsequent reversal of fortune with the abrogation of New Mexico's allegiance to the government of Mexico and its appropriation as a territory of the United States is also part of the iconography of the mural. Pointing to the panel depicting that historical moment, Ulibarri said, "Here you see how five years after the Texans' invasion, General Kearny marches in and, standing on a rooftop overlooking the plaza, proclaims New Mexico as a U.S. territory. Everyone calls this a bloodless victory, but it wasn't bloodless at all. There was a good deal of resistance. The soldiers who were left in New Mexico after Kearny started his march to California were supposed to keep order, but instead they began stealing livestock from the Hispanic settlers in the villages outside Las Vegas. When five men were involved in killing a soldier in one such raid, they were caught, accused of homicide, and taken to Santa Fe for a public hanging. The soldiers, of course, were never accused or punished for theft."

Moving on to the next scene, Ulibarri continued his narrative: "Now comes the Santa Fe Ring—more land-grabbers. Here is where you get to the Gorras Blancas. This is the most important chapter in our history and the one that changed New Mexico forever. We are the only state in the union that still has land grants—or what's left of the original ones that weren't taken away illegally. That's because the Gorras Blancas brought the land-grabbing to a standstill. It was a victory for the people. That's why here in Northern New Mexico we have a certain pride that you don't find anywhere else in the Southwest." He went on to explain how Juan José Herrera and his two brothers, Pablo and Nicanor, formed the Gorras Blancas and organized the resistance: "They were doing much more than simply protesting the appropriation of the land by Anglo ranchers. Juan José was a prominent labor leader, and Pablo Herrera was instrumental in forming the People's Party—el Partido del Pueblo Unido. This was not just a Hispanic thing. There were many poor working-class Americans who were on the side of the Gorras Blancas just like there were whites that were part of the Civil Rights movement. Also, there was no shortage of Anglo settlers who married in and became part of the culture. It was about the people who came to exploit, and the people who came to settle. It was fundamentally a class thing: rich against poor."

When I told Ulibarri that I had read *The Devil's Hatband,* the novel in which his second cousin, Daniel Aragon y Ulibarri, tells the Gorras Blanca story in gripping detail, he replied that he had heard the same history firsthand from his grandmother. That was because his family property is in the Gallinas Canyon at El Porvenir where Nicanor Herrera spent his last years. His grandmother, who was a young woman at the time, knew him well. "She was able to give me story after story," he said. "They even lived in the same house. Besides that, it turns out that I am related to the Herrera brothers on both sides of the family."

Ulibarri views the Chicano movement as the successor resistance to that of the Gorras Blancas. On another day when I had stopped by the Casa de Cultura art studio in the high school I saw Tiny Martinez's portrait propped against the wall so that Ulibarri could draw his face as realistically as possible on the final panel of the mural. "Tiny was on the side of the Brown Berets," he said. "Some people here thought of them as hoodlums, but they were also heroes. We also have to deal with the revolution that went on at Highlands University and the students who called themselves the Muralistas Norteños de Aztlan. Their names—Freddy Trujillo, Alonzo Garcia, and Samuel Aragon—and that of their teacher Jesus Aragon should be remembered. The mural they did inside the student union building depicted Che Guevara, and on Burris Hall they painted three mestizo faces above the Aztec pyramid and a group of Chicanos carrying signs saying '¿Que pasó?' in protest against the administration of the new president Gilbert Sanchez. That and another mural at West Las Vegas High School got painted out at the same time. It showed beautiful Aztec dancers and aspects of the mestizo heritage along with skeleton soldiers with banners saying, '18,000 Chicanos muertos en Vietnam.' " For Ulibarri and others, the murals' removal in 1975 is a dark stain on the history of Highlands, and this is one reason why he feels Casa de Cultura's new historically revisionist mural should pay homage to those heady days of radical protest.

Miguel Angel and his wife Georgina had come into the room at this point as had Mayor Alfonso Ortiz, who wanted to see what was going on. Ulibarri showed the mayor a sketch on the wall depicting the zia,[3] the four-rayed New Mexico sun symbol in red against a yellow background, the colors of Spain. "That's the part that will be painted by the offenders who are over in the detention center," he said, adding "There is a lot of talent behind those bars. They are community too."

Conducting the mayor through the same sequence of scenes he had earlier described to me, Ulibarri stopped in front of the panel of the Gorras Blancas. "We're going to get in as much about the Gorras Blancas as possible," he said. You know, this whole idea of private property in a capitalist society like the United States is very foreign to us. That's the history we are trying to teach the community." Georgina, who was standing nearby, added with ideological contempt, "I'm glad I never went to high school and had to study the garbage they taught as American history."

When I called Ulibarri later to make sure that I had gotten my facts right, I said I was curious about the images depicted within the mural since their emphasis on the Chicano movement seemed somewhat at odds with the prevailing local attitudes about race, which esteems Spanish colonial culture while downplaying its mestizo elements. Making no distinctions between northern New Mexican Hispanics and south-of-the-border Latinos, his answer was both political and pedagogical. "Mural art reflects the passion, knowledge, culture, and social views of the time. Historically the poor get no media coverage, nor do they have any means to publish their views or opinions. Murals are nothing short of an illustrated diary of the poor. They provide another way of teaching history."

Although a sympathizer with the plight of all races, Ulibarri is as proud of his Basque heritage and as deeply rooted as other Las Vegans with ancestral ties to Northern New Mexico. When I visited him at his family compound in El Porvenir, I remarked that the book I was writing was fundamentally about the nature of place and that I was trying to understand what I call the "placeness" of this part of the world. I asked him to tell me what he thought about Las Vegas in this light. He paused and then said with considerable thoughtfulness, "Well, there is place and space. They are not the same thing at all. Space is boundary, acres. My personal feeling about living here is that I was raised to consider this part of Northern New Mexico as place. Place is where my great-grandfather planted corn; it is something that is just part of me. The people from around here see it that way. I feel very strongly that what we have here is place, not space."

MARTÍN MONTOYA

Like Rock Ulibarri, Martín Montoya is a man whose art and life are inseparable from this part of the world. He is rooted here not only because of his Hispanic heritage but also by a deeply felt personal choice. Unlike Ulibarri's mural art, his work is devoid of political narrative; rather, it is simply an expression of his own happy spirit. A prolific painter, he is an occasional muralist but usually paints in acrylic on canvas. His studio is a tiny windowed nook in his mobile home in the village of Tecolote, where I went to visit him one day. As we talked for an hour in the shade of his makeshift porch, I began to realize that his subject matter is everywhere—in his head and in the land and sky around him. Art for him is all about place, for he experiences an innate vitality in the quotidian and paints whatever he sees in the ordinary here and now—his dog, his white pickup truck, the village church.

Tecolote is notorious for its longstanding feud, beginning when the second generation of land grantees started to argue among themselves over access to various parcels of the common land. By now the history of the dispute is as unfathomable as the legal case in Dickens's *Bleak House.* Montoya, who belongs to one of the contending families, is philosophically inclined to keep himself above the fray. "After all," he said, "no one really owns the land; we're all just tenants on this earth. Someone is always taking, and this goes on over and over again as life changes. All that matters is experiencing the moment. Who knows what will happen this afternoon? Yesterday is already distorted in your mind. It is an illusion, too." He said that he was glad to subsist on very little as long as he and Maria and their young son had enough to live on. "I feel that all I want to do is just produce and produce and produce art. I have this drive that requires me to express what I feel." When I remarked that no one can sustain such intense creativity day after day, he replied that for him just looking at the sky is a kind of spiritual replenishment that builds artistic capital.

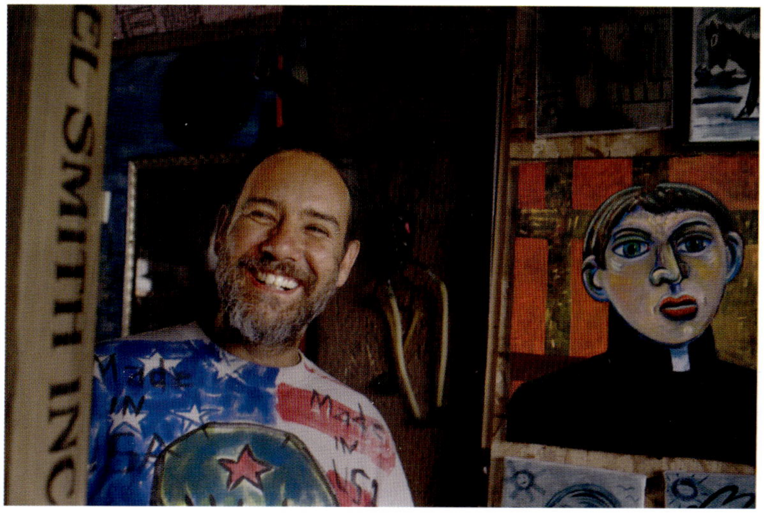

Martín Montoya

Montoya is also a sculptor, and he applies the word *decorative* to both his painting and sculpture. He sees no separation between art as design and art that fulfills his desire to represent the exuberance inherent in everyday objects. "Art is the jewels of the home," he told me as we stepped inside. I felt as if I had indeed entered a jewel box. The four small rooms of the mobile home were crowded and dark, but they did not seem so. Everything—everything—in the house seemed to be part of a giant three-dimensional collage. There was a group of cast-bronze and carved-wood sculptures by the front window. The window looked as if it were made of stained glass because every pane was painted over with colorfully vibrant, cheerful images. In the kitchen, refrigerator art had spread to cover the walls and doors. Maria, who like Martín was wearing a hand-painted T-shirt, showed me the bedroom where their son was watching television. The Montoyas were married twenty-one years before he was born, and the depth of their love for this only child was palpable.

Although they have a place in Las Vegas where they live in the winter, Montoya told me that he doesn't really think of himself as part of the community. "I don't get out. I just do art. When society loses art, as ours is doing now, we lose the human element. We have to let the spirituality of art—that's different from the icons of religion—come in. It opens doors. Art has the key. Look, Van Gogh didn't paint landscapes; he painted the energy of life. I hope my art inspires somebody. It is what allows me to be me, which is something that is not very easy to do in this world. But I believe in it and live my life by it."

PHIL LUCERO

Even though it is customer-dictated for the most part, body art is another form of self-expression. Phil Lucero, the proprietor of the House of Pain, is a tattoo artist whose passion for his vocation equals Montoya's. On the evening when I stopped by his shop he was tattooing the left bicep of his fifteen-year-old son. For now the young man's forearm was bare of tattoos because he plans to enlist in the Marine Corps, and the military won't accept recruits with tattoos below the elbow.

Almost all of Lucero's body, including his face and shaved head, are covered with tattoos. When I asked him why the numeral 63 covered almost the entire top of his shaven head, he replied, "That's the year my grandpa died." Pulling up his shirt, he showed me a realistic portrait of a young man. "That's my younger brother. He passed away a couple of years ago. It's like a loving memory piece. My buddy, who is a real good tattoo artist, did it. Pretty soon I am going to tattoo a collage around it with some of the things he used to say." Pulling up his pant leg to reveal his left calf, which bore the image of a mustachioed man wearing glasses and a black Stetson hat, he continued, "Here is a portrait of my dad."Then he showed me a colorful clown with a red nose and green hair on his right thigh, saying, "A friend did this one a long time ago when I was first getting started."Turning around and lifting his T-shirt to show me his back, he remarked, "See the Last Supper. That's an old tattoo. I wish I had known what I know now about tattooing before I got that one."

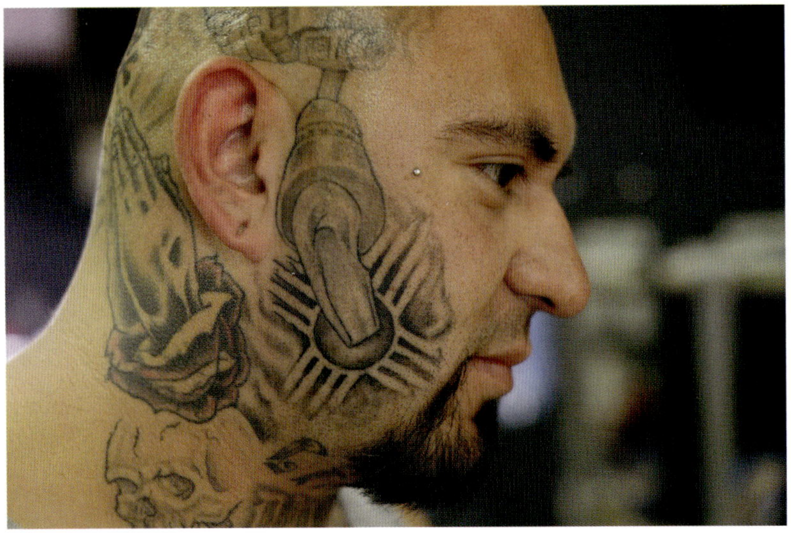

Phil Lucero

When I asked him what had made him want to become a tattoo artist in the first place, he replied, "I was a troubled kid growing up and was always getting sent to my room. My only outlet was to draw. My dad worked for the prison system, and he would being home some of the tattoo machines the prisoners had made. Then I started building my own machines with stuff like a motor from a Walkman and other weird parts. After that I began doing tattoos on myself. Now that I have my own business, of course, I only use high-tech equipment."

As we talked, Lucero's passion for his art became increasingly apparent. "I really like to draw, and the art industry—I love it. I go to conventions all over the world and learn from other artists. You see many kinds of specialties: black-and-gray work, color work, bio-mechanical work, and lots of different styles of body art: Japanese koi fish and cherry blossoms, Samoan and Polynesian tattoos, just about everything. Right now the thing I am getting into is portraits like the ones my buddy did on me. I buy a lot of magazines and make drawings in my sketchbook of the faces I want to transfer onto skin."

When I inquired about the business side of Lucero's work, he said, "It's good protection. I make somewhere between sixty thousand and seventy thousand dollars a year. And the important thing is I am doing what I love. I look forward to coming to work every day. I've always loved art, and everything I've done since I left high school has been art. I used to do silk-screening and other things related to art before I got apprenticed to become a licensed tattoo artist. I opened this shop in 2004, but I didn't do the tattoos on my head and face until about four years after I knew that I was a stable business owner and wouldn't have to go look for a job somewhere else." Pointing to the wall where customers can pick out standard tattoo patterns, he said, "I do that kind of stuff and also cover-ups. I always tell people not to have their girlfriend or boyfriend's name tattooed on them, but some of them want to go ahead anyway. Then when they have broken up they come in and have me do a cover-up tattoo. But what I really want to do is custom draw the images that are in my head, the things I think up myself. That's when tattooing gets to be real art."

Fascinated, at Lucero's invitation I leaned over the padded massage table on which his son was lying to get a better view of the machine he uses as his artist's tool. "See, there are coils that run up carrying the electric current," he explained. "Then at the end you have the needle. When I dip it into one of these ink caps, it draws the ink up just like a hypodermic. When I release it I have to be careful to puncture the skin at just the right angle so it won't spread out and make a blotch." To get a better view of the piece he was tattooing on his son, I walked around to the other side of the table. Lucero explained, "It's an embellishment of the skull I already tattooed on his arm." Pointing out what he calls the blood line—a series of pink dots where the skin had been pricked to outline a design corresponding to the one on a piece of paper he occasionally held up to the light, he explained, "You can see what I am doing on this side is matching up the grenade that's already been tattooed on the other side of the skull." When I asked him how long it takes to do such a tattoo, he replied, "We've been here now around three and a half hours. When we did the skull in the middle, he was lying here for eight and a half."

Hygiene is a critical part of body art, and Lucero is scrupulous about using sterile equipment and wearing rubber gloves. I watched his son, who had just risen from the table where he had been getting tattooed, swab it with an antiseptic solution. He then threw his father's used needles into a lined garbage can. "We can't be too careful, Lucero said, "There's HIV and hepatitis, so we have to be cautious and treat everybody as if they were infected in order to be sure we're not transmitting a disease to some other person." Pointing to a framed certificate on the wall, he told me, "We have to keep our license up to date. This place is inspected once a year. They have to check our chemicals and make sure all our supplies meet the state's standard."

As I got ready to leave, I remarked on the prevalence of tattoos today. Lucero said, "You're right. It used to be that only pachucos, prisoners, and people in the military had tattoos. Now that's not true. I've given my mom four tattoos, and my buddy gave her another one the other day. Hey, this has been nice talking to you. Why don't you come in sometime, and I'll give you a tattoo—for free!"

MARGARITO MONDRAGÓN

Las Vegas has its own representatives of the venerable art of the santero, the maker of devotional icons for churches and moradas. Thanks to a commercial market for this northern New Mexican indigenous art form, these self-taught artists continue to produce bultos (the carved and painted wooden sculptures depicting saints), Cristos (crucifixes), and retablos (devotional paintings). Along with weavers, *colcha* embroiderers, decorative tin designers, jewelers, and furniture makers, several santeros exhibit at the annual Spanish Market, the juried traditional Hispanic arts festival sponsored by the Spanish Colonial Arts Society in Santa Fe.

One day I called Margarito Mondragón, currently one of the most active Las Vegas santeros, at his home on Ninth Street next to the Gallinas River. Born in Ocaté in 1950, Mondragón moved to Las Vegas as a small boy and considers himself for all intents and purposes a native of the town. "My wife Gloria and I are living in the same house my mother bought back then. It was a wonderful place to grow up. I used to play by the river. It was our jungle, our swimming hole, our place to go fishing." He and Gloria, who is a former schoolteacher, were married after their senior year in high school, and for twenty-five years Mondragón worked for the New Mexico Department of Transportation as an operator of bulldozers, rollers, and other kinds of heavy equipment. When he was eligible for his pension in 1988, he retired from road building, but three years later when he discovered that, in spite of his love for fishing, he still had time on his hands, he became a santero. He says that he now makes a better living than he did when he worked for the highway department.

Mondragón is among the santeros who regularly exhibit at Spanish Market. In 2007 his retablo depicting the Father, Son, and Holy Spirit was the image used on the market poster, and his work can be found in the Museum of Spanish Colonial Arts in Santa Fe, the Regis University Collection in Denver, and the Rough Riders Museum in Las Vegas. Recognition as an artist and the sale of work to collectors are gratifying, but he still feels that his art is more spiritually inspired than market-driven.

His stories behind some of the pieces he has carved prove the point. When I stopped by his booth at the 2010 Spanish Market and admired the work on display, he said, "I did this Sacred Heart of Jesus where you open up the heart and find Christ inside at the time my son was going to have a big open-heart surgery operation. He came through, and I think that praying this way was a help. When my daughter got laid off from work, I was doing a Saint Joseph. I prayed to him to find a job for her, and when I finished the piece she got one." Holding up a *nicho* (a small tabernacle for housing a saint) with a miniature deerskin rug laid like a welcome mat on its base, Gloria confirmed the efficacy of praying to these holy intercessors. "Inside is the Virgin," she said, opening the carved latticed doors. I had never seen an image of Mary with a red protuberance from her forehead. "That's a blood-covered thorn," Gloria explained. "When Christ went to his Crucifixion a thorn fell from his crown. It's there to show her suffering. Last week my son called to say that my daughter-in-law had cysts in her liver. I prayed that she would get better and then closed the doors of the nicho. The next day he called and said that the doctor had given the wrong diagnosis, that she had gallstones, not cysts. I opened the doors then because the favor had been granted." Nonbelievers may look askance, but the succor that the santos provide to pious Catholics is an active part of their faith. "I have to believe," said Gloria. "I know that the saints guide our prayers."

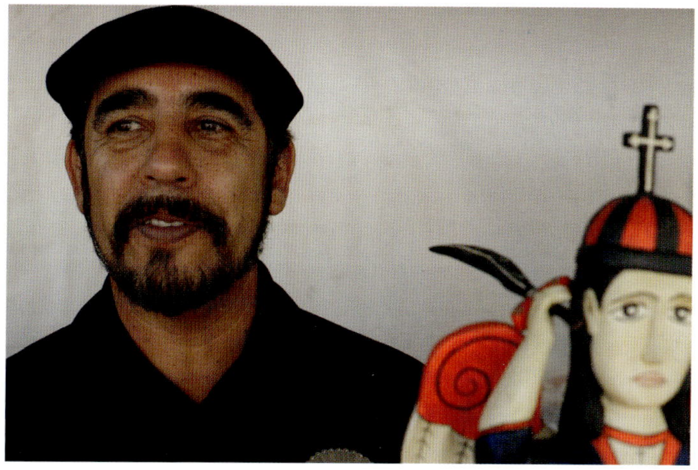

Margarito Mondragón

Mondragón's largest and most significant work to date is of Las Vegas's patron saint, Our Lady of Sorrows. Commissioned by the city, this life-size bulto stands in the center of a circular bed of flowers near the eastern entrance of the plaza. I had noticed it with a degree of surprise on a previous visit to town, and when I stopped by their booth at the 2012 Spanish Market to say hello to Margarito and Gloria, I asked them to tell me more about the genesis of this unusual piece of sacred art. Showing me a scrapbook of the work in progress, he explained, "It happened this way. They were pruning a lot of old trees that are dying, cutting them down to about eight to twelve feet off the ground. Joseph Baca who runs the radio station had been talking about making sculptures out of those tree trucks, and I said I would be willing to donate my work if I could carve one. They told me I could go ahead."

As we leafed through the photos in the scrapbook, Mondragón discussed how he had worked on a scaffold with a chain saw and chisels to make the form of the saint emerge from the tree. Pointing to a photograph showing the rear side of the

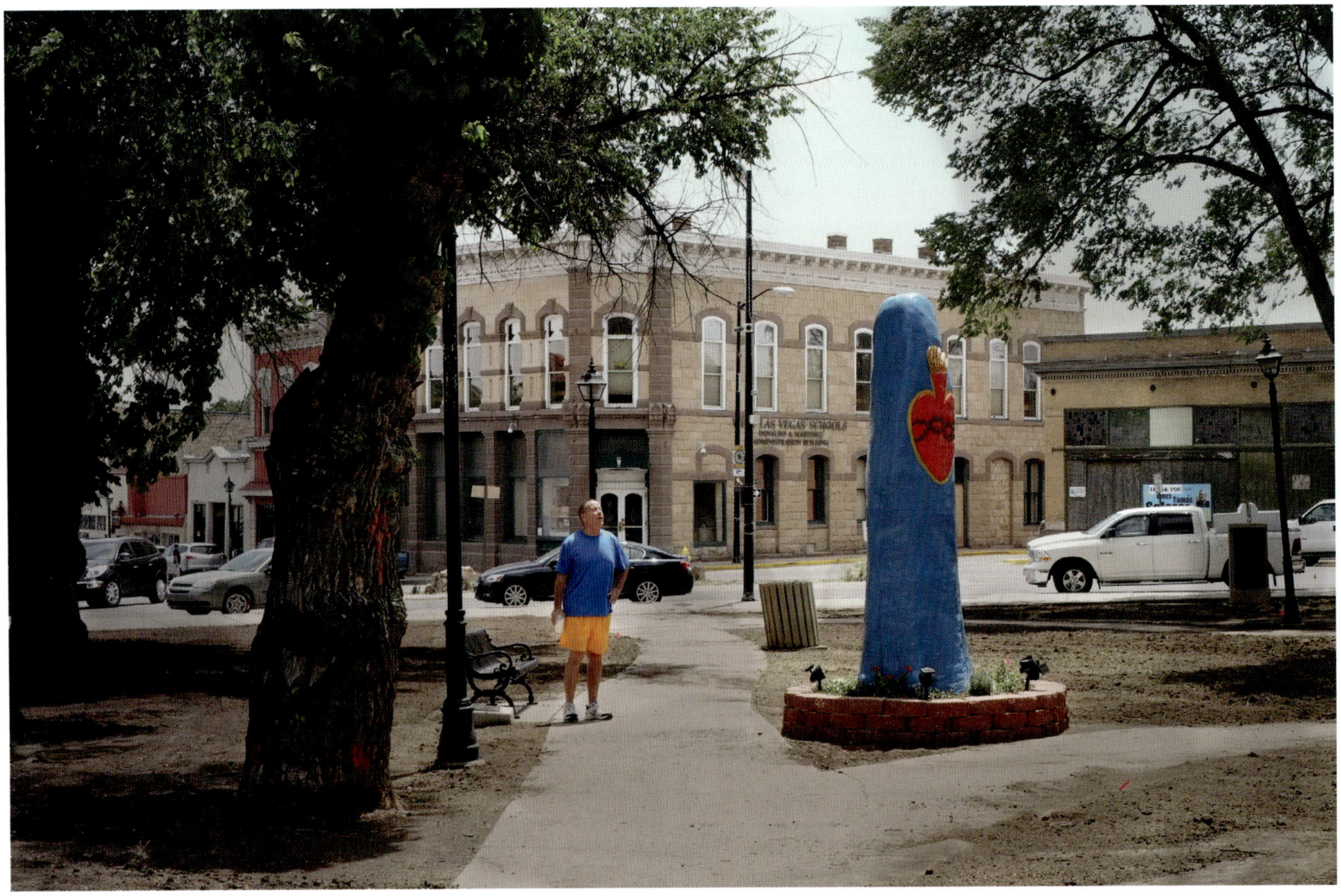

Margarito Mondragón, "Our Lady of Sorrows"

figure as it was just beginning to become discernible, he said, "Here is when I began to see this face, which looks something like Christ with a long beard. That is how I decided to put the Sacred Heart of Jesus on the back of Mary's robe rather than on her breast, which is where you usually find it." When I asked if there had been a ceremony of consecration when the work was completed, Mondragón answered, "The Penitente brotherhood came and sang hymns."

On the day I visited the Mondragóns in their home, he invited me to step into the galley space off of the living room. As I looked around, he called my attention to a sculpture he says he will never sell. It is the first bulto he ever made, an unpainted figure inspired by a divine miracle: "I was going to collect firewood one day when I saw the image of Christ's face in one of the logs. I carved away some of the outside and put a piece of barbed wire around the forehead for a crown of thorns. I could see that there was a tear in the eye. I knew then that I was meant to be a santero."

Mondragón believes, furthermore, that in taking up the santero's calling he was aided by another miracle. "I had never carved before," he told me, "and then one day after I had started on my own, I was showing my work at the Colorado Springs Spanish Market, and a little man came up to me, and asked, 'Do you carve?' When I said yes, he told me that he had some tools he would like to give me. He actually went sixty miles back to Pueblo where he lived and then returned with what must have been two thousand dollars' worth of tools. He said I could have them for a hundred dollars, and he wouldn't take more even when I offered it. I had never seen him before and I couldn't figure out why he had done this for me. But then I understood. I believe he was Saint Joseph because Saint Joseph is the patron saint of carpenters and wood carvers." Mondragón added that he later found out that his great-grandfather and great-great-grandfather had been santeros, which provided a further incentive to continue to fulfill his God-given talent.

After I had viewed some of his recent pieces, Mondragón took me out to the mobile home that serves as his studio in back. This was his mother's apartment when she was alive, and he says that he feels her spirit here watching over him. A faded marriage photograph of his parents above his worktable attests to her continuing presence in the room. He then showed me a retablo that was a work in progress—a white-clad, winged figure helping a child across a bridge. "We are all born with a guardian angel to watch over us," he said with matter-of-fact conviction.

Pointing to the guardian-angel retablo, he explained the technique of the santero. "First, I carve the image and then cover it with gesso, which I make from a rabbit glue that has been soaked for twenty-four hours and then cooked. All my colors are natural earth pigments. For the skin, I use a light dirt that I dig up along the roadside seventeen miles south of Santa Fe." On a nearby shelf I noticed some jars of pulverized stone—azurite for vivid blue, lapis lazuli for sky blue, cinnabar for red, malachite for green, nickel titanium for yellow, pure titanium for white. "These are my mineral pigments, which I reconstitute to make paint," he said. "I get them online from Kremer's in New York. Then when I am finished I cover the piece with a varnish that I make from the pitch of the piñon trees from around here, which has been soaked in alcohol. After that I rub beeswax over everything to give a nice soft glow."

Gloria welcomed us back into the house, pointing with pride to the kitchen cabinets attesting to her husband's skill as a woodworker. Before we said goodbye, she opened the refrigerator and handed me some homemade flour tortillas. Margarito gave me a bag full of apples that he had just picked from the tree outside. On the way out I took a last look in the gallery off the living room where the santos on display are for sale—all except the piece of natural wood in which Mondragón had discerned the face of Christ, the sign for him to dedicate his life to the art of the santero.

Shopkeepers

NEITA FRAN WARD

Neita Fran Ward, a pretty blonde with cornflower-blue eyes and a personality as shining as her abundant silver jewelry, is an active member of Las Vegas First, which is made up of the small-business owners who are attempting to foster Las Vegas's commercial revival through tourism and the arts. She owns WarDancer Designs & Gallery, which now occupies the newly renovated Veeder Building on the west side of the plaza. A relative newcomer to Las Vegas, Ward is from Tyler, Texas. She is married to Bill Ward, a tall, good-looking motorcycle buff and competitive archer who spends weekdays in Mosquero, New Mexico, a tiny village on the northeastern edge of San Miguel County, where he is superintendent of schools.

As she explained to me one day when I dropped into her shop, her decision to relocate in Las Vegas coincided with her success in fulfilling a dream. She was determined to give a Native American jeweler the opportunity to exercise his talent on a full-time basis. The fact that there are very few Native Americans in Las Vegas—in contrast to Santa Fe, there are no extant pueblos nearby—makes it surprising that her somewhat mystical search ended here. She told me how it happened: "I would go to archery tournaments with Bill and set up card tables offering for sale some of the Navajo silver-and-turquoise jewelry I had collected. I'd sell everything and then go out and buy more to take to the next tournament. But I wanted to do something besides just selling what I bought. You see, I'm a very spiritual person, and I began to know that I had to find one Navajo jeweler and help him. It was not about me, but about him becoming famous, having an avenue for selling his jewelry. So I would go to Indian Market every year in Santa Fe. I would look the ones who were there in the face. I saw nothing. Then one day—it was July 21, 2001, one month after I moved here—I was in the beauty parlor, and someone sitting in the next chair said, 'Wait a minute, I know just the one for you. His name is Brian Billie. He comes from a family of jewelry-makers in Gallup and lives in Las Vegas now.' " Ward called Billie on the phone, and made a date to meet him. "The minute I saw him, I just knew that this was the one. I'm certain that there was a spiritual path leading me to him."

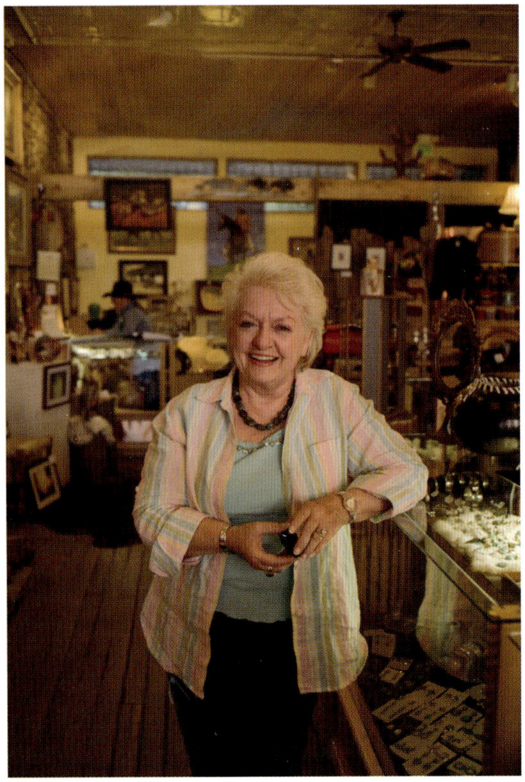

Neita Fran Ward

Ward has a great deal of jewelry in her gallery besides that of her protégé and a variety of the kinds of objects tourists traditionally collect, such as kachina dolls, Pendleton blankets, Spanish Colonial tinwork, and other kinds of local arts-and-crafts items. But Brian Billie's bracelets, rings, and other links are given pride of place in one of the front cases. She explained how their partnership works: "I buy the stones and the silver. Then I tell him what I'd like him to do, and he makes something that is better than I could ever have dreamed. Aren't these cuff links just beautiful?"

Ward's business is one of a small handful that cater to tourists passing through Las Vegas or staying over at the Plaza Hotel. "Tourists are my mainstay," she told me. "Seventy percent of my business comes from tourism. I do have local customers, but they are few and far between." She also has an interior design business, which she calls Valerosa. "That means brave and valiant," she translated.

I realized the degree to which she needed to armor herself with these traits when I heard how strongly her entrepreneurship had been resisted in some quarters. "The Chamber of Commerce here is a joke," she said, "and I resigned from the Economic Development Commission board because they weren't interested in doing any of the things that need to get done if the town is to succeed. Of course, the fact that I'm blonde, blue-eyed, and a Texan doesn't make it easy." This being the case, Ward is an obvious target for some Las Vegans' animus toward outsiders. She gave me a particularly ugly example: "It was Christmastime, and a package came containing a blackened doll that was meant to be me burnt in effigy. There was a piece of cardboard tied around its neck with the word 'Death' on one side and 'Muerte' on the other. I know there's an underground faction here in New Mexico that practices black magic, but I am a Christian, and they can't touch me. I get lambasted all the time by angry people. You can't ignore them but you just have to understand that it comes from jealousy and lack of power."

TITO CHAVEZ

When I am in Las Vegas I often stop by the Bridge Street art gallery and crafts shop owned by Tito Chavez and his wife, Mary. Chavez, who is a jeweler, comes from a family that has lived in Las Vegas since the town's founding in 1835. One day as we sat and talked at a table in back where he was polishing some silver earrings, I learned how he had started making jewelry during his student days at the University of New Mexico but had not turned this avocation into a full-time career for many years. After earning a graduate degree in education at the University of Michigan, he stayed on in that state working with the Catholic Migrant Ministry, an organization with the mission of getting child workers out of the fields and into school. There he met Mary, who was with the Protestant Migrant Ministry. The two married, and in 1972 when he received an offer to teach at the Las Vegas High School, they took up residence with his extended family in their large house on North Gonzalez Street. Today a designated landmark on the National Register of Historic Places, it was built in 1875 by Miguel Romero for his youngest daughter, Juanita, Chavez's maternal great-grandmother. The Chavezes' two children, William Carlos, named for the poet William Carlos Williams, and Anita Frances, grew up in Las Vegas. The earrings I was watching Tito polish had been made the evening before by the students at the United World College, where he teaches an evening class in jewelry making. They were intended for an auction to benefit an organization that assembles relief supplies for disaster victims.

Chavez told me how he and Mary decided to open a shop while he was still teaching school. In 1992 they moved from their location on the southwest corner of the plaza in what is now the headquarters of the Las Vegas police to their current establishment on Bridge Street. Originally built as a merchant warehouse in the late nineteenth century, in the years prior to the consolidation of East and West Las Vegas into a single municipality it had been the West Las Vegas City Hall as well as a booking station for petty criminals. Pointing to three large cages of steel latticework, Chavez explained that these were once jail cells. Now they serve as storage bins. Glancing toward the ceiling, he said that when he and Mary bought the building it was in obvious need of repair but that the second-floor renovation had to be postponed when the back wall caved in and emergency reconstruction was necessary.

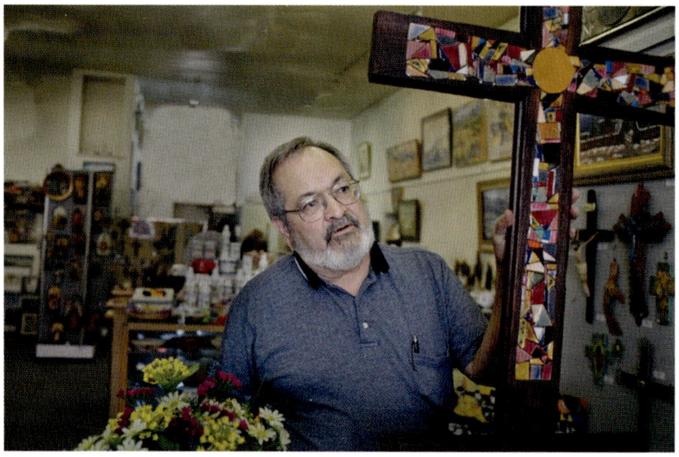

Tito Chavez

The glass-topped cases in the front of the shop display Chavez's work—silver rings, bracelets with semiprecious stones, chased brooches with inlay—but the rest of the shop is filled with a variety of artwork and craft objects. Looking around I saw pottery vases, bowls, and dinnerware as well as paintings, sculptures, and numerous retablos and bultos by a local santero whose work the Chavezes admire. Sometimes they organize gallery shows of other artists' work as well. That day one wall was covered with an exhibition of colorful ceramic crosses. "Here is one I made from an old door frame," Tito said pointing to a large wooden cross with a mosaic made up of small, multi-colored enamel plates.

It was the weekend of Halloween, and costumed children were coming in the door holding out plastic pumpkins for trick-or-treat candies. "Well," Tito said, "I have to get busy now because I'm involved in planning the big La Llorona festival that is taking place tomorrow." I remembered from my earlier conversation with Elmo Baca the folk tale of La Llorona (the Weeping Woman) who, in the local version, roams the banks of the Gallinas in search of the children she drowned in a fit of jealousy. The night before All Souls Day was obviously a time when she would be abroad to frighten children who strayed near the river.

Mary called out, "Tito, I'm in here taking care of customers, so you've got to get outside and help." A table had been set up on the sidewalk and covered with a colorful cloth printed with the kinds of skulls one sees in Mexico, where Día de Los Muertos—the Day of the Dead—is a national holiday, elements of which are seen widely throughout Hispanic New Mexico and around the world. In its pure Latin form it serves as a kind of family reunion of the living and the dead in local camposantos. People gather and light candles on their relatives' graves, which they have decorated with elaborate floral arrangements and strewn with marigolds, their strong odor helping to draw the spirits of the deceased out of the ground. It is also celebrated in people's homes, where private altars adorned with molded sugar figures, paper flowers, and statues of the Virgin and saints have been constructed as temporary shrines. Clothed wood and plaster skeleton dolls representing the reawakened dead are sold in shops, and everywhere street vendors sell skull-shaped sugar candies. Here on Bridge Street a dim echo of this important Mexican holiday was to be found spread out on the top of the sidewalk table. Standing next to them a striking woman with henna-dyed bangs was handing out tubes of colored sugar paste to passing children who were then invited to decorate them.

"I'm Bambi Doe Blake," she said when I introduced myself. I asked her why the life-size cardboard figure next to the children crowded around the table was that of Frida Kahlo instead of La Llorona. "I'm a big Frida fan," she said. "I have all her movies and her books. I even have a collection of rare Frida paper dolls and Frida comic books by the nephew of Diego Rivera. I go on eBay all the time and buy Frida things. Here is the latest, it's a Frida Day of the Dead scapular bracelet," she said, holding out her wrist, "and these are Frida earrings." I noticed a Frida-with-monkey pendant on a chain around her neck. "That's because I have a pet monkey at home," she explained.

Blake, like Chavez, is a Las Vegan who has lived for a period elsewhere, in her case upstate New York, where she ran a B&B cum antiques shop before returning fifteen years ago to settle in the house that had been built by her paternal grandfather on Valley Street. "Let's go inside Tito's," she said, "I want to show you my Frida dolls. They have been featured in seven or maybe eight magazines." I gazed at the folk-art Fridas she had created and told her with sincerity that I thought she was a very talented artist. "Oh, not like Tito, but yes, I guess I am a little bit of an artist," she modestly replied. "She's a very good artist," Mary Chavez interjected, drawing my attention to a wall on which several dolls larger than the ones in the case were pinned. "These are my Mother Mary dolls," Blake told me. "Here is Mary with a monkey, and this one is María del Mar—she looks like a mermaid—and this one is dressed in a fabric from Afghanistan that I found, and the one over there has a dress decorated with tiny shells and glass beads from India. The one here is my stick doll, and she was featured in *Sunset Magazine*," she said, pointing to a figure with tree twigs representing arms and legs. "I love them all."

I was particularly drawn to the beautiful faces of these dolls, all of which were similar except for the way Blake had painted their expressions. "I took a santo and made a mold of the face," she explained. "It was one of the old plaster-of-paris saints that was broken, and I cast my faces from that one mold." As I admired the Mother Marys, Blake exclaimed, "I am always so excited when somebody buys something I have made. I think to myself, 'Oh, they chose mine when there are so many other things they could have bought instead!' "

Like Chavez, Blake likes to teach her skills to others. "I have five girls who come over to my house as apprentices. We cook and sew and make things," she said. "You're welcome to come over, too, sometime. I'll show you my big collection of dolls made in Japan in the 1920s. Sometimes I just pick them up and hold in my arms, I love them so much." I said that I might indeed like to do so when I was next in Las Vegas, at the same time making a mental note that Christmas was not far away and perhaps I would come back to Tito's to do some holiday shopping.

The Sound of Music

Not surprisingly, the music of Northern New Mexico has its own distinct flavor, a blend of traditional regional pieces colored by the influence of Tex-Mex mariachi favorites, as well as other American idioms such as rock and jazz. The musicians who play in the gazebo at the plaza and at concerts and parties elsewhere use Hispanic tradition in original ways, making new arrangements of existing songs and composing original ones. Especially when set to words, these pieces display some of the same beliefs and emotions that imbue the lives of Las Vegans.

New Mexican music owes a large debt to Alberto Nelson Sanchez, better known as Al Hurricane, the legendary guitarist and bandleader from Albuquerque. Hurricane, today widely regarded as the "godfather" of New Mexican music, forged his musical brand in the 1960s. It derives from an eclectic fusion of Cumbia's tropical flavor, Cuban big band influence, disco dance rhythms, *ranchera*'s balladic quality, and waltz, polka, and bolero tempos, plus the *grito*—a kind of trilling yell that often punctuates musical interludes. It also contains mariachi and corrido elements,[4] as well as rock and roll rhythms. Although it is similar in some respects to mariachi music and has appropriated many mariachi songs, *la musica norte mexicana* has a different instrumentation plus the amplification afforded by electric guitar, keyboard, and accordion[5]. Percussion is provided by drums[6] and a *guitarrón* (bass guitar). Trumpets are not as prevalent as in mariachi bands, although trumpeters do play in some New Mexican bands. Occasionally, a saxophone, representing the influence of jazz, will be incorporated into pieces.

While some Las Vegas musicians are indebted to Al Hurricane's innovations, there are others who represent a simpler style based on local folk tradition. Among these is Steve Sanchez, the leader of the band called Amistad, meaning "Friendship."

STEVE SANCHEZ

I went to see Sanchez one day in his home in Sapello, a ranching village a few miles north of Las Vegas. He explained that his father had been a musician and that he had founded Amistad as a way of connecting not only with him but also with his ancestral roots in the area. "I started by wanting to record some of the music I had learned from my dad," he explained. "We started with four musicians—Raymond Durrán, who plays the keyboard and does vocals, my wife, Deborah Sarah Sanchez, also a vocalist, and Lawrence Gomes and me on guitar. When we cut our album *Paz y Gozo* (Peace and Joy) in 2009, we got Donny Tesso, a great Albuquerque musician who plays the bass guitar, to be our producer. He was also our bass percussionist along with Chris Lopez on drums and chimes."

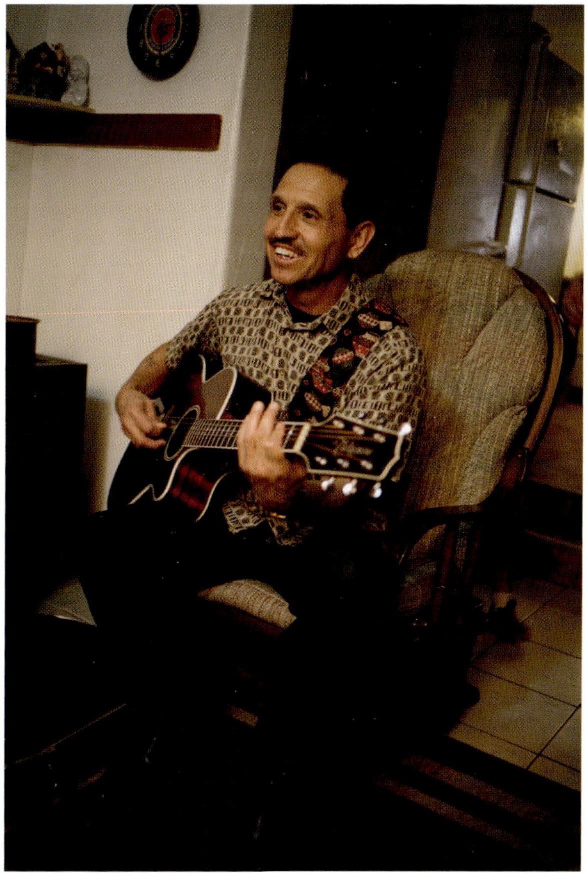

Steve Sanchez

Sanchez's music is not only rooted in the folk ballads, polkas, and other regional music he learned from his father but also in a deeply felt spirituality. According to him, "It's about culture and the people who came into this area and brought their own traditions from Europe and Mexico. I like to do arrangements of the old songs, but I give credit to the Holy Spirit for my inspiration. It is amazing to listen to my song "Purificamé" (Purify Me) being played on radio stations and hear people say how much they love that piece. I am surprised, but the band gives full credit to Jesus Christ for the honors the song has received."

When I spoke with Tesso, who played for several years in Al Hurricane's band and has seen the more dissolute side of a musician's life, he told me that he feels the power of Sanchez's spirituality and is grateful to him for helping him to keep clean of drugs as well as for the opportunity to be his producer. On the back cover of *Paz y Gozo,* the first album they did together, he pays him the following tribute: "I truly know God sent you to me to help me and guide me. It can only be something Divine that allowed me to make each song evolve into what they are now. Each time I sat in front of the keyboard for each song, the ideas and structure just came out. Your talent you inherited from your dad is Heaven-sent. You play the guitar from the heart and your style is unique." To me he explained. "He's so good that all I did was to get a couple of guys from Albuquerque to play with him so we could surround him with sound. Steve's talent is really raw—raw meaning he just knows the basics—but what comes out just oozes, it's so beautiful."

Sanchez said to me that the band works on an ad hoc basis doing gigs such as weddings and fiestas, but that increasingly he gets his deepest satisfaction from playing with Ray Durán every Sunday in his church. Called Cornerstone, the church is one of several similarly named nondenominational charismatic churches in the United States and abroad. Like Cornerstone churches in other places, it has a service that begins with a participatory concert of twenty minutes in which the congregation sings, claps, and sways as various evangelical lyrics are projected on a screen behind the two musicians. Sanchez explained, "It isn't entertainment but part of worship. To me it is not music but rather praising God with his gift to me. I love to play the big-band tunes and it was wonderful for Amistad to be one of fifteen bands invited to play with others from around the state in the New Mexico Hispanic music competition, but it doesn't compare with playing my music in church." As I sat one Sunday in a pew next to his wife Debbie and their two grandchildren, Esperanza and Michael, I witnessed the inspiration he and Durán brought to the service with such songs as "Help Me God to Live One Day at a Time." When they played "Raising the Last Day's Army"—the church's motto—the congregation stood and swayed with arms outstretched before Pastor Mark Saiz began to stride up and down the aisle using enthusiastic body language as he preached his lengthy sermon with fundamentalist fervor. As heads nodded in beatific assent to the hortatory words the minister frequently substantiated with prophetic passages of biblical scripture, I understood where Sanchez had found inspiration for his particular blend of northern New Mexican tradition and evangelical church music.

ANTONIA APODACA

After church I went with the Sanchez family to the Smiling Faces Restaurant on Grand Street, and following a big lunch consisting of a tamale, an enchilada, a taco, beans, and sopaipillas fresh off the stove, we paid a call on Antonia Apodaca, a musician who is something of a northern New Mexican legend. When we arrived she opened the gate to one of the old properties on South Pacific Street that stretch from the placita of a family compound to the acequia madre. A petite woman of eighty-eight with curly jet-black hair, she was dressed in colorful regalia and made up with lipstick, rouge, and mascara. After we parked she led us to a small adobe house that her son Maximilian found for her after her own home on the Apodaca family property in the village of Rociada near Mora burned to the ground just before Christmas 2010. She recounted how this calamity came about when a strong gust of wind caused the hot chimney pipe to start a fire on the roof while she was cooking eggs, chicharrones, and chile for breakfast one morning.

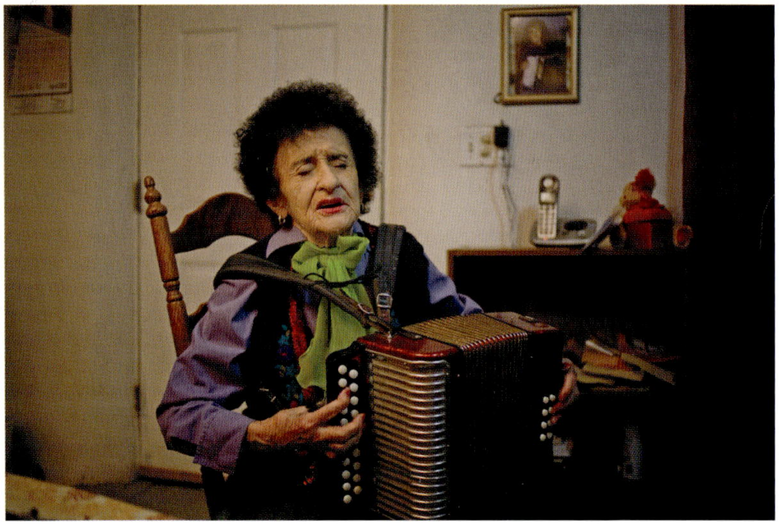

Antonia Apodaca

As soon as we entered her cozy living room she showed me several large framed photographs on her wall. Three were of her sons in military uniform and one of herself as a young woman playing the accordion. She invited us to sit down and immediately picked up the same accordion that, along with her guitar, she had managed to carry out the door as she escaped from the fire. Punctuating conversation with song the same way she had when I had called on the telephone to see if I could meet with her, she began playing and singing a number of familiar tunes, mostly in English but sometimes with repeat verses in Spanish. There was "Rancho Grande," "Home on the Range," "Oh My Darling, Clementine," and, after she learned that I was born in the Lone Star state, "The Yellow Rose of Texas" and "San Antonio Rose." "Isn't that pretty?" she would ask in the brief pause between one song and another. I tried to remember the steps to "Put Your Little Foot," the polka she played for us and watched Debbie lead young Esperanza and Michael in some other dances as Sanchez accompanied her on the guitar. As he played and sang with her, she kept saying, "You're so good, I'm going to take you with me when I go to Washington." She explained to me that she was planning to travel there sometime soon for a repeat performance of the concert of New Mexican music that she gave at the Smithsonian Folklife Festival twenty years ago, mentioning proudly that at that time she had also performed at the White House for the first President Bush. Not surprisingly, she is a star attraction on the annual program in the Santa Fe plaza during Spanish Market where she and her band, Trio Jalapeño, represent the indigenous music of this part of New Mexico.

After the Sanchezes left, Apodaca, who plays four other instruments besides the accordion, picked up her guitar and gave me a solo concert. Switching back to the accordion, she sang more songs, punctuating the intervals in between with fragments of her life history. "I was just eleven and my daddy took me to town and we saw this old busted accordion with a hole in the bottom. It sounded like this," she said, pumping the bellows back and forth without fingering the keyboard. There was a wheezing sound like labored breathing. "Well, you know what I did? I stuck my skinny little knee in the hole just like this," she said, demonstrating how she had inserted her knee into the hole. There were more wheezing sounds followed by a little tune. "See, I put my skinny little knee in there, and everyone was so surprised that I could make the notes come out and was playing this song. Then my daddy said, 'I'll buy you a little accordion and take you over to Santa Fe so you can play at the La Fonda Hotel.' That was in 1936, and I have been playing ever since." She picked up the accordion once more in order to express some regional philosophy in the lyrics and song of her own: "Chile in the morning, chile in the evening, chile makes me happy, all the time."

STEVE LEGER

Steve Leger is the proprietor of Love Music, a large white building on the east bank of the Gallinas River at the place where Bridge Street turns into National. He is a musician and a bandleader and gives lessons on the trumpet, flute, and drums. One day when he was not too busy with students and customers to sit down and talk, I stopped by his store with its huge eye-catching red heart painted on the exterior wall. He offered me a chair, pulling up another beside it. Looking around at the various drums, guitars, and other musical instruments for sale, I asked him to describe the Las Vegas musical scene. He answered, "We used to have dinner clubs where they played a lot of big-band jazz and brought in Tex-Mex groups. They had large horn arrangements that were more sophisticated than country music. But that's all gone. What my group, Los Tropicales, does now is mainly play for weddings and events in the plaza here and the one over in Santa Fe. We played for a big celebration at Highlands recently, and when they tented the gym inside, it felt like being in a cabaret."

I wanted to know if the music of Los Tropicales represented some aspect of the style of Northern New Mexico. "Not really," he answered. "It has elements of that, of course, but the group started out a dozen or more years ago as an outgrowth of a non-local band with that name. What we play is more like Latin music with Cuban bolero rhythms and with a percussion beat that gives it a somewhat tropical flavor. We like to incorporate a little jazz, and our lyrics, which are in Spanish, have some of the romantic character of the popular songs of the 1950s. It's dance music for the most part, and it is fun for us to blend in different styles like rock and western."

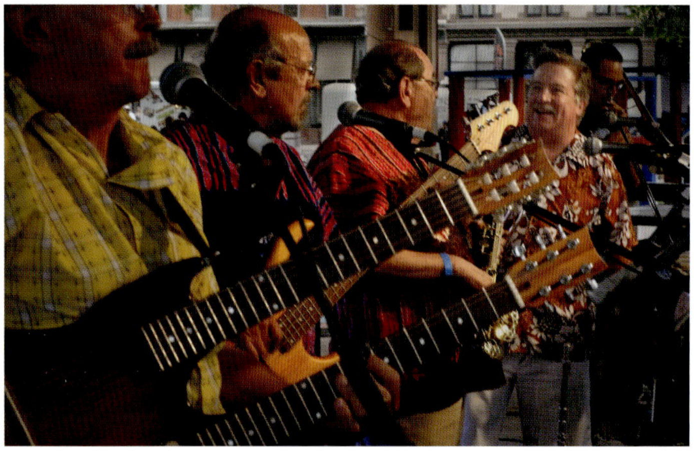

Steve Leger and Los Tropicales

On the covers of the two Los Tropicales CDs I bought while I was in the store, Leger and the other members of the band—Michael Romero (lead guitar), Leroy Lucero (vocals and bass percussion), Lee Norman Gonzales (vocals, sax, and rhythm guitar), and Leger himself (trumpet, flute, percussion)—are dressed in Hawaiian shirts. The sensuous tropical islands quality of the quartet's brand of music is evident in songs like "Besos," "Dulce Amor," "Mi Bebi Tu Requerdo," and "Un Viejo Amor." With a slower beat than mariachi music, these songs have the same flamenco overtones, trumpet riffs, and often the same words as ones sung by mariachis. In essence, the most important difference lies in the fact that their slower tempo is that of a ballroom dance rather than a spirited serenade.

When I brought the conversation back to the subject of regional music, Leger said, "Don't get me wrong. I like our northern New Mexican style. I'm from Las Vegas, and it's what I grew up with. Some of the old songs we play have been around here forever, and we just arrange them in our own style, using three-part harmony in a quartet format. We like to hark back to the trio style of Eydie Gormé and to jazz by adding the trumpet, percussion, bass, and sometimes the saxophone. Just like there are lots of different varieties of potatoes, there are lots of kinds of music, and it is fun to add some of outside influences to what's always been a strong native folk tradition."

ANDRÉ GARCIA-NUTHMANN

At Highlands University André Garcia-Nuthmann, a trained singer and pianist, teaches mostly classical music. Using students and outside community talent, he also directs some of the amateur theatrical performances that constitute the backbone of Las Vegas's local entertainment. As we sat down together one afternoon in his office at Highlands I remembered with particular pleasure attending his production of Mozart's one-act singspiel *Bastien and Bastienne* in the ballroom of the Plaza Hotel.

The son of a Mexican father and German mother, Garcia-Nuthmann was born in El Paso, Texas, and moved to Las Vegas at the age of six when his father accepted a position as a Spanish teacher at Highlands University. Although his father became interested in the kind of northern New Mexican music played by Antonia Apodaca and founded an *orquesta típica*, a band that plays popular songs, Garcia-Nuthmann's passion is for baroque music. "I love Bach and Telemann," he said, adding, "Mozart is also an important part of my life."

As he was growing up, Garcia-Nuthmann's love for Las Vegas was not as straightforward as his love for music. "To be a teenager at Robertson High School in the 1960s," he said, "was very difficult if you wore glasses, played the piano, didn't go out for sports, were confused about your sexual identity, and just plain didn't fit in. But it made me very strong and determined, and these things didn't affect me in the long run. But back then I was really anxious to leave this place. I was fortunate because Robertson had a great principal who let me go to summer school and graduate a year earlier than the rest of my class. I am also lucky because my family was completely behind me and only cared that I could support myself if I chose to have a musical career."

Garcia-Nuthmann attended Southwestern University in Georgetown, Texas, where there was a excellent music department. "My major was in piano," he said, "and the organ was my minor instrument. My first church job was playing the organ, but after earning two degrees in piano, I realized that I was more talented as a singer." Asked to build a choral

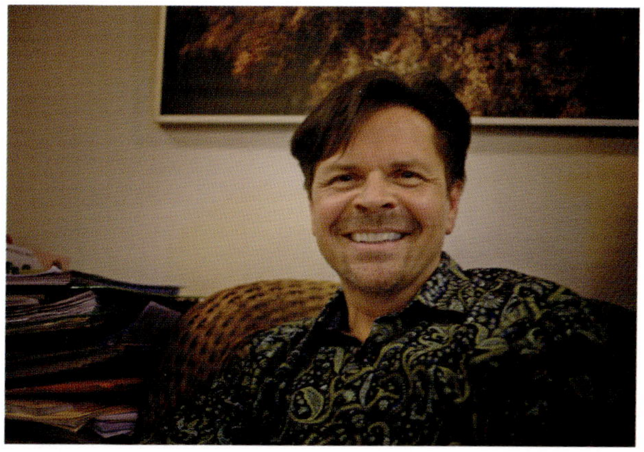

André Garcia-Nuthmann

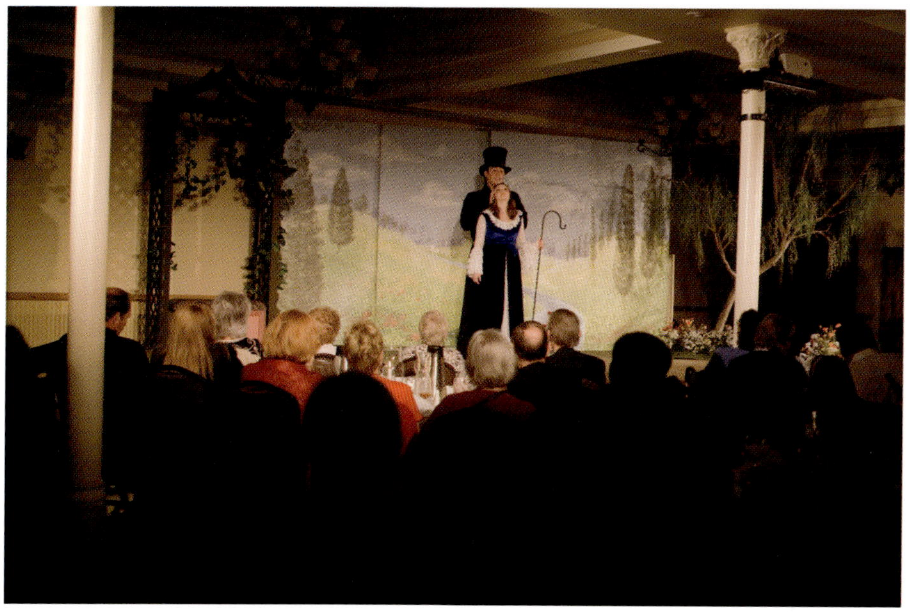

Performance of Mozart's Bastien and Bastienne, Plaza Hotel

program and voice studio at Highlands, he decided to go back to graduate school and obtain a doctorate in vocal music. He has sung with the Santa Fe Desert Chorale, one of the country's most distinguished a cappella groups, and been a guest conductor for the Santa Fe Symphony Orchestra and Chorus. But it was clear from his animated conversation that his passion for teaching is equal to his passion for the music of the baroque period. "My whole goal is to try to inspire people to become part of this wonderful world of music. I honestly come to my job every day with a smile. When I left at nineteen I swore I would never come back to Las Vegas. I certainly never expected to end up living here, but it has turned out to be the best thing I ever did. I really have such a great respect for this community."

Stage and Screen

If Las Vegas lacks the cultural attractions of Santa Fe—world-class opera, chamber music, theater, multiplex movie houses, a performing arts center—it has something else in the way of entertainment: an abundance of local talent. In addition to the productions of the Nat Gold Players, there are numerous other homegrown events throughout the year. Some of these, such as the Miss Las Vegas contest and the Highlands Homecoming Pageant, take place in the Ilfeld Auditorium, which also offers a program of weekly movie nights known as Cineflix.

CYNTHIA RILEY

Like Garcia-Nuthmann, Cyn Riley has found a rewarding place for herself in the life of Las Vegas through the performing arts. She teaches theater at both Highlands University and Luna Community College and is the head of the Nat Gold Players, an amateur theatrical group that stages three original productions during the course of the year. "Over the Edge," the annual summer show with a script she develops with another local writer, Karyl Lynn, might be characterized as a town roast—a spoof in which the community makes fun of itself. "Last year we wrote radio jingles about local businesses and incorporated some jazz players in the play," she told me one day as we sat in her office following the class I had observed her teach at Luna. "We are part of Theater New Mexico, a statewide community organization that has competitions every other year. This past year we won, which was a great feather in the cap of Las Vegas."

Cynthia Riley

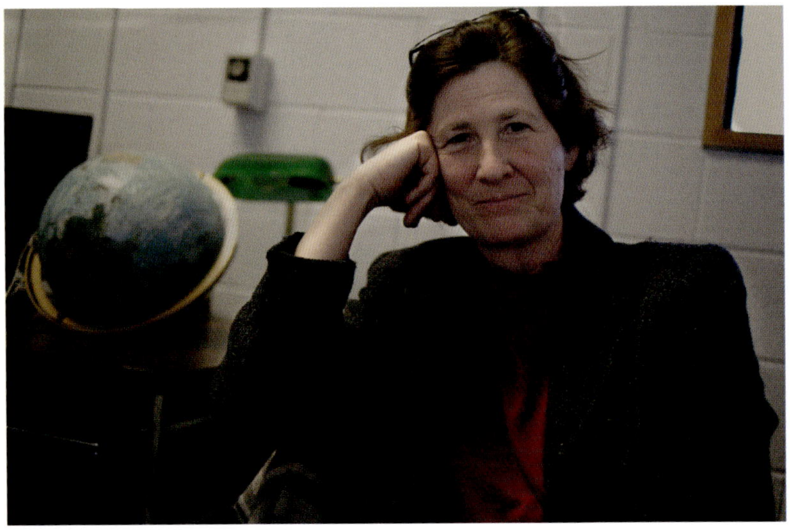

The cast for "Over the Edge" consists of a group of regular adult performers as well as students recruited from Riley's classes and some teenagers who act in school plays and enjoy drama as an extracurricular activity. "We get people from every walk of life," she told me. "We have a woman who works for the Sanitation Department, for instance. Our youngest cast member last year was eleven and our oldest eighty-nine. Men actors are often hard to find, however." In addition to "Over the Edge," the Nat Gold Players stage "Box Seats," an annual series of ten-minute-long original plays, and an hour-long program billed as "A Little Light Music," which the group presents in December in the Presbyterian Church on Douglas Street.

I asked Riley how she came to reside in Las Vegas. She replied, "I didn't live here at the time, but I got acquainted with the place in the 1980s when my mother and dad, Carroll Riley, who is a well-known Southwestern anthropologist, moved here. I was in and out all the time. During that period I got a bachelor's degree in theater and a master's degree in writing from the University of Alabama. Then, in 1994, I moved here for good."

Like her friend Garcia-Nuthmann, Riley feels that she has found the perfect niche in which to fulfill her twin passions as a local-entertainment producer and teacher. "After last year's 'Over the Edge,' " she said, "some of the kids got the theater bug and decided to start their own company called Clearly Confused Productions. I encouraged them to go ahead, and they did. They wrote a script, rehearsed forever, and then performed their first show, called *Reflections on Alice,* which included middle-school as well as high-school students."

Characterizing Las Vegas as a place and her role in the life of the community, she concluded, "I grew up on a farm in southeastern Missouri, and I think that I really understand the culture of rural Northern New Mexico. I connect with the sensibility you find here. There is a reverence for the arts and a sense of ceremony and entertainment as forms of art. When I first moved to Las Vegas I was warned that as an Anglo woman I would not be accepted. But I have never, ever, ever felt that that was the case. This is a very special place where every person I met was kind and respectful. There is a graciousness and warmth that's part of the Hispanic culture, and the people here have always made me feel very welcome."

THE PLAZA

There are historic photographs showing wagon trains pulling to a stop in the original plaza, a dusty square where townspeople, traders, and teamsters gathered. The coming of the railroad was responsible for its conversion into a tree-shaded park, but this did not change its function as the heart, and some might say the soul, of Las Vegas.

Sometimes the plaza feels deserted, but not often nor for long. On nice days teenagers hang out there after school. Musicians often perform in the bandstand as do dancers and stunt skateboarders who like to fly over its steps in wide gliding jumps. Its most festive use is during the three days of fiestas. Planned by a special

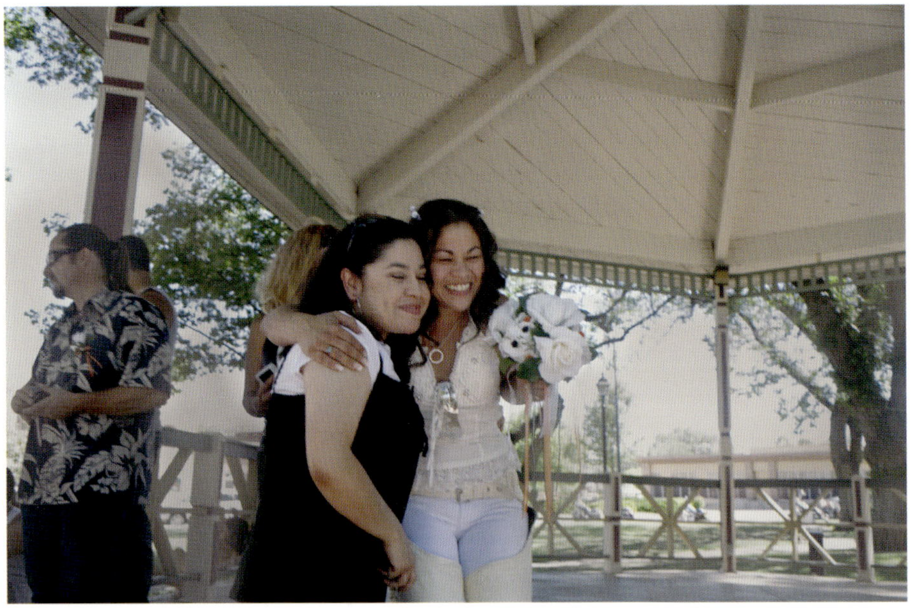

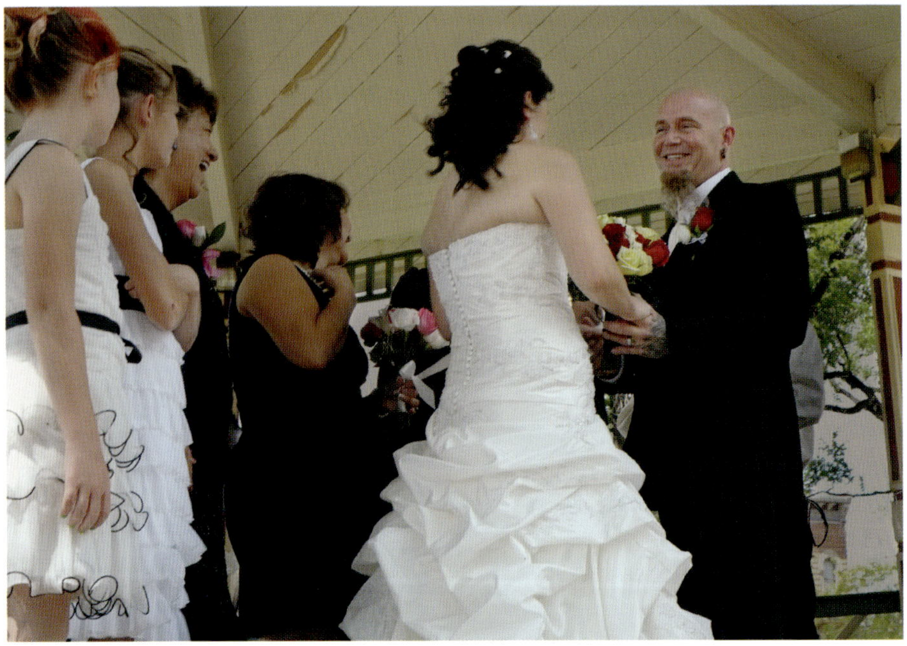

committee over the course of the year, the extended holiday begins with the Fourth of July parade, which starts in New Town and ends in the Old Town plaza, where the fiesta queen—traditionally a young Hispanic woman who has been crowned the previous evening at a Mass at Our Lady of Sorrows—reigns over an audience of all ages seated on blankets, collapsible canvas chairs, and park benches. The perimeter of the plaza is surrounded by food vendors selling roasted corn, funnel cakes, ribbon fries, and other popular fiesta fare. Happily noshing, the crowd is treated throughout the day and evening to a full program of performances by local entertainers. Once, as I watched the swirling skirts of the beautifully costumed women and girls who are part of Lori Bovia's Los Zapateados dance group, I was reminded of something I had read about the days when the arrival of a Santa Fe Trail caravan in this same plaza would be celebrated with a fandango, a dance with clicking castanets and ringing tambourines.

On other occasions I have found myself in the middle of a wedding party. One Saturday afternoon I witnessed the vows of a bride and groom in traditional attire,

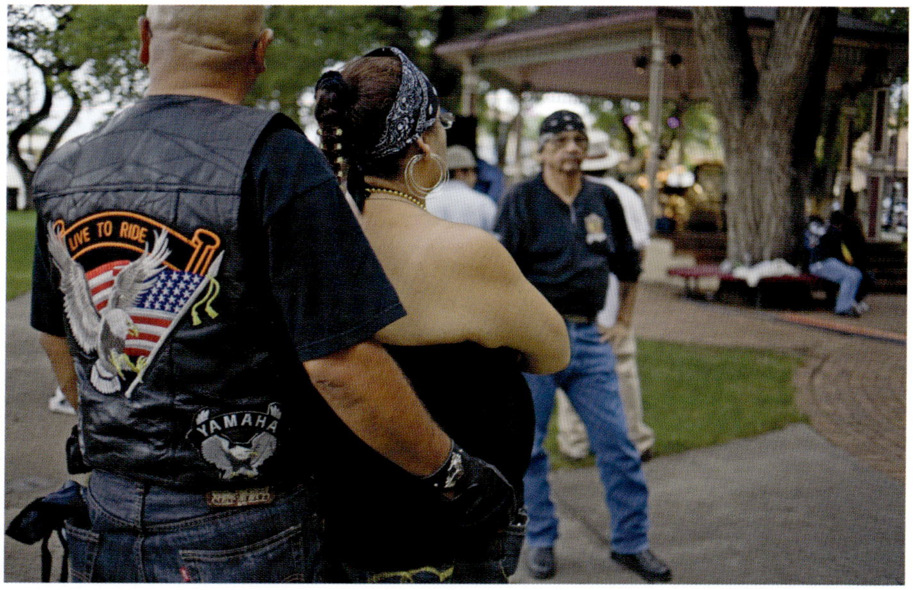

Bikers

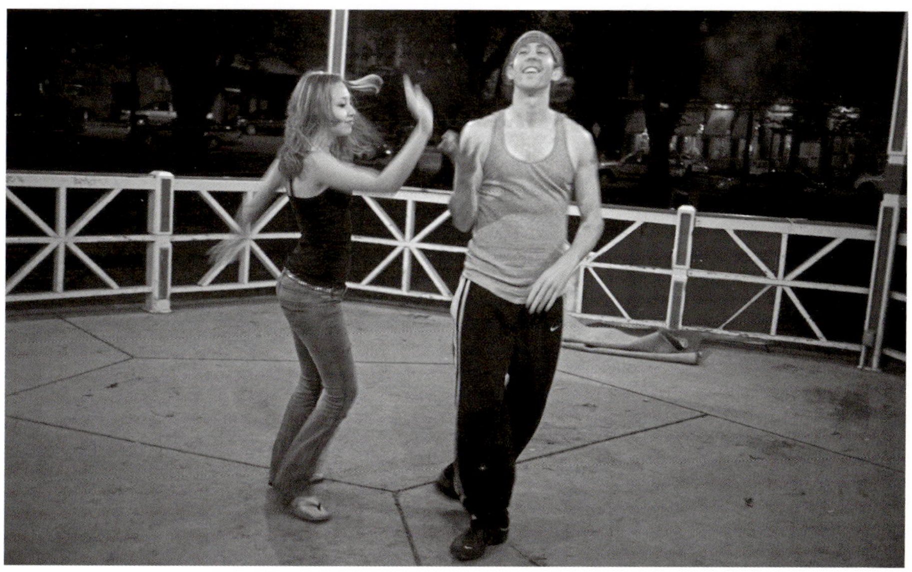

Dancing in the Dark

and on another I got there just in time to see the bride, who was dressed in tight white jeans and fringed chaps, receive a joyful post-nuptial hug from her best friend before she and the groom jumped on his motorcycle and circled the plaza three times. Trailed by an entourage of friends who were also cyclists, they then sped off to the reception in a banquet hall on the edge of town.

The plaza is also a regular venue for motorcycle rallies. Bikers from hundreds of miles away and even a few from foreign countries roar into town on their gleaming Harleys, BMWs, Hondas, Yamahas, and Kawasakis, many of which are decorated with flaring flames and other artistic detailing. Knots of fellow bikers are gathered around admiring vintage models and ones that have been modified in original ways. There are some female bikers but most of the women—and there are many—are wives or girlfriends who have come as passengers on the backs of men's motorcycles. There are vendors selling food, T-shirts, and a variety of motorcycle gear from kiosks. Some of these are set up as temporary tattoo parlors. Bands play throughout the day, and amplified music blares pretty much nonstop. But the real highlight of the rally is the announcement of the winners of the tattoo contest. Everyone claps as these champions display biceps, backs, and shoulders or roll up pants to expose leg art.

Late one evening as I was walking across the plaza, I stopped beside the bandstand to watch a boy and girl who were dancing all by themselves with sexy verve to the sounds of a portable CD player. I was the only bystander. I stood there a long time in the dark taking photographs of the pair, realizing once more the perennial significance of this small public space in the life of Las Vegas. Swaying to their music, I thought to myself, "Well, this certainly beats hanging out at the mall!"

Newcomers are attracted to the small-town ambience of Las Vegas, its relaxed pace, simple way of life, and relatively low cost of living. In addition, the Northern New Mexico light, the immensity of blue sky, the beautiful mountain scenery, and the recreational opportunities—skiing, hiking, motorcycling, trout fishing, hunting—are important assets. For people who are retired, self-employed, or have noncommuting jobs, Las Vegas's comparatively bargain-rate real estate is an incentive to settle, especially for those who like to renovate old houses or own small businesses. Because of low rental and purchase costs, such newcomers are buying historic homes and investing in vacant commercial buildings on Bridge Street and Douglas Avenue. While their desire to have the town remain New Mexico's anti–Santa Fe is strong, their presence is evidence of the hope that Las Vegas may be in the process of successfully reinventing itself economically. Moreover, since Northern New Mexico is a region that has been hospitable to the hippie subculture since the 1960s, Las Vegas and its environs have provided a congenial home for a handful of civil rights and community activists, back-to-the-land types, and unconventional personalities.

Free Spirits and Rolling Stones

PATRICIA LEAHAN

For Pat Leahan, who runs the Las Vegas Center for Peace and Justice on Sixth Street, settling in Las Vegas was the result of a spiritual call rather than a reasoned decision. "Here is how it happened," she said when I asked her to explain. "I was raised in a blue-collar family who were very social-justice oriented. I got my college degree and trained in social work. I was living and teaching in Minnesota when two of my friends and I decided to come to New Mexico for a vacation. As we drove up Interstate 25 from Albuquerque and came to Cochití Pueblo where the whole landscape just opens out and you see the Sangre de Cristo Mountains in the distance, I could feel my heart chakra opening up. I had this powerful sense that this was an extraordinary and unique place. There is something about the whole of Northern New Mexico—about San Miguel Country and Mora County, too—that feels incredibly spiritual to me."

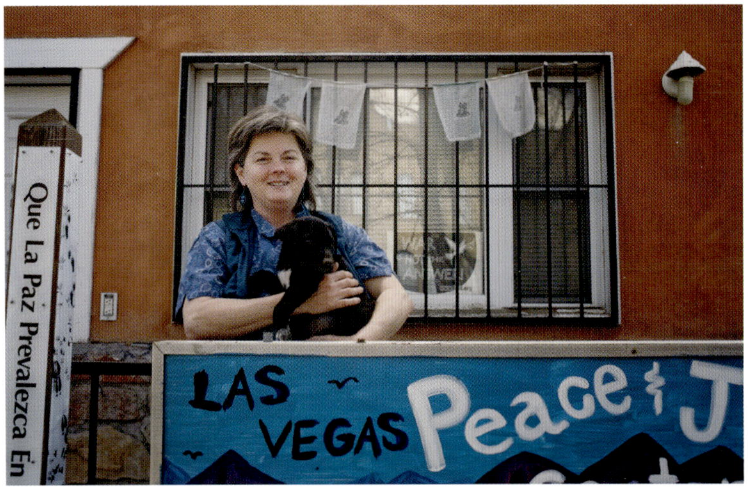

Patricia Leahan

When I urged her to continue the story of her immigration to New Mexico, she said, "I belong to the Society for Spirituality and Social Work, which is an organization that creates connections, innovative approaches, and mutual support among social workers pursuing a variety of spiritual paths. When I found out about a conference that was being held by the society where two professors from Las Vegas were speakers, I thought, 'Wow! I had no idea that there was this little town with a university where there were people doing social work.' I went to the conference, and while I was there I looked them up. When they told me, 'Las Vegas is not for everyone,' I got really intrigued. I went back to Minnesota, where I was perfectly happy with my job and didn't have any intention of leaving and going someplace else. But many months later my two friends and I got the travel bug, and we decided to come back to New Mexico. Again, as we were driving north from the airport in Albuquerque, I could just feel my heart opening inside of me. I have always had an open heart, but this was really shocking: the greens were greener somehow and everything around us was charged with a spiritual energy. Somehow, I felt I was being pulled there by an invisible force. I could just feel the history. After driving around the plaza a couple of times, we started down one of the narrow old streets, and then another miracle occurred: I saw one of the ladies I had met at the conference. My friends said, 'Follow her!' so we did. She stopped, and when I got out of the car and came over, she remembered me. Again, a miracle: She said that she was going out of town and asked us if we would like to house-sit, and we were thrilled to accept this offer right out of the blue. What she told us about Las Vegas at dinner that night was that it was a place where kids, dogs, and the mentally ill run free. Well, these are three of my favorite creatures on the face of the planet! So the next day I walked over to Highlands and met with the dean and associate dean of the School of Social Work. They said they were looking for someone to teach there, and then all of a sudden on the spot they offered me a job.

I had to think hard about leaving Minnesota. For a while I resisted the idea, but my friends were all for the three of us moving out. When I made my decision, I thought, 'Whoa! I can't believe I am really moving here!' It's funny because now they're gone, and I am the only one left."

Leahan said, "Getting settled turned out to be a seamless process. The first house we saw was affordable, and there was a place on University Drive owned by two women that sold the kind of food I want to put in my body. It's called Semilla Natural Foods. Somehow I continued to feel that I was being guided. Teaching these kids here was really a beautiful experience. The class environment was completely different from the one I was used to. The majority of my students were female, Hispanic, and Native American. Some of them were single moms who were taking care of a grandma who was dying, raising a child, and getting a degree all at the same time. What is great is they don't feel oppressed like other people of color; they don't want to assimilate but just better themselves and stay in their own cultural tradition. I just loved teaching where there were no biases against different ethnic groups or different types of persons. The kids were so real, so honest. I connected immediately with the town and its strong combination of humility and strength, and here I am fifteen years later."

Leahan's decision to leave the teaching career she found "way cool" was, like her coming to Las Vegas, the result of an epiphany. "One day when I was walking down Bridge Street I heard this voice right here," she said pointing to her left ear. "I couldn't tell who or what it was, but it was so intense. I knew it was a heavy moment. I went and sat in my car, put my head back, and listened to it. It said that I should go and start the Peace and Justice Center. There was already a committee for Peace and Justice, which I was on, but my sister had just been diagnosed with cancer. Since she didn't have insurance, along with the rest of my family I was helping pay her medical bills. I was in a zombie state and resisted listening to the voice, which said I was to do this and that it was going to be soon. I drove over and told my friends at Semilla Natural Foods what was going on. They immediately said, 'Yes! Yes! We'll support you; we'll see that you have groceries every week.' This was in April 2004, and on May 15, with absolutely no money, I resigned from my job. Then, while I was sitting in Library Park, a friend pointed out this place and said it was for rent. I really believe in miracles, because when we decided to take it, a doctor who has faith in our work came along and said, 'I'll pay the rent for the first year.' We still didn't know how we were going to run the place, but then a lady came to me and said, 'I have no money, but I'll help find people who want to invest in you.' She drafted a letter that we sent to thirty people asking them to buy shares."

Since the term *shares* usually implies equity and it seemed to me that this form of capitalization was a tenuous proposition under the circumstances, I asked if the organization had been set up as a charitable 501(c)(3) corporation. The idea was repugnant to Riley. "Nobody has equity or gets tax-deductions for contributions," she said. "We won't take any government money or have anything to do with bureaucracy. I am not going to consult any official guidelines or be tied down in other ways before I offer someone help. We have no budget and no savings account, but somehow we get by, and for eight years I have never missed paying a bill. It's all just occurred because of a series of miracles." She gave me an example: "On the day we were supposed to pay a $200 bill for the printing of our brochure we were one dollar short, but at five-fifteen, just before Semilla's closed, a woman came in and left four quarters in the cookie jar that had been set on the counter for contributions. When one of the owners pointed her out to me as she was leaving, I ran down the street after her to tell her 'You're our Dollar Lady!' Things like that that keep happening all the time."

Leahan explained another novel economic practice that keeps the Peace and Justice Center afloat. "We started a barter currency," she said. "Everyone pays five dollars a year and gets barter bucks. When I go to the Farmer's Market and need eggs, the woman I buy them from takes half cash and half barter bucks, which she can then use at the stand where they sell soap. I don't send out notices. I don't have to keep track. It just so clean: there are no bills or anything like that."

When I wanted to learn more about the activities of the center, she handed me the miraculously funded brochure encouraging volunteer participation and donations to the Peace and Justice Center. She then reviewed the four areas of mission it enunciates: Access, Education, Advocacy, and Solidarity. "Access is about physical space. We give research assistance on social justice issues. We get Highlands to let us hold meetings, and the Presbyterian Church is good about that too. The computer over there is donated, and people who don't have their own computers can come in here and check their e-mails and go online." Pointing to a bookcase, she said, "There is our library, where people can come and learn about things like permaculture and organic gardening. In the area of Education we focus on voter registration, environmental justice, and instruction on how be a conscientious objector. At the same time we give support and information to our military families. We hold forums where the United World College students come and teach about their countries. Last week our UWC student volunteers went to the firehouse and learned some cool stuff about what it is like to fight fires, and at the same time the firefighters learned what it is like in places like Jordan and Palestine. Under Advocacy we organize community actions such as the candlelight vigil we held at the plaza when the United States started bombing Iraq. We work on protecting and strengthening our civil liberties and support our local unions. For instance, the workers at the hospital formed a union three years ago, and the administration still refuses to sit down and negotiate. We are trying to give visibility to this issue. As far as Solidarity goes, we work with other groups such as the Casa de Cultura, the Northern New Mexican Hispano Coalition, Project PeacePal, the Animal Support Center, the Bartos Institute for Constructive Engagement of Conflict, and Las Vegas CARES, which stands for Citizens for Affordable, Responsible Energies."

When I asked Leahan to be more specific about the social problems of Las Vegas, she said, "Yes, drugs, alcohol, and domestic violence are issues. But I believe in my heart that this community is no worse than any other community. It's true that individuals need to take responsibility for their troubles, but it is our whole society that is culpable. Funds for the important things are always being cut. We don't have a detox center, and it isn't right for people to have to drive to Albuquerque or Denver to get help."

In spite of the political, environmental, and social problems she sees around her, Leahan remains optimistic. "We are a small community, and that is an advantage. It means that we are more caring for one another." About her own future, she remarked, "I am very spiritually directed, and that voice inside may one day tell me I have to go do something else. But right now I am happy to be living in the present here in this place, and I'm glad when I go to bed at night knowing that I have pulled off another day. But it's really not about me. It's about the community. I'm the co-director of the Peace and Justice Center; the community is the other director. They are more than half of the equation. I guess I provide the energy and the zest, but it is really the community that sets the agenda. I know it sounds too good to be true, but I am glad you were here to witness the miracle of this place because you wouldn't believe it otherwise."

ROBERT MORRIS

Bob Morris, whose studio and living quarters used to be on the same block as the Plaza Hotel, typifies the born-mobile American who makes an impromptu decision: "Hey, this would be a nice town in which to live for a while." Cheerfully suited to his rolling-stone lifestyle, Morris has since moved away, and no one I have spoken with seems to know where he is living now.

What I gleaned from him about his previous history is that he grew up in Iowa and lived in Sonoma, California, for a number of years, working as a dental ceramicist making caps for broken teeth. Deciding to turn his artistry into a broader channel, he became a painter and moved to Pátzcuaro, Mexico, where he lived for a few years before returning to Sonoma. One day he saw advertised on the Internet a good deal on a trip to Mexico City. That was for him sufficient reason to pull up stakes. Driving east from California, he stopped in Las Vegas, walked around the plaza, which in his eyes resembled the plaza in Pátzcuaro and —somewhat improbably—reminded him of the Zócalo, the Aztecs' great pre-Conquest central plaza that still forms the heart of Mexico City. "That was it," he said. "Right away I took this place on the plaza, the landlord fixed

Bob Morris

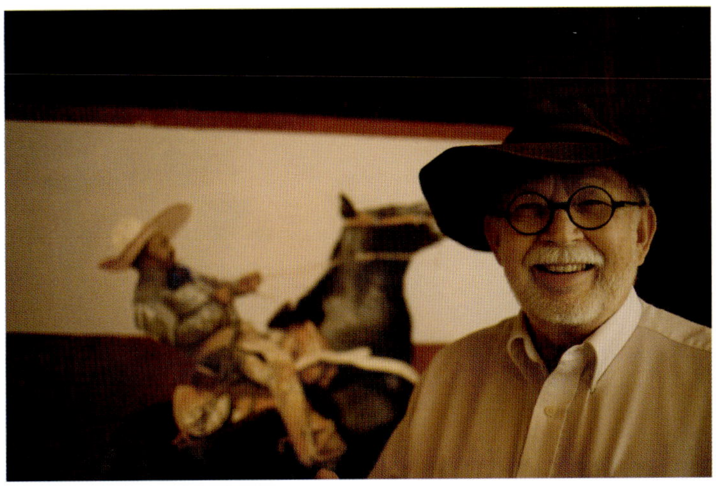

it up, and here I am," he said amiably as we stood chatting on the sidewalk in front of his studio cum art gallery with its big "Zócalo" sign over the door.

With a friendly wave he invited me to enter. Inside I saw a series of pastel portraits of Native Americans and oil paintings of *charros*—traditional Mexican horsemen—on the walls. When I asked him about his art, he replied, "My cowboy art's been dragging along, following me for a while. Then when I was in High Point, South Carolina, showing some stuff, I got another idea. While I was there, I went to a powwow up in the hills. I met an old Indian lady and told her about an idea I had to paint one person from every tribe in America. She brought her granddaughter—the one you see in the portrait over there on the easel—and also her nephews to meet me. They all wanted to get painted. So from that point I started. Now I go to powwows all over the country, take pictures of people in native dress, and work from these," he said, showing me several snapshots. He claimed his goal was to sell the Native American portraits as a collection to a museum or casino. I hope, wherever he is, that Bob Morris may have succeeded in realizing his dream.

ELIZABETH DEMARE

Like Leahan and Morris, Elizabeth deMare settled in Las Vegas as a matter of impulsive choice. A striking woman with a full-bodied mane of natural blond hair she claims to have never cut, she was born and raised in New York City, graduated from St. John's College in Santa Fe, and fell under the spell of Northern New Mexico. A resident of Las Vegas for over twenty years, she lives on Tecolote Street in a house that is part of the West Side compound she owns.

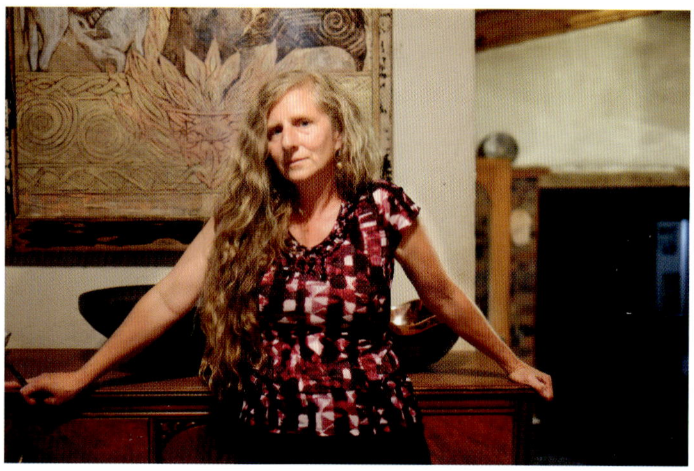

Elizabeth deMare

Sitting on a wide overstuffed sofa beneath the vigas of her large, high-ceilinged living room, an entire wall of which is lined with shelves and glass-topped cases containing a large miscellany of handcrafted objects she has collected over the years, I asked why she had chosen to live in Las Vegas. "I could go anywhere," she said with some vehemence, "Nothing made me have to be here. I actively *chose* to be here." I asked her how she picked Las Vegas, and she answered with a laugh, "My sense of geography is so poor I discovered it by accident when I drove here with my sister, thinking we were headed for the Strip. When we ended up in this Las Vegas instead, I immediately loved the place. Then every time I came back I just felt like I was coming home, so in 1989 I decided to move here with my boyfriend."

Proudly unconventional, deMare considers herself a crossover person, an Anglo who has tried to become assimilated into Las Vegas's dominant Hispanic culture. She says, "Here right on my own property I have this little community of people who all know each other. The rest of the neighborhood is one of nice little adobes and a lot of mobile homes where people don't feel they have to lock their doors." When I inquired about her family, she said she had three children fathered by two different Hispanic men. "I never found anyone I wanted to marry, but in contradistinction to some of the members of my family back East, I didn't think that meant that I shouldn't have children. The men I picked weren't good partners, but they are very loving with the kids, and I don't have issues with either of them."

What was her opinion of Las Vegas as a burgeoning arts community? "I think the town is in danger at the moment," she said. "You have a lot of people coming into the area, living in the East Side enclave, people of retirement age who don't have families here and are not really part of the town. In some ways that's good for the arts community and means more galleries, but here things depend on how deep they run. What we have now is just something that is parked on top. Actually, we could be a very strong arts community, but we don't project our true abilities, which are at a very high level. We are the worst self-promoters on the face of the planet." However, in contrast to Santa Fe, Las Vegas in deMare's eyes is utopian. "Santa Fe is a dysfunctional mess," she said flatly. "Here you wouldn't walk by somebody and not acknowledge they are a human being and you are a human being." When I asked her to describe the particular character of the town, she replied, "Yes, there is definitely some bad stuff like the macho-ness among young men with big dogs and little cars, but here in Las Vegas we are grand masters of an unsung kind of public art, the art of living together for generations. The inertia of all that history is one of the best things about the place. It's like a big strong tree with deep roots. It doesn't blow around much."

BIRDIE JAWORSKI

From 2008 until 2010 when Birdie Jaworski left Las Vegas and moved with her family to Albuquerque, she and deMare published a free weekly newspaper called *Gallinas*, the name referring of course to the river but with the additional connotation of "chicks." The paper's masthead read: "Celebrating Northeastern New Mexico's Arts, Culture, Community, History, and Entertainment," and the issues, which were themed to various holidays or aspects of regional culture, were indeed celebratory in spirit as well as entertaining and informative. Publication was entirely a two-woman operation. Jaworski and deMare edited the stories of their contributors, wrote their own, took photographs, got local businesses to place ads, did the layout, and then drove north for an hour on Interstate 25 to Raton where a print shop ran off 5,000 copies, which they then proceeded to distribute at more than 200 stops throughout Mora and San Miguel counties.

Jaworski's story about finding Las Vegas demonstrates the large role the Internet now plays in directing personal destiny. Living in California, she and her husband, Daniel Jencka, who builds harpsichords and used to play in different venues throughout the town, wanted to find somewhere less expensive where they could raise their three sons. They went to www.myspot.com, filled out the online questionnaire, and up came Las Vegas, New Mexico, as an ideal small town with an excellent climate, beautiful scenery, and low cost of living. They drove out to see for themselves and decided that this would be a perfect place to settle.

A prolific writer, inveterate blogger, and former representative for Avon cosmetics—her 2007 book *Don't Shoot: I'm Just the Avon Lady!* describes this phase of her career—Jaworski is first and foremost a storyteller. On her Web site, she proclaims, "It's our job to write about people. Some of the people I write about have no one to tell their story. But I have someone. Me! And you! We can write about people who need us, and we can write about each other." Since blogging is the easiest form of self-publication, right after moving to Las Vegas Jaworski established the Web site mytinyvegas.com where she used to post "Stories from Meadow City," cultural vignettes where her natural exuberance was given free rein. Now published in book form, *My Tiny Vegas* (2009) is a compendium of these stories. Readers will find that her breezy narratives are based on the experience of the moment and often describe the landscapes and people she has encountered on short road trips in the San Miguel County countryside, frequently in the company of her children.

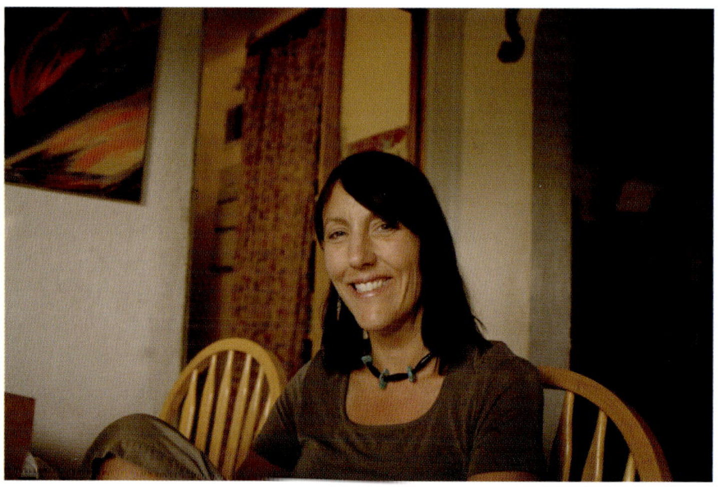

Birdie Jaworski

To say that Jaworski's writing style is colorful is something of an understatement. The opening paragraph of the first story in *My Tiny Vegas* reads: "The road to San Augustin passes nothing, nothing but a pistol-pitted sign welcoming travelers to county road C-24, nothing but dry wind and green-gold prairie, the asphalt twisting in deference to property line and gulch, pockets of fattened cows standing bored sentinel. I drove slower than the speed limit, my son riding shotgun, and watched the sun fall from my ears to shoulder in the rear view mirror." Weaving this kind of scenic observation with human interest, she draws sympathetic portraits of people and their relationship to the land. In this case, her story was about Huero and Eva Gonzales who grow sweet corn, which when roasted in their backyard *horno*, is turned into *chicos*, a northern New Mexican delicacy.

Like deMare, Jaworski characterizes herself as a crossover person. She briefly served as the director of the Las Vegas Arts Council but resigned partly because, as she put it, "all the people in charge are Anglos, and they have what is basically an Anglo agenda." Public events do not necessarily act as a means of melding cultures, according to her. She pointed out that for the most part Anglo and Hispanic people don't go to the same town functions, except perhaps for the Fourth of July parade, the kickoff for the three days of fiestas that constitute a Hispanization of the all-American holiday. With regard to town politics, she exclaimed, "You ought to see the signs at election time; people put out placards for opposing candidates next to each other in the same yard! That's because everyone is related to everyone else." According to Jaworski, Anglos spend a lot more time on jury duty than Hispanics because lawyers can't find anyone Hispanic to serve on a case who is not a relative of the defendant.

When I asked her how she would describe Las Vegas, Jaworski said, "Sometimes the place drives me crazy, but I love it here. It's great for my kids. It's not like California. No one has a lot of money, you don't have to schedule activities for them, and they all have fun just hanging out with their friends after school. And then there are just so many stories. I get to meet all these interesting people because of publishing the paper. I guess I'm stuck here now, but not in a bad way. You just have to let go and embrace the place and then you can begin to understand it." Shaking her head, she immediately contradicted herself, "No, you can't ever *really* understand this town."

I was sorry when a few months after this conversation I learned that Jaworski had moved to Albuquerque, but I recently reconnected with her on her current Web site, which is called "Birdie Jaworski Dot Com, Baby!: A Bird with Words." Her stories also appear on another Web site called "Camp Strange," which is hosted by the online publisher wikinut. If you click on the "About Birdie" tab on this one, you will learn that "Birdie loves salsa dancing, staring folks down with her left eye, yodeling, playing banjo, whomping her kids' butts at the Japanese game of Go, and making exotic crafts out of popsicle sticks." With a profile like this, it is obvious that when it comes to discerning the meaning of place, place is personality and the Internet a new kind of residence. Place in Jaworski's case is what you write wherever you happen to be.

MICKEY DOWLING

In the 1970s when the Reagan Administration determined that new psychotropic drugs could stabilize mentally ill persons sufficiently to turn them over to clinical care as outpatients, homelessness rose in many American cities. In Las Vegas those that left the State Hospital did not end up on the street but rather in boarding houses where they sleep dormitory-style and are fed three meals a day. For these services, their monthly Social Security payments are transmitted to their landlords, who retain most of the check, give them a small weekly allowance, and send them out on the street after breakfast. Fortunately, in Las Vegas there is a place where they can spend their mornings in friendly acceptance, comfort, and comradeship. This is the Richards Center of the Mental Health Association of New Mexico on Bridge Street, which is run by Sheila Silverman and Mickey Dowling. Both Silverman and Dowling maintain that they are themselves mentally ill, a condition they say can't be cured but only stabilized, which is their current situation.

Like most people who haven't socialized with the mentally ill, I was hesitant at first about walking into the center, but Dowling gave me a friendly smile and a hand-

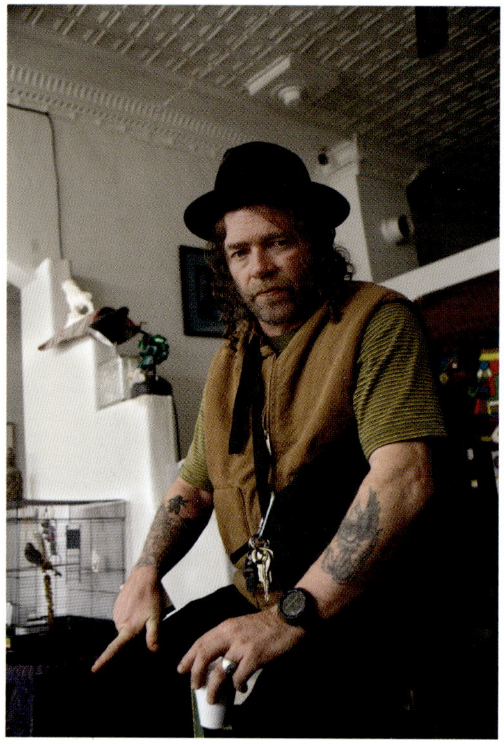

Mickey Dowling

shake when I introduced myself. I noticed the sunniness of the room, the houseplants in the window, the colorful art on the walls, and a parakeet chirping in its cage. While we were talking he greeted everyone coming in the door by name, asserting to me as a truculent aside, "Here we only call people by their names. You label jars, not people. Outpatient mental institutions and caseworkers call them 'clients,' and hospitals and therapists refer to them as 'patients.' The PC term is 'recipient.' That's why the system sucks. None of those professionals do shit on weekends, but we're here seven days a week. I see myself as a peer, not a professional."

I asked Dowling to tell me something of his own life story. "I'm pretty much a ding-dong," he said. "I was a train tramp, not a thumb bum," meaning that he rode the rails rather than hitchhiked. "Train tramps are called wing nuts because other bums think they are kind of screwy. I didn't hang out very much with road dogs, except for girl road dogs, because guy road dogs are always looking for a team player, and that's trouble for two when they get busted for doing something stupid like stealing." Dowling said that he never stole but was able to work the system, amassing food stamps from several state agencies across the country and selling them at a discount. Since stores receive a premium from the government when the stamps are redeemed, many small grocery owners are willing to buy them. And because stamps come in dollar denominations, a food-stamp customer can get coin change.

He confided, "You can go in one store and then another, buy a can of malt, an Atomic Fireball, one banana, whatever, and get silver back. I had some other good tricks. For instance, I'd go to Target (he likes to Frenchify the name, pronouncing it Tar-jay) and get a little immersion heater to heat liquid—hobos call those stingers. You always find electrical outlets in parks, so I could heat things that way. Or I'd go to a hardware store and buy some spigots and then get a shampoo nozzle at a pet store or a Wal-Mart. At night I'd go behind a restaurant where they had hoses to clean stuff, strip naked, and take a shower. But when I was laying up in the woods, I'd get pretty filthy."

As the door opened, he called out, "Hey, Frederico! What's going on, Big Fred? What's going on next Tuesday? It's April first, the day the eagle shits!" To me he explained, "The Social Security checks come in on the first day of the month. It's payday, so I won't see much of a crowd next week."

A young man with a friendly grin, who had been watching me for a while, wanted to talk. He said he was brought from Española to the State Hospital in Las Vegas by his parents and had stayed there for ten years before he was let out and placed in a boarding house. When I asked him what he thought of the town, he said, "Las Vegas is a beautiful place to live. What I see is more mental people, and there are doctors here. I've been suicidal, but the meds are helping me a lot. Last night I dreamed about having my own apartment. I dreamed I had a job and was working. I wish I could drive a bit and get rid of the mental bipolar."

Dowling invited everyone who came in to say hello to a large rabbit in a cage in the back corridor. While it was being admired, I asked him to tell me more about his former way of life. He said that when he was a hobo he carried a backpack and would sleep in a tent when he was not sheltering in a train car. He would sometimes live in a roadside camp but always had the urge to go into town. "The hobos who don't leave camp," he said, "are the ones who are shooting dope all the time. For me, it was a visual thing. Who's going to look at pigeons and sagebrush all day?"

During his vagabond days, Dowling gravitated to places like Salt Lake City because of their cultural amenities, explaining, "There are libraries in cities, and I always sought them out. Don't get me wrong. I'm a lazy brain. I didn't go there to read philosophy, but I wanted to look at newspapers and magazines in order to keep up with the world. In cities a homeless person learns where it is safe to go for the night. I've slept on the grounds of four state hospitals. Nobody is going to look for a hobo there. Then when it got cold in the winter I'd go to the Organ Mountains east of Las Cruces and camp in the desert with the snowbirds."

Taking in this education in the lifestyle of the down-and-out itinerant, I realized that for Dowling place is really nothing more than whim, ingenuity, and opportunity. You get a notion to head in a certain direction, you survive by your wits, and then you grab a particular circumstance such as government funding for a mental health program to set up residence for a time wherever that might land you. It Dowling's case, Las Vegas was the place.

Chapter Nine: Feeding Las Vegas

Food is an essential ingredient of the culture of place, and that of Northern New Mexico is an important part of Las Vegas's identity. Here a celebrity-chef-run restaurant or sushi bar would be a distinct anomaly, for in the same way that Las Vegans shun other aspects of Santa Fe's sophistication they also express a decided preference for home-style northern New Mexican cooking.

La Comida

At first taste, northern New Mexican cuisine does not seem especially different from Mexican food, but this is not the case. Although, like the indigenous fare of all of preconquest North America, it is corn- and bean-based, there are subtle variations that make it a distinct regional variant. In the rural areas around Las Vegas corn is turned into chicos, sweet-tasting dry kernels, by being smoke-roasted in an outdoor horno, an oven than looks like an adobe beehive. It also becomes posole, the basis of a rich, savory stew, by being soaked in an alkaline solution of powdered lime and water and then allowed to dry out after the kernels have sufficiently swollen. Although similar to hominy, which is made by soaking corn kernels in a weak solution of lye made from leached hardwood ashes, posole has a more intense flavor. Christmas wouldn't be Christmas in Northern New Mexico without steaming bowls of this traditional food.

Protein-rich blue corn is an ancestral variety, one that is still grown in the Southwest. Soaked in limewater like posole and hulled, it becomes (as does white corn processed in the same way) *nixtamal*, which when ground into meal, or *masa,* forms the basis for blue tortillas. *Frijoles* (beans) are a staple served with practically every meal. When these cooked legumes are mashed, seasoned, and cooked again in a skillet, they become *frijoles refritos,* refried beans. New Mexico specializes in a particular green chile,[1] which is roasted in late summer, as well as a variety of hot red chiles, which are harvested in the fall, dried, and ground into a fine powder or plaited into ornamental *ristras*. Both dried-red and roasted-green chiles are the respective bases of the sauces served over enchiladas made from either blue- or white-corn tortillas. People who want both order "Christmas," for one red- and one green-topped enchilada.

Besides corn tortillas, flour tortillas are commonplace in Northern New Mexico. They form the wrapping for burritos or are served on the side like bread. Another regional specialty, *sopaipillas*, are puffy, air-filled, deep-fried bread triangles or squares that can be stuffed with a meat and bean mixture or eaten plain with honey drizzled on top. *Sopa,* a bread pudding that is also called *capirotada*, is served as a special Christmas and Lenten dessert.

In addition to these dishes, *biscochitos*, the delicate anise- and cinnamon-flavored cookies introduced by the Spanish settlers, are traditionally made at holiday times or for weddings. Jesus Lopez says that his mother, Mama Lucy, was unsurpassed in the art of making biscochitos: "She would roll out the dough and cut it into strips and then cut the strips into small squares. Then she would use a paring knife to make small cuts around the edges so that they would flare out when baked." According to him, although it is sprinkled with sugar and cinnamon, a biscochito is much more than a sugar cookie; rather, it is an indigenous delicacy, one that is "very, very unique to Northern New Mexico." As a boy he also liked to watch his mother make *empanaditas*, another holiday pastry. The dough for these is cut into circles, which are folded and crimped after being filled with meat, piñon nuts, and spices.

Family Business

Almost all the eating establishments in Las Vegas are in the Mama Lucy tradition not only in their menus but also in the fact that they are small, family-run businesses—even the McDonald's franchise at the corner of Mills Avenue and Seventh Street. Talking over breakfast or lunch with the owners of several well-established favorites, I learned that many not only employ several immediate relatives in their operation but are themselves the children of restaurateurs and hope that their children will follow in their footsteps. While eating various delicious items on the menus of these establishments, I was able to appreciate their popularity and observe how they function as everyday social venues for loyal customers. I also came to understand how hard local food-service people work to make their businesses thrive and succeed economically.

CHARLES SANDOVAL

At breakfast and lunchtime Charlie's Spic & Span Bakery & Café on Douglas Street is probably the busiest place in Las Vegas. When Charles Sandoval bought the restaurant from Carmen Fernandez in 1998, it was much smaller but just as popular as it is today. "It was started in the 1950s and Carmen owned it for thirty years, so there have been only three owners during its sixty or so years of existence," Sandoval explained one day when he was able to take a break and sit down with me at one of the booths that line the walls of the restaurant. "People have always loved this place," he said. "A lot of our customers remember coming here with their parents and grandparents."

Mama Lucy is credited with bringing down the "tortilla curtain," attracting students from Highlands University and other East Las Vegas residents to her famous café on the plaza, but Sandoval can boast with assurance that "the Spic & Span has always been known as Tortilla Heaven. They are the best thing that ever happened to this restaurant. Carmen used to roll them by hand, but now that we sell about a hundred dozen a day, I am going to have to buy another machine in order to turn them out fast enough." Knowing that as usual I was about to buy a bag of the large, still-warm flour tortillas that I could see being rolled onto the big griddle behind glass cases filled with donuts and cream puffs, I said that I had no trouble believing it. "Yes," Sandoval replied, "I think I've built up the place quite a bit."

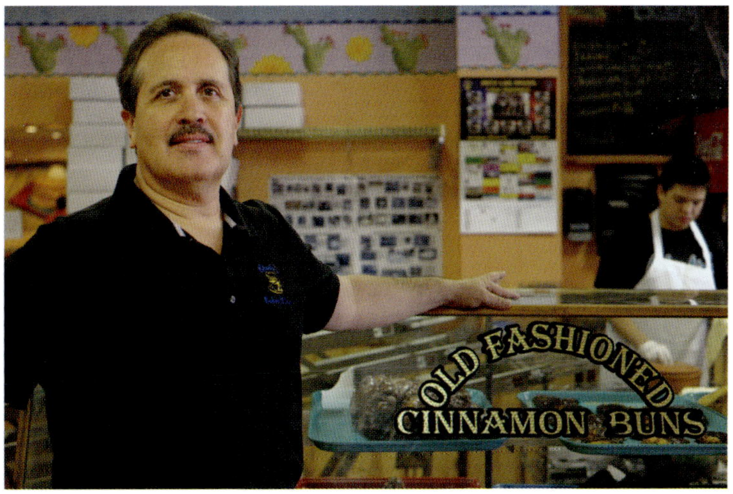

Charles Sandoval

Along with the famous tortillas, the temptingly displayed baked goods are a profitable sideline. "I have a cake decorator and two bakers in back," Sandoval told me. "We have to begin making the donuts at four in the morning, because it's a four-hour process mixing the dough, letting it rise, cutting it into shapes, letting these rise, and then putting them in the hopper and cooking them at a hundred degrees in oil. It's a lot of work and it gets hot back there, but it's worth it. People also like our cakes, and we do a good deal of catering. December's a big month. We make a huge amount of empanadas then."

For its dining customers, the Spic & Span offers traditional New Mexican food—burritos, enchiladas, posole, rice, beans, huevos rancheros. (I like to order the vegetarian enchiladas and always waver between choosing "red or green.") To handle the sit-down customers who flock to enjoy this popular fare, Sandoval expanded the restaurant's size. "It used to be just this little place, one room that was part drugstore, but I doubled our space by opening up the wall of the building next door. I also opened a room downstairs, which is used for parties." Looking around, I admired the colorful walls, which are decorated with big, bold paintings of food. "My son does the murals," Sandoval said. "He just graduated from Highlands, and right now he is headed off to Kansas to get a master's degree in art."

The Spic & Span serves around eight hundred customers a day. Other events such as the Cinco de Mayo celebration, Highlands graduation, and Mother's Day bring in over a thousand. But the restaurant is not Sandoval's only business. "We have the franchise for the Dairy Queen out on the highway north of town," he told me. "My wife runs that." He agreed when I said that being in the food business certainly entails a lot of hard work. "It does," he answered. "I'm here by six o'clock every morning, and it is at least a twelve-hour day seven days a week. We close at five thirty because that's when things slow down around here. I wish we could get back some of the activity there used to be in the evening in this part of town. I hope they will renovate the SERF next door. It would be nice to have a movie theater there again, and it would also be good if there was something like a bowling alley nearby."

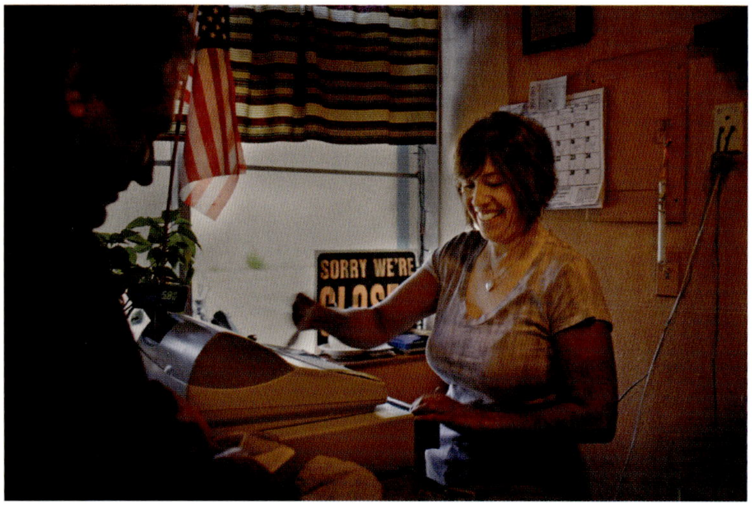

Esther Loera

ESTHER LOERA

Esther Loera, the owner of El Encanto Restaurant at the northeast corner of the plaza, told me, "I learned everything from my grandmother." In the 1950s her grandparents, Aurora and Gregorio, had a restaurant on Bridge Street. In 1980 her parents, Louis and Andrea, moved to Trinidad, Colorado, where they operated two restaurants before moving back to Las Vegas in 1999. In the meantime, Esther took a job as a waitress at Tillie's Kitchen on South Pacific Street. Wanting to be her own boss, she decided to buy El Encanto when it was put up for sale. Her mother, who has now been a chef for more than thirty years, is the chief cook, and her husband doubles as cashier and waiter. Her children Carlos, Yolanda, and Lucero also help out, and her grandchildren are usually in the back somewhere.

When I have breakfast at El Encanto, almost invariably sitting nearby are several policemen, since this is their established gathering place before reporting for work at their headquarters on the opposite side of the plaza. El Encanto's breakfast menu includes huevos rancheros, fried-egg burritos, and pancakes. In addition, Loera does catering on the side. "I love to bake," she told me. "Biscochitos are my holiday specialty, and we do a lot of parties at Christmastime and also weddings."

KAREN PETTINE

The Hillcrest Restaurant on Grand Street is another morning meeting spot. Here, every day of the week a group of men, including Democratic County Chairman Marty Suazo, gather for breakfast at a round table in the corner. It might appear to be Las Vegas's current political hub, but without an all-controlling patrón like Tiny Martinez, the restaurant does not really function as an auxiliary party clubhouse as Mama Lucy's once did. Rather, it is where several of the chief players in town and county affairs exchange news and opinions that inform, but do not strictly govern, local politics.

Like Esther Loera, Karen Pettine, the owner, was born into the restaurant business. Her family were farmers in Kansas until the Dust Bowl days in the 1930s, when they followed her older sister Vera and her husband, who had moved to Washington state to pick fruit in the orchards. While we sat in a booth and talked after the morning breakfast crowd had left, she said, "We lived in Seattle and, as things got worse and worse during the Great Depression, my mother worked in a downtown coffee shop, and Vera opened a restaurant near the Boeing air field where I would go as little girl and stand on a milk carton and look over the counter at what they were doing in the kitchen. Then my mom got tired of waiting on tables and opened her own restaurant downtown in the industrial section where the bus depot and the warehouses were. The men in my dad's family were bakers, and during the war he got a job training shipboard bakers in the Navy commissary. But before going to work, he would get up at four o'clock and come to my mother's restaurant to get the yeast rolls started."

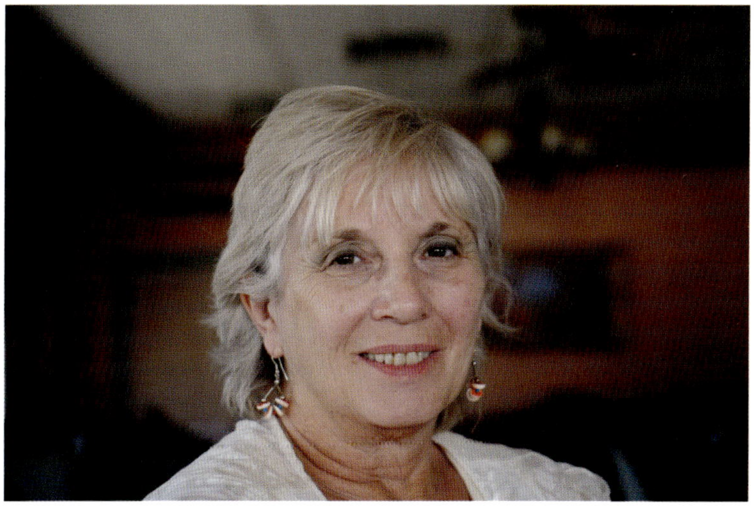

Karen Pettine

The construction of Seattle's freeways in the 1950s and 1960s forced Pettine's mother to sell the restaurant when the state condemned the site for a right-of-way. This precipitated the family's move to Las Vegas at the invitation of her brother-in-law who had bought the restaurant, which was then called the 85 Coffee Shop because of its location on Highway 85 (now Interstate 25). According to Karen, "It was a burger-and-shake place and was very popular with the teen crowd; we still have the original juke boxes from the 1950s. All the motels were starting to grow up along this stretch of the highway, so we found ourselves in the right location at the right time. My uncle had built the four-room apartment upstairs," she added, pointing to the ceiling overhead, "and in 1964, after my parents sold their house in Seattle to get the down payment, we took over the restaurant from him and moved into the apartment. I was very excited because for the first time in my life I had my own bedroom."

In 1974, while Pettine was in the middle of her senior year at New Mexico State University studying commercial food management, her father suddenly called and said that he was tired of being in the restaurant business and ready there and then to sell the Hillcrest to her and her brother, an Air Force veteran who had also studied the culinary arts. She persuaded her father to let her have a few more months to finish college, while she and her brother managed to scrape up the $75,000 that allowed her parents to retire. Today the thriving restaurant has been remodeled, and while the coffee shop is the same size as before, there is a large room for evening dining in the back. In addition, Karen and her brother bought the former gas station property next door, which provides them with an ample parking lot as well as the opportunity to operate a bar-lounge adjacent to the restaurant. "We have a good business," she said. "This is partly because Las Vegas is a day's ride between Phoenix and Denver, and all the snowbirds always stop here. It's really wonderful when they tell us that they love this place and have been coming for years."

One afternoon I came back when Pettine was free to sit down with me for a few minutes. As we chatted in the back dining room, an employee came in and asked her how to pack the food that was to be picked up shortly. Referring to the shelter a few blocks south on Grand Avenue, she replied, "It's for the Good Samaritan. We send food over to them every day." At the time this conversation took place, news was in the air that the bank mortgage lender had announced the default of Wid Slick's Plaza Partnership Ltd. and that its repossession of the Plaza Hotel was imminent. I asked Pettine how she felt about the town's future in light of this. "It is just a terrible thing what is happening with the Plaza," she said. "None of us knew what a special historic place this town is, and then thirty years ago Wid and Kak Slick came along and made us understand the asset we have here. More than anyone else, they are responsible for what has happened to bring Old Town back to life. We all owe them so much for making Las Vegas what it is today."

MANUEL MARTINEZ AND LUISA AND KENNETH PACHECO

In 2008, at the same time that Wid Slick was renovating the adjacent historic Ilfeld Emporium in order to double the size of his hotel, Manuel Martinez opened Plaza Burgers on the opposite side of the park. I like to eat lunch there sometimes because the hamburgers are thick, juicy, made of freshly ground meat, and served with ribbon fries—long spiraling curls of potato. Luisa Pacheco and her husband, Kenneth, operate the place along with Martinez, who is Kenneth's father. One day when I was passing by I stepped in the door and found that Luisa was not too busy waiting on tables to chat with me for a few minutes. "Me, my husband, my mom, my best friend, my father-in-law, my little boys, Kenneth and Keith—we are all here," she said, adding, "I have a lot of fun. It's our home away from home." Kenneth, who had walked over to the side of the room where we were talking, said, "I was working over at the body shop that my brother Orlando started, but I got out of that when my dad asked me to help him open up a place on the plaza like the one my grandfather used to have on Highway 85 in the forties and fifties."

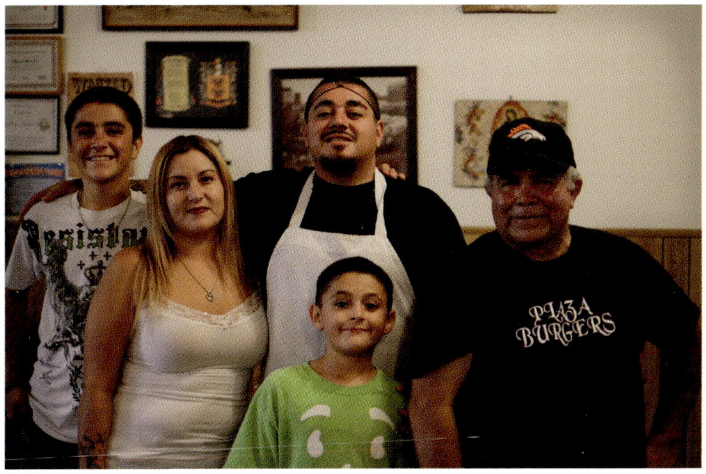

The Martinez-Pacheco family

Martinez, who sat down with me after I had ordered lunch, elaborated, "My dad used to have a place over on this side of town when 85 still ran along South Pacific Street. After Interstate 25 rerouted the old highway to the south, he closed the first place and opened another one down on Grand. But I didn't go into the restaurant business with him after I graduated from high school. Instead I ventured into construction, motels, nightclubs, and other stuff before I retired. Then I heard there was a store on the plaza for rent, so I walked over to my sons' body shop and asked Kenneth, 'Do you want to make hamburgers?' The body shop wasn't making any money, so he said yes. That was on June 28, 2008, and we needed to open by the Fourth of July weekend. Ralph Garcia, who owns the Rialto on Bridge Street, and I are real good friends, so I went to him and said, 'I need some chairs.' He opened the door to a room in the back of his restaurant and told me, 'Take what you need.' I didn't have a restaurant license, so I went to the fire chief and the head of the health department, and because they knew me and the fact that my family had been in the restaurant business, all I had to do was show them the menu and they said, 'OK, we know you can run a first-class joint.' We did a little bit of modifying inside and were open by July 4—just one week after we signed the lease. Now, a year later, we've outgrown our first place up the block, and we're here a few doors down in this bigger one with a five-year lease and an option to buy."

I wondered how they had been able to build a clientele so quickly. "Well," Martinez replied, "We had an automatic following of at least 200. Our family here in Las Vegas is 500 strong. We do have our differences, but we're very clannish and we all stick together and help each other when we need to. And then it's about friendly service, good quality, and good quantity. Our loyal customers are what keep us going."

"These are really nice fat burgers," I told him, taking another bite. The cheeseburger I was eating with so much relish along with a pile of ribbon fries comes with lettuce, tomato, onion, and pickles. But because this is New Mexico, Plaza Burgers also serves jalapeños on the side. In addition, they make a taco burger, which is called the Keith Special after Martinez's grandson. But these are just small concessions to the regional palate. "We don't serve New Mexican food because we don't want to compete with Ralph or any of our other friends who are in the restaurant business," Martinez told me. "We all like each other. Sometimes one of us will bring the others a piece of cheesecake, or if somebody has made posole we'll all be given a bowl."

At that point, business started to get lively, and Luisa was going from table to table taking orders from customers who had just walked in the door and seated themselves. Martinez said, "I've got to get back to the kitchen now." When I asked if I could follow him and see for myself what went on there, he replied "Sure." As I watched Kenneth feeding potatoes one by one into the cutting machine, I was fascinated with the way the spiraling blade would unfurl each into a long ribbon. "When customers ask how we do these, we tell them that we have a little monkey in the back," he said with a laugh. Meanwhile, Martinez was flipping burgers on the grill. "Our meat is a lot cleaner than McDonald's," he bragged, "because we get our own beef daily. Everything we use here is completely fresh. We don't use anything that has been frozen. That's the secret of our success."

After lunch when things were less busy, I sat down with Martinez under one of the red-umbrella-shaded tables on the sidewalk. Next to us his grandsons Keith and Kenneth were struggling to make a homemade puzzle of linked pieces of wood unfold from a stacked center so as to form a cross. It was tricky to figure out, and Manuel looked on with affectionate pride, giving the boys bits of advice as they kept trying. "This is why we are doing this," he confided. "We're building the business for these guys. They're going to run it someday."

RALPH GARCIA

One morning while lunch preparations were under way in the kitchen, I visited the Rialto Restaurant on Bridge Street and met with the owner, Ralph Garcia. "I bought this location, which was then a dry-goods store, in 1974," he told me. "I was only twenty-eight at the time. In 1977 I purchased the building next door, which is now the bar attached to this place, and later the one just up the street, which my son Abraham now runs. We also own the courtyard in between, and that's where we have a patio bar and do a lot of catered events. You can see if you look at historic photographs of Bridge Street that there used to be bars all over the place, but ever since the state began to have strict controls and you had to purchase a liquor license, they started to close one by one. I now own four bars altogether, which we operate under one license because we have all our locations incorporated as a single business. In thirty years we have never been cited for a single infraction. Now, ever since the police got so strict with DWI enforcement, the revenue we get from selling liquor has dropped by probably 80 percent. But our restaurant business is good, and that keeps us going."

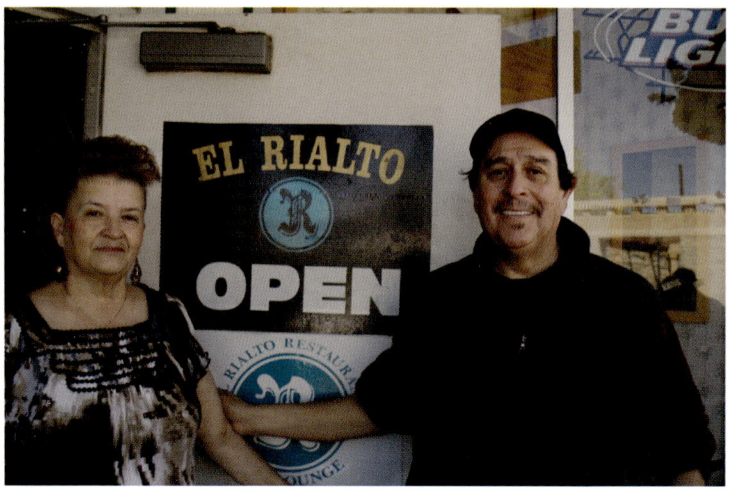

Frances and Ralph Garcia

Ralph Garcia was born and raised in Las Vegas and attended Highlands University. His wife, Frances, is as closely involved as he is in the day-to-day running of the Rialto. "We're at a point now," he said, "where the kids are grown, and we're going to retire and get some R&R, and let them run it. It's a tough business. I get up seven days a week at four in the morning and am here until we close at eight-thirty at night. After that a second manager takes over until 1 A.M., and then I'm back five hours later."

Garcia said, "The Rialto menu is comprised of the foods we used to eat as children: flour tortillas, posole, beans, chiles, homemade tamales, sopaipillas—all native northern New Mexican food, not Tex-Mex." I observed that the Rialto is just one of a handful of restaurants in Las Vegas that is open for dinner and that the place always seems crowded. "The secret," he told me, "is this. If you are in the hospitality business, you have to maintain high standards. You must have clean restrooms, and you must treat the staff well. They have to be trained and well groomed, the food has to come out at a certain temperature, and it has to be good. Right now my wife is the Number One chef, and she has Abraham helping her back in the kitchen. It's like this," he summarized, "We started with just four walls, struggled for the first five or six years, and gradually built the business. We've worked hard, and this town has been good to us."

ADELITA LUJAN

Probably one of the attractions of Las Vegas for the movie industry is the old-time appearance of Bridge Street. The faded white-and-red neon sign with scalloped edges set at a right angle to the sidewalk, with "CAFE" in fat capitals running vertically beneath a horizontal arm that says "ESTELLA'S" in smaller letters, announces even more visibly than the Art Deco Kiva movie theater on the opposite side of the street that time stopped here somewhere around the middle of the twentieth century. This is true because Adelita Lujan hasn't changed anything much since she decided in 1999 to return to Las Vegas with her husband Joseph and their son and daughter Zachary and Mericele in order to run the restaurant her grandmother Estella and grandfather Luis had started in 1950.

Adelita Lujan with B. J. Garcia

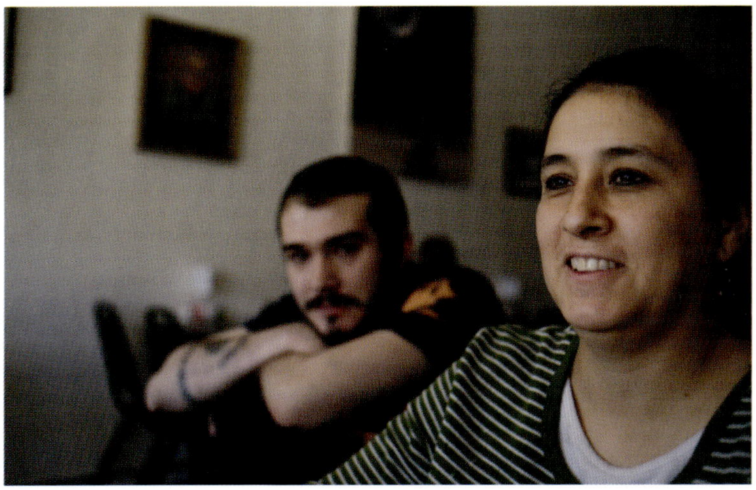

There is an old-fashion red-and-white Coca-Cola machine in the corner near the front window and a long row of backless, round-seated, plastic-covered swivel stools beside the lunch counter. A color photograph of Estella, various santos, family photos, old posters, and a variety of knickknacks adorn the walls and fill the shelves of several cabinets. It is an unusual décor, bearing no resemblance to the kinds of stock historic photographs and period items with which some restaurants are embellished.

Rather, coming into Estella's is like entering someone's personal world. And that is, as it happens, the case.

As we talked over coffee one day, I asked Lujan to tell me about her grandmother Estella, the history of the restaurant, and how she came to run it now. "Back in the 1970s," she said, "after my grandma had been operating the restaurant for around twenty years, she was trying to clean some of the things sitting on the top of that tall cabinet over there behind the lunch counter one day, and she fell and broke her hip. But even though she had chronic pain after that, it did not stop her from carrying on the business with the help of my grandpa and my dad." Pointing at the white-painted stairs that rise to an opening in the pressed-tin ceiling, she said, "It was cold up there and expensive to heat, so after she broke her hip it made sense for her and my grandpa to move downstairs and live in the back of the kitchen. You have to understand, this place was always their whole life—literally. Estella hardly slept, just took naps." When I wondered why she didn't go to bed like other people, Lujan shot back, "Have you ever run a restaurant? It's on your mind all the time. You get up in the morning at four to wash the beans and start cooking them. Then you have to prepare the dough for the sopaipillas, start two kinds of chile sauces—red and green—grate cheese, chop the lettuce and tomatoes, boil and shred the chicken, cook the pork for the tacos, fry the tortillas for tostados, make guacamole—it's a *lot* of work! That didn't mean that my grandparents weren't involved in town politics or didn't have fun. My grandfather ran the bingo, and sometimes they would hold little dances back here where the kitchen is now."

Estella's Café

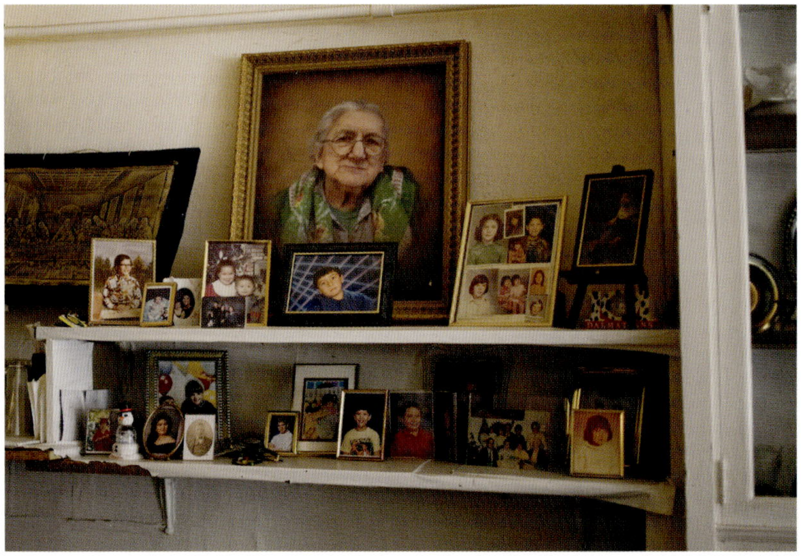

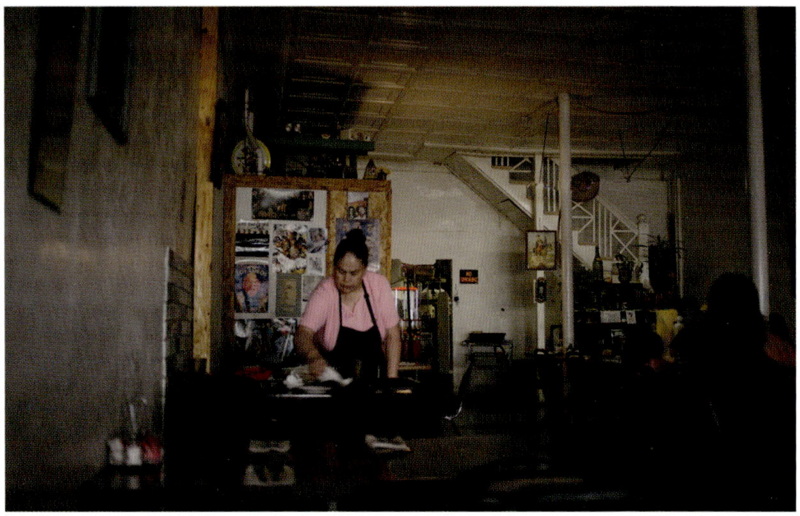

Bringing her story up to the present, Lujan said, "In the mid-nineties I'd come up from Albuquerque a lot with my kids Zak and Mericele to see them. That was when my grandparents were really slowing down. My dad kept asking his three daughters to come back and help him take care of the restaurant.

At first I said I wouldn't, but every time I came up I would hear them worrying about how they were going to pay bills if they had to close the place. I could never get it off my mind. I was so concerned about them. My husband wasn't too keen on moving up here, but one day I just told him, 'We're going to live in Vegas. I've got to help my grandma.' This was in 1998, and Grandpa had just died. Joseph said, 'Well, OK,' and that was it. We came home." I wondered why it was she rather than one of her sisters who had decided to run the restaurant. She thought for a moment before she answered, "Because I am the one who cared."

When I asked her why the restaurant had such a timeless quality, Lujan replied, "This was my grandparents' home, and these were just Estella's knickknacks, anniversary presents and that sort of thing. She would move stuff around from time to time, rearranging her pictures, statuettes, vases, pitchers, and other possessions. We do the same, so the place doesn't seem stale and keeps on being fresh to our eyes. But it is still all her things you see around here. We don't add anything of ours except every once in awhile. The only things we never move are the santos. They always stay in exactly the places where they have always been."

Lujan fetched a pile of family albums from a cabinet by the stairs. As we leafed through the photos of her relatives taken at various family functions, she pointed out Estella and Luis in the center of the group in one picture. "They are sitting there at the table that was always reserved for the family. Everybody that came in always knew not to take that one."

Before I left Estella's, I told Lujan that the book I was writing was not just about Las Vegas but about the meaning of place in people's lives. "That's so coincidental that you said that," she said. "Just a couple of days ago, we were playing this game back there in the kitchen. You know how certain cities have a word or some sort of saying that describes them, captures their essence—'Vibrant' for New York and I don't know what for LA, maybe 'cool'? So I asked the guys to think up a word that describes Las Vegas. Someone said 'hardship,' another said 'no change.' Somebody called it 'struggle,' someone else called it 'a place to be.' Really, it was a nice little thing to do, just a one-day exercise while we were all working." I asked her what her word for Las Vegas was. There was a long pause. "My word? I guess I didn't put down anything for myself," she admitted. There was another pause. "Well?" I encouraged. Finally she looked up and said, "Home."

Chapter Ten: Appraising Las Vegas

Las Vegas remains in a state of uneasy stasis, a puzzling phenomenon. The long arm of history falls as a shadow over the town because the signs of its prosperous past are so apparent. Its abandoned buildings, evidence of former better times, betoken economic failure and at the same time invite recovery. Although its population continues to decline and its future is uncertain, the pull of place keeps this dream alive. Nevertheless, there are those who came to stay but are now leaving. Some of them fault what they believe to be the town's intractable ills, inbred nature, and political corruption. In addition, there is an unsettling demographic trend as college-educated young people from long-established families are lured away by the kind of job opportunities that do not exist in Las Vegas. Militating against economic revitalization is the belief on the part of many—though not all— Hispanic residents that greater tourism, new businesses, and start-up industries could bring a population increase that might upset their prevailing hegemony in town politics.

Las Vegas's poverty is an obstacle to recovery, but low incomes and crime are only one side of the coin, self-reliance and hard work being the other. Because of these and other assets, there are those who see the half-full rather than the half-empty glass and believe in the possibility of a brighter future for Las Vegas. For them it is a dream to which they have pledged their aspirations, their efforts, and their lives. The two major issues they face are whether Las Vegas will have a future that is sustainable in terms of its economy and basic resources—most notably jobs and water.

Free Speech

People are as opinionated in Las Vegas as anywhere else. Because it is a small, isolated town, Las Vegans' worldview tends to be inward-focused. Although, as is true everywhere else, access to global technology is breaking down communications barriers, many residents' attitudes are still clannishly colored by prejudice against Anglos. Even some Hispanic latecomers say they are made to feel like permanent outsiders. But the willingness of many Las Vegans to share their opinions and often inspirational life stories with me has proved that this is far from categorically true.

TOM MCDONALD

The *Las Vegas Optic* is owned by Landmark Community Newspapers, a sixteen-paper chain with headquarters in Shelbyville, Kentucky. Assigned by the company to run the paper seven years ago, Tom McDonald is a relative newcomer, a Southerner whose origins are readily apparent from his accent. An enthusiast by nature, he said on the day I dropped by his office to meet with him, "This is one of the most interesting towns I have ever worked in. It has a rich cultural flavor and is one of the most generous communities I know. I think it has great potential but also some deep-seated problems such as a high rate of illiteracy, property crime, and violent crime to some degree. Being part of the West makes it, in my opinion, a live-and-let-live sort of place, but there are undercurrents of resentment and a 'We don't want to be like Santa Fe' attitude, which has a certain legitimacy but stymies economic development."

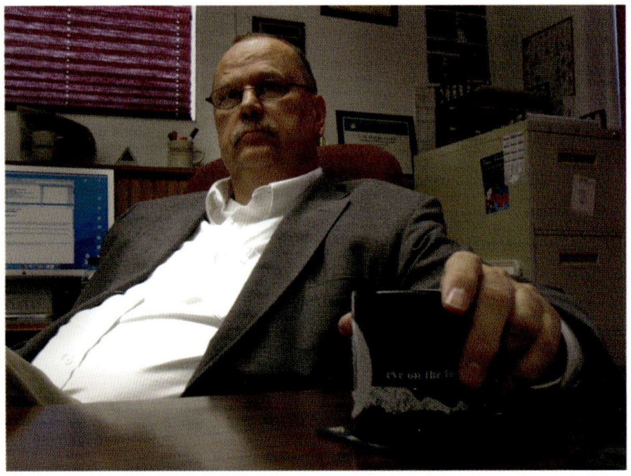

Tom McDonald

I asked McDonald if being an outsider had posed a problem for him. "Sometimes there is a letter writer who bashes me," he replied, "but a lot of people like the fact that we are writing with a level of independence and challenging the power structure. Since I have come here, the paper has angered some politicians, but there are a lot of people out there who appreciate the fact that the newspaper has an independent voice. It's like this: we're not combative at every turn but at the right turn. The patrón system is pretty much a thing of the past, and the ones who want transparent government, open government, and honest government have accepted me, even though I am an outsider."

I asked McDonald to characterize Las Vegas further. "The community is left-leaning but devoutly Catholic at the same time. It has very strong social principles. There has always been a difference in temperament between Anglos and Hispanics, Anglos being more openly defiant of the status quo and Hispanics more deferential and less activist by nature. Perhaps that is because the Church fosters a culture of obedience. And don't forget the hippies. They were a big thing in Northern New Mexico a while back; we still have several of them living here."

I brought up the topic of school-district consolidation, one of the political hot buttons in Las Vegas. "Having two separate school districts in a town this size just doesn't make sense," he said. "I'm for consolidation, and I think that more than anything else this would help heal the divisiveness that is felt in so many ways in this town. It would have a huge psychological benefit. I'd like to see us pass on to the next generation a level of unity that hasn't existed to this point."

When I went back home, I picked up an editorial I had cut out of the *Optic* a few weeks before, in which McDonald analyzed Las Vegas in terms of the recently published 2010 census. "We're in God's country," he wrote. "Beautiful land, good people, rich in culture and diversity, with a live-and-let-live approach to getting along. So why are more people leaving than coming in?" He pointed out that the new demographic—a loss of 812 people, or 5.6 percent of the town's population over the past decade—was not an encouraging sign. He explained this dispiriting news as part of the normal migration pattern that draws people toward places of greater opportunity, but he added, "It's more of a problem here than in many other communities. A lot of small towns and cities have actually maintained or grown their populations by replacing the old agricultural jobs with twentieth- and twenty-first-century opportunities. Small manufacturing facilities, rock-solid mom-and-pop retail stores, and vibrant business districts keep a lot of small towns across the U.S. economically healthy, but here, it seems we have more failures than successes." He then pointed to the crucial fact that Las Vegas has reached its maximum potential growth in terms of available water resources, which is a serious problem for the existing population and an obvious deterrent to increasing its size. But the real problem, he concluded, was this: "We are a divided community. Even the Gallinas River, that modest waterway flowing through the heart of our city, divides us between East and West. And that's just the most obvious division. There are also cultural, economic, social, and political divides, which might shift from time to time, but they never go away." I would like to think that these words were simply admonitory, for it was clear to me from our earlier conversation that, like many others with whom I have spoken, McDonald has not given up on Las Vegas as a place of possibilities.

JOSEPH AND LORETTA BACA

The story of Joseph Baca, the owner with his wife Loretta of the local radio station KFUN, shows Las Vegas to be indeed a place of possibilities. The independent station serves the community and its surrounding areas with news, talk programs, and promotion of other small businesses and not-for-profits with social-service and cultural causes. Joseph's own story, as told in his autobiographical *Blessings in Disguise: Early Sorrows and Lasting Miracles in the Town of Las Vegas, New Mexico* (2011), is inspirational. It is, he admits, a story that is not all that uncommon in Las Vegas, except perhaps for the will he was able to exert in order to overcome the severe disadvantages of an abusive father, dire poverty, and lack of encouragement to strive for achievement.

Baca's book begins with the words "As a young boy I hated the home and family I was born into. I felt so alone, lost and condemned to failure." He then goes on to talk about the many beatings he and his brothers endured as a result of the chronic alcohol-

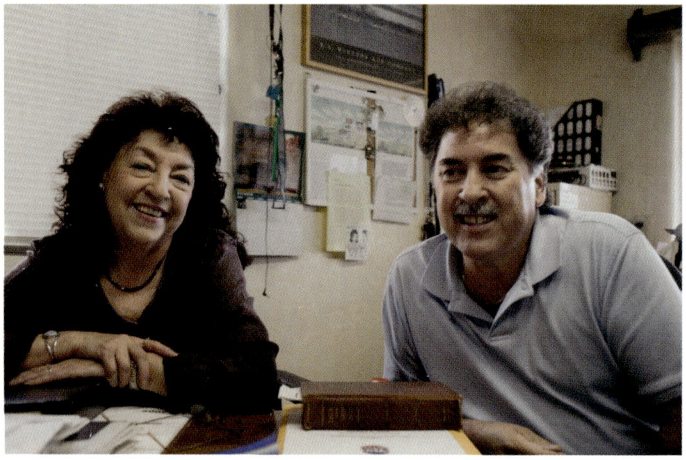

Loretta and Joseph Baca

fueled rage of their father, known as El Willé, concluding "We had to stand up for ourselves and take whatever came our way, good or bad, or in between." His was a family of nine children who slept in a single room in one large bed "packed in like sardines." For clothes he depended on the charity of neighbors who donated their hand-me-downs as well as on his ingenuity in stealing items left overnight on people's clotheslines. With his father's words, "You'll never amount to anything," constantly dinned into his head, the fact that he would one day own his own business was as inconceivable as holding a winning ticket in a million-dollar lottery. As it happened, both of these seemingly preposterous events came true.

"The lottery was just the icing on the cake," he told me one day when I met with him and Loretta at the KFUN station on top of Radio Hill. "The real blessing is that I was able to let go of the fear and animosity I had when I was growing up and that I am happy with who I am today compared with where I came from. Another blessing is working here together with my wife and our two sons. Some people think it is odd that I dedicated the book to my dad as well as to my mom. That's because I know now that something happened to him when he was little, and since he wasn't able to overcome it he was filled with rage and anger, which he took out on his family. I can even say now that I love him and that it is a shame that we never got to really know one another."

Because of his topsy-turvy home life, Baca had poor study habits, bad grades, and little incentive for finishing high school. A stint with the Job Corps, remedial summer classes to catch up with his grade level, and a few kind words from the summer school principal motivated him to stay in school and graduate from West Las Vegas High School in 1966. After that he worked with his friend Bobby Ortiz at Ortiz's photography studio and while photographing the dancers at a place called Blue Light City, he met Loretta Sedillo. Baca claims that her sympathetic understanding of what he dubs his uncertain past became the biggest blessing of his life: "How healing it is to be able to express things that are locked up inside you and that you fear to release because of censure."

Although they liked to drive around town in her white Chevy Impala with big tail fins listening to rock 'n' roll music (some of it emanating from KFUN), their dating life eventually veered from partying with friends to Bible study together. This was the beginning of their transition from the Catholic faith to the kind spiritual life offered by evangelical religion. They moved to Arizona, where they attended the church of "one of many ministers who brought themselves down with their own misconduct and secret shame all during the sixties," but this did not deter them in their joint quest for spiritual fulfillment and, for Joseph, the realization that he needed to release the haunting demons of his past and face life with new confidence. He claims to have taken the first step on that path on February 25, 1967, the day he married Loretta.

Making their way in the world, Joseph got a job in Tucson installing carpets and Loretta found employment at McClellan's Department Store in a nearby mall. They continued to attend prayer meetings, while Loretta's pregnancy confirmed "our spiritual trust in the higher power that surrounded us with light." To save money they lived in a camper trailer loaned to them by friends during the months when they were waiting for the birth of their son Michel, who was delivered by Joseph.

In 1969 the young family moved to Albuquerque, where the Bacas' daughter Annette was born. Joseph spent weekdays working as a carpet layer in the new community of Rio Rancho, and Loretta got a job in the carryout section of a Mexican restaurant near their home. They enjoyed their lives as parents; however, without a church affiliation or prayer meetings to attend at this time, Joseph began to be haunted again by his past. His anger erupted into drunken behavior not unlike that of El Willé. Ashamed—"I didn't treat my Loretta with the respect she deserved," he told me as she gently laid her hand on his arm—he continued to seek a way to be spiritually grounded. It was at this point that the Bacas experienced an important shift in their mutual religious life. After witnessing the extravagant and risible showmanship of a revival minister in a coliseum outside Albuquerque, they suddenly realized that "our world, the real world was within *and* without, but you didn't need to search for it outside yourself; it would come to you if you were patient."

Joseph wanted to move back to Las Vegas then, but knowing that "this wouldn't be good for my head or for our marriage," he allowed Loretta to dissuade him. Shortly after their second son, Joseph Baca, Jr., was born in 1975, they decided to move to Snohomish, Washington, where they opened their own carpet business, A-1 Carpet and Floor Covering. In Snohomish they formed many spiritual friendships with other families, but all during their time there they knew that they wanted to come home. After almost five years they agreed that the time had come, and in 1979 they sold their company, rented a U-Haul trailer, and returned to their roots. Joseph attempted to establish some kind of healing friendship with his father, but El Willé's fury at life had not subsided, as he demonstrated by gathering up all the family photos Joseph had sent him during the years they were away and dumping them in a paper bag on his doorstep. By this time, however, Joseph had let go of his own anger and was focused on getting a good job. Eight months after being hired part time by the radio station KNMX to use his bilingual skills on the morning wake-up show, he found out that the owner of KFUN, Dennis Mitchell, wanted to hire a full-time Spanish program director and Spanish announcer. As it happened, Mitchell also needed a receptionist and traffic controller, a job that Loretta quickly learned.

At the same time she discovered her own broadcasting abilities hosting a program of country music from 5 to 7 P.M. Monday through Friday evenings.

Radio brought Baca into the public eye, and for twelve years he served as a city councilman. By 1992, however, unhappy not to have a stronger say in the running of the station, he left to become the manager of a furniture rental business. Six years later he accepted Mitchell's offer of a full-time job while simultaneously asking him if he would consider selling KFUN and its sister FM station KLVF to his employee. Working for Mitchell, he fed his faith in himself by saying out loud every morning when he arrived at the station at 4:30, "Good morning, KFUN and KLVF, I love you, and one of these days I am going to own you and you are going to be mine." His dream appeared to evaporate when Mitchell sold the station to a longtime broadcasting partnership, and Baca was left in charge of running it almost single-handed. Fortunately, the new owners hired Loretta and their younger son, J. R., to work with him. Fate—or as Baca would say, his guiding angel—smiled on him when the principal partner, who wanted to build a new station in Santa Fe, decided to offer KFUN and KLVF to Baca.

I noticed on the wall behind the desk where he and Loretta were sitting a framed pencil sketch depicting a man and woman in deep conversation. "That is Loretta and me in the Ore House Restaurant in Santa Fe trying to figure out how we are going to buy KFUN and KLVF radio," Baca said. "What you see is the drawing on the napkin that the man at the next table, who had been watching us, made that day because we had caught his attention by looking so serious." Community First Bank answered their prayers with a loan of $450,000, and Mitchell's agreement to leave $100,000 of his proceeds from the original sale of the station in the bank furnished the couple with the necessary collateral to move forward with the purchase of KFUN/AM. They hired J. R. and his older brother, Michel, to help them run the business, sell advertising, do spot commercials, host live programs, and stream the top-of-the-hour news they get as an affiliate of ABC. Their next challenge was to come up with the $650,000 they needed to buy the FM station. The bank supported their efforts once more, but only after prolonged negotiations with the FCC in Washington to have the KLVF license reassigned to Las Vegas (Santa Fe was the city of license at the time) did the Bacas end up with the possible ownership of both the AM and the FM stations—and a debt of $1.2 million.

Most people would call it luck, but Baca thinks of the news he got from the convenience-store cashier he asked to check the lottery tickets he was holding as an answered prayer. With a $1 million win deposited in Community First Bank, he and Loretta were able to buy the FM station outright along with the additional piece of land on Radio Hill they wanted in order to build a new station. It still amazes her, but not him, who truly believed he would win the lottery some day, to think that all this was made possible by the purchase of a $2 ticket.

One has to love being a broadcaster as much as Joseph does to be cheerful about getting up at three every morning. Such early rising is necessary in order for him to scan the news and other information that has appeared on the computer overnight and to prepare the commercials and select the music that will be aired that day. At 6 A.M. the station goes live with the weekday show hosted by Martha Johnsen. "Everyone loves Martha," Baca said. "Some of them don't even want to get in the shower when she is on the air. Her show is made up of music, news, weather, and whatever else she wants to talk about that is on her mind that day, even something like an earring she has lost. Then my show starts at 7:30. It is mostly informational. I do the New Mexico newscast and then, like Martha, I talk about all sorts of everyday things that are happening in town or to me and my family. Once it was our dog, Pepito, who got lost. People here love their pets, so wherever I went they kept asking if the dog had been found. I also play a lot of taped commercials, mostly ones advertising local businesses, since revenue from this source is what keeps us going. We also find slots for people from the community who want to go on the air. Besides Martha we have Jesus Lopez with his regular Monday Las Vegas history program and Neita Fran Ward who does a show called the New Mexico Arts Collection. Pete Campos, who is now president of Luna, came to me and said he wanted to have a regular time slot, and there are several not-for-profit organizations who like to promote their causes. For instance, on Saturday mornings from 10 to 11 we have Pat Leahan, who runs the Peace and Justice Center and works with some of the kids at United World College. Because, thanks to the wonders of computer technology, we are able to broadcast all over the world, she gets lots of former UWC students calling in talking about their experiences in such places as Iraq and Libya. We were even able to make it possible for one of our talk-show hosts who was going abroad to stream his program for three weeks from Germany. And now we have just added a second Web site that will allow worldwide streaming, because if you are not on the Internet nowadays, you are being left behind."

KFUN further extends its outreach to the entire community by giving locals who have something to say or sell random free airtime. "We always let people know that we have the airwaves open for anybody who has something legitimate they want to share. We like to give time to CASA, a court-directed program that helps abused kids now in foster homes. Ride to Pride, which works with children with special needs is another organization we support. They teach them how to groom, ride, and get over their fear of horses. It is a real healing experience for them. There are other charities we help with things like selling tickets to events. That's the special part of radio. We know we are touching people's hearts and lives."

Glancing at his wife, Baca concluded, "Of course, I couldn't do any of this without Loretta. She is the one who really runs the station. She answers the phone, puts together the commercials, and decides which members from the community-at-large get airtime. She also broadcasts her own program of country music. Michel and J. R. are another huge asset. Loretta and I are now able to go home at five rather than at midnight because they are here to take over."

Positive Action

The Citizens Committee for Historic Preservation—usually referred to by its acronym CCHP—is a not-for-profit organization whose agenda is community improvement through the renovation of the town's physical fabric. Formed in 1979, CCHP has as its mission statement "To protect, preserve and promote the cultural landscape and historic buildings of Las Vegas and to develop a sense of community and connection to the past." A volunteer-run not-for-profit organization, it operates out of a storefront on Bridge Street. To date CCHP has nominated more than 900 structures for inclusion on the National Register of Historic Places. Its members have also worked with town officials on creating a historic buildings ordinance and obtaining Certified Local Government (CLG) status, an official designation that allows the city to receive federal and state funds earmarked for historic preservation. It organizes such events as the annual "Places with a Past" tour and a Christmas House Tour. CCHP also hosts periodic seminars, workshops, and lectures on local history and historic preservation. The group offers a series of self-guided tours both in brochures and online, and these were a valuable resource for me when I was first discovering Las Vegas's rich cultural and architectural heritage by walking through the town's nine historic districts. In addition to receiving this kind of on-site education, I have spent several enjoyable hours poring over the CCHP photo archive, which contains approximately 3,000 images of early Las Vegas.

DOYLE DAVES

Doyle Daves, a member of the board of CCHP, was born in 1936 on a ranch near Clayton, New Mexico. A graduate of the class of 1959 at Highlands, he became a chemist and academic administrator. Upon retirement in 2000 from Rensselaer Polytechnic Institute in Troy, New York, he moved back to Las Vegas. Like others with a strong attachment to the place, he looks at the abandoned buildings as tremendous opportunities for town betterment. For him the Castañeda Hotel, the Navajo Textiles building, and many other empty structures of architectural distinction present significant challenges to the fulfillment of CCHP's ideal for a Las Vegas renaissance capitalizing on the town's considerable historic assets.

From his years as a student at Highlands, Daves remembers when Las Vegas wore a very different face. "There were wonderful parties at the Castañeda Hotel; we used to go there all the time," he reflected. "Now it is all boarded up. It's been up for sale for several years, and the owner, who is the sole occupant, just keeps the bar open a minimum number of hours so the liquor license, which is valuable, won't expire. If only the right buyer would come along, the sale and renovation of the Castañeda would be as symbolically significant for East Las Vegas as the restoration of the Plaza Hotel was for West Las Vegas thirty years ago." He added with resignation, "I don't know when that will happen. In Las Vegas history repeats itself over and over and over. It's all about controlling the place. It's true that we don't want to be like

Santa Fe or Taos, but we do need to grow local businesses in order to have a thriving community. We're losing population at the moment at a steady rate, which is not good for a town of this size. It may be that we are at a crisis point. We somehow have got to convince young people that if you do it right, you can make a living here. I'm a firm believer in small steps. It's all about attitude and expectations."

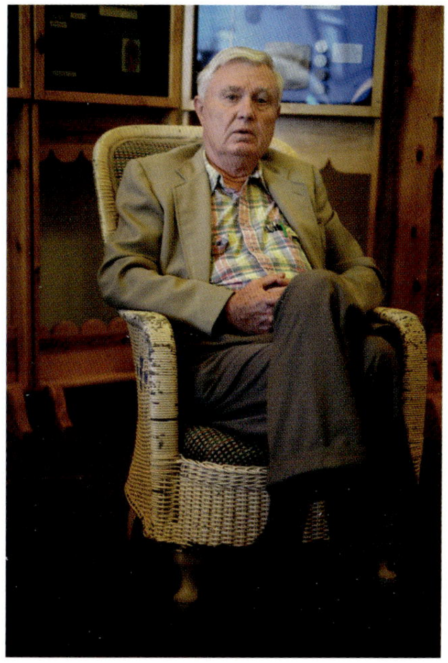

Doyle Daves

As I had learned many times before I met with Daves, when one speaks of attitude in Las Vegas, conversations inevitably veer toward Tiny Martinez. "Tiny made the town explode," Daves said. "Some overdue reforms occurred, such as opening up more jobs for Hispanics, but Highlands and Las Vegas have not yet recovered their former importance as a university and as a community. Today it's hard for some people to give up the ideas they grew up with, but it's important to realize now that the whole culture of the country with regard to minorities has changed since Tiny's time. The kids of today are the most tolerant generation we've ever produced. Lots of Hispanics are sick and tired of things being the way they are, but they are not willing to do anything. Mayor Ortiz is part of the generation that saw the old system die. Now he would like to inspire the youth of the town to make it a better place. He wants to see the next generation get interested in making a difference. That's the only way we're going to move forward."

The attempt to conserve and restore historic structures is seen by many Hispanics as mainly an Anglo enterprise. As my conversation with Daves continued, I remembered something Jesus Lopez had said to me earlier, "Don't forget, I lived on the plaza when I was young. Over the years I've seen these renaissances come and go. People move here from the outside, they fix up some abandoned buildings and open up shops, but then after a few years they leave. They just can't make it in this place."

Most resistance to the commercial restoration of the town is somewhat more nuanced, and there are Hispanics such as Tito Chavez who have renovated buildings and opened businesses on Bridge Street. Yet the notion that change is not in the interest of the community runs deep. One interpretation of the continually reiterated refrain "We don't want to be like Santa Fe" is that Las Vegans do not care to have their town to become a mecca of tourism and international art and culture. As we have seen, however, this does not mean that *local* art and culture are not thriving. One of the brightest lights in this regard is the presence on Bridge Street of that endangered species, the independent bookstore.

NANCY COLALILLO

To find an apparently thriving owner-run bookstore anywhere these days is a pleasant anomaly. In this regard Nancy Colalillo's Tome on the Range seems almost too good to be true. A small stage in back for children's events and adult programs and a couple of comfortable sofas for reading in front, on one of which the store cat lies curled up, provide a homey, inviting atmosphere. At the counter Michael Siewert, the store manager, goes out of his way to help customers.

Tome on the Range opened in 1996, two years after Colalillo moved to Las Vegas from her native New Jersey. Like other relatively recent arrivals, she had choices of where to relocate, and when I went to see her, she enumerated her reasons for picking Las Vegas with strong conviction: "Little towns like this just don't exist in this country anymore. It's a real community; the scale and color of the surrounding landscape are exhilarating in the way a lot of people from the East with their idea that everything has to be green just can't understand. I like the fact that it's not a big city like San Francisco or a place like Santa Fe with lots of culture from the outside. We're homegrown; we don't import our culture; there's a do-it-yourself approach here that I really appreciate. We have wonderful artists in Las Vegas; I have a house filled with their work. We have a high school band that is on a college level, a theater group, lots of musical events. One thing's for sure: I'll never go back to New Jersey."

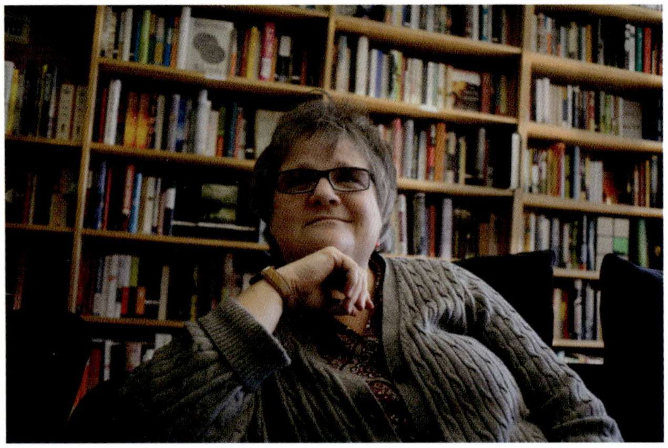

Nancy Colalillo

Colalillo is obviously a member of the upbeat group of outsiders who have attached themselves to their adopted hometown with visionary passion, having decided to commit their entrepreneurial creativity and financial resources toward its betterment. She admits that the independent bookstore today is indeed obsolete and that Tome on the Range would have to close if she did not subsidize it personally. Like the building on Bridge Street she renovated to house her bookstore, its existence can be viewed as an act of historic preservation. "I'm fortunate," she explained, "I was left an inheritance. I believe that reading is important, and I can't think of a better thing to do with the money I have. Literacy, culture, and urban renewal all combined in one small business in a regrettably dying industry—this seems to me to be an admirable form of philanthropy."

JAMES MONTOYA

As I was finishing this book, I went to the Hillcrest one morning for breakfast. Marty Suazo was at the corner table as usual, and next to him was James Montoya, another regular. At age seventy-one, Montoya has had a longtime involvement with Las Vegas politics. A retired policeman, he was able to tell me how law enforcement, criminal justice, and legislation have worked through politics over the years. "Tiny, Judge Armijo, Senator Dennis Chavez, Senator Joseph Montoya—these were people who made a big difference in Las Vegas and the rest of New Mexico," he said. "I would bring offenders to court when Tiny was district attorney. I learned a lot from him about the importance of preserving our culture and civil rights and about wisdom in the legal sense. He liked me because I tried to put people's lives first. Most people didn't know what a big heart Tiny had. He wanted power and control so that he could help the people. I spoke at his funeral and thanked him for what he did to make Las Vegas a better community." Montoya went on to explain, "You see, in this sense the word *patrón*, which is often misunderstood in its English translation, has a very good meaning. Remember, it's all we had. Don't get me wrong, the American system is one of the best government systems in the world, but you have to have somebody who listens, someone who can lead on behalf of the people. It is the same way at home. We are a very family-oriented culture, and there has to be a head of every family."

When I said that I was trying to find a way to describe both Las Vegas's commonalities with other places and its unique indigenous cultural values, Montoya replied, "You have to understand how Northern New Mexico has stood apart as a separate culture within American society. We were actually never really part of the United States. That goes back to the land-grant system. We were always different, and even today with everything going on all around us we are still are a very conservative society with our own traditions, culture, and religion. We are also special in the sense that we have a lot of history and most of it has been good history. One thing that stands out in my mind is that we are the most democratic city in the whole country because when something happens in Las Vegas everybody knows about it. How much more democratic can you be!"

According to Montoya, the flip side of Northern New Mexico's culture of poverty is its culture of self-sufficiency. "Unlike other parts of the country, we know how to deal with depression and inflation," he remarked. "That's because we've always been poor. Drive around the countryside here, and you'll see big woodpiles next to the houses. You can tell that there are lots of people who are not in the mainstream and don't have any kind of modern heating. So they go out and chop firewood. We know how to build and fix things because we have to. We are a very creative people. We make sculptures and all kinds of art. We know how to live on the land. We are still an agricultural people, and things like cattle-raising are part of our independent way of life. We live with the government but we are not part of it."

"Don't get me wrong," he continued. "We're proud to be Americans. I've served in the army like a lot of other men around here, but we don't like the way the country is run by big corporations. Here's the thing: we are educating the children in the American way and yet the corporations are exploiting us. We are providing the kids here with excellent higher education at Highlands, and then those who graduate are being hired to go elsewhere. That's why we are losing population. It's also the reason why we are having a hard time getting our local economy to become less dependent on government jobs."

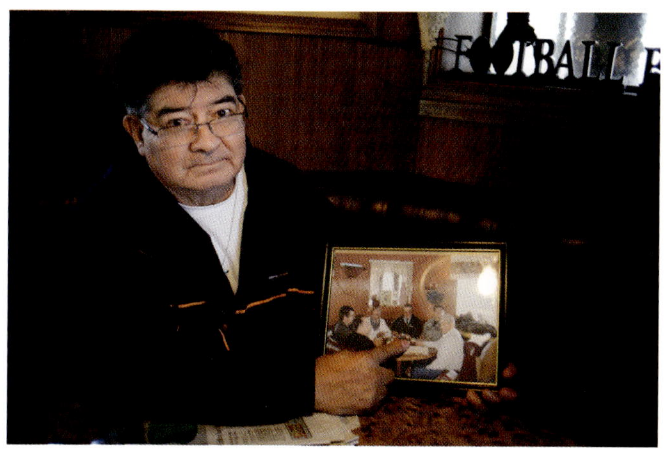

James Montoya

"Isn't resistance to change on the part of a large segment of the community part of the problem?" I asked. Montoya answered, "Certain people would like to see Las Vegas remain the same, but the majority want to go forward and become a better community. There is more diversity here than you realize. It's not just Hispanics against outsiders anymore. We know how to get along and help each other." I mentioned that I had nevertheless heard some negative remarks about the economic development promoted by so-called outsiders. "Not everybody feels that way," he replied. "I think Wid Slick has done a wonderful job; he kept Old Town alive. There is nothing wrong with investors coming in and improving our tourist economy. And we have more than just our Hispanic history to sell. New Town and Railroad Avenue have some great buildings like the Castañeda Hotel that are also assets to be exploited. We need to bring these parts of town alive."

Montoya agreed when I suggested that tourism alone could not bring back the kind of prosperity Las Vegas had once enjoyed. But looking into the future, he believes that wind farms and solar energy development offer new opportunities both for job growth and power for light industry. "We have natural resources that haven't yet been exploited," he said. "There is still a lot of gas and oil underneath the ground. Look at the scenery all around us. We have the mountains, the desert, forests, wonderful fresh air. There isn't a more beautiful place in the world than Las Vegas! And we have lots of room for growth. People of wealth are going to want to come and live here. We need to involve them politically in improving the community." Tempering this optimism, however, is Montoya's recognition of the area's Number One resource deficiency: water. "Without water you can't have much growth," he admitted. "The Gallinas is drying up, and we are going to have to tap more aquifers or import water from somewhere else."

For Montoya environmental solutions and faith go hand in hand. "I have learned that faith heals," he said. "Now archaeologists and historians are going back and understanding that the earth is always being destroyed in so many ways. But I believe that people are now coming to understand that there has to be a Supreme Being and that we have souls as well as bodies. Here we are a religious community, and there is power in that. God will help us preserve what we have and move forward. Our culture is fortunate to have faith, and nothing is greater than that. What they say is true: faith can move mountains."

Montoya went on to describe how the morning gathering at the Hillcrest provided a means of achieving Christian action through political will. "I'll give you an example," he said. "When my best friend, Henry Sanchez, was mayor, he used to sit at this table every morning. He and I were spiritually connected. I told him one day when he was running for mayor and I was walking all the streets campaigning for him that I had seen elderly ladies come to the door with heavy coats on because they had no heat. It was right here at this table that I encouraged him to start the Love Your Neighbor program, which was the first thing he did when he was elected."

Pulling down from the ledge at the back of the banquette a framed photograph of a group of men sitting around Sanchez, Montoya turned it so I could read the inscription on the back. It was signed by one of the regulars, Travis Regensberg, a subcontractor from Mora, and addressed to "my friend Henry y mi Tocallo." "Read it," said Montoya. "This will tell you what this table is all about." Putting on my glasses, I read aloud: "Even though we may not have seen eye-to-eye on every issue or political view, we agreed to disagree. But the one vision we did share was that in which to help with the simplest needs on which to live. 'It is the Christian way.' " Taking my hand as we got up to leave, Montoya said, "When you write your book, give the people who read it the meaning of what the community is really like: it's generosity, caring, and everything that goes with it."

Acknowledgements

In writing this book my first debt is to the people whom the reader has met in these pages. The title recognizes my role as student: I could not have "learned" Las Vegas to the degree that I, a non-native, have over the past five years without the friendly candor of many of its citizens. It is through our conversations about their lives and the meaning of Las Vegas as a place to each of them that I have been able gain some understanding of this special town and the rest of Northern New Mexico as a unique part of America's landscape, history, and culture.

Several readers of the manuscript have provided factual information, corrections, and valuable suggestions as to its narrative structure. These include Anthony Alofsin, an architect, author, and professor of architectural history at the University of Texas, as well as a former resident of Northern New Mexico; Christopher Wilson, J. B. Jackson Professor of Cultural Landscape Studies at the University of New Mexico School of Architecture and Planning in Albuquerque; Las Vegas native Elmo Baca, chairman of the board of the New Mexico Humanities Council and program associate, Cultural and Heritage Projects, New Mexico Main Street program; Marcus Gottschalk, an authority on the pioneer merchants of Las Vegas; and cultural geographer, conservationist, author, and photographer Don Usner.

In addition to the constructive criticism offered by these readers, native Las Vegan Bernie Lopez, former director of the New Mexico Arts Division (now known as New Mexico Arts), the Consortium for Pacific Arts and Culture, and a member of the National Council on the Arts, gave me insight into the nature of the town, both past and present. Katherine Slick, former State Historic Preservation Officer and Historic Preservation Division Director for the State of New Mexico and a guiding force in the initial stages of the restoration of Old Town Las Vegas and the Plaza Hotel, provided me with helpful information as I was setting forth on my examination of the Las Vegas's wealth of historic architecture. Jill Cooper Udall furnished valuable background knowledge of political New Mexico and introduced me to important Las Vegans involved in governmental affairs. Another early advisor, Elmer Martinez, community development director for the City of Las Vegas, helped me gain an understanding of Las Vegas from a city-planning perspective. Robert Mischler, emeritus professor of anthropology at Highlands University, chair of the City of Las Vegas Design Review Board for Historic Properties, founding member of the Citizens Committee for Historic Preservation, and chair of the Friends of the City of Las Vegas Museum and Rough Rider Memorial Collection, made me familiar with past and ongoing efforts to preserve historic Las Vegas. Linda Gegick, the museum's administrator, shared her in-depth knowledge of the town's architecture through conversation and the loan of the landmark-by-landmark survey of Las Vegas's historic districts.

Maurilio E. Vigil, emeritus professor of political science at New Mexico Highlands University, spent several hours giving me a valuable tutorial in the history of Las Vegas. Eric Romero, professor of Indo-Hispanic Studies at Highlands, helped by educating me in Northern New Mexico's land-based economy, ranching heritage, and culture of communalism. Ernest Quintana's guided tour and explanation of Las Vegas's water issues and the workings of Northern New Mexico's acequia system was similarly instructive. Christina Semik and Patrick Alarid brought me into contact with important individuals active in the life of the Catholic Church. Musician Donny Tesso's knowledge of the heritage, rhythms, styles, and bands of Northern New Mexico was crucial to my understanding of this core element of regional culture. To all of these mentors I say, *"muchas, muchas gracias."* My thanks also go to Joseph Gonzales, the "ambassador" of Las Vegas whose dependable presence in and around the plaza has given me much timely information about what is happening in town.

In addition, I want to express gratitude to photographers Tony O'Brien, Ed Ranney, and Clifford Ross, whose critical review of my work helped me to make the final selections found in the book's portfolio of images. I am further indebted to Joanna Hurley, editor, publicist, agent, and publisher specializing in photography books for much good advice and to Lisabeth and Frank Davis, who welcomed me on various occasions to their ranch in the Gallinas Canyon and gave me the opportunity to photograph Las Vegas and its regional environs from above in Frank's open-cockpit aircraft.

In terms of the book itself, I thank Mary Wachs, editorial director at the Museum of New Mexico Press, for her helpful comments, astute queries, and general oversight and skill in guiding it through all phases of production. I also extend my gratitude to editor Julia Moore for her sensible advice and gentle nurturing of the manuscript as it progressed toward completion. I am similarly appreciative of Beth Hadas's careful copy editing and David Skolkin's outstanding talent as a book designer.

Finally, I thank the board and supporters of the Foundation for Landscape Studies, an organization whose mission is to foster an active understanding of the meaning of place in human life, for assisting in the publication of this book. In addition to the many Las Vegans who have befriended me throughout my quest, my principal debt of gratitude is to my husband Ted Rogers, whose appreciation of the people of Las Vegas and the remarkable landscape of Northern New Mexico has encouraged me at every stage of this journey.

Elizabeth Barlow Rogers
New York City

Notes

NOTES: INTRODUCTION

1 . With the omission of the preposition, the title echoes that of Robert Venturi and Denise Scott-Brown's landmark book *Learning from Las Vegas*. By looking with a friendly eye at the commercial strip of Las Vegas, Nevada, with its symbolically expressive signs and building shapes—conventionally considered as kitsch—its authors and their student collaborators offered a contrarian perspective that helped change the course of architecture and usher in the period known as Postmodernism in the years following the book's publication in 1972.

NOTES: CHAPTER 1

1. Although an Amtrak train between Chicago and Los Angeles stops in Las Vegas, the station is now a visitor center, making it necessary to buy a ticket online or on board from the conductor.

2. Chris Wilson, *Architecture and Preservation in Las Vegas,* vol. II, Citizens' Committee for Historic Preservation, (Las Vegas, NM, 1982): 109.

3. *Ibid.,* p. 115

4. *Ibid.,* p. 117

5. The Tecolote land grant was conferred by the Territorial Deputation in 1824 following a petition by Salvador Montoya and five associates for a tract of land whose boundaries comprised "on the north, the Cueva; on the east, the Pueblo, on the south, the Puertecito de las Gailinos; and on the west, the Cañada de Tres Hermanos."

NOTES: CHAPTER 2

1. The Spanish Crown granted encomienda lands to certain favored persons who were then expected to extract labor, gold, and other forms of tribute from native populations. It was, in effect, a form of slavery.

2. See Malcolm Ebright, *Land Grants and Law Suits in Northern New Mexico* (Albuquerque: University of New Mexico Press, 1994): 24–25.

3. Colloquial Spanish of the region alters several words beginning with v to b. Hence, just as *baca*—an extremely common surname in Northern New Mexico—is a linguistic transformation of *vaca* (cow), so the word *vado* (ford) became *bado*.

4. New Mexico State Record Center and Archives, Santa Fe, 2004–2011.

5. Anselmo F. Arellano and Julian Josue Vigil Arellano, *Las Vegas Grandes on the Gallinas 1835–1985* (Las Vegas, NM: Editorial Telaraña, 1985): 6–7. According to historian Marcus Gottschalk, the C. de Baca family did not formally renounce rights to the land until 1860, when the heirs of Luis C. de Baca were given five large tracts of land by the United States Senate in return for a quitclaim of the original Las Vegas grant.

6. See Arellano and Arellano 1985: 9–13, for an extended discussion of Father Leyba's efforts to secure socially beneficial colonization of northeastern New Mexico in the years following Mexican independence from Spain.

7. As quoted in Arellano and Arellano 1985: 11.

8. The honor roll of Las Vegas's first settlers, courtesy of Jesus Lopez, is as follows: Juan Pedro Archuleta, Arcenio Baca, Juan José Baca, José Guadalupe Baca, Tomás Baca, Simón Blea, José Antonio Casaus, Foribio Crespín, Juan Crespín, José de Jesús Durán, José María Durán, Manuel Durán, Francisco López, José Lucero, Juan de Dio Maese, Antonio Martín, José Martín, José María Martín, Juan José Martín, Juan Nepomuceno Martín, Miguel Martín, Miguel Martín II, Santiago Ortega, Teodocio Quintana, Cruz Rendón, Miguel Rendón, Rafael Rendón, Antonio Romo, Simón Romo, Rafael Sarracino, Eulogio Segura, Felipe Tafoya, Antonio Ulibarrí, Faustin Ulibarrí, José de Jesús Ulibarrí, and Pablo Ulibarrí.

9. Serving as a formula for colonial settlement, Book IV of the Laws sets forth rules that served as planning principles, building regulations, and design guidelines. They dictated that a town site should be in an elevated and healthy location and furnished with fertile soil, sufficient water, adequate land for farming and pasturage. They further specified its configuration with a church facing a central plaza, which was enclosed by attached houses of uniform appearance forming a protective wall that could serve if necessary as a defensive fortification. A grid of streets running from each corner of the plaza was to be laid out to accommodate future town growth.

10. In 1882, when a unified government combining both East and West Las Vegas was created, Miguel Romero became the town's first mayor. Two years later, when the territorial legislature passed a law requiring new municipal incorporation, Romero decided that, rather than challenge it, he would concede East Las Vegas to Anglo-American governance so that the family could maintain absolute rule in West Las Vegas and the rest of San Miguel County.

11. Anselmo F. Arellano, *Through Thick and Thin: Evolutionary Transitions of Las Vegas Grandes and Its Pobladores*. Unpublished manuscript, University of New Mexico, December 1990: 79.

12. Jesus Lopez, *Nuestra Historia* column in the *Las Vegas Optic*, October 21, 2011.

13. For a comprehensive description of the architecture around the plaza, see Ellen Threinen, *Architecture and Preservation in Las Vegas: A Study of Three Districts,* Vol. I (Las Vegas, NM: Citizens Committee for Historic Preservation, 1977): 14–21.

14. The Raynolds brothers were pioneer bankers who, like other entrepreneurs, kept one step ahead of the railroad as it moved westward toward Las Vegas. Their Las Vegas bank was preceded by other, more temporary banks they had set up as new rail towns sprouted along the route. They were probably under the impression, as were many other people, that the railroad would locate somewhere on the existing town site rather than a mile to the east, in which case they would have probably chosen to locate in New Town.

15. William J. Parish, *The Charles Ilfeld Company: The Rise and Decline of Mercantile Capitalism in New Mexico* (Cambridge, Mass.: Harvard University Press, 1961): 93.

16. The school is also known as the Armand Hammer United College of the American West, after the philanthropist who purchased the property for this purpose.

17. Eventually, in 1944, the Storrie Project Water Users' Association came into existence. Still the operating entity today, it administers a system of water-sharing between its members, most of whom now use industrial agricultural methods to farm their land. For a detailed narrative of the Storrie Project, see Malcolm Ebright, *Storrie Lake State Park: History of Title and History of the Town of Las Vegas Land Grant* (Santa Fe: New Mexico Commission of Public Records, 2009): 32–40.

18. Because New Mexico is the only part of the country where land ownership still harks back to grant conveyances before statehood, this issue remains contentious.

19. Arellano 1990: 126.

20. According to many older Hispanics in Las Vegas with whom I have spoken, they were forbidden to speak Spanish in school when they were young, a stricture that was often harshly enforced. Although this racist policy would be considered deplor-

able now, Hispanic children did become bilingual at an early age. Ironically, today Spanish is taught in school, since many young people no longer hear it at home and are in danger of losing their ancestral tongue.

21. Arellano 1990: 145.

22. Ebright 1994: 218–19.

NOTES: CHAPTER 3

1. University of New Mexico Press, 1954.

2. First published in 1972, *Bless Me, Ultima* eventually became part of the Big Read community reading program of the National Endowment for the Arts. It was made into a stage production in 2009 by a Chicano theater company in Denver, turned into a full-scale play by the Vortex Company in Albuquerque the next year, and then made into a movie, which was released in 2012.

3. Judge Luis Armijo (1887–1942) was one of the most powerful patrones in the history of San Miguel County. I was told by one informant that during the thirty years he held the reins of absolute authority, Judge Armijo exercised control of every school board and every county, city, and town office. No mayor or city council member—indeed, practically no one—did anything without his permission. It is common knowledge that, while serving as district attorney, the judge sold land grants from the bench. But he could at the same time, if he so chose, adjudicate cases involving land ownership in favor of present holders. According to John Pope, author of "New Mexico's Man for All Seasons," *Bar Journal,* May–June 1996, "It has been said that during trials, particularly quiet title actions when numerous old timers would testify as to fences and boundaries, that the cadence of the trial could be interrupted to renew acquaintanceships and exchange news. This was done by the attorneys, witnesses and the judge." It is in this light, which illustrates how the favors bestowed by patrones served as means of ensuring absolute allegiance, that Martinez's story about the retention of his family's property can be best understood. The patrón tradition continues to exert influence on Las Vegas politics today, although to a much lesser degree than in the time of Judge Armijo.

4. Daniel T. Kelly, with Beatrice Chauvenet. *The Buffalo Head: A Century of Mercantile Pioneering in the Southwest*. (Santa Fe, N.M.: Vergara Publishing Co., 1972. Reissued, Santa Fe: Historic Santa Fe Foundation/Museum of New Mexico Press, 1985).

5. Kelly: 10–11.

6. Kane acquired the *Las Vegas Optic* in 1921 and owned the paper until 1947.

NOTES: CHAPTER 4

1. Akin to the myth of story of Medea, the legend of La Llorona—the Weeping Woman—recounts how a young woman named María drowns her children in order to live with her lover, is rejected, kills herself, and is barred from heaven and condemned to wander the earth forever in search of her little ones. Prevalent in Mexico and Puerto Rico, it has its localized version, which goes like this: María is walking along the Gallinas one day with her two children. Looking up at the bridge, she sees her handsome husband ride by in a carriage with a beautiful woman. In a fit of jealous anger over his betrayal, she takes revenge by drowning the children. In remorse she then throws herself in the river. Since then her ghost has walked along the riverbank in a long white robe, and listeners can hear her wailing lament. Las Vegas youngsters have always been warned not to go near the river after dark for fear that La Llorona will snatch them.

2. Ellen Threinen, *Architecture and Preservation in Las Vegas,* Vol. I. (Las Vegas: Citizens Committee for Historic Preservation, 1977).

3. Las Vegas was one of five municipalities in New Mexico to be designated a Main Street community in 1986 soon after the program was initiated. The program had operated only sporadically over the years, so this was in effect a re-designation.

4. Created in 1985 under the auspices of the National Trust for Historic Preservation's program of beautification and revitalization of principal commercial thoroughfares of historic significance throughout the country, New Mexico MainStreet operates as an interagency collaboration between the State's Economic Development Department, the Department of Cultural Affairs, and the Tourism Department. The Arts and Culture District is therefore the recipient via the local MainStreet office of funding falling within the guidelines of the state MainStreet program.

5. The district includes most of the city's nine historical districts and the campus of Highlands University.

NOTES: CHAPTER 5

1. At the beginning of 2012 Father Brasher was reassigned to the New Mexico parishes of Holy Family in Roy and St. Joseph in Mosquero. He was replaced as priest at Our Lady of Sorrows by Father Douglas Mitchell.

2. Called the De Salle Institute, the school was founded by the Christian Brothers in 1888. The site where it stood on the west bank of the Gallinas River is now occupied by West Las Vegas High School and West Las Vegas Middle School.

3. New Mexico is the only state that still recognizes both Pueblo water rights and historic Spanish land-grant law and, as a corollary, the original communal system that governs the allocation of water on the basis of seniority.

4. An acre-foot is the volume of one square acre of water to a depth of one foot, which equals 43,560 cubic feet or 325, 929 gallons.

5. As recounted in Chapter Two, the Storrie Project, as it came to be called after the engineer who completed it in 1921, originated in the early years of the twentieth century as one of a series of then-popular irrigation schemes intended to attract farmers to the arid West with the offer of an interest in land adjacent to a body of dammed water. For various reasons, including the high cost of transportation, political complications arising from the ownership rights of the upstream acequia owners, and a short growing season, the small farming operations around Storrie were not successful. Through a foreclosure sale, most of the 17,000 acres the Las Vegas Land Grant board had originally sold for the project ended up in the ownership of the Storrie Project Water Users Association and is today owned by farmers who use industrial agricultural methods.

6. I also heard that his withdrawal from the campaign had been the result of a threatening phone call from someone opposed to non-Hispanic involvement in town politics.

7. The coalition is dedicated to stopping upstream pollution caused by corporate exploration for natural gas through "fracking," the fracturing of subsurface geological strata within the Las Vegas watershed, an activity for which the state engineer has already issued drilling permits.

NOTES: CHAPTER 6

1. The institution is part of a statewide system of hospital facilities.

NOTES: CHAPTER 7

1. I understood what Lujan meant when I went on the Internet later and looked at what Montana has to offer: Kicking Yellow, Toad, Pear Green, Hannibal, and Lost Island, "a newly formulated Montana Black line paint with an even faster drying finish and an improved valve system without losing the quick coverage you have come to know from the earlier paint line." And, proving that graffiti is no longer considered an illicit punk activity, Molotow boasts an artist line "dedicated to fulfill huge surfaces in a fast way. Developed ten years ago in cooperation with some of the most renowned street artists worldwide, it revolutionized the spray can technology fundamentally and is still affecting the street-art scene."

2. The incident he was referring to was essentially a land grab on the part of the Anglo settlers in Texas who had ventured forth after Texas had established independence from Mexico with the intention of claiming the neighboring territory and overthrowing the Mexican government in Santa Fe. Instead of acquiring New

Mexico as part of the newly formed Republic of Texas, however, the aggressors were captured and sent down to Mexico City, where they were imprisoned for a year before being repatriated.

3. The zia is so called because it originated at Zia Pueblo. This emblem of native New Mexican culture was later adopted as the state's symbol. Hence, it is in the center of the New Mexican flag.

4. There are bands of performers plus singers of pure mariachi music in and around Las Vegas, and instruction in this distinctly Mexican idiom is available locally. Often mariachis will play brief enthusiastic bursts of music in church as an accompaniment to the service. The corrido is a narrative song about heroes and villains that is an epic version of the *ranchera* ballad.

5. The popularity of the accordion in the Spanish Americas can be attributed to the influx of German and Austrian immigrants in the nineteenth century.

6. Drums, which are associated with Cumbia music, are of African origin and were brought along with the slaves of the Spanish conquerors of the New World.

NOTES: CHAPTER 9

1. Chile is spelled with an *e* in New Mexico. Elsewhere the chile pepper is spelled "chili."

Selected Bibliography

Arellano, Anselmo F. "Through Thick and Thin: Evolutionary Transitions of Las Vegas Grandes and Its Pobladores." Unpublished manuscript, 1990).

———, and Julian José Vigil. *Las Vegas Grandes on the Gallinas 1835–1985*. Las Vegas, N.M.: Editorial Telaraña, 1985.

Beier, Florence. *Reaching for New Rides: Stories from My Life.* San Mateo, Calif.: Beier & Associates, 2007.

Beimer, Dorothy Simpson. *Hovels, Haciendas, and House Calls: The Life of Carl H. Gellenthien.* Santa Fe: Sunstone Press, 1985.

Dary, David. *The Santa Fe Trail: Its History, Legends, and Lore*. New York: Alfred A Knopf, 2000.

deBuys, William. *Enchantment and Exploitation: The Life and Hard Times of a New Mexico Mountain Range*. Albuquerque: University of New Mexico Press, 1985.

Ebright, Malcolm. *Land Grants & Lawsuits in Northern New Mexico.* Albuquerque: University of New Mexico Press, 1994.

Drumm, Stella M., ed. *Down the Santa Fe Trail and Into Mexico: The Diary of Susan Shelby Magoffin 1846–1847.* Lincoln: University of Nebraska Press, 1962.

Garcia, Eloy, J., Jr. "The Chicano Student Movement at New Mexico Highlands: An Interpretive History." M.A. thesis, New Mexico Highlands University, 1997.

Gregg, Josiah. *Commerce of the Prairies.* Norman: University of Oklahoma Press, 1954.

Jaworski, Birdie. *My Tiny Vegas: Life Between the Sangre de Cristo Mountains and the Great Plains.* Charleston, S.C.: CreateSpace, 2009.

Kelly, Daniel T., with Beatrice Chauvenet. *The Buffalo Head: A Century of Mercantile Pioneering in the Southwest.* Santa Fe, N.M.: Vergara Publishing Co., 1972. Reissued, Santa Fe: Historic Santa Fe Foundation/Museum of New Mexico Press, 1985.

Nahm, Milton. *Las Vegas and Uncle Joe: The New Mexico I Remember*. Norman: University of Oklahoma Press, 1964.

Parish, William J. *The Charles Ilfeld Company: A Study of the Rise and Decline of Mercantile Capitalism in New Mexico*. Cambridge, Mass: Harvard University Press, 1961.

Perrigo, Lynn I. *Gateway to Glorieta: A History of Las Vegas, New Mexico*. Boulder, Colo.: Pruett Publishing Co., 1982. Reprint, Santa Fe, N.M.: Sunstone Press, 2010.

Threinen, Ellen. *Architecture and Preservation in Las Vegas,* [vol. I]. Las Vegas, N.M.: Citizens Committee for Historic Preservation, 1977.

Wilson, Christopher. *Architecture and Preservation in Las Vegas*, vols. II and III. Las Vegas, N.M.: Citizens Committee for Historic Preservation, 1982 and 1984.

Index